GREECE IN THE TWENTIETH CENTURY

GREECE
in the
TWENTIETH CENTURY

Editors
THEODORE A. COULOUMBIS
THEODORE KARIOTIS
FOTINI BELLOU

Hellenic Foundation for European and Foreign Policy

(*ELIAMEP*)

FRANK CASS
LONDON • PORTLAND, OR

First published in 2003 in Great Britain by
FRANK CASS PUBLISHERS
Crown House, 47 Chase Side
London N14 5BP

and in the United States of America by
FRANK CASS PUBLISHERS
c/o ISBS, 920 NE 58th Avenue, Suite 300
Portland, Oregon 97213-3786

Website: www.frankcass.com

British Library Cataloguing in Publication Data

Greece in the twentieth century
  1. Greece – Politics and government – 20th century 2. Greece
    Foreign relations – 20th century 3. Greece –Economic
  conditions – 20th century 4. Greece –Social conditions –
  20th century
  I. Coluloumbis, Theodore A. II. Kariotis, Theodore C.
  III. Bellou, Fotini
949. 5'076

ISBN 0-7146-5407-8 (cloth)
ISBN 0-7146-8340-X (paper)

Library of Congress Cataloging-in-Publication Data

Greece in the twentieth century / editors, Theodore A. Couloumbis,
  Theodore Kariotis, Fotini Bellou
    p. cm.
  "Hellenic Foundation for European and Black Sea Studies"
  Includes bibliographical references and index.
  ISNBN 0-7146-5407-8 (cloth) – ISBN 0-7146-8340-X (pbk.)
    1. Greece–History–1974– I. Couloumbis, Theodore A. II. Kariotis,
  Theodore C. III. Bellou, Fontini. IV. Hellenic Foundation for European
  and Black Sea Studies.

DF850.G695 2003
949. 5'076–dc21   2003043430

Typeset in ClassGaramond, 10.5/12pt by Frank Cass Publishers
Printed in Great Britain by MPG Books Ltd, Bodmin, Cornwall

Contents

List of Figures

List of Tables

Notes on Contributors

Ino Afentouli is a journalist specializing in foreign affairs. Born in Alexandria, she has studied law and political science in Athens and Paris and has written numerous articles on European Affairs and Foreign Policy. She is the author of *May '68: Twenty Years After* (Athens: Odysseus, 1988); and *The Europe We Want* (Athens: Sideris, 1997). She is currently academic officer at NATO Office of Information and Press, NATO HQ, Brussels.

George Babiniotis is Professor of Linguistics at the University of Athens, Rector of the University of Athens and President of the Philekpaideftiki Etairia (Arsakeia–Tositseia Schools).

Fotini Bellou holds a PhD from the Department of War Studies, King's College, London, and is currently International Relations Analyst at ELIAMEP, Athens. She specializes in Greek foreign policy, European Security, Transatlantic relations and issues concerning international crisis management. She is Managing Editor of *The Journal of Southeast European and Black Sea Studies* (ELIAMEP–Frank Cass).

Theodore A. Couloumbis is Professor of International Relations at the University of Athens and Director General of the Hellenic Foundation for European and Foreign Policy (ELIAMEP).

Van Coufoudakis is a Professor of Political Science and currently serves as the Dean of the School of Arts and Sciences at Indiana University–Purdue University, Fort Wayne. He has written extensively on the politics and foreign policies of Greece, Cyprus, and the foreign and security policy of the US in southeastern Europe.

Thanos P. Dokos received his PhD from the University of Cambridge and has held research posts at the Hessische Stiftung Friedens und Konfliktforschung, Frankfurt, and the Center for Science and International Affairs (CSIA) at Harvard University. He was also a NATO Research Fellow (1996–98). He served as the Director for Research,

Strategic Studies Division, Hellenic Ministry of National Defense and as an Advisor on NATO affairs at the Ministry of Foreign Affairs. He is currently the Director of Studies at the Hellenic Foundation for European and Foreign Policy (ELIAMEP).

Anna Frangoudaki, PhD of the University of Paris V (1975), is Professor of Sociology of Education, Department of Early Childhood Education, University of Athens. Her main research fields and publications are on social inequality and ethnic discrimination in education, the Greek diglossia, analysis of school textbooks and ethnocentrism in education.

John Iatrides was educated in Greece, the Netherlands and the United States and served with the Hellenic National Defence General Staff and the Prime Minister's Press Office. He is Professor of International Politics at Southern Connecticut State University.

Anna Karamanou has served as the State General Secretary for Equality and has also worked as an expert for the European Commission, in the Equal Opportunities Unit, representing Greece in two European Networks (1983–90 and 1992–96) for the promotion of women's rights. She is a founding member and general secretary of the 'Political Association of Women', Secretary of the Women's Section of PASOK since 1994, and Vice-President of the Socialist International Women since 1996.

Theodore Kariotis teaches economics at the University of Maryland University College, where he has received two teaching awards. He is also teaching public policy at the MBA program of the R.H. Smith School of Business of the University of Maryland.

John Koliopoulos is Professor of Modern History, School of Philosophy, Aristotelian University of Thessaloniki. He is the writer of *Brigands with a Cause: Brigandage and Irredentism in Modern Greece, 1821–1912,* and *Plundered Loyalties: Axis Occupation and Civil Strife in Greek West Macedonia 1941–1949.*

Ioannis M. Konidaris is Professor of Ecclesiastical Law; Director, Section of History, Philosophy and Sociology of Law, Department of Law, Faculty of Legal, Economic and Political Sciences, University of Athens. Major publications include *Legal Theory and Practice Concerning the Jacob's Witnesses in Greece, 1987; Church and the State in Greece, 1993; The Conflict Between Law and Canon and the Establishment of Harmony Between Them, 1994; Ecclesiastical Atacta, 1999* and numerous articles on Ecclesiastical Law and History of Law.

Costas B. Krimbas is a Professor in the Department of History and Philosophy of Sciences, University of Athens.

Charles Moskos is Professor of Sociology at Northwestern University, Evanston, Illinois, holding the Anderson Chair in the College of Arts and Sciences. He is the author of *Greek Americans: Struggle and Success*. In 1999, he was elected to the American Academy of Arts and Sciences.

Byron Theodoropoulos, Ambassador (ret), has served in numerous countries and organizations including Turkey, Canada, the EU and NATO. He was the General Secretary of the Hellenic Ministry of Foreign Affairs (1976–81) and was the Chairman of the Central Negotiating Committee for Greece's accession to the EEC. He has written extensively on Greek Foreign Policy, Greek–Turkish relations, and the Cyprus issue.

Loukas Tsoukalis is President of the Hellenic Foundation for European and Foreign Policy (ELIAMEP). He is also Professor of European Integration at the University of Athens. His former appointments include: Professor (Venizelos Chair) at the European Institute of the London School of Economics and Political Science; Director of European Economic Studies, College of Europe, Bruges; University Lecturer and Fellow of St Antony's College, Oxford; and Editor of the *Journal of Common Market Studies*. He is the author of many books and articles, including *The New European Economy* (Oxford University Press).

Aristotle Tziampiris has studied politics and international relations at the London School of Economics and Middlebury College. He is currently Lecturer at the Department of International and European Studies, University of Pireaus and Research Fellow at ELIAMEP. He is the author of numerous essays on European, Greek and Balkan History and foreign policy. Most recently, he has published *Greece, European Political Cooperation and the Macedonian Question*.

Thanos Veremis is Constantine Karamanlis Professor of Greek and Balkan History at Fletcher School of Law and Diplomacy, Tufts University, and Professor of Political History at the University of Athens. He is a member of the Board of Directors, ELIAMEP.

Foreword

The end of the Cold War, the adoption of a single European currency, the expectation that Cyprus will join the European Union in 2004, and a prolonged period of domestic 'modernization': each of these developments indicate that it is an appropriate time to review our understanding of the politics and policies of contemporary Greece. This remarkable dynamism in the domestic and external context of the nation points to the need to re-examine old assumptions and conditions. Periods of rapid change often sustain an ambiguity of interpretation, as we cling to traditional notions without being able to fully comprehend the significance of the 'new', distinguishing the permanent from the temporary. This book is thus an opportune occasion for both Greeks and her foreign observers to take stock and consider future challenges.

Certain visions of Greece have dominated the lens when analysing her. At the risk of some crude characterization, let me suggest that the traditional view has fixed on the following key characteristics. First, Greek foreign policy has been beset by a fundamental ambiguity over its relationship with the West and the 'Great Powers' of the day, stemming from its own strategic position and domestic cultural/political cleavages. Thus, Greece is not able to define a clear and stable relationship with the USA or NATO, and she is an uncomfortable member of the European integration process. Secondly, the Greek state at home is a 'colossus with a feet of clay': obese, and often dysfunctional. Statism is endemic: there are no cultural barriers to its extension, nor is there adequate space for independent institutions of civil society to flourish. Thirdly, political culture is marked by patron–client mentalities, with the traditional role of 'notables' overtaken by modern mass parties. Political participation revolves around the dominance of charismatic leaders, able to stir up intense passions based on old and unresolved social divisions. Thus, wilful domestic leaders are not to be seen in a vacuum: the emotions they engender are based on the legacies of social and political conflict. As a result, domestic politics can lurch from one crisis to another.

These are perhaps the most important images of how the modern Greek state evolved after 1945. So, how relevant are they today? The contrast over the long term is rather remarkable. As Couloumbis argues in this book, one of the key changes to have occurred in Greece is the increasing consensus over her role with the West. The old clashes of identity and ideology have greatly abated: Greece is more at ease with belonging to the West. Moreover, Greece is firmly within the European Union. Where are the 'anti-Europeans' now? Their voice in the established party system is weaker and less influential. The disturbances that arise in Greece's relations with the West in relation to foreign policy are now regional: how to deal with the break-up of Yugoslavia and how to secure Greece against Turkey. The divergences on Bosnia and Serbia, and even perhaps on an independent 'Macedonian' state, now do not seem so intense. And, 'rapprochement' with Turkey has broken out in recent years. The latter is not unrelated to the stalemate on Cyprus seeming likely to be broken. After almost three decades of inertia and false breakthroughs, it is a stunning change to acknowledge that Cyprus is on the verge of joining the European Union. This act may yet open up a solution to the division of the island that has lasted since 1974.

Moreover, the European integration process that Greece joined, rather half-heartedly, in 1981 has changed beyond recognition. The single European market and the adoption of the 'euro' are at the core of an external pressure – a 'Europeanization process' – that has fundamentally challenged the traditional domestic lethargy and dominance of the Greek state. From financial liberalization to market deregulation, low budget deficits and a fully independent central bank, state-economy relations in Greece have been transformed. In addition, Greek public policy is now developed in the context of a European-based process of policy-learning and peer-pressure. The so-called 'Open Method of Coordination' developed by the EU has added to the mutual surveillance of Economic and Monetary Union (EMU) to shape a common agenda of structural reform. Politically sensitive programmes of privatisation and pension reform are now placed within this external monitoring process. External discipline can crucially strengthen the domestic reform momentum, as seen earlier with EMU.

The contributions to this volume also map out the changes to the strength and role of civil society in Greece, the liberalization of television and radio, and the advances in education (with yet more Greeks experiencing the cultural impact of studying at foreign universities). These exemplify the changes underway in Greek society at the start of the twenty-first century. Their full significance could have been barely predicted twenty or thirty years ago. Moreover, the high emotions of electoral campaigns in the pre- or post-junta years, through to the early 1990s, can often appear to be almost part of a lost world. Today's

electoral battles seem much more sober, with voters having grown more
sceptical of rhetorical promises and more distanced from past struggles.
While there remain valid concerns about participatory structures and
the cultural attitudes towards leadership, again the shift from the past is
striking in the way internal party democracy has developed.

We do not have to make crude claims about Greece's blanket convergence with northern or western Europe to appreciate how far her
politics, economy and society have travelled since the 1970s. These are
very significant changes to her foreign policy and the domestic role of
the state. Of course, there are important continuities with the past, but
today Greece is probably more comfortable with the present than she
has been for generations. The new challenge is, indeed, of
Europeanization: not some simplistic sense of conformity with an
imposed model, but the ability to adjust to the external pressures of
open and flexible markets, while preserving and, where possible, deepening social solidarity. 'Modernization' and 'Europeanization' have
once again become synonymous for Greece and it is here that the test
of state strength and efficiency will be seen. Europeanization is also a
challenge to Greece's foreign policy-making, as the EU extends its
competences into the security field and thus recasts the agenda of
Greco-Turkish relations and of Cyprus.

The core theme of this new book is of the need to break out of the
conceptual frames of the past and to adjust our understandings to
current realities. There is no more important dimension to this adjustment than to ascertain the contours of the Europeanization process
experienced by Greece today. This book is a valuable start to the task of
re-examining old assumptions and conditions.

Kevin Featherstone
Eleftherios Venizelos Professor of
Contemporary Greek Studies
Director, Hellenic Observatory
London School of Economics and Political Science

February 2003

Acknowledgements

The editors wish to thank all contributors whose chapters have ably analysed and evaluated different aspects of Greece's society and polity of the past century. Special thanks go to Elizabeth Phocas, the Deputy Director of the Hellenic Foundation for European and Foreign Policy (ELIAMEP), for her thoughtful comments and ideas regarding the structure and substance of the volume.

We also thank warmly Dr James Ker Lindsay for his instrumental contribution in improving the readability of our volume. ELIAMEP staff members Irene Glypti, Georgia Kapsogeorgou, Vasilis Kousoulas, Marina Agelaki, Panos Lambrides, Gerasimos Koutsogiorgos, Fay Karantza and Ioanna Frangeskaki have offered invaluable and cheerful assistance throughout and deserve our gratitude.

Last but not least, the editors thank Frank Cass Publishers and ELIAMEP for their sponsorship and professional expertise.

Theodore A. Couloumbis
Theodore Kariotis
Fotini Bellou

February 2003

Introduction

THEODORE A. COULOUMBIS,
THEODORE KARIOTIS and FOTINI BELLOU

Looking through the contents of this volume the reader will discover that our contributors point to the theme of *metamorphosis*[1] in the long and tortuous road of twentieth century Greece. There has been, especially since 1974, a drastic change in Greece's political, economic and social profile in the direction of progress (development/modernization).

Yet the image of Greece, at home and abroad, is suffering from a heavy case of 'conceptual inertia'.[2] This is not a phenomenon peculiar to Greece. Individuals, groups and societies often describe themselves by employing a rearview mirror. When, for example, American and Russian political analysts continue to characterize contemporary US–Russian relations by using a Cold War framework, they are suffering from the syndrome of conceptual inertia.

Conceptual inertia in Greece has heavily infected individuals and centres involved in analysis and learning. There are still some thinkers who equate contemporary Greece with the greatness and glory of Ancient Athens. A number of other cognoscenti still tend to attribute to the country patterns and characteristics that were relevant to the 1897–1974 period. They still see Greece, therefore, as a fragile state at the crossroads of great conflicts; a country that is small, isolated, internally divided, surrounded by dangerous neighbours and totally dependent on the great powers. The Balkan Wars, two World Wars, the Asia Minor adventure (1921–22) and the catastrophe that followed, as well as the two major political schisms of the twentieth century, have left deep scars in the minds of most Greeks. Foreign occupation (1941–44), the civil war (1946–49), poverty, mass emigration and foreign interference (especially by the British and Americans) in Greece's political affairs, explain occasional sentimental outbursts and reflexive responses such as those that accompanied President Clinton's visit to Athens in November 1999.

As long as conceptual inertia shapes our self-awareness in poetry, literature, cinema, theatre, the mass media and – generally – in Greek political discourse, antiquated images will continue being transmitted and often magnified abroad, especially in major Western centres of activity. Using as a source, sometimes selectively, our own self-perception, non-Greeks have described us as a people who are 'different' and who tend to cause 'headaches'. Some have gone as far as to argue that we should not have been admitted to the European family of advanced democracies.

Among the top priorities for Greek intellectuals today is to update objectively the image of their country. Greece, after 1974, has developed economically at a high rate and can be classified as belonging within the ranks of the well-to-do and privileged nations. According to most recent statistics[3] it is placed 23rd among 189 states ranked in terms of the quality of life index – on a par with countries such as Italy, New Zealand, Spain, Cyprus, Israel and Malta. Following consistent and austere policies Greece has managed to secure entry into the European Economic and Monetary Union, placing inflation, deficits and debt within the limits specified by the Maastricht criteria. The wounds that were caused by the great political divisions of the past (especially the civil war) have finally healed and democratic institutions have been functioning effectively since 1974. Concurrently, accession to the European Community in 1981 – the European Union (EU) today – has contributed to the qualitative and quantitative upgrading of our society, economy and polity.

Unlike the rest of our EU partners, however, we are still surrounded by a fragile and dangerous region. Our great challenge is to prevent ourselves from sliding into the role of an adversary in a zone of nationalist and secessionist conflicts that have been the product of populist leaders (e.g. Slobodan Milosevic, Franjo Tudjman, Alija Izetbegovic – in order of descending culpability) as well as structural problems of social and economic underdevelopment. Fortunately, in the years 1992–95, we resisted the 'irredentist temptation' which could have entangled us in a multi-front confrontation that could have started with weak neighbours such as Albania and Former Yugoslav Republic of Macedonia (FYROM) but which would have invited – almost certainly – Turkey's military intervention.

Today, having removed the issue of Skopje from our foreign policy agenda, we need to work hard in the direction of gradual normalization of our relations with Turkey. This does not mean that Turkey has ceased to pose a revisionist challenge. Unfortunately, its political ambivalence and the growing internal problems it faces may still lead our eastern neighbour to become involved in costly adventures. Our strategy, therefore, must ensure adequate deterrence – based on modern and tested armed forces – while simultaneously cultivating régimes of tension reduction by proposing clusters of confidence-building measures and drawing Turkey into the multilateral institutional networks afforded by the EU and NATO.

As Greece (already a member) and Cyprus (heading for accession) deepen their ties with the European Union, while inviting Turkey (a candidate for EU accession) to do the same, the networks of interdependence will take root and Greeks and Turks – as was the case with the French and the Germans after the Second World War – will move safely into the zone of cooperation and peace. Should Turkey, for a variety of reasons, fail to accomplish its own metamorphosis, we have no reason to follow her in that choice. Having rid ourselves of the syndrome of conceptual inertia, with a sense of balance and with clear vision, we should press on with the premises of Jean Monnet and remain part of the solution, rather than being part of the problem, in the Balkans and the Eastern Mediterranean.

The chapters of this volume cannot be easily summarized given their depth, richness, idiosyncrasies and special insights. The focus throughout this volume is on twentieth-century Greece. The reader will notice some unevenness among the various chapters in terms of the closing date of each treatment. In the interest of avoiding additional delay in publication the editors have opted not to update certain chapters, thus not covering the latest developments. The theme of painful adjustment to change is a thread that runs through all of them. Part I of the volume is a chapter by Thanos Veremis and John Koliopoulos, which offers an insightful examination of the evolution of the Greek nation and its identity. Language and religion, as well as residence and 'descent', have proved to be the key ingredients shaping the consciousness of the Greek nation following the 1821 War of Independence from the Ottoman Empire. The process of hellenization of the southern Balkan Orthodox Ecumene is presented in this chapter as a mode of ethnic formation towards a concrete national identity. Importantly, as the authors explain, this process was attained by means other than force, specifically by the modernizing structures that hellenization brought into particular areas as well as by the self-awareness it enshrined in terms of belonging to a community anchored by an illustrious past.

Part II focuses on the geostrategic setting in which Greece formulated its international relations. Theodore Couloumbis begins with an overview of domestic factors that have influenced the formulation of Greek foreign policy and continues with an examination of the country's foreign policy priorities. He argues that political schisms between Royalists and Republicans, and at a later time between Communists and Nationalists, plagued Greece's political life from 1915 to 1974, inviting frequent military and foreign interventions in politics.

The second part of his chapter focuses on the behaviour, not necessarily the rhetoric, of political leaders (Constantine Karamanlis and later Andreas Papandreou) whose conduct encouraged democratic political discourse and manifested the country's Western political outlook. Greece's Euro-Atlanticist orientation is today the paramount foreign policy priority for a country no longer torn by ambivalence as to its role in the world. The maintenance of a sufficient military balance for purposes of deterrence in the Greek–Turkish nexus of relations is the second foreign policy priority. Constructive relations with neighbouring countries in the Balkans and the Mediterranean region aimed at contributing to the establishment of a region of stability is another foreign policy priority for Greece, while relations with the United States occupy an equally critical position.

An analysis of the rationale behind the making of Greece's strategic choices is offered by Thanos Dokos. His chapter provides a careful examination of Greece's defence policy since the end of the Second World War. Emphasis is given to the post-Cold War era which has generated a new set of threats and risks for Greece. From a strategy of external balancing during the early Cold War period (mid-1960s) which was oriented mainly by the country's membership in NATO, Greece has moved to a strategy of internal balancing, namely the strengthening of its armed forces, which was dictated primarily by its security dilemma *vis-à-vis* Turkey. Greece's European orientation is of profound importance in the new strategic regional and international setting and has been substantiated in practice by a growing commitment to structural adaptation in security and political issues. In addition, there has been an alteration in the understanding of Greek decision-makers regarding the salience of the country's participation in multilateral peacekeeping forces. Hence, from being an inactive observer in the early 1990s, Greece has evolved into an energetic participant in a number of UN/NATO peacekeeping operations (Bosnia-Herzegovina, Kosovo, etc.) and has responded positively to the practice of the 'coalitions of the willing' regarding its participation in international peacekeeping missions (as was the case in Albania in 1998). Nowadays Greece perceives itself as being a *status quo* country playing the role of a stabilizer in the region.

A number of thematic analyses present the parameters which have deeply affected the formation of Greek foreign policy. The chapter by John Iatrides examines the evolution of US–Greek relations since the end of the Second World War. Emphasis is placed on the supportive US role during the reconstruction years of the 1950s onwards. Occasions in which Greek public opinion became particularly sceptical of Washington's role in Greek affairs are noted with a specific reference to the controversial (lukewarm and frequently supportive) US attitude towards the Colonels' junta. These were times of serious friction in the relations of the two countries. From the Greek perspective, strong griev-ances against Washington emanated from the latter's policy of detachment following Turkey's invasion of Cyprus in 1974 and the continuing occupation of 36% of its territory. By 1974 the salience of the previously constructive US role towards Greece was seriously ques-tioned in the view of many Greeks and it took several years before a positive image could be restored. Washington was always considered the key global actor with strong influence and ability to play *inter alia* a mediating role in Greek–Turkish relations. On the other hand, Washington had frequently indicated its disenchantment with Greece, especially during the years of Andreas Papandreou's rule, when his neo-Marxist ideas as well as anti-American and anti-Western utterances created an ambiguous climate towards Athens within the American foreign policy-making community. Iatrides concludes that despite occa-sions of mutual disenchantment, relations have evolved positively, with Washington being currently perceived as an important and instrumental ally of Greece. Needless to say, some segments of Greek public opinion remain highly critical of some US foreign policy actions in Greece's immediate region, as had been the case of NATO's air campaign during the Kosovo crisis in 1999.

Van Coufoudakis presents a detailed analysis of the evolution of the Cyprus issue as a factor affecting Greek foreign policy, especially towards Turkey. His treatment of the Cyprus Question unveils the way in which economic and strategic concerns of great powers, especially the United States and Britain, prevented rather than encouraged an effective resolution of the Cyprus Question. Specifically, the problem remains an issue not only bewildering Greek–Turkish relations but also presents a case exposing the ineffectiveness of international crisis management. For Coufoudakis, America's fixation on Turkey's strategic importance helps explain a systematic tilt in the latter's favour.

Another important dimension in Greek foreign policy concerns rela-tions with the Balkan states. Aristotle Tziampiris examines Greece's relations with its northern neighbours with central focus on the Macedonian Question. The latter, according to this author, reflected the way in which partisan politics in Greece proved instrumental in the flawed handling of a dispute, thus tarnishing Greece's image. Tziampiris concludes that in the last few years there has been a policy shift in Athens manifesting a more rational and pragmatic attitude towards the Former Yugoslav Republic of Macedonia (FYROM) and other Balkan countries in general. This has rendered Greece in the eyes of its northern neigh-bours as a reliable regional stabilizer, in contrast to the early 1990s.

An examination of Greece's domestic transformation in key areas is dealt with in Part III. Fotini Bellou discusses the democratization process that was augmented in Greece after 1974 and the way in which charismatic political leaders, as well as the country's membership in the European Community, later the European Union, proved to be the catalysts in the consolidation of democratic institutions and practices. By the end of the century, Greece had managed to attain a belated yet considerably developed civil society, even if its full realization is yet to be accomplished.

The negative effects of a patron–client system, which had plagued the Greek polity for decades, are noted by a number of authors. There is agreement on the role of clientelism and the paternalistic state that caused considerable delays in the process of the country's democratic consolidation with a civil society undergirded by a strong market economy. An important dimension reflecting the level of consolidation of democracy regards the role of free media in the political landscape. Ino Afentouli examines the way in which the relationship between the state and the media evolved in the last few decades. Régime change, *metapolitefsi*, after 1974 encouraged the development of free media while the operation of private electronic media was permitted only in the late 1980s. Although today's media in Greece follow the pattern of development observed in other Western countries, the road towards a decentralized media landscape is not going to be without obstacles.

Costas Krimbas, in his chapter focusing on science, technology and the environment, argues that although Greek scientists are of a particularly high standard, research has not progressed to the levels that could capitalize effectively on the human potential of Greece. The presentation of the achievements of Greek scientists in almost all aspects of scientific development and a number of successful environmental projects indicate that human potential can be particularly promising, if the state increases the levels of investment in research. This applies not only to medical research but also to research projects regarding the application of new technologies and the protection of the environment. In sum, Krimbas argues that there should be greater focus on sustainable development.

Another important dimension related to the process of a democratization in a European society is examined in the chapter on education in Greece by Anna Frangoudaki, who presents a careful historical analysis of the educational system in Greece. Frangoudaki posits that a previously underdeveloped educational system, which had been the privilege of the wealthy, has experienced a dramatic transformation in recent years. A considerable change took place as early as 1964 when the spoken language was established as the language of education, compulsory school attendance was extended to nine years and new curricula were introduced aiming to reflect rational approaches to culture and society. Following *metapolitefsi* in 1974, and especially in the 1980s, changes in education enjoyed a new momentum. Modern textbooks, adapted to new realities and democratic values, were introduced, while the system of enrolling students to higher education became more inclusive. Certainly, deficiencies always appear and this presents an important challenge to both state and society, as it does in most Western European countries. This points to the need for a constant effort to adapt the Greek educational system to the needs of a rapidly evolving information age.

The need for educational and cultural adjustment to new realities, as these are posed in the context of the European Union melting pot, is stressed by George Babiniotis. The author illustrates the importance of Greece's cultural and linguistic characteristics in the context of the European Union. He believes that the utility as well as the character of a language should be preserved and respected in the multicultural EU society in which Greece is a member. For this reason, European policies should encourage younger generations to fashion multilingual education, which in turn would strengthen rather than weaken the purposes and objectives of the European Union.

Respect for cultural and religious differences has been a concept that touches a chord in modern times. Admittedly, this has introduced new perspectives in discourse of Greek society. The Greek Orthodox religion has been an important aspect in Greek identity formation and historically it has played a considerable role in the self-definition of the Hellenic nation. On the other hand, religious freedom and tolerance are key aspects of a democratic society. This is the basic premise that Ioannis Konidaris advances in his chapter regarding Church and State relations. In a rare analysis of the legal underpinnings of this relationship, the author offers a detailed presentation of the separate roles that inform the two institutions. In addition, the legal status regarding religious tolerance, as this is contrasted to proselytism, is elaborated. The chapter, needless to say, offers an excellent platform upon which one can assess and evaluate the issue of removing 'religions affiliation' from police-issued identity cards.

Part IV of the book deals with the economic and scientific development of Greece in the last century. The chapter by Theodore Kariotis examines at some length the economic development of Greece, which has fared quite well in comparison to its neighbouring countries. Three factors appear to have contributed substantially to this: the defeat of the communist forces in the wake of the Civil War in the late 1940s, the economic penetration of the United States in major economic activity in the 1950s and, finally, Greece's membership of the European Community in 1981. The author supports his thesis with a number of economic figures in which the progressive evolution of the Greek economy reflects increasing levels of development. Analysis offers a detailed account of the progress taking place at both the macro and microeconomic level. However, as the author elaborates, this process of dramatic economic development has not evolved in a way that could also attain appropriate levels of income distribution. Kariotis argues that income inequality in Greece, as is the case in most developed countries, in all likelihood will unleash negative consequences that could function at the expense of further development. For this reason he recommends policies that sustain economic development and social welfare. In other words, as is advocated by other authors in this volume, structural transformation towards an open market economy cannot ignore social cohesion.

Another perspective reflecting on the degree of democratization in Greece regards the role of women in society. In her chapter, Anna Karamanou offers a concise presentation of the slow but steady incorporation of women into the functional procedures of society as well as the way in which discrimination on grounds of gender is being gradually eliminated in Greece. Today females amount to 57% of the student population in Greek universities, 40% of the workforce, while there has been a dynamic breakthrough in all scientific and vocational fields. In addition, 75% of the workforce in the legal profession and the civil service are female. However, in fields traditionally occupied by males, especially positions related to political decision-making, the deficit in female representation is more than apparent. The chapter also analyses the manner in which Greece's membership in the EU has contributed towards the reduction of gender discrimination against women.

Part IV concludes with an analysis of the Greek diaspora in the United States constituting a distant yet vital component of the Greek nation. The chapter by Charles Moskos provides key historical evidence regarding the periods of Greek mass immigration to the United States. According to the most recent census (1990) figures, one million persons claimed to be of Greek ancestry while two-thirds of them were entirely of Greek ancestry. A substantial number of Greek immigrants have distinguished themselves in American society both in politics and business. The author comments on the role of the Greek Church in preserving the Greek traditions in the United States by the creation of philanthropic groups and culturally oriented societies. The latter, as the author advocates, has helped preserve the Greek consciousness abroad, while on several occasions it has sought to influence the formation of American foreign policy positions to Greece.

Part V concludes with two prospective analyses of the road ahead. These chapters discuss the two strategic areas that have proved to be instrumental in the setting of Greece's foreign policy priorities and the country's political and economic transformation (i.e. Greek–Turkish relations and Greece's future in the European Union). In his short but thought-provoking chapter, Byron Theodoropoulos makes some particularly sober remarks regarding Greek–Turkish relations. The seasoned diplomat raises questions regarding the wisdom of Greece's past and recent policies towards its eastern neighbour, but points out the dangers on the road ahead, in case Turkey continues to conduct its foreign policy under the veil of suspicion underpinned by revisionist tactics challenging the territorial *status quo* in the Aegean.

On an equally pragmatic footing, Loukas Tsoukalis discusses Greece's efforts to adjust to EU membership and the difficulties that have accompanied this endeavour in the last two decades. Greece's entry into the euro-zone in January 2001 required significant shifts to the country's political and economic system. Adjustment to the 'euro' standards required the government to demonstrate strong political will, as it was more acutely illustrated after 1996, in order to rein in a hitherto clientelist system, both in politics and the economy. Greece, Tsoukalis argues, has entered a long and difficult phase of structural reform, by reducing considerably the state-controlled sector of the economy, overhauling the social security system and adjusting Greek public administration to the rapidly shifting reality of European integration and globalization. There is still a long road to travel in this direction with many obstacles on the way. In an insightful argument reflecting many of the premises advanced in this volume, Tsoukalis suggests that the appropriate mode of governance and international behaviour for the country should be analogous of the EU norm. Accordingly, Greece will need to combine further reforms at home with careful diplomacy abroad. Domestic transformation can succeed when structural reforms are coupled with policies based on social cohesion. In addition, a foreign policy that is conducted primarily through compatible alliances, formal or *ad hoc*, will prove to be a good recipe for Greece well into the twenty-first century.

NOTES

1 We have borrowed this term from William Hardly McNeil's excellent book entitled *The Metamorphosis of Greece Since World War II* (Chicago: Chicago University Press, 1978).
2 T. Couloumbis, 'The Syndrome of Conceptual Inertia', *Kathimerini*, Athens, 8, 11 (1998).
3 UNDP, 2000.

PART I

1

The Evolving Content of the Greek Nation

THANOS VEREMIS and JOHN KOLIOPOULOS

The notion of a newly born nation is a convenient starting point to the question of the identity of the 1821 insurgents. The major themes in this respect are terms such as *ethnos* (nation) and *genos* (people), as well as the idea of the necessary space for the new nation state referred to as *epikrateia* (domain). The meaning of the term *ethnos* in revolutionary Greece is elusive and, more often than not, misleading: it was frequently used in the sense of the Orthodox Christians, irrespective of their mother tongue, or in the sense of the term *genos*, as well as in the sense of nation state.[1] Religion and residence, as well as language and 'descent', were used in various combinations to define the identity of the members of the insurgent nation.

Religion was one determinant on which everyone agreed, while residence was accepted only in determining citizenship. Language was only grudgingly conceded for spreading Greek education to all the Orthodox subjects. One aspect of the early debates on the criteria for defining the 'newly born' nation, was the lack of consensus on any single criterion or combination of criteria. Two conflicting trends, a 'modern' and a 'traditional', clashed over the suitable criteria for defining the new nation and the identity of its members, the former favouring language, while the latter insisting on religion. Eventually, religion prevailed as the dominant criterion for defining the modern Greek nation while irredentist ideology became the hallmark of its modern history.

Most significant for the growth of a modern national identity and ideology, what came to be known as the 'Great Idea' (*Megali Idea*), projected the state as the arbiter of Greek fortunes. Eventually the nation state, it secured unchallenged supremacy in the ideological restructuring of the traditional Greek world outside the state's boundaries and succeeded in forcing the Ecumenical Patriarchate to relinquish its leading role in the Greek world.

However, before this 'Helladic' ideological imperium was established, the Greek nation state had first to develop a coherent ideology out of the diverse ideas put forward in insurgent Greece. Religious differentiation from the Turks was no longer sufficient in the new political framework. It was, above all, essential to define modern Greek identity in relation to the other Orthodox peoples in the Balkans, Bulgars, Albanians and Vlachs, with claims to the same lands. What was the relation of the Greeks to these 'others', and who were the Greeks?

The name *Hellenes* for these post independence Greeks was irresistible and perhaps unavoidable, in view of the early and strong identification with ancient *Hellas*. *Graecoi* was also recommended as a conscious departure from *Romaioi* or *Romioi*, which were still in use in insurgent Greece but too much identified with the nation's eastern antecedent. *Graecoi* was thought to be most appropriate and in accord with Western usage.[2] The denomination *Hellenes* prevailed, because it was thought to be most appropriate for the 'descendants' of the ancient Greeks; this notion, however, undermined the potential appeal of the modern Greeks to their co-religionists in the Sultan's dominions, whose antecedents could not be traced as far back as those of the Greeks. This departure from tradition, which reflected the conscious effort to resurrect the classical past in as many ways as possible, in conjunction with the inelegant parting from the Ecumenical Patriarchate, vitiated the very vision of a Greek cultural imperium over the other Orthodox Christians of the East, and at the same time dug a deep ditch between popular culture and the 'new state culture'.

How could the Greeks present themselves credibly as leaders of all the Orthodox Christians of the East, when their choice of name signified a turn to an antecedent that placed language at the centre of national identity and made it the major, if not the sole determinant, of that identity? Was language alone, even as highly esteemed a language as Greek among non-Greek speaking co-religionists, an adequate instrument for the establishment of the new Greek empire? All the declarations that the insurgents had been fighting for, 'the faith and the cross' and for the establishment of a 'Christian nation', were these solemn protestations made to dupe those who had always been suspicious of Greek aims?

These were legitimate questions for the non-Greek speaking Orthodox Christians of the Ottoman Empire to pose and for the Greeks of the time and subsequent times to answer. The crux of the matter was this: how could the Greeks possibly aspire to build a Western nation state based on their own language as the primary determinant of identity and hope to incorporate and accommodate the non-Greek speaking Orthodox Christians in that nation state as their equals? For more than 50 years no one had real cause to either ask this question or try to answer it. Albanian-speaking Suliots and Hydriots, Vlach-speaking Thessalians and Epirots and Slav-speaking Macedonians had fought in revolutionary Greece along with the other Greeks, and no one had thought that non-Greek speakers were any less Greek than Greek speakers. When most of the northern Greek fighters settled in southern Greece as refugees, they were not made to think that they were lesser Greeks for speaking little or no Greek, the ongoing debate on Greekness and Greek identity notwithstanding. Essentially, this question was never posed before the Greeks met the Bulgars in the north as competitors; even then, however, the real issue was circumvented by superimposing 'sentiments' or 'consciousness' on language.

The vision of a Greek Christian empire, however, was no longer a driving force behind the objectives and actions of those who held power in the 'model' kingdom. At best it was a harmless fantasy, at worst a show of bravado put on for the benefit of the masses who still held fast to that vision. The protagonists of the 'first' Greek war of liberation were now comfortably established as army generals, senators and ambassadors, decorated by the Greek and foreign monarchs, while their progeny were manning the civil service and were well on the way to giving the country an indigenous but thoroughly Westernized intelligentsia. This generation of Greeks offered the nation a truly modern theory of Greek history and nationality. Building on existing scholarship and working in the changed atmosphere of the 1850s and 1860s, Spyridon Zambelios and especially Konstantinos Paparrigopoulos were able to construct a historical edifice that survived the onslaught of many subsequent historiographers and served the reconstruction of the union as no other theory has.[3]

Some of the major and lasting contributions of the Zambelios–Paparrigopoulos school have been: i) the restoration of Byzantium in the history of Eastern Christendom and of the Greek nation; ii) the establishment of the cultural continuity of the Greek nation in time and in space; and iii) the convincing projection of the modern Greek nation as a cultural community consisting of all the linguistic groups and peoples it has incorporated in its long history from antiquity to modern times. All three concepts reaffirmed contemporary opinion about culture as the primary determinant of modern Greek national identity and placed that identity on what appeared at the time a safe and solid course of national development.

Paparrigopoulos' concept of Greek history and the modern Greek nation provided the principal arguments in support of Greek claims to the Sultan's European and Asia Minor dominions. It also strengthened the conviction of the generation of Greeks that confronted the Turks and the Bulgars in the period between the Congress of Berlin (1878) and the Treaty of Lausanne (1923), that the Greek cause rested on solid historical and moral ground. Subsequent developments and particularly the insecurity associated with a long and vulnerable border and the presence of minorities claimed by neighbours as their brethren, derailed these concepts and arguments from their old cultural tracks.

The Greeks of the interwar period were led to believe that all people inhabiting Greece were or ought to have been Greek, not only in sharing the same culture, but also in speech. Greek national ideology and assumptions about the Greek nation were led, under the influence of the threat from Bulgaria and international communist sedition, into a narrow path which did not allow differences in speech or in any other way. The broad and all-embracing approach to national identity of the nineteenth century, which did not distinguish Albanian, Vlach, Slav or Turkish speakers from the dominant Greek-speaking component of the nation, had given way to a narrow interpretation of modern Greek identity. Before settling down for the more modern approach, which defines the modern Greek nation as a cultural community embracing all the linguistic groups that the Greeks have incorporated and absorbed in their history, Greek officials would frown upon what had come to be considered dangerous deviations from the model Greek and manifestations that negated the homogeneous nation. The Greek state of course did not invent assimilation, nor did it remain attached to such national visions longer than others in the West. Suppression of Slav Macedonian speech in Greece came much later than the ordeal of such 'others' in the West as the Huguenots, the Moriscos, the Irish or the American Indians, but was followed by the ordeal of the Jews, the Gypsies and the Blacks.

A disgruntled group of intellectuals, who included Ion Dragoumis and looked back to an idealised and fictitious pre-independence past, turned back to the Greek kingdom as the 'beacon' of the West in the East and searched in that past for guidance to re-fashion the Greek nation. There was only a slight and subtle shift from the traditional position on the Greek nation, but this shift cast doubts on the Western liberal tradition as the proper premise for the nation. Violent death before the rise of fascism saved Dragoumis from seeing his ideas seized upon by the theorists of the Metaxas dictatorship between 1936 and 1940, and turned into ideological caricature.[4]

The content of Greek nationalism was transformed during the interwar period. The Asia Minor debacle of 1922 that put an end to the largest Greek community outside the realm, signified the end of Greek irredentism and the beginning of a parochial definition of 'Greekness'. At the same time the Comintern decided in 1924 that Greek, Bulgarian and Serbian inhabitants of the geographic region of Macedonia ought to unite into an autonomous whole under Bulgarian tutelage. The decision initially split the Greek Communist Party before it fell in line with the Comintern, but its ultimate compliance made it the target of much abuse by the state. Besides threatening the established social order, the communists were viewed as conspiring to cede territory from the national body. The 'danger from within' was an entirely new threat to a state that had known only external adversaries. The fear of encirclement on both external and internal fronts forged a mentality that looked for overt and covert enemies. Whereas during the years of irredentism state ideology reflected a generosity of spirit towards potential convertees and tolerance for ethnic idiosyncracies, the interwar state pursued its mission in history. The exclusive relationship with antiquity became one of the two legitimising elements of ethnicity. The other was ideological purity.

The new content of Greek nationalism was a negative reflection of the communist creed. Class analysis and Historical Materialism that cut across national distinctions indirectly shaped the future of the Greek state's ideological orientation. The Greek Communist Party (KKE) provided the state with ample opportunity to persecute it. In 1931, responding to the Comintern's insistence that it should 'wage the struggle for the right of true self-determination of the nations, including secession',[5] the KKE accused Greece of being 'an imperialist state, which conquered by force entire regions inhabited by other nationalities ...'[6] The Liberal government of Eleftherios Venizelos had already drafted laws in 1929 which authorized the persecution of those whose thoughts and acts were believed to undermine the social order.

In the elections of 1936 the KKE received 5.76% of the votes and sent 15 MPs to Parliament who held a pivotal 'balancer' role between the conservative and liberal parties. This development diminished the popularity of the Parliamentary system among the supporters of the two larger parties and rendered the long-standing dictatorship of Greece's Italian neighbour all the more attractive.

The Metaxas regime of 1936–40 featured some of the trappings of its contemporary dictatorships but failed to secure the enthusiasm of a public that defied regimentation. The fragmentation of Greek society by familial and patronage loyalties precluded the dissemination of 'collectivistic nationalism'.[7] Metaxas' doctrine was based on the general will and the nation state as the highest repository of liberty. The regime was defined as the 'Third Civilization', succeeding the Classical and Byzantine traditions and combining elements of both.[8]

Since most ethnic groups in Greece were conservative in their political affiliations and declared their identification with the nation, they did not suffer from the regime. The traditional benign relationship of the major anti-liberal political forces with ethnic groups in Greece was thus carried over to the Metaxas government.[9] The blatant exception to this rule were those Slavonic speakers of northern Greece who had viewed Asia Minor refugees settled in Greek Macedonia in 1923 as their natural adversaries. Not only were refugees given the coveted property of the exchanged Turks, but the destitute Asia Minor Greeks enjoyed preferential treatment by the state. The above reasons and the high-handed methods of the Metaxas functionaries in the north, who considered the ethnic Slavs politically suspect, compelled the latter to shift their loyalties to the Communist Party. Thus the Comintern decision of 1923 became a self-fulfilling prophecy with some 'help' from the Greek authorities.

During the Second World War Eastern Macedonia and Thrace were annexed by the Bulgarian forces in the name of a united Macedonia and Thrace. The western part of Macedonia was occupied by Italian and German forces that gave the secessionist element a free hand. The about-face turn of Nazi collaborators after the departure of the Germans brought them once more within the ranks of the communist guerillas – Greek and Yugoslav. The civil war of 1944–49 pitted the loyalist Slavonic speakers who fought on the side of the Greek army, against the secessionists, who joined the ranks of the communist-controlled 'Democratic Army'. The latter's defeat signified the exodus from Greece of people who had placed their hopes first on an autonomous Macedonia under Bulgarian tutelage, and subsequently on a Socialist Republic within Tito's Yugoslavia.[10] Throughout the post-war years, the voting patterns in western Macedonia, where most of the present day Slavonic speakers reside, have favoured right-wing parties.

The Greek Civil War polarised society, politics and ideology. This did not occur under conditions of dictatorial rule in a state which, in spite of various constitutional irregularities and extraordinary measures, continued to observe the essential rules of parliamentary democracy. The Communist Party that abstained in the 1946 elections and called upon its followers to defy their outcome, was outlawed following the outbreak of hostilities, but all the other parties continued to operate undeterred by the Civil War and the social challenges confronting post-war Europe. Ideological polarization left little margin for middle-class leaders and the intelligentsia to deal with issues other than those of Greece's national identity and its place in western Europe.

State ideology (legitimised by the parliamentary system and trans-mitted through the channels of education and state-controlled radio stations) presented an image of Greece as a besieged nation warding off communist adversaries and upholding Western values. Yet no principled argument was propagated concerning liberal values and political toler-ance. There emerged therefore a form of nationalist fundamentalism, which unlike nineteenth-century irredentism was defensive, exclusive and parochial. With the state apparatus, a cluster of agencies developed, filled with functionaries (policemen, military personnel and other guar-antors of public order) who enjoyed relative freedom from public scrutiny. Liberal attempts to dislodge these functionaries from power in 1964–65 provoked the wrath of the Crown and encouraged military cabals ultimately bringing about the 1967–74 military régime.

The functional relationship between Greece and its Western allies was challenged by the advent of the Socialists in power. The anti-Western undertones in PASOK's pronouncements, after three decades of almost uninterrupted official loyalty to the US and its European allies, partly reflected the sentiments of those that had been excluded from public life due to their left-wing affiliations. It also reflected widespread disappointment with the West's failure to censure the military junta between 1967 and 1974. Even traditional nationalists opted for PASOK because its criticism of the West stroked the self-esteem of the Greeks traumatized by the military dictatorship and the Cyprus disaster that was its natural consequence. Although Andreas Papandreou's verbal defection from Atlantic solidarity created a negative climate against Greece in Western official quarters, a substantial segment of the Greek public was thrilled by this manifestation of independence *vis-à-vis* the powerful states of the world.

The collapse of communism in south-eastern Europe generated a widespread revival of nationalism in the region. Memories of wartime annexation of Greek Macedonia and Thrace by Bulgarian occupation forces were rekindled and all parties (except the KKE) united in opposition to the Macedonian denomination adopted by Greece's newly independent neighbour. Greek foreign policy *vis-à-vis* the naming of the Former Yugoslav Republic of Macedonia became hostage to popular sentiment and international confusion. By the mid-1990s the outburst of defensive nationalism subsided as the perception of the 'brotherless' and besieged nation was replaced by a new-found national self-confidence. The consolidation of democracy, improvement of relations with all the Balkan states and the convergence of Greece with EMU (Economic and Monetary Union) criteria, marginalized the nationalist deputies in parliament and established a moderate mainstream in politics.

The Church, after a century and a half of compliance with state policy, has through its prelates chosen to contest the prerogatives of the Greek government to draft legislation that removes religious affiliations from public identification cards. The paradox lies in the fact that the Church is rebelling not against state supervision but the likelihood of a putative separation with the temporal authorities. Having identified with the national ideology, although at the expense of its ecumenical credibility, the Church will continue to grasp its affiliation with the state as a life preserver in times of competing material diversions.

DEFINING MODERN GREEK IDENTITY

Defining modern Greek national identity has never been an easy undertaking. Greeks have been adding new terms or new meanings to old
terms and shuffling more or less the same criteria from generation to
generation, adding new ones without always dropping those which
might appear to be in conflict with the old. These shifts of meanings and
definitions of terms and criteria were, of course, the result of changing
needs and circumstances.

The 'other' is normally a useful concept in distinguishing and defining group self-perceptions. By identifying the others, one expects to
arrive at a relatively secure definition of a group. In the case of the
modern Greeks this approach is anything but safe because some of the
others have been thought to be 'less' other than the rest, or not other at
all. The other Orthodox Christians, the Latin or Western Christians and
the Muslims have been the three principal 'others' for the Greeks and
are a convenient point of departure for a discussion of the subject.

The definition of the Greeks and the others in the first Constitution
of the War of Independence, although it refers to them as citizens of the
nation state in the making, does provide some important clues as to the
criteria in use for distinguishing them from the others. The relevant
article (Art. 2) laid down that 'those indigenous inhabitants of the
domain of Greece who believe in Christ are Greeks'.[11] This definition,
however, soon proved inadequate for the needs of the fledgling nation
state. Were Catholic Greeks of the Aegean Islands as Greek as the
Orthodox Greeks? They were in political terms, and only grudgingly so
and with grave misgivings in ideological terms. Similarly, were non-
indigenous Western Christians equally Greek if they chose to settle in the
'Greek domain' permanently? They were, according to the Constitution,
but not as far as the Orthodox Church was concerned. Lastly, were
indigenous Muslim Turks as Greek as the rest if they chose to convert to
Christianity, as many did to avoid expulsion? They were and were not.
Orthodox prelates welcomed such converts but lay revolutionary leaders
were very reluctant to consider them other than opportunists who would
turn against the Greeks if the opportunity arose.[12]

Religion, or more accurately, Eastern Christianity, was the principal
qualification and criterion of Greek national identity. Residence in the
'Greek domain' was the second qualification; but no sooner was residence laid down as a determining factor of Greek identity than it
presented the Greeks with a series of questions on which there was no
agreement and never has been ever since. What did, after all, constitute
the 'Greek domain' during the War of Independence, when the fortunes
of war changed radically and swiftly? Were the districts that had
revolted against Turkish rule the only constituent lands of this domain?

Another important determining factor of Greek identity, language, was introduced one year later by the second revolutionary constitution, no doubt as a major step in the desired Western orientation of the fledgling nation state in Europe's south-eastern fringe. The conclusion was amended to provide also for 'those coming from abroad who have Greek as their mother tongue and believe in Christ'.[13] This amendment, however, which was intended to modernise the nation's definition of its identity, was silently dropped in the next revolutionary constitution.[14] Yet language as a determining factor of modern Greek identity would never stop exercising a powerful influence on all subsequent efforts to come to grips with the intractable question under consideration here. Though never admitted openly, language became a powerful instrument in the hands of the Greek nation state in its drive to Hellenize the multilingual lands it gradually detached from the Ottoman Empire in the course of one century.

The *heteroglossoi* or *heterophonoi* (heterolinguals) of the initial Greek national state, principally Albanians and Vlachs, caused no embarrassment to Greek nation state builders. At the time, no other Balkan nationalists claimed either of the two as their brethren. Besides, after many centuries of cohabitation, both the Albanians and the Vlachs of southern and central Greece had been comfortably Hellenized in most respects and, in some cases, in speech as well. Moreover, both had generously contributed in the making of the Greek nation state in the southern Greek peninsula, the Vlachs in the Greek Enlightenment and the Albanians in helping win the war against the Turks; and both identified with Greek national aims and future irredentist objectives. Finally, both Albanians and Vlachs were numerous enough not to be frowned upon, let alone discriminated against. Other heterolinguals, the descendants of the Slavs of Macedonia, a fair number of whom fought in southern Greece with distinction after the collapse of the uprisings in southern Macedonia in 1821 and 1822, and who were given land to settle in the independent Greek nation state, were again not differentiated from the rest of the Greeks. They were referred to as 'Bulgarians' or 'Thracian-Macedonians', and were thought to be Bulgarian-speaking brethren. They, too, identified with the Greek nation state no less than the Greek-speaking Greeks of the time. In any case, most heterolinguals of Greece of the time, and later times, spoke and, in many cases, wrote enough Greek not to feel excluded from the rest of the Greeks. The Greek-dominated Orthodox hierarchy and the dominant position of Greek education and language in commerce in the Ottoman Empire were respectable and unassailable endowments for the nation state to draw upon for many decades to come. The role of the language in becoming a major instrument of acculturation into Greek citizenship cannot be exaggerated, although its beneficiaries have often taken this for granted. The Greek state will probably continue to neglect, as it has done in the past, this formidable asset in its care.

The *heterothreskoi* or *heterodoxoi* (heteroreligionists), essentially the Jews and the Muslim Turks and Albanians, were not discriminated against politically, although they were clearly differentiated from the other Greeks; and though free to exercise their religious duties, they – and every religious community for that matter, except the Orthodox Christians – were not allowed to proselytise. On the status of the heteroreligionists Greek nation state builders displayed an insecurity disproportionate to the threat these inhabitants of Greece posed at the time, and subsequently, to the state religion. No doubt Orthodox prelates were instrumental in this unwarranted display of insecurity with respect to heteroreligionists. This insecurity, however, seems to have had deeper roots than the expected opposition from Orthodox prelates to allow the heteroreligionists complete freedom of action. Koraes, who opposed all restrictions to political and human rights and was no admirer of protected state religion, expressed the liberal position of the time on the subject as follows:

> After letting them freely practice their religion, inside their temples or the temple precincts, we should encourage them to believe that they would gradually be granted full political rights, as they prove themselves capable of enjoying them; because these rights we can neither deny them, nor is it completely safe to grant them immediately. With such gradual progress, instead of turning them into enemies, we shall make them sincere friends of the commonwealth, so much so as we are in a way offering them what we do not owe them.

Because, he explained, the Jews no more than the Muslims had not fought for the freedom of the land.[15]

Others were also the Roma; but such they were, and always had been, everywhere in Europe. The perpetual fleeting outcasts of sedentary society were no more 'other' in newly-independent Greece than in most lands of the time and subsequent times. Like the transhumant Sarakatsan and Vlach shepherds, Gypsies were considered enemies of organized human society and state security; unlike the Sarakatsans and the Vlachs, however, who were never thought to be other than backward Greeks, Gypsies were never considered members of the Greek nation.

Language as a determining factor appeared to be waning and religion to be waxing as the Enlightened and Westernised intellectuals gave way to the Romantics of post-Revolutionary Greece. Romanticism and a growing sense of superiority over the other peoples of the Ottoman

Empire, on account of commercial competence, accumulated wealth, superior education and a growing re-Hellenization of lands lost in the past to foreign invaders, were responsible for associating the Greeks with the Ecumenical Patriarch's spiritual domain – until the challenge of the Bulgars in Macedonia forced Greek thinkers to come up with new arguments where old ones were thought to be of no use. The Bulgars, by claiming the Orthodox Slavs of Macedonia as their brethren on account of their Slav language, dealt a serious blow to Greek claims to the land. Language as determining factor of identity as an argument in support of claims to unredeemed lands and their inhabitants was dropped altogether, but not education for the 're-Hellenization' of Greeks who had 'lost' their mother tongue in the centuries of foreign invasion and rule. Indeed, Greek education, more accurately Greek schools in the irredenta, flourished in an impressive way.

Religion, too, as a determining factor was no longer a convincing argument and had to be refined. In the new situation what was important was not Orthodoxy as such, but adherence to the Ecumenical Patriarch; and the Bulgars and all those who adhered to the Bulgarian Exarch were 'schismatics'. The Ecumenical Patriarch was the true and legitimate head of the Ottoman Orthodox, and adherence to the Ecumenical Patriarch was a prerequisite of Greek identity. Descent was another 'unfailing' determining factor of identity. This argument was thought to be unassailable. Who else but the Greeks could put forward the oldest and most illustrious titles to the land and its people? *Prior tempore, fortior jure*. The 'Bulgars' and 'Thraco-Bulgars' of past days now became 'Bulgarian-speaking Greeks' (Voulgarophonoi Hellenes) with striking 'Greek features'.[16] They were Greeks by descent and by remaining loyal – those at least who did remain loyal – to the Ecumenical Patriarch.

In the case of the Slavs of Macedonia or the Slav Macedonians, a further and even more 'unfailing' determinant of identity was put forward at the time – self-identification or 'conviction' (*syneidesis* or *phronema*) – which marked a further departure from the initial course of national development charted by the men of the Greek Enlightenment. Self-identification was the most important determining factor of identity. It was a most useful construct, and was seized upon by modern Greek nation state builders and has never been relinquished. Consciousness or 'conviction' was the ultimate proof of a person's identification with a community and loyalty to it. All the other determining factors, language in particular, were of secondary importance; what really mattered about a person's identity was his or her sharing of sentiments.

This new Western import was thought to be modern, democratic and reasonable. Thus, Greek identity rested on the paternal faith or the maternal tongue, on time-honoured customs, but above all on a person's right to choose it. Greek nation state builders were convinced that they possessed an irrefutable argument against all those who questioned the Greek identity of non-Greek speaking Orthodox in the irredenta and subsequently in the northern 'New Lands' of Greece. When 'descent' was uncertain or impossible to prove convincingly, self-identification was the ultimate answer. Little did the Greeks of the time think of the inherent dangers in the concept of self-identification as a determining factor of identity; of the danger, in particular, of identity becoming a subject of interpretation, transformation or manipulation by agencies or people other than those immediately concerned; or of the danger of this concept being applied to define someone's 'correct' political affiliations.

For the time being, the Greeks of free Greece could indulge in defining their brethren of unredeemed Greece, primarily the Slav Macedonians and secondarily the Orthodox Albanians and the Vlachs. Primary school students were taught, in the 1880s, that 'Greeks [are] our kinsmen, of common descent, speaking the language we speak and professing the religion we profess'.[17] But this definition, it seems, was reserved for small children who could not possibly understand the intricate arguments of their parents on the question of Greek identity. What was essential to understand at that tender age was that modern Greeks descended from the ancient Greeks. Grown up children, however, must have been no less confused than adults on the criteria for defining modern Greek identity. Did the Greeks constitute a 'race' apart from the Albanians, the Slavs and the Vlachs? Yes and no. High school students were told that the 'other races', i.e. the Slavs, the Albanians and the Vlachs, 'having been Hellenized with the years in terms of mores and customs, are now being assimilated into the Greeks'.[18]

On the Slavs of Macedonia there seems to have been no consensus. Were they Bulgars, Slavicized Greeks or early Slavs? They 'were' Bulgars until the 1870s and Slavicized Greeks, or Hellenized Slavs subsequently, according to the needs of the dominant theory. There was no consensus, either, on the Vlachs. Were they Latinized Greek mountaineers of late immigrants from Vlachia? As in the case of the Slavs of Macedonia, Vlach descent shifted from the southern Balkans to the Danube, until the Romanians claimed the Vlachs for their brethren; which made the latter irrevocably indigenous to the southern Balkan mountains. The Albanians or 'Arvanites', were readily 'adopted' as brethren of common descent for at least three reasons. Firstly, the Albanians had been living in southern Greece, as far south as the Peloponnese, in considerable numbers. Secondly, Christian Albanians had fought with distinction and in considerable numbers in the War of Independence. Thirdly, credible Albanian claims for the establishment of an Albanian nation state materialized too late for Greek national theorists to abandon well-entrenched positions. Commenting on a geography textbook for primary schools in 1901, a state committee found it inadequate and misleading. One of its principal shortcomings concerned the Albanians, who were described as 'close kinsmen of the Greeks'. 'These are unacceptable from the point of view of our national claims and as far as historical truth is concerned', commented the committee. 'It must have been maintained that they are of common descent with the Greeks (Pelasgians), that they speak a language akin to that of the Greeks and that they participated in all struggles for national liberation of the common fatherland.'[19]

In 1908, just as the Young Turks were embarking on their pronunciamento that was intended to transform the decaying Ottoman Empire, another national committee deciding on geography textbooks for Greek children gave the following definition for the Greeks of Asia Minor:

> Greeks are those who speak Turkish but profess the Christian religion of their ancestors. Greeks are also the Greek speaking Muslims of Asia Minor, who lost their ancestral religion but kept their ancestral tongue. As far as the inhabitants of Asia Minor, who are Muslims and speak Turkish, are concerned, only reliable historical evidence or anthropological studies can prove their Greek descent and their distinction from the non-Greek Muslims.[20]

Neither language nor religion, therefore, were reliable and decisive determinants of Greek identity; what was reliable and decisive was descent – where descent could be established with the assistance of historical evidence or anthropological study. History initially, archaeology and folklore eventually, were mobilized to support the theory of the modern Greeks descending from the ancient Greeks. The language and, when language was of no use, the ancient 'stones', the mores and customs of the inhabitants were reliable witnesses of the Hellenic past living into the modern Greek present. Conquerors and settlers of past centuries had been absorbed and assimilated by the culturally 'superior' Greeks. What was left from the turbulent past of foreign invasion and conquest were foreign place names and linguistic pockets here and there to remind modern Greeks of the centuries of foreign captivity or settlement.

Who, then, were the 'others' after a century of debate about the determining factors of modern Greek identity? The Osmanli Turks, who had invaded the Greek lands and were temporarily 'camping' in these lands, were certainly others; so were Jews and Gypsies, who guarded their particular identities, and foreign-born Catholics or Protestants. Greeks were all the rest, including the Hellenized Albanians, Slavs and Vlachs and not excluding even the *heterothreskoi* or *heteroglossoi*, whose

Hellenic descent could be safely established or whose Greek conscience could be determined.

Interesting clues on the question of 'others' in the Greek nation state can be derived from the naturalisation provisions of the state's early and formative years, which reflect official views on who could be granted Greek citizenship, and how. Initially, and before the question on who could be appointed to higher state positions and who could not, foreign-born Greeks became Greek citizens on appearing before and registering with any local Greek authority. Aliens were required, before being granted Greek citizenship, to reside in Greece for five years, to acquire immovable property in Greece and possess a worthy character. The residence requirement was eased in 1827 – three years, instead of five – no doubt in order to attract people to a country whose population was decimated by massacre, epidemics and famine.

As in all nation states, naturalization legislation in Greece has been based on *jus soli* or territory law and aimed at creating a homogeneous people. In Greece, however, as in Germany and certain other European countries, *jus sanguinis* or blood law, has always been decisive in defining Greek citizenship; which provides a further clue in the question of Greek nationality and national identity. The 1823 and 1827 revolutionary Constitutions, as well as the 1835 and 1856 laws – and the 1955 law – on Greek citizenship, clearly differentiated the Greeks from the others with respect to nationality. Foreign-born Greek *homogeneis* or simply *homogeneis* (Greek nationals) were, and still are, preferentially treated when it comes to citizenship. The Greek nation, in other words, although it created the Greek nation state, according to official theory, could not possibly be associated solely with that state; and although the Greeks followed the usual path of one nation one state and one state one nation, the Greek nation existed and exists not only within the confines of the Greek nation state.

If others before then had imagined, reconstructed or invented their modern identities, the modern Greeks could have done no less. What mattered, for themselves, their neighbours and the 'others', were not so much the 'objective' or 'subjective' criteria they used as determining factors of their national identity, but a certain nervousness and panic in the projection of these criteria after the appearance of serious contenders for the lands of the Ottoman sultan in the last quarter of the nineteenth century. The select nation on the south-eastern fringe of Europe, which would act as a beacon of light in the East and would civilize its less fortunate brethren in the region, became the threatened, insecure and 'brotherless' nation of late nineteenth century. Would the modern Greeks have felt that language became the sole determining factor of their identity? Perhaps. This, however, required a different beginning from the one the Greeks had had in the 1820s. It certainly required a national course less subservient to Orthodoxy and more anchored in the Enlightenment. Not that the two were incompatible; indeed, some of the more serious and solid enlightened thinkers were Orthodox prelates. Orthodoxy was used by Greek Romantics to penetrate the worlds of Orthodox peasants and turn them into Hellenes with the Greek language as their instrument.

Language, therefore, became a medium and an end in itself. What surprises the student of modern Greece is not so much the grandiose and somewhat deceptive project of Hellenizing of the Orthodox Ecumene of the southern Balkans as such, but that this project was realized in large measure. The price, of course, of this national course was high for the modern Greeks no less than for their former brethren and the 'others'; it has not been, however, without benefits to everyone concerned. The imaginatively constructed Hellenic Ecumene in the southern Balkans may well have trampled on the rights and sensibilities of the 'others' in the region. The Orthodox Ecumene, however, was no less imagined, and the temporal state it was subservient to, the Ottoman Empire, was not exactly a paradise for subject peoples, for the Greeks no more than for their Orthodox 'brethren'. Two of the prime benefits of this Hellenization of the southern Balkan Orthodox Ecumene have been the modernization it brought into backward areas and the sense of pride it gave in terms of belonging to a community anchored in an illustrious past. Neo-Orthodox thinkers may well lament the alleged 'integral' and orderly life of the pre-national Orthodox community of the southern Balkans. What they both choose not to see is that this penetration and transformation of the Orthodox community of past days has primarily been achieved by means other than force.

NOTES

1. D. Zakinthou, *I Politiki Istoria tis Neoteras Ellados* (*Political History of Modern Greece*) (Athens: 1965) pp. 37–56 [In Greek].
2. *Ephemeris ton Athinon* (*Athens Daily*), August 1825 in A. Lignos (ed.), *Archion Hydras* (*Archive of Hydra*), viii, Piraeus, 1934, pp. 312–13.
3. K. Th. Dimaras, *Konstantinos Paparrigopoulos* (Athens: Morphotiko Idryma Ethnikis Trapezas, 1986).
4. I. Dragoumis in Phillipos Dragoumis (ed.), *Ellinismos mou kai oi Ellines, 1903–1909* (*My Hellenism and the Greeks*) (Athens: 1927) [In Greek].
5. G. Mavrogordatos, *Stillborn Republic: Social Coalitions and Policy Strategies in Greece, 1922–1936* (Berkeley: University of California Press, 1983) p. 234.
6. *Ibid.*
7. C. Sarandis, 'The Ideology and Character of the Metaxas Regime' in R. Higham and T. Veremis (eds), *The Metaxas Dictatorship: Aspects of Greece 1936–1940* (Athens: ELIAMEP, Vryonis Center, 1993) p. 161.
8. *Ibid.*, p. 150.
9. For a well-rounded account of the tension between the Liberal Party and ethnic-religious minorities and the latter's support for the conservatives forces in Parliament, see Mavrogordatos, *Stillborn Republic*, pp. 226–72.

10. Y. Koliopoulos, *Leilasia Phronymaton* (*A Pillage of Convictions*), (Thessaloniki: Vanias Publications, 1994).
11. See the doctoral dissertation of Elpis Volgi on the content of Greek citizenship since independence 1821–56 now in progress at the University of the Aristotelian University in Thessaloniki.
12. *Prosorinon Politevma tis Ellados* (*Preliminary Constitution of Greece*), Corinth 1822, Article 2.
13. Correspondence of insurgent Greek government in *Archia Ellinikis Palingenesias* (*Archives of Hellenic Regeneration*) 1, (Athens, 1971) pp. 289–90, 293–4, 389.
14. *Nomos tis Epidaurou* (*Epidauros Charter*), (Hydra: 1824) Article 2.
15. *Politicon Syntagma tis Ellados* (*Political Constitution of Greece*), (Troezen: 1827), Articles 4 and 6.
16. A. Koraes, *Peri ton Ellinikon Sympheronton Dialogos Dyo Graekon* (*A Dialogue of Two Greeks on the Interests of Greece*), (Hydra:1825), Article 2, p. 93.
17. C. Koulouri, *Historia kai Geographia sta Ellinika Scholia: 1834–1914* (*History and Geography in the Greek Schools*) (Athens: 1988) p. 225.
18. *Ibid.*, p. 378.
19. *Ibid.*, p. 463.
20. *Ibid.*, p. 531.

PART II

2

Greek Foreign Policy: Debates and Priorities*

THEODORE A. COULOUMBIS

TOWARD A NEW ERA IN GREEK FOREIGN POLICY

Students of the foreign policy behaviour of states have been generally divided into pro-theoretical and non-theoretical orientations. The former prefer to advance their arguments in abstractions and generalizations, to classify, compare and evaluate foreign policies of nation states and to search for deeper causes of phenomena leading to war and peace. The latter are impatient with generalizations, find real life too complex to be categorized in abstract terms and generally treat each issue as *unique*, subject to its own rules or dynamics.

Alexis de Tocqueville brilliantly captured the essence of the debate between theorists and practitioners of foreign policy as follows:

> I have come across men of letters who have written history without taking part in public affairs, and politicians who have concerned themselves with producing events without thinking about them. I have observed the first are always inclined to find general causes, whereas the second living in the midst of disconnected daily facts, are prone to imagine that everything is attributable to particular incidents and that the wires they pull are the same as those that move the world. It is to be presumed that both are equally deceived.[1]

The working hypothesis of this chapter, admittedly closer to the pro-theoretical orientation, is that the foreign policy of Greece cannot be understood, explained and evaluated in isolation from the behaviour of a plethora of variables which include quality of leadership, size and strategic location of a country, level of economic and political development, quality of life, societal cohesiveness as well as external variables which address the interests and objectives of regional actors and, need-less to say, great powers.

Our proposition is that the so-called burden of history is not neces-sarily going to spill over into the twenty-first century profile of Greece. The country, as we will argue below, has experienced a dramatic change in its social, political and economic structures which renders it less vulnerable to the voices of home-grown populist politicians and/or the demands and interferences of great powers.

The Greek transformation, juxtaposed with the drastic alterations in the post-Cold War contours of the international system, calls for a fresh look in understanding Greece's place in a changing world. Suffice it to say, at this point, that the centre of gravity of Greece's external activity is moving more and more toward geoeconomics and away from geopolitics.

GREECE'S TRANSITION TO THE 'CENTRE' FROM THE 'PERIPHERY'

The year 1974 is the gate connecting two different eras in the history of twentieth-century Greece. In the period 1909–74 the small and strate-gically located country experienced considerable turbulence in its external and internal relations. Economically, it was classified in the category of poor, agrarian, raw material producing, trade dependent and externally indebted – in short, underdeveloped. Politically it was polar-ized, functioning with personalist and clientelist political parties whose main purpose was to distribute the largesse controlled by a hypertrophic state sector. Deep schisms – pitting royalists against republicans and communists against nationalists – marked the years from 1915 to 1974, resulting in frequent military interventions in politics. Accordingly, dictatorial rule was imposed in 1925–26, 1936–41 and 1967–74. A bloody, destructive and socially traumatic civil war, in 1946–49, scarred deeply the body politic and the society of the country. Given the insta-bility and fragility of its democratic institutions – constantly challenged by competing models of monarchical authoritarianism and communist totalitarianism – Greece during this long period was classified by politi-cal scientists in the 'praetorian zone' together with states such as Spain, Portugal and Turkey, as well as countries in Central and South America.[2]

In its external relations, in the cauldron that was Europe of two world wars, totalitarian ideologies, competing nationalisms and the holocaust, Greece was also actively involved in international conflicts such as the Balkan Wars (1912–13), the First World War, the Greek–Turkish War (1921–22), and the Second World War. All these adven-tures, which were very much a reflection of general turbulence in Europe (and particularly in the Balkans), affected the delimitation of the boundaries of Greece which were formally defined in 1923 (the Treaty of Lausanne) and 1947 (the Treaty of Paris).[3]

Given its strategic location in the Mediterranean and the Balkans, Greece throughout its modern history was subject to the competing bids for Great Power penetration. Its near total exposure by sea placed the small state under the direct influence of whatever Great Power exercised naval control in the Mediterranean (Great Britain before 1947 and the United States after that time). In the area of Greek–Great Power relations, political scientists classified Greece among those states with penetrated (dependent) political systems.[4]

The collapse of the Colonels' dictatorship triggered by the Cyprus imbroglio in the summer of 1974, opened the gates on to a new era. The infrastructure for change had already been put in position, given the high (highest in the OECD) rates of economic growth in the 1950s and 1960s, the rapid urbanization of the population (a product of the civil war, immigration, emigration and economic development), and the consequent creation of a sizeable middle class.

Constantinos Karamanlis, returning in 1974 from political exile and possessing strong political instincts and considerable foresight, presided over a remarkably smooth transition process that led to the establishment and consolidation of durable and, with the passage of time, adequately tested democratic institutions. The deep divisions of the past were gradually bridged leading to the effective reintegration of Greek society: the question of the monarchy was resolved in a free and fair plebiscite in December 1974, removing a thorny symbol that had for decades polarized a revolutionary Left against an authoritarian Right. More importantly, the vanquished in the Greek civil war were permitted to re-enter the political process through the legalization (and participation in the November 1974 elections) of the Communist Party(ies). Also, the handling of 'dejuntification' in 1974–75, confined primarily to coup leaders and those responsible for the ordering and execution of torture, prevented the upsurge of a new schism between the 'ins' and the 'outs', thus putting an end to the long cycles of mutual revanchism in the Greek political arena, while reducing the opportunities (as well as removing the causes) of patron–client relationship between warring political parties (or coalitions) within Greece and the Great Powers competing for influence through local clients.

The government's (Karamanlis') decision in 1974–75 to redress the imbalance of forces between Turkey and Greece – an imbalance so dramatically manifested by the near effortless Turkish invasion of Cyprus – reflects the deep impact that the prospect of EC accession exercised on post-1974 Greek foreign policy. Following the Colonels' coup in Cyprus, which offered Turkey an opportunity to invade and partition the island republic, the Karamanlis government had three options: the first was to go immediately to war with Turkey. But the dictators, paradoxically, had kept Greece militarily exposed by leaving the eastern Aegean islands undefended and at the mercy of a Turkish military operation. The second option was to seek a truce so as to gain time and, later, mount a massive rearmament programme so as to force the Turks at an opportune moment to withdraw their occupation army from Cyprus. Had this option been chosen, Greece and Turkey would have initiated a chain reaction of revanchist wars of the Arab–Israeli variety. Needless to say, a climate of high tension and protracted conflict would not have permitted Greece to secure membership in the EC. The third option was to arm the country for purposes of adequate deterrence of future Turkish revisionist contingencies in Cyprus, the Aegean and Thrace and to employ in parallel a mixture of political, economic and diplomatic, but not military, instruments in order to secure a viable settlement in Cyprus and the Aegean.

Karamanlis opted for the third of the strategies outlined above. He had been summoned from self-exile in Paris in late July 1974 to help rescue a sinking ship. He had become firmly convinced that Greece's destiny would have been bleak outside the greenhouse of democracies which had been carefully erected by the masterbuilders of European integration. In order for Greece to qualify for entry into the European Community, it (like France, Germany and others) had to abandon concepts and policies such as irredentism or other forms of territorial revisionism and to accept the challenges of functional integration and economic interdependence which were at the heart of the grand European experiment.

Despite the spirited debate that had preceded entry into the EC in the years 1976–79 (PASOK had been at that time heavily opposed to Greek membership), in the 20 years that have elapsed since January 1981, the EC has become nearly universally accepted by the full range of political parties as the centrepiece of Greece's external relationships. Furthermore, one can safely propose that EU accession has had a deep and generally positive impact on nearly every aspect of Greek economic, political and social performance.[5]

In the field of foreign policy, we can advance the proposition that EC membership in the 1981–2000 period has served Greece both as a diplomatic lever and as a restraining mechanism. For example, Greece adopted a stance of 'conditionality' by using its membership in the EC as a lever designed to convince Turkey that Turkish–EC relations cannot be normalized unless the occupation of Cyprus is terminated. EC membership status was also employed *vis-à-vis* the Former Yugoslav Republic of Macedonia (FYROM) in the early 1990s in order to prevent the latter from monopolizing (in the Greek view expropriating) the historic name of Ancient Greek Macedonia. Simultaneously, however, the EC has functioned mainly as a restraining instrument. Membership in an elaborate structure that is highly institutionalized required the abandonment of some of the trappings of undiluted sovereignty and national independence. Both with respect to Turkey (as we suggested above) but also in relations with its northern neighbours (especially FYROM), Greece found itself, like Odysseus, tied to a European Community mast permitting it to resist the tempting siren songs of atavistic nationalism and irredentism. Without the mast the Greek ship of state could have veered off course and into the rough of the Balkan vortex, becoming a part of the Balkan problem rather than serving as part of the solution together with its 14 EC partners.

FOREIGN POLICY PRIORITIES IN THE EARLY YEARS OF THE TWENTY-FIRST CENTURY

The post-Cold War period (let us better call it the 1990s) appears to have falsified the prophesies of both the global order and the global disorder schools of thought.[6] Early in the twenty-first century, the world appears to be moving toward a new variant of *bipolarity* defined primarily in economic rather than military/political/ideological terms. One pole comprises advanced, industrial and democratic states while the second pole groups regions of the Third World and the former Soviet bloc that are plagued by economic scarcity and underdevelopment as well as by political systems that vacillate between traditional authoritarianism, unstable democracy and praetorian managerialism.

Greece belongs institutionally to the pole of stability but, unlike its remaining EU partners, it borders on a region of fluidity and real or potential conflict north and east of its frontiers. Therefore, the gamut (nearly) of political parties as well as an overwhelming majority of public opinion have supported, increasingly since the mid-1980s, the process of Greece's multidimensional integration into the mechanisms and institutions of the Western family of nations.[7] The dominant paradigm premised on multilateralism and reflecting Greece's foreign policy priorities could be summarized as follows:

The first priority of foreign policy since 1974 has been the consolidation of democracy and the adoption of an economic convergence strategy (with the more advanced EU partners) designed to safeguard Greece's historic European option. In their efforts to secure full integration into the 'hard core' of post-Maastricht Europe, policy makers, whether drawn from the ranks of New Democracy (in government between 1990 to 1993) or of PASOK (in government since October 1993), have avoided the so-called dilemma between a Europeanist and an Atlanticist profile. They have opted instead for a Euro–Atlanticist stance (akin to the British, Portuguese and Italian models) recognizing that there is adequate complementarity in a strategy that pursues political and economic integration through the European Union and, simultaneously, relies on NATO for the provision of the collective defence and security values.

The second (first from a defence and security standpoint) priority in foreign policy is the maintenance of a régime of sufficient military balance in the Greek–Turkish nexus of relations. Since 1974 (following the Turkish invasion and continuing occupation of northern Cyprus) all political parties have perceived Turkey as posing a threat to Greece's territorial integrity in the Aegean and in Western Thrace. In this connection, bipartisan policy has called for the maintenance of an adequate balance of forces (especially in the air and sea) while avoiding highly destabilizing and economically costly arms races. NATO has been repeatedly urged by Greek officials to consider seriously the development of an intra-NATO dispute settlement mechanism which would help resolve differences peacefully as well as strengthen the appeal of the Atlantic Alliance as a collective security organization in addition to bringing a collective defence providing institution.

Under the Simitis government (but also under New Democracy rule in 1990–93), the stance *vis-à-vis* Turkey's oft-declared European option has been to move away gradually from a strategy of *conditional sanctions* and toward one of *conditional rewards*. In other words, Greece, especially following the Helsinki (December 1999) European Council meeting, openly declared its readiness to lift its objections (given its veto power in the EU) to the building of a close relationship between the EU and Turkey, provided the latter abandons its threats of going to war over the Aegean question and contributes substantively toward a functional and mutually acceptable solution to the Cyprus problem permitting the reunification of Cyprus as a federal, bizonal and bicommunal state that is also a member of the European Union and NATO.

The remaining foreign policy priorities involve relations with post-communist Balkan neighbours and with the non-EU and non-NATO states of the Mediterranean region. In the case of the Balkans, after a painful interlude (1992–95) of near involvement in a regional imbroglio, Greece has opted for a multilateralist foreign policy (together with its EU, WEU, OSCE and NATO partners) designed to contribute to successful transition policies toward democracy and a market economy in each of the states north of its borders. After smoothing its troubled relations with Albania and FYROM, while continuing to cultivate good relations with Bulgaria and Romania, Greece has also proceeded to adopt a purely equidistant stance (*vis-à-vis* Serbia, Croatia and Albania) on the questions of Bosnia and Kosovo respectively. In this respect, Greece has joined Western peacekeeping and peace-enforcement initiatives in Albania, Bosnia and elsewhere in former Yugoslavia. This included its mid-May 1997 participation in partnership for peace military exercises on the territory of FYROM and the midsummer 1998 NATO exercises in Albania, together with troops from the United States, Italy and Turkey, among others.

The processes of EU and NATO enlargement, especially after the welcome changes unfolding in post-Milosevic Yugoslavia, fit well with Greece's strategic objective of encouraging stability and peace in the Balkan region, thus distancing the unpleasant contingency of having to face a second diplomatic/military front in addition to what has been widely perceived as a clear and present danger emanating from Turkey. Further, Greece's substantive support and involvement in EU regional developmental programmes fits the strategy of a multilateral and stabilizing presence in the Balkans.

With respect to Greece's role in the Mediterranean, the multilateralist formula applied to the Balkans is the orienting principle for Greek foreign policy in this region as well. Here the opportunities for NATO and EU initiatives are more than apparent. The Euro–Atlantic community has every incentive to extend the values of security and cooperation into this structurally unbalanced region (where the EU North is rich and demographically stable while the non-EU South is economically disadvantaged and demographically explosive). For the time being the EU/MEDA fund, which has amounted to the very substantive sum of 4.7 billion Ecus for the 1995–99 period, is a concrete and much needed first step in a gradual convergence strategy designed to facilitate economic and political development in the disadvantaged littoral states of the non-EU Mediterranean South (Mediterranean Politics 2000).

Greek policy makers believe that NATO offers excellent opportunities for military cooperation (beyond confidence-building measures) between the alliance and critically important eastern Mediterranean states such as Egypt, Jordan, Israel and Cyprus. The opportunities for substantive cooperation between NATO and these states will increase geometrically if the nexus of Greek–Turkish difficulties is adequately addressed and Cyprus is permitted to join the ranks of NATO and the EU (given the overwhelming benefits that such a prospect ensures for both communities on the embattled island).[8]

Finally, in Greece's list of priorities, the relationship with the United States occupies a critical position.[9] There has been a dramatic improvement in the United States–Greek relationship during the 1990s. One could argue that the profile of this relationship from 1947 (the Truman Doctrine) to 1974 (the collapse of the Athens dictatorship) had been of the classical patron–client variety. The United States, a dominant superpower, and Greece, a strategically located but internally divided small state, could not have avoided the centre-periphery dependence relationship. It was, indeed, decisive American intervention in the 1947–49 period which prevented a communist take-over in the Greek Civil War. The victors, the majority in Greece, were indeed grateful, and Harry Truman's statue was erected overlooking a central and busy Greek boulevard. However, the vanquished, a sizable minority, viewed the United States as an 'evil Empire' that had been responsible for their final defeat in 1949.

In the 1950s, 1960s and early 1970s, Greek–American relations were adversely affected by a constantly escalating Greek–Turkish conflict over the fate of the island of Cyprus. Perceptions in Athens were that the United States was systematically tilting in favour of Turkey (whose strategic value was heavily exaggerated by American strategic thinkers). Anti-Americanism assumed even greater proportions by what the Greek people considered an American stance of benign neglect (if not outright support of the dictators) during the 1967–74 period when Greece was placed under the oppressive régime of the Athens Colonels. The Greek military régime not only violated basic human rights but also triggered a criminal coup against President Makarios of Cyprus (15 July 1974) which – in turn – led to the Turkish invasion and the subsequent occupation of 37% of Cypriot territory.

In the years following the restoration of democracy in Greece (1974), despite the anti-American rhetoric of Andreas Papandreou and his left-of-centre political party (PASOK), the image of the United States began to improve again. The gradual consolidation of democracy, the incorporation of the vanquished of the Civil War into the political process, continuing economic development, entry into the EU (January 1981), the alternation of left-and-right-of-centre parties in power, and the establishment of strict civilian control over the Armed Forces, have permitted Greece to move in the direction of becoming a 'civil society'. Pluralistic discourse, the rise of independent and antagonistic media (radio and television that had been previously state controlled) have also permitted the kind of complex public exchange that reduces dogmatism and challenges Manichean (light vs. darkness) over-simplifications.

ASSESSMENT AND PROSPECTS

Looking at the record of Greece at home and abroad the optimist would say the glass is half full, the pessimist would report it as half empty, and the pragmatist might say to both 'get a smaller glass'. The arguments that optimists tend to employ include the following: Greece's domestic conditions (political and economic) have improved considerably since the days of the Papandreou succession saga (November 1995 to July 1996); the country has a prime minister with a pragmatic and

Eurocentric orientation who has managed to establish control over his party while enjoying a comfortable majority in parliament and projecting a moderate image abroad; New Democracy, the party of the loyal opposition, under a youthful and modernizing leadership, has lowered somewhat the tone of criticism on vital foreign policy questions, abandoning a 'tradition' of automatic dissent on all issues in order to score points with the permanently frustrated Greek public.

For the optimists the big bet will be won if Turkey begins and sustains a process of transformation that will lead to democracy at home and peace with its neighbours – especially its prospective EU partners. Following a series of crises (Imia, S-300s, Ocalan) that had brought the two countries to the brink of war, Greece and Turkey have launched what has been inelegantly referred to as 'earthquake diplomacy'. Two soft-speaking and personally compatible ministers – George Papandreou and Ismail Cem – have agreed to disaggregate the Greek–Turkish dispute and have been promoting a step-by-step tension reduction strategy which has already produced a number of agreements in areas of 'low politics', such as immigration control. The optimists' objective, ultimately, is to address high political questions in a climate that will be rid of the threat of force as an instrument of policy. The optimists emphasize that all this has been happening while the inflation rate in Greece has fallen to the 2.5% mark and the remaining Maastricht (EMU qualification) criteria have been fully met.

The pessimists, wearing dark glasses, would shake their heads and dismiss the above as reflecting a mixture of utopian thinking and mirage-making. For the pessimist, EMU membership has been attained at the expense of the poor and disadvantaged in Greece. Turkey is continuing, despite Madrid and Helsinki, to escalate its revisionist demands in the Aegean and in Cyprus, and the 'good boy' approach adopted by the current Greek government is being perceived in Ankara and elsewhere as a sign of weakness. Exhibiting a longing for the now gone 'strong, proud and charismatic' leadership, the pessimists are sounding the alarm for the declining Greek population that is becoming decadent, consumerist, selfish and, at best, indifferent. Greece, for the pessimist, still has a chance to survive if it arms itself well, abandons wishful thinking, trusts less the so-called solidarity of its European partners, and embarks on an international crusade condemning Turkey for its miserable human rights record and for its reliance on force to attain its foreign policy objectives.

At first sight, one might think that both approaches make sense and, in Nasreddin Hodza fashion, might pronounce them both right! Obviously both optimists and pessimists have similar long-range objectives: they both want a neighbour that respects the international *status quo* in the Aegean and permits the peace process in the Republic of

Cyprus to continue as accession talks for Cypriot admission to the European Union are proceeding toward their logical conclusion. Both optimists and pessimists have no illusions about the chances of Turkey (given the current fluidities and contradictions in its society, economy and polity) opening the gates of a historic reconciliation with Greece. Both optimists and pessimists agree that effective deterrence *vis-à-vis* Turkey depends first and foremost on the maintenance of a sufficient balance of power, while avoiding – if possible – a costly and destabilizing arms race. But here the similarities end.

The optimists believe that a policy of European integration adds considerably to Greece's diplomatic calculus of deterrence. The pessimists, on the contrary, are unilateralist and ethnocentric in orientation. The optimists argue that a policy of tension reduction is to Greece's advantage given its privileged condition in political and economic terms. The pessimists retort that time is working in favour of the rapidly growing (in population and military prowess) Turkey. Between the lines, one reads in the pessimist argument that eventually war is inevitable and their conclusion is *si vis pacis para bellum*. Finally, for the optimists, the argument is ultimately summarized with 'how can we avoid war without losing in peace'.

This writer shares the problematique of the optimists and believes that the objective of Greece should be to engage Turkey in a patient, clear-sighted and long-range campaign in order to convince it that its own best choice is the Euro-Atlantic community of nations. This strategy calls for a collectively orchestrated stance of offering 'conditional rewards' to our complex and vacillating eastern neighbour. The Turks will hopefully realize that Europe offers them the best future and that in order to join its family fully, they must abandon rusty, geopolitical instruments of statecraft. The desired result may take time but there seems to be no better way whether one wears rosy or dark glasses.

If the optimists, experiment eventually succeeds, Greece will be free of its Turkish preoccupation, and by contributing fully to the stability and democratization processes in the rest of the Balkans it will be able secure its highest values: peace, democracy and economic development. While supporting substantively the processes of enlargement of the EU and NATO in its troubled neighbourhood, Greece will continue its quest for the further deepening of the institutional structures of its European family. Having finally anchored in the relatively safe port of interdependent democracies and advanced economies, Greece will continue facing the multitude of risks and challenges of a global system that carries with it awesome structural problems, not least of which is the growing gap between the rich of the global north and the poor of the global south.

NOTES

*This is an updated as well as revised version of the author's chapter entitled 'Strategic Consensus in Greek Domestic and Foreign Policy Since 1974' in V. Coufoudakis, H. J. Psomiades and A. Gerolymatos (eds) *Greece and the New Balkans: Challenges and Opportunities* (New York: Pella, 1999).

1. Cited in G. T. Allison *Essence of Decision: Explaining the Cuban Missile Crisis* (Boston: Little Brown, 1971) p.i.
2. W. H. McNeil, *The Metamorphosis of Greece Since World War II* (Chicago: University of Chicago Press, 1978); N. P. Diamandouros, *Cultural Dualism and Political Change in Post-Authoritarian Greece* (Madrid: Instituto Juan March de Estudios e Investigaciones Avanzados en Ciencias Sociales, 1994); T. Veremis and M. Dragoumis *'Greece'*, compilers, 17 (Oxford: Clio Press, 1998).
3. R. Clogg, *A Concise History of Greece* (Cambridge: Cambridge University Press, 1995).
4. P. A. Petropoulos, *Politics and Statecraft in the Kingdom of Greece 1833–1843* (Princeton: Princeton University Press, 1968); T. A. Couloumbis, J. A. Petropoulos, H. J. Psomiades, *Foreign Interference in Greek Politics: A Historical Perspective* (New York: Pella Publishing Co., 1976); T. M. Veremis, *The Military in Greek Politics: From Independence to Democracy* (London: C. Hurst & Co., 1997).
5. P. Kazakos and P. C. Ioakimides, *Greece and EC Membership Evaluated* (London: Pinter Publishers, 1994); L. Tsoukalis, *The New European Economy: The Politics and Economics of Integration* (Oxford: Oxford University Press, 1981); L. Tsoukalis, *The New European Economy Revisited* (Oxford University Press, 1997).
6. F. Fukuyama, *The End of History and the Last Man* (New York: Free Press, 1992); A. Ch. Kupchan and A. Cl. Kupchan. 'The Promise of Collective Security' in *International Security*, 20 (1995), pp. 52–61; P. H. Huntington, *The Clash of Civilisations and the Remaking of World Order* (New York: Simon and Schuster, 1996); Z. Brezinski, *Out of Control: Global Turmoil on the Eve of the 21st Century* (New York: Scribner, 1993); 'What Comes after the "Post-Cold War" World?' *Foreign Policy*, 119, 2000.
7. C. Lyrintzis, 'Political Parties in a Post-Junta Greece: A Case of Bureaucratic Clientelism' in G. Pridham, *The New Mediterranean Democracies* (London: Frank Cass, 1984), pp. 99–118; M. Spourdalakis, 'Political Parties in the Greek Literature', *European Journal of Political Research*, 25 (1994) pp. 499–518.
8. T. Dokos, 'Greek Defence Doctrine in the Post-Cold War Era' in V. Coufoudakis *et al.* (eds) *Greece and the New Balkans: Challenges and Opportunities* (New York: Pella, 2000).
9. M. Stearns, *Entangled Allies: US Policy Toward Greece, Turkey and Cyprus* (New York: Council on Foreign Relations, 1992); T.A. Couloumbis, *The United States, Greece, and Turkey. The Troubled Triangle* (New York: Praeger, 1983); N. A. Stavrou (ed.) *Greece under Socialism: A NATO Ally Adrift* (New Rochelle, New York, 1988); A. Papachelas, *The Rape of Greek Democracy: The American Factor 1947–1967* (Athens: Estia, 1997); V. Coufoudakis, 'Greek–Turkish Relations, 1973–1983: The View from Athens', *International Security*, 9, 4, (Spring 1985), pp. 185–217; J. O. Iatrides, *Greece in the 1940s* (Boston: New England University Press, 1981); H. J. Psomiades and S. Thomadakis (eds) *Greece, the New Europe* and *The Changing International Order* (New York, Pella, 1993); T. Kariotis (ed.) *The Greek Socialist Experiment: Papandreou's Greece, 1981–1989* (New York, Pella, 1992); Coufoudakis, Psomiades and Gerolymatos (eds) *Greece and the New Balkan, passim.*

3

Greece in a Changing Strategic Setting

THANOS P. DOKOS

This chapter begins with a presentation of Greece's strategic position in the Balkans and Eastern Mediterranean and continues with a concise review of Greece's security policy from the end of the Second World War to the end of the Cold War. It will show that Turkey has dominated Greece's security agenda since the early 1970s, while the Cyprus issue – a problem that has severely affected the two countries' relations – had already emerged in the 1950s. In the post-Cold War era a series of 'new risks' in Greece's immediate security environment, namely the Balkans, have emerged while 'old threats' stemming from Greece's eastern neighbour, namely Turkey, did not cease to exist. Actually, in the post-Cold War era, Turkey remains the main concern of Greece's security policy and the driving force behind most foreign policy initiatives.[1] However, Greek security policy vis-à-vis Turkey started being reformulated in the mid-1990s due to Greece's new strategic needs and priorities. Finally, the analysis will focus on Greece's security challenges and priorities in rapidly changing domestic, regional and international settings and Greece's security prospects for the twenty-first century.

The main argument of the chapter is that Turkey has been the main concern of Greek security policy and the driving force behind most foreign policy initiatives.[2] Until the mid-1960s, Greece relied heavily on the US and NATO for protection against the perceived threat posed by the Warsaw Pact. This reliance on 'external balancing' resulted in a certain loss of security autonomy.[3] Since the mid/late-1960s, Greece's emphasis was on 'internal balancing' (through the strengthening of its Armed Forces) and to a lesser degree through membership in NATO and a bilateral relationship with the US (mainly as a result of Turkey's membership to the former and its 'privileged' relationship with the latter).[4] In the last decade or so, Greece placed increased importance on its 'European card' (membership to the European Community/Union and the WEU). This resulted in a certain loss of political and economic autonomy (although this may be seen as part of a larger process of integration and is certainly not limited to Greece but extends to other members of the EU).

GREECE'S GEOSTRATEGIC POSITION IN THE BALKANS AND EASTERN MEDITERRANEAN

Today the post-Cold War global structures are in a state of flux. Analysts and policy makers in small countries are attempting to identify and to predict trends as well as to recommend policies of adjustment to emerging global patterns. The challenge for Greece, a rather small,[5] democratic, internationalist, western, free-enterprise oriented, strategically located and *status quo* country, is to safeguard its territorial integrity and to protect its democratic system and values.[6]

Greece is located at the crossroads of three continents (Europe, Asia and Africa). It is an integral part of the Balkans (where it is the only country that is a member of the European Union, the WEU and NATO) and is also in close proximity to the Black Sea and the oil-rich regions of the Middle East and the Caucasus. The Aegean Sea is an important shipping route, connecting the Black Sea with the Mediterranean, and a major transit route for the transportation of energy products (after the construction and operation of pipelines from Central Asia and the Transcaucasus). Furthermore, Greece's position in the Eastern Mediterranean enhances its strategic importance.[7] The Mediterranean region constitutes a crucial area of contact (a 'faultline') between what is described by many analysts as the emerging great division of the world: the North and the South.

The Mediterranean has always been a region endowed with special significance. It has been either a familiar route of trade and culture, or a faultline between hostile states and civilizations. Its strategic importance was eclipsed twice in history, once by naval technology which shifted the traffic of sea commerce to the Atlantic, and the other during the Cold War, when the central front of the continent attracted most allied attention. In the past NATO and the West had generally regarded the Mediterranean as a peripheral strategic theatre. This is rapidly changing, however.

As a result of two 'cataclysmic' changes – the end of the Cold War and the collapse of the Soviet Union – the Mediterranean, the Middle East and much of their surrounding regions are in the midst of a rapid geopolitical evolution without, however, a clear direction. Analysts discern an 'arc or triangle of crisis, extending from the Balkans, to Central Asia–Transcaucasus and the Middle East'. The majority of

régimes in those regions are or will soon be faced with a crisis of political legitimacy.[8] Furthermore, and this is of great interest for Greece, the
transition from loose bipolarity to polycentrism, after the end of the
Cold War, has increased the autonomy of regional actors and has led to
the intensification of peripheral disputes. The new environment presents
the 'actors' with new dangers and opportunities.[9]

Greece's strategic position accounts for its membership (in 1952) in
NATO. During the Cold War Greece provided an essential link in
NATO's south-eastern flank. Turkey, for example, could have been
isolated from the other NATO members if Greece had not also participated in the Alliance. In the opinion of many Greek decision makers, the
country's strategic importance to the West has been underestimated and,
at times, even neglected. Successive Greek governments have, however,
continued to contribute to Western defence strategy, despite periods of
difficult relations.[10]

According to a recent RAND Corporation study, Greek strategic
space is wide, encompassing Europe, Eurasia, the Middle East and the
Mediterranean as well as transatlantic relations. At the broadest level,
Greece will also be affected by the complex of trends described as 'globalization'. The contemporary strategic environment is characterized by
a series of functional issues that cut across traditional geographic lines,
leading to a greater degree of regional interdependence (although this is
true more for the Mediterranean than for the Balkans). It is also argued
that the strategic environment around Greece is being shaped by the
development of new lines of communication for energy, and other non-
energy infrastructure projects. [11]

THE EVOLUTION OF GREECE'S NATIONAL SECURITY POLICY

Due to the rather anarchic nature of the international system, small
states, with their limited capabilities, are trying to deal with their security problems through the development of strategies based on balancing
(internal and external) and/or bandwagoning. As small states have fewer
options and less freedom of manoeuvre than the great powers, to
promote its security interests most effectively, Greece has sought to
aggregate its voice and to integrate its policies with those of its European
Union partners and its NATO allies.[12]

Historically, the main strategic dilemma for Greek decision makers
was whether to ally themselves with the sea power dominant in the
eastern Mediterranean or the land power dominant on the Balkan
peninsula. In most cases, mindful of their responsibility for the defence
of 2,000 Greek islands, stretching from the Eastern Aegean to the
Adriatic Sea, have chosen to ally themselves with sea power.[13]

During the late 1940s and early 1950s, the difference between conservatives and liberals (the communists had been outlawed as a result of the Greek Civil War) on security issues and NATO was one of emphasis. Both groupings basically believed that Greece's main security threat emanated from its northern borders and that communism (external and domestic) threatened mutually cherished values. NATO was viewed, therefore, as indispensable for the defence of the country and the US was treated as Greece's natural ally and guarantor.

Greek governments, given the dependence on the US, yielded on most issues in the field of national defence. Since the years of the Civil War (1946–49) Greek security arrangements were closely identified with American foreign policy. The Greek armed forces were exclusively equipped with American arms and the hundreds of officers who received graduate military training in the US welcomed the continuity of their host country's influence on the Greek armed forces.[14]

As has been pointed out

> This led to the limitation of Greek defence and foreign policy options. Greek policy makers were ineffective in capitalizing on Greece's strategic assets and value in order to promote Greek national interests. Consequently, the US and NATO took for granted Greece's commitment and downgraded its strategic significance. Such policies and assessments had negative effects on the Greco-Turkish political and strategic balance.[15]

The orientation of Greece's defence until the mid-1960s was based on the US credo that the main security concern was one of internal rather than external nature. The Greek armed forces (in contrast with the Turkish ones) were primarily supplied and organized to face a domestic communist threat. According to NATO planning, Greece was only expected 'through certain limited accessories to cause some delay to Soviet and satellite forces in case of global war'.[16]

With the relaxation of international tension in the late 1960s, perceptions of a domestic communist threat, supported by Greece's communist neighbours (except former Yugoslavia) diminished considerably, while a confrontation between Greece and Turkey became more likely (especially after the 1964 and 1967 Cyprus crises).

Even as early as the late-1950s, NATO's southeastern flank has been experiencing periodic cycles of great tension. The emergence of the Cyprus problem in the 1950s, with the Greek–Turkish crises of the 1960s, the Greek junta-sponsored coup of 1974 and the Turkish invasion and occupation of the island (which continues to the present day),[17] has been complicated by a series of Greek–Turkish frictions in the

Aegean region, caused by Turkey's pressure for the revision of the Aegean *status quo*. This led to the re-orientation of the Greek defence doctrine, with the official declaration of the 'threat from the East' as the main security concern for Greece.

The restoration of democratic rule in 1974 was, indeed, a major turning point in Greek security policy. This new period of Greek political history, lasting from 1974 to the present, has been characterized by the diversification of Greece's external relationships, including a relative weakening of its ties with the US in favour of closer economic and political integration into Western Europe and improved relations with Eastern Europe.

The re-orientation of Greece's security doctrine (followed from the necessary re-deployment of forces from the north to the Greek–Turkish border in Thrace and the islands of the Aegean), in the aftermath of the 1974 crisis (a process that began, however, in the mid/late-1960s), led to an instinctive de-emphasis towards developments within the Warsaw Pact. During the late 1970s and the 1980s there was little evidence that Greek security planners had been concerned about any danger of direct attack by Warsaw Pact forces on Greece's narrow and difficult-to-defend land-strip in Thrace and Macedonia.

THE POST-COLD WAR SETTING: THREATS AND CHALLENGES

In the post-Cold War era Greece is faced with what she considers as a major security threat and a number of risks: the threat is perceived to emanate from her eastern neighbour (Turkey)[18] and the risks are seen as resulting from Balkan and Mediterranean instability.[19] Furthermore, Greece is involved in a highly emotional dispute on the issue of the recognition of the official name of FYROM and is concerned about respect of human rights of the Greek minority in Albania. It should be noted, however, that there has been significant progress in Greek–Albanian and Greek–FYROM relations during the last two to three years.

(a) The Turkish Threat

Major events in the modern history of Greek–Turkish relations (i.e. post-1922 period) include the Lausanne Treaty (1923), the Venizelos–Ataturk détente in the 1930s (and the 1930 Friendship Treaty and the Naval Arms Control Protocol), their NATO membership in 1952, the 1954 'Balkan Pact', the emergence of the Cyprus issue in the mid-1950s, the Istanbul pogrom ('Kristalnacht') of September 1955 (which, together with the events of 1964 led to the expulsion of the Greek minority from Istanbul), the Zurich–London agreements on the creation of an independent, federal state in Cyprus, the Cyprus crises of 1963–64, 1967 and 1974 (when an abortive coup staged by the Greek dictatorship against the president of Cyprus, Archbishop Makarios, in 1974 offered Turkey a much sought-after pretext to invade the island and keep it divided it for the past 26 years), the closure of the Halki Theological School by Turkey (creating serious problems for the survival of the Constantinople Ecumenical Patriarchate), the dispute on the delimitation of the continental shelf which led to the 1976 and 1987 crises (when Turkey sent survey vessels in disputed waters), and the unsuccessful 1988 *rapprochement* effort in Davos between Andreas Papandreou and Turgut Ozal which, however, produced the Papoulias–Yilmaz agreements (better known as the Vouliagmeni and Istanbul Memoranda) establishing general principles on Confidence-Building Measures (CBMs) in the Aegean (unfortunately, both memoranda were never implemented).[20]

The 1990s witnessed a number of bilateral crises including the declaration of the Joint Defence Doctrine between Greece and Cyprus, the October 1994 declaration of a *casus belli* over the possible extension of Greek territorial waters by Prime Minister Tansu Ciller, which then became official policy through a Resolution of the Turkish National Assembly, the Imia (Kardak for Turkey) crisis which brought the two countries to the brink of war, the dispute over the planned deployment of the surface-to-air missiles (SAMs) S-300 in Cyprus, the introduction by Turkey of the so-called 'Grey zones theory', disputing the Greek sovereignty over more than 100 inhabited and uninhabited islands in the Aegean (including the inhabited island of Gavdos south of Crete), and the Ocalan crisis[21] (for Greece's handling of the incident, the term 'fiasco' would be more appropriate).[22]

Since September 1999 there were some positive developments such as the so-called 'earthquake diplomacy', the Greek agreement in Helsinki to Turkey's candidacy for EU membership, the signature of nine 'low-politics' bilateral agreements, the continuing discussion of a number of Confidence-Building Measures, the establishment of a multinational peacekeeping brigade (the Southeast European Brigade/SEEBRIG, with a Turkish Commander and a Greek Deputy Commander and Political Director, with alternation of command posts), the establishment of NATO's new command structure (during the Dynamic Mix exercise, Turkish troops landed on Greek soil and Turkish fighter aircraft and the whole exercise was conducted very smoothly, in contrast to the Destined Glory exercise taking place in Turkey a few months later when Turkish objections to the agreed scenario forced the Greek contingent to leave the exercise, causing a mini-crisis in bilateral relations).

The current *rapprochement* with Turkey is a very important development and needs to be analysed in more detail. As mentioned above, the
dark picture started changing during the Kosovo conflict, when the two
governments reached an understanding that an improvement of relations was necessary. Greek Foreign Minister George Papandreou and his
Turkish counterpart Ismail Cem prepared the ground for an official
rapprochement that was greatly facilitated by two unexpected events:
the catastrophic earthquakes in Turkey and Greece in August and
September 1999 respectively. The swift Greek reaction to the Turkish
tragedy spectacularly changed the mood and led to a similar Turkish
reaction after the Athens earthquake. Both countries, either through
official channels or through private initiative, rallied to the side of each
other dispatching medical supplies, equipment and rescue teams to alle-
viate the plight of earthquake-torn Greeks and Turks.

The December 1999 EU Summit in Helsinki saw what was described
by other European states and the US as a courageous decision taken by
Greece. Athens accepted the granting of EU candidate status for Turkey,
attaching only two conditions (in addition, of course, to the
Copenhagen criteria that apply to all candidate countries). Firstly,
Turkish claims concerning grey zones in the Aegean and the dispute over
the delimitation of the continental shelf had to be submitted to the
International Court of Justice in the Hague by 2004, if all other efforts
fail, and secondly, that the accession of Cyprus to the EU would not be
conditional to the resolution of the Cyprus problem.

In January and February 2000 Foreign Ministers Papandreou and
Cem visited each other's capitals and signed a total of nine bilateral
agreements on 'low politics' or 'low confrontation' issues. These agreements concerned tourism, culture, the environment, trade and
commerce, multilateral cooperation (especially with regard to the Black
Sea and Southeast Europe regions), organized crime, illegal immigration, drug trafficking and terrorism.

Those 'low-politics' agreements are perceived by both countries as a
very positive development and constitute a good basis for building a
solid bilateral relationship. However, progress on the more substantive
issues touching the core of bilateral problems ('high politics') will be
neither automatic nor easy. Although both sides, with the encouragement of the EU, NATO and the US, have appeared willing to discuss, in
principle at least, various Confidence-Building Measures and conflict
resolution proposals, there is strong 'inertial' opposition, especially in
Ankara.

The current *rapprochement* between Greece and Turkey remains
nascent and fragile and it seems that it constitutes the epi-phenomenon
of the two states' actual relationship.[23] Both countries have not moved
from their firm positions regarding 'high politics' issues. The Cyprus

problem, issues related to the Aegean sea, and the prospects for a short term resolution of their conflict over these issues, most of which are considered by Greece as unilateral Turkish revisionist claims, are still rather low.

The nature of the threat: The perception of a potential military threat from Turkey has been widely shared by public opinion and reflected in expert debates as well as Greek security planning[24] for – at least – the last two decades.[25] The 1974 Cyprus crisis can be regarded as the major turning point in post-Second World War Greek security considerations: the Turkish invasion and subsequent occupation of the northern part of Cyprus was for Greece a highly traumatic experience, but also a basis for 'new thinking' in terms of security.[26]

Greek security planners are concerned about Turkey's revisionist aims towards Greece expressed through official statements, diplomatic initiatives and military actions (including the deployment of its armed forces). Geography and its small population in comparison to that of Turkey further increased Greek insecurity.

As one analyst points out, 'Turkish official declarations, usually making headlines in Greek mass media, have been intensifying Greek fears. For instance, the Turkish Prime Minister Demirel stated in 1975 that "... half the Aegean is ours. Let the whole world know that this is so ... We know how to crush the heads of our enemies when the prestige, dignity and interests of the Turkish nation are attacked". Turkish official references to a "growing Turkey" and to the 21st century as the "era of Turkism" have caused escalated concern. Moreover, direct challenges (e.g. "the group of islands that are situated within 50 km of the Turkish coast ... should belong to Turkey"), as well as indirect questioning of Greek sovereignty over the Aegean islands have been viewed with great alarm. Furthermore, Greece has proposed on several occasions a bilateral non-use-of force pact, which has been rejected by Turkey, thus reinforcing the perception of Turkish intentions to use military force at an opportune moment against a member of the same alliance.'[27]

Turkish 'revisionist actions' include violations of the Greek airspace, refusal to submit the delimitation of the Aegean continental shelf to the International Court of Justice, threats of war in case of Greek extension of the territorial waters limit from six to twelve miles (according to the provisions of the 1982 Law of the Sea Convention) and challenges of the Aegean *status quo* as codified by a number of international treaties (1923 Lausanne Peace Treaty, 1932 Agreement between Turkey and Italy, 1947 Paris Treaty). The latter led to the Imia crisis in January 1996.

The dispute concerning the width of Greek airspace began in 1974, with Greece insisting that the width of its airspace has been ten miles since 1931 and Turkey responding that it has not and will not recognize the ten-mile Greek air limit (Turkey also refuses to submit flight plans when its military aircraft enter the Athens FIR region). The frequency of violations of Greek airspace by Turkish military aircraft (frequently overflying Greek islands) has considerably increased in the last few years, but even more troubling has been the tendency to engage in mock dogfights, increasing the probability of a real air engagement with possible escalatory effects.

Greek policy makers see Turkey as backing its 'non-friendly' intentions with significant military capabilities. Since 1991 Turkey has launched an impressive modernization programme of its armed forces. It has acquired advanced fighter (a fleet of up to 320 F-16) and transport aircraft, attack and transport helicopters, Main Battle Tanks (MBT), Armoured Infantry Fighting Vehicles (AIFV), Multiple Launcher Rocket Systems (MLRS), frigates, submarines, etc., while it has developed the capability to co-produce some of the above weapon systems. Such a sizeable increase in military expenditures in an era when other European states, the US and Russia have been cutting their defence budgets in an effort to benefit from the 'peace dividend', was a cause for concern for neighbouring countries, including Greece.[28]

The full implementation of Turkish armament programmes threatened to fundamentally alter the bilateral Greek–Turkish balance of power, despite Greece's economic 'sacrifices'. Unless successful external balancing (through diplomatic means/manoeuvring) can offset the Turkish prospective military superiority, the only option for Greece will be to follow Turkey in a costly and destabilizing arms race, which could create economic problems in both countries and accentuate their security dilemma. Military expenditures constitute a heavy burden for the Greek economy, at a time when Greece is completing the implementation of an economic austerity programme and has just joined the European Monetary Union (EMU).[29] Defence expenditures are, to a certain extent, responsible for the country's budget deficit, as well as Greece's lower- than-desired level of social services. On the other hand, the existing arms race places a very heavy burden on Turkey as well, faced as it is with chronic high inflation and considerable social and political problems (which contribute to the increase of popular support for the Islamic Refah/Fazilet Party).

According to Greek security planners and analysts, the focal point of any Greek–Turkish armed conflict was expected to be the Aegean islands, Greek Thrace (to 'protect' the Moslem minority), and Cyprus (with an extension of the occupation zone southwards or even an attempt to control the whole island), or even simultaneously in more than one theatre.

One of the major Greek concerns was the contingency of a Turkish seizure of Greek islands in the eastern part of the Aegean. This move could result from a number of factors such as, for instance, a Greek extension of the territorial waters limit from six to twelve miles, according to the provisions of the 1982 Law of the Sea Convention. Turkey has repeatedly threatened that such an act would be considered a *casus belli*.[30] Particularly worrisome is Turkey's insistence that a number of Greek islands in the Aegean and the Dodecanese revert to a status of total demilitarization, ignoring Greek claims for the right of self-defence against Turkey's Fourth (Aegean) Army and large landing craft fleet (over 70 craft).

The Moslem minority (around 120,000 or just over 1% of Greece's total population), living mainly in Greek Thrace (northeastern Greece), consists of 49.9% Turks, 33.6% Pomaks and 16.5% Gypsies.[31] Occasional threats – in certain extremist quarters – calling for intervention in Thrace aiming 'to liberate their oppressed kin' have not been matched by Turkish governmental authorities. There is concern, however, that, under certain circumstances, Turkish territorial aspirations *vis-à-vis* Greek Thrace may in the future become the most important challenge to Greek security.[32]

(b) Instability in the Balkans

The end of the Cold War affected Greek security in a profound way. Although its strategic value was probably enhanced, she was faced with considerable fluidity and uncertainty in her northern borders. Yugoslavia's disintegration and civil war released a variety of explosive ethnic, political, social and economic tensions and were the subject of considerable concern in Athens. Proximity and the fear that Balkan instability, whether limited to former Yugoslavia or more general, would inhibit the integration of Greece within the European mainstream created a sense of vulnerability. The economic parameters of the problem were quite significant. Greece had relied on road and rail communications through Yugoslavia for some 40% of its trade with the European market. Prolonged disruption of this vital link has had direct economic consequences for Greece, as had the imposition of EU sanctions against the Yugoslav federal government. Greek authorities estimated that the imposition of sanctions resulted in losses of up to $10 million per day.[33]

Furthermore, it was feared that a violent disintegration of the southern part of the former Yugoslavia could engage outside powers into the conflict, or trigger the flight of waves of refugees into Greek territory. There are nearly one million economic immigrants in Greece – nearly two-thirds originating from Albania. In a period of recession and high unemployment, large numbers of illegal workers place an extra pressure on the already strained Greek economy.

Greece's Balkan interests are for reasons of geographical proximity and historical connections more vital than for any other EU member state. Being the state that was comparatively the most affluent, stable, democratic and well connected with the West in the region, Greece was ideally situated to play the role of interlocutor in the troubled Balkans, but failed to play this role for several years, for reasons that will be explained below.

Greek views on its security interests were not affected by irredentist claims on its neighbours or fear of secessionist tendencies within its territory. The Greek government has renounced all territorial claims on Southern Albania,[34] and has never expressed any territorial ambitions *vis-à-vis* FYROM. However, as a result of the collapse of former Yugoslavia, Greece became involved into a dispute over the official name of the newly independent 'Former Yugoslav Republic of Macedonia' (FYROM). Greece failed to persuade its allies and international public opinion about the correctness of its position on the 'Macedonian' question. Athens was unable to explain that more than history and historical heritage was at stake, and that its main concern is, in the long term, the possible re-emergence of revisionist claims, as indicated by the name, the flag and certain provisions of FYROM's Constitution. Domestic political considerations prevented the acceptance by Greek political leaders of a compromise solution (and also created in some circles the mistaken impression that Greece had territorial designs over FYROM).

The embargo (which was not applied 'very strictly' anyway) imposed on FYROM by Greece had economic cost for FYROM and political (and to some extent economic) cost for Greece. In September–October 1995, as a result of a mediating effort by the US, Greece and FYROM reached an agreement for the termination of the embargo, the change of FYROM's flag and the provision of assurances for specific articles of its Constitution. Although the issue of FYROM's name will be negotiated separately, it is expected that a compromise agreement will be reached. Both countries are quickly proceeding to full normalization of relations, including economic cooperation and Greek investment in FYROM. FYROM officials readily recognize that, because of its geographic location and its membership to the EU, Greece is a natural economic partner for their country. In fact, because of its role as a buffer state against the likelihood of an irredentist 'Greater Albania', Greek officials consider the safeguarding of FYROM's territorial integrity as a vital interest for Greece.

Greek–Bulgarian consultations on security matters had been encouraged by the sense of insecurity felt by both countries in relation to Turkish military power and political interests in the Balkans (Bulgarian–Turkish relations had been particularly difficult as a result of the mistreatment of the large Turkish minority under communist rule in the mid-1980s). In this context, commentators begun to talk openly of an Athens–Sofia axis.[35] Bilateral relations reached a high point in 1986 with the 'Declaration of Friendship and Cooperation', which provided for consultation when the security of either country was in danger (a provision exercised by the Greek side during the Greek–Turkish crisis of March 1987). This *rapprochement* was in the framework of Greece's policy of external balancing for the perceived Turkish threat. Greece adopted a policy of 'vigorous balancing' with Bulgaria, that is improvement of relations with a third power short of an alliance.[36]

More recently, as Greek concerns about Bulgaria's potential role in the so-called 'Macedonian' separatism have grown, and political relations between Sofia and Ankara have steadily improved (not the least because of Bulgaria's military weakness after the dissolution of the Warsaw Pact), Greek–Bulgarian relations deteriorated. However, during the last three years, a process of improvement in Greek–Bulgarian relations has been again in motion, as Bulgaria is adopting a more balanced approach in its relations with her two NATO neighbours.

In the 'post-Dayton' era, Greece is attempting to play a stabilizing role in the Balkan area by formulating a comprehensive and cooperative approach to the region's problems. The changes introduced to the Balkan political scene since the end of the Cold War, the collapse of communism, the break-up of former Yugoslavia and the emergence of a number of successor states, clearly highlight the magnitude of the stakes that the new regional environment has brought to the fore; they also render imperative the need to define an appropriate strategy to meet the new threats and risks that the twenty-first century will entail.

GREEK NATIONAL SECURITY POLICY IN THE POST-COLD WAR ERA

Greek defence policy should be examined in the broader context of Greek security policy, which has the following components: its main security concerns emanate from its problematic relationship with fellow NATO member Turkey, its exposed geographic location in the Balkans, as well as the fact that Greece is not connected by land to any of the other EU countries; proximity to three former communist countries (Albania, Former Yugoslav Republic of Macedonia/FYROM, and Bulgaria) undergoing a period of transition (political and economic) that could under certain circumstances go out of control (as the recent example of Albania demonstrated); and a strategic location which has historically involved this small state in great power antagonisms.

To deter threats to its security, Greece relies on internal (strong armed forces) and external balancing (participation in all West European security and political organizations [NATO, WEU, EU] and signature and adherence to practically all multilateral arms control agreements and international export control). More specifically, to deter the perceived Turkish threat, Greece, for many years, relied mainly on international law and agreements, as well as the mediating role of the US, NATO and the UN.[37] As this policy proved rather ineffective, Greece began to place more emphasis on internal balancing (through the strengthening of its armed forces) and less on membership in NATO and the bilateral relationship with the United States (mainly as a result of Turkey's membership to the former and 'privileged' relationship with the latter). In the last decade or so, Greece placed increased importance on its 'European card' (membership to the European Community/Union and the WEU). Today, Greece relies on a mixture of diplomatic manoeuvring, the strengthening of its armed forces and its membership to the EU in order to balance Turkish military superiority.

(a) Military Doctrine

Greece's military doctrine is defensive, in accordance with NATO's posture. The objective is to deter any threat or actual attack against Greece and to protect Greek national interests. Greece, as a *status quo* country, aims at persuading any revisionist power that the cost–benefit analysis would not be favourable for the latter in the event of aggression.[38] The doctrine of forward defence has been adopted by the Hellenic Armed Forces, due to the country's geography (inadequate defensive depth in Thrace and many islands in the Aegean). On the tactical level, doctrine may have a defensive or a counter-offensive orientation, according to circumstances.[39]

After the impressive performance of the US Armed Forces in the second Gulf War, Greece has decided to reorganize its land forces, with emphasis on smaller units (from divisions and regiments to brigades and battalions), with increased mobility and firepower (in an effort to apply a version of the Air–Land Battle Doctrine).[40]

In 1994 Greece and Cyprus announced the Doctrine of the Joint Defence Area. According to this doctrine, as long as Turkey maintained an occupation force of more than 30,000 troops and heavy military equipment in Cyprus, Greek and Cypriot defence would increase their level of cooperation. In this context, any attack against the Republic of Cyprus would constitute a *casus belli* for Greece. The initiative (actually a policy of extended deterrence) currently being materialized had a clearly defensive character and aimed at averting or facing an eventual aggression against the contracting parties through improving cooperation and joint training between the armed forces of Greece and Cyprus.[41]

Greece is aiming at the qualitative improvement of its armed forces. According to former Minister of National Defence Tsohatzopoulos,

> Considering the dimensions of our country, the condition of our economy and the demographic problem, quantitative armaments competition with any hostile power would constitute a particularly costly effort for Greece with an uncertain outcome. Emphasis, therefore, should be put on quality, by adopting a modern strategic and operational doctrine (with emphasis on combined/joint operations), improving personnel training, restructuring combat units (with the aim of successfully carrying out defensive operations, but also to transfer operations on enemy territory), obtaining the necessary modern weapon systems (smart weapons and especially force multipliers) and rapidly integrating them in our armed forces. The main element of our defence planning is the achievement of maximum cost-effectiveness. We also intend to gradually increase the participation of domestic defence industry in armament programmes for the Greek armed forces.[42]

Greece is exploring the possibilities of the RMA, trying to adapt selected concepts, doctrines and technologies to its national security needs. The main challenge for the Hellenic Armed Forces will be to develop a new military strategy based on new doctrines and technologies, not simply integrate new weapons systems to the existing strategic doctrine. The first step in the direction of substantially improving joint planning and operations and inter-service cooperation was the adoption (December 2000) of a new command structure that would give increased authority to the Chief of the Hellenic National Defence General Staff in both peace and war and would curtail the role of the Services' Chiefs, upgrading at the same time the role of regional commanders.

The next step would consist of a gradual movement from platform-centric to network-centric armed forces with the final objective of creating a 'mixed', multi-mission force and the creation of a smaller, more efficient mixed force of professionals and conscripts.

The officer corps: The current system is designed to guarantee the civilian control of the armed forces, an issue of great significance after the 1967 *coup d' état* and the seven-year military dictatorship that followed. According to the Greek Constitution (which was partially revised in 1985), the President of the Republic is the Supreme Commander of the armed forces, but his powers have a largely symbolic character.

Decisions are taken by the Prime Minister and his government. The Government Council on Foreign Affairs and Defence (KYSEA) appoints the Chief of HNDGS and the Chiefs of Staff and takes all the important procurement decisions.

The military had repeatedly intervened in Greek political life during the twentieth century, on three occasions establishing a dictatorship (in 1925, 1936 and 1967). After the restoration of democracy and the trial and incarceration of the leaders of the 1967 *coup d'état*, officers have consistently refrained from intervening in political life.

It is accurate to state that the officer corps, especially before 1967, had viewed itself as 'embodying the national ideals of Greece and equated the goals of the armed forces with those of the nation'. Furthermore, 'the self-perception of the military as an indispensable instrument of progress and modernization stemmed in part from the variety of social programs and economic development projects in which the armed forces had been employed since 1945'.[43] As a consequence of the suffering of many officers and their families during the Civil War, the political attitude of the armed forces has been strongly anti-communist and pro-conservative. Time and the process of national reconciliation have altered to a large extent the strong pro-conservative attitude of the military.

Earlier studies had reached the conclusion that 'civil control over the military has not advanced at a pace similar to that of the West European democratic states' and that 'generally the Greek military tends to reflect a historical development that has more in common with the other Balkan and Eastern Mediterranean states than it does with its West European allies'.[44] It appears that the above conclusions are no longer applicable, especially in reference to the post-1974 period. After the restoration of democratic rule in 1974 and the limited purge in the Hellenic Armed Forces, civil control over the military has never been in question. The role of the military has been scrupulously limited to defence matters and all significant decisions concerning national security issues are made by the government.

Today, it would be wrong to compare the Hellenic Armed Forces with those of any of its neighbours. By virtue of their organization (based mainly on NATO standards), strict non-interference in politics and civil control and professionalism, they have very much in common with the armed forces of its Western European partners and allies.

Defence expenditures: Since 1974, when Turkey invaded Cyprus and occupied 37% of its territory, Greece has maintained a high level of defence expenditures (with an average of 6% of GNP, which is the highest among NATO countries).[45] High military expenditures and intensive training have been deemed necessary to compensate for

Turkey's quantitative advantage in military equipment and manpower. Although there is consensus among major political parties and the Greek people that this 'sacrifice' is necessary for national defence, military expenditures constitute a heavy burden for the Greek economy at a time when Greece is implementing an austerity economic programme in order to join in the next phase of the European Monetary Union. However, as a result of the Imia crisis and the Turkish announcement for a (ten-year) $31 billion armament programme, Greece responded with a (five-year) $14 billion programme.[46]

TABLE 1: THE ARMED FORCES OF GREECE AND TURKEY

	Personnel	MBT	APC/ AIFV	Artillery[a]	Fighter aircraft	Combat helicop- ters	Major surface vessels	Sub- marines
GREECE	160,000	1,735	2,400+	1,900+	423	20	15	8
TURKEY	610,000[b]	4,200+	3,800	2,900+	505	36	22	14

Source: *The Military Balance 2000–2001 (IISS)* and *Jane's Sentinel Security Assessment: The Balkans* (2000).

Notes: ᵃ Excluding mortars
ᵇ Excluding the Jandarma

TABLE 2: NUMERICAL LIMITS UNDER THE CFE TREATY

	Greece	Romania	Bulgaria	Turkey[47]
MBT	1,735	1,375	1,475	2,795
APC-AIFV	2,498	2,100	2,000	3,120
Artillery	1,920	1,475	1,750	3,523
Combat aircraft	650	430	235	750
Attack Helicopters (2000)	65	120	67	130
Personnel	158,621	230,248	104,000	530,000

Source: *The Military Balance 2000–2001 (IISS)* and *Jane's Sentinel Security Assessment: The Balkans* (2000).

(b) Greece's External Balancing Efforts

1. Greece's participation in NATO: Greece has been a member of NATO since 1952 and remained a member of the Alliance until 1974, when it decided to withdraw from the military structure of NATO in protest to NATO's perceived acquiescence to Turkey's invasion and occupation of

Cyprus. After lengthy negotiations Greece was fully re-integrated to the Alliance in 1980, with the Rogers Report. However, the provision of the agreement for the activation of the land and air headquarters in Larissa (LSE and 7ATAF) was never implemented due to Turkish objections, creating, therefore, a 'gap' to the Alliance's military structure in its Southern Flank.

Unfortunately, Greece has for a long time not been participating fully in most NATO exercises in the Aegean, due to the inability – as a result of Turkish objections – to reach agreement over the issue of including the (forces stationed at the) Greek island of Lemnos in these NATO exercises.[48] It should also be mentioned that both Greece and Turkey veto each other's annual share of NATO funds for infrastructure purposes. Hopefully, a comprehensive settlement of differences separating Greece and Turkey will enable all parties concerned to revitalize the activities of the Atlantic Alliance in this sensitive strategic region.

Today Greece participates in the Standing Naval Force Mediterranean (STANAVFORMED), which consists of destroyer/escort ships and will be at the core of SACEUR's Multinational Maritime Force in a period of limited aggression. Furthermore, she is contributing one division to the ACE Rapid Reaction Corps (ARRC) and will participate in the Multinational Division in the Southern Region – MND(S).[49] Greece is also contributing troops to the ACE (Allied Command Europe) Mobile Force (AMF). Finally, the E-3A aircraft of NATO's Airborne Early Warning Force are manned by integrated crews from 11 nations, including Greece. The E-3A component maintains Forward Operating Bases and Locations in Preveza, among others. There is also a number of NATO NADGE installations in Greece.

Greece fully supported the efforts for the internal adaptation of NATO, providing for the establishment, among others, of a Southern Command with four Sub-Regional Commands (Spain, Italy, Greece, Turkey) and two Component Commands (Air & Naval in Italy). The Larissa-based SRC is already in operation.

During the April 1999 Washington Summit, Greece's Prime Minister, Costas Simitis, stated that

> A successful review of NATO's strategic concept will serve as the necessary tool for the harmonious transition of the Atlantic Alliance from an era of confrontation to one of integration and cooperation. Collective defence and indivisibility of security remain valid, as in the past … As we have turned the page on East–West confrontation, Russia has become NATO's strategic partner. It is impossible to think of a viable European security structure that does not take into account both the political and geostrategic importance of Russia and

the contribution that this country can make to security and stability in Europe.[50]

2. *Greece and the WEU*: In 1995 Greece became the tenth member of the WEU. Initially seen as the European pillar of NATO, WEU's role was 'upgraded' by the Maastricht Treaty and the objective is for it to become the defence arm of the European Union.[51] Subsequently, however, the decision was made to incorporate the WEU into the EU. The WEU ceased to exist in January 2001.

Greece supported an expanded security role for the WEU, as a means towards strengthening of the European defence 'identity' within a strong NATO of two pillars. In this framework, Greek forces would have been available for participation into WEU's multinational land and naval forces,[52] whose missions would include crisis management, peace-keeping operations and protection of WEU nationals abroad.

The Greek position is that the development of a common European foreign and security policy should be based on continued close cooperation and reliance on NATO and should allow, through its procedures, European states, collectively and individually, to shoulder their share of responsibility in trying to promote peace and stability in Europe and the development and well-being of its people. However, in matters directly affecting European member states of NATO and only indirectly non-European member states, the former should have prime responsibility. Furthermore, the creation of a mechanism, in the framework of the EU, is necessary for defining the mission and the required force structure if IFOR- and KFOR-type forces are to be deployed in the future. Greece is a strong supporter (and willing contributor) of the newly created European Rapid Reaction Force.

3. *Participation in international organizations, arms control treaties and export control régimes*: Greece is now a member of most international organizations: the United Nations, the European Union, NATO, the Western European Union, NACC, the Organization for Security and Cooperation in Europe (OSCE), the Council of Europe, and the Black Sea Economic Cooperation.

Furthermore, it has signed practically all multilateral arms control agreements and is a member of all international export control régimes. More specifically, Greece is a signatory of the 1925 Geneva Protocol, the Antarctic Treaty, the Partial Test Ban Treaty, the Outer Space Treaty, the Non-Proliferation Treaty (NPT), the Seabed Treaty, the Biological Weapons Convention, the ENMOD Convention, the 'Inhumane Weapons' Convention, the CFE Treaty and the Chemical Weapons Convention.

A brief reference should be made to Greece's non-proliferation

TABLE 3: GREEK PARTICIPATION IN INTERNATIONAL, POLITICAL AND SECURITY
ORGANIZATIONS, TREATIES AND AGREEMENTS

	Year
United Nations	1945
European Union	1981
NATO	1952
Western European Union	1994
NACC	1991
CSCE/OSCE	1975
Council of Europe	1952
Black Sea Economic Cooperation	1992
Geneva Protocol	1931
Partial Test Ban Treaty	1963
Antarctic Treaty	1987
Outer Space Treaty	1971
Non-Proliferation Treaty	1970
Seabed Treaty	1985
BW Convention	1975
Enmod Convention	1985
Inhumane Weapons Convention CFE Treaty	1989
Chemical Weapons Convention	1993
London Suppliers Group	1991
Australia Group	1990
IAEA	1957
MTCR	1993
Wassenaar Arrangement	1994

Source: Hellenic Ministry of Defence (2001).

policy. Greece signed the NPT in 1968 and signed a safeguards agreement with the International Atomic Energy Agency (IAEA) in 1970. Despite its exporting virtually no nuclear items, Athens complies with the Zangger Committee's 'trigger' lists and will apply safeguards in the eventuality of transhipments of nuclear technology through its territory. It is also observing the Nuclear Exports Guidelines and is a member of the 'London Club', the Australia Group for the Control of Chemical Exports and the Missile Technology Control Régime (MTCR). It has also signed the Chemical Weapons Convention and is preparing to fully implement the treaty's provisions.[53]

Greece was a member of COCOM and is participating fully to the successor régime, the Wassenaar Arrangement. In Greece's view, however, police-type measures are not adequate. The root cause of the alleged security threat providing the motives for the acquisition of weapons of mass destruction must be addressed. A political solution to a brewing conflict constitutes the most effective arms control measure. In this context, the European Union (especially if it becomes more closely integrated politically) can play, along with the US, a very important stabilizing role in the Mediterranean, and the post-Gulf War Middle East and Greece's traditionally good relations with the Arab world (and, more recently, with Israel) might constitute a complementary factor in facilitating such a process.

4. Greek–US defence relationship and bilateral relations with other countries: In 1953, the first defence cooperation agreement between Greece and the US was signed, providing for the establishment and operation of several American military installations on Greek territory. The only operating facility today is that of Souda Bay, providing direct operational support for the US Sixth Fleet in the Eastern Mediterranean.[54]

The Hellenic Armed Forces were built up progressively after the Second World War with British and US aid. In the post-Second World War period, Greece received more than $3 billion in military aid from the US. The majority of the armed forces' major weapon systems were furnished by the US, and the American influence in organization, doctrine, training, uniforms, etc. has been considerable. After 1974, and in view of the Greek–Turkish conflict, Greece tried to lessen its dependence on the US, turning to France as a partial defence alternative. However, as pointed out below, the US remains the main source of defence equipment for the Hellenic Armed Forces.

In 1964, Greece received for the first time military aid from Germany, in the framework of assistance to other NATO members. Under the cascading process, a result of the CFE Treaty, Greece (and Turkey) has received, since 1991, a large number of main battle tanks, armoured personnel carriers, artillery pieces, mortars and other equipment.

Greece has signed a number of defence cooperation agreements with several NATO countries such as the US, UK, France, Germany, Spain, Norway, etc. Recently, Greece has also signed agreements with several former Eastern bloc countries in the framework of the Partnership for Peace Initiative, as well as with a number of Mediterranean states.

In the foreseeable future, Greece will continue to import defence equipment from the United States (especially as far as land and air force weapon systems are concerned), but there will be a gradual Europeanization of defence procurement. The possibility of defence cooperation with Russia and Israel and the purchase or co-production of equipment is another possible option for Greek procurement.

5. Greek participation in peacekeeping operations: In recent years, Greece has evolved from a firm, but rather inactive supporter into an active participant of United Nations peacekeeping efforts and operations. Greek military personnel have participated in peacekeeping operations in Somalia (UNSOM I), Bosnia-Herzegovina (IFOR & SFOR),[55] Albania (Operation ALBA), Kosovo (KFOR, with a sizeable contingent), FYROM (Operation Essential Harvest) and Afghanistan (ISAF) and as observers in other missions in Kuwait, Northern Iraq, Western Sahara and Abkhazia.

Greece is also prepared to participate in the UN-readiness system[56] and will soon create an all-volunteer Unit for Peacekeeping Missions. It would be ready to contribute troops for a peacekeeping force in the Middle East, if the negotiations between Israel and Syria are successful, as well as in prospective UN peacekeeping forces in Abkhazia and Nagorno-Karabakh. As already mentioned, Greece is an active participant in the Southeast European Brigade, a multinational peacekeeping unit. Greek officials believe that in the future we will witness more and more peacekeeping operations by 'coalitions of the willing'.

6. *Transnational threats*: Greek strategic analysts are beginning to deal with the so-called 'new asymmetric threats' and Greece was certainly shocked and deeply saddened by the terrorist attack against the US. The predominant feeling is that this is not a clash of civilizations, West against Islam, but a war of the civilized world, including many Muslim countries, against the fanatics and the zealots. There is no doubt that Greece is firmly in the Western camp and will fulfil all obligations resulting from its membership of NATO and the EU.

Greek officials will have to re-assess to a certain extent their security priorities and assessments. Issues of high concern include the proliferation of weapons of mass destruction, theatre and 'national' missile defence, terrorism (both conventional and new forms: NBC and cyber-terrorism) and the resulting need for increased bilateral and multilateral intelligence and police cooperation, transnational organized crime, with special emphasis on drug trafficking, religious extremism, pollution of the environment and illegal migration.

More specifically on the issue of (international and domestic) terrorism, Greece, in view of the 2004 Athens Olympic Games, will need to complement the existing political will with the further improvement of the competence and an increase at the level of professionalism in its security services, a process that has been underway for the past two to three years with US and British assistance.

GREEK SECURITY IN THE TWENTY-FIRST CENTURY

Greece, despite being a member of the EU and NATO, is geographically situated in a conflict-prone region (Balkans and Mediterranean) where the use of force in inter-state relations may be considered as an option. Greek foreign policy officials and decision-makers, in an effort to formulate a policy that would both promote Greek national interests and be compatible with the policies of the EU and NATO, are assessing developments on a number of issues of high importance, including: EU's Common Foreign and Security Policy (ESDP) – an issue of critical importance for Greece – and Greece's contribution to the European Rapid Reaction Force, EU and NATO enlargement, the Transatlantic relationship, burden-sharing in the context of NATO and the gap in military capabilities between the two pillars of the Alliance, relations with Russia, new asymmetric threats in NATO's Southern Flank and general concern about the South as zone of instability in a region of vital interest for the West.

Greek membership to NATO and its strategic relationship with the US would be essential in facing potential regional challenges. Indeed, for Greece, a functional security relationship with the US based on mutual interests would be a valuable asset in times of regional instability. In this framework, Greece is willing to contribute politically and militarily to the Alliance's efforts to deter out-of-area threats in the Balkans and the Mediterranean (in the framework of NATO's Strategic Concept, adopted at the Washington Summit in April 1999).[57] However, because the Greek foreign policy élite perceives the US as a benevolent force, which has a moral duty to serve as an example in the international system, there is concern about the rather strong signs of unilateralism in US foreign policy.[58]

In the context of North–South relations, Greece is slowly becoming more actively involved in the shaping of EU's Mediterranean policy on the basis of its traditionally good relations with Arab countries and its recently, if belated, improved relations with Israel (and has played a minor role in the peace process by hosting meetings between Israelis and Palestinians). Furthermore, in the 'post-Dayton' era, Greece is attempting to play a stabilizing role in the Balkan and Black Sea regions by formulating a comprehensive and cooperative approach to the region's problems. In this context Greece will serve as a guide and facilitator for the eventual entry of Serbia, FYROM and Albania to NATO and especially, the EU.

Relations with Turkey will continue to remain a top priority issue of Greek foreign and security policy well into the twenty-first century. Unfortunately the short-term prospects for a Davos-III (or Camp David process) between Greece and Turkey are very uncertain. Problems in EU–Turkish relations could have a negative impact on Greek–Turkish relations. Furthermore, there are also problems of cohesion and stability in Turkey's coalition government and domestic politics in general. In view of the scepticism in Greece about Turkey's real intentions, what will be the next step? One should have lower expectations, but continue the process with careful, well-planned and well-prepared steps and involve the civil society, private citizens and NGOs, but also the business persons in both countries to the maximum extent possible.

It is very likely that Cyprus will be included in the group of new members during the EU's next phase of enlargement. The decision will be made in December 2002 or June 2003. If both communities join the EU together, the benefits for Turkey would be obvious and significant: it would boost its relationship with the EU, enhance its international prestige as producer, not consumer, of security, strengthen the détente process with Greece, challenge the perception/allegation that the EU is a Christian club and, in a very symbolic development, render Turkish into an official language of the EU.

At the same time, Greek security planners stress the need for caution. It is argued that, based on the fundamental strategic principle that 'Intentions may change very quickly but (military) capabilities remain', Greece should be prepared to maintain a relative military balance with Turkey. Therefore, to deter the perceived Turkish threat, at least until Turkish policy towards Greece changes in a fundamental way, Greece's emphasis will continue to be on internal balancing (strengthening of its armed forces through increased emphasis on quality with the adoption of a modern strategic and operational doctrine with emphasis on combined/joint operations, improved personnel training and acquisition of modern weapon systems, including smart weapons and force multipliers) and to its membership of the EU.

In the 1980s, the perception of many Western governments and foreign analysts was that 'reactionary' policies, unreliability and unpredictability were the dominant characteristics of Greek foreign policy. In the 1990s and early twenty-first century there is no doubt that the pattern has been a more pragmatic, reliable, rational and multidimensional foreign policy, placing emphasis on multilateral diplomacy.

NOTES

1. According to a former US Ambassador to Greece, 'it would be only a slight exaggeration to say that Greek foreign policy for 160 years has taken no major initiative that was not, directly or indirectly, intended to create a more favourable balance of power with Turkey'. See M. Stearns, 'Greek Foreign Policy in the 1990s: Old Signposts, New Roads' in D. Constas and N. Stavrou (eds), *Greece Prepares for the 21st Century* (Baltimore: Johns Hopkins University Press, 1997) p. 60.
2. *Ibid.*
3. The notions of balancing and bandwagoning were first presented by Kenneth Waltz in his classic work *Theories of International Politics* (Reading, MA: Addison-Wesley, 1979) p. 168. *Balancing* is forming an alliance or building up resources to oppose an aggressive, threatening state. *Bandwagoning* is joining up with the aggressive power to appease it or gain favourable treatment from it. On the balancing vs. bandwagoning debate, see also S. Walt, *The Origins of Alliances* (Ithaca, 1987); *Security Studies* (Special Volume), 1, 3 (Spring 1992); and P. Tsakonas, *Balancing and Bandwagoning Reconsidered. Weak States' Alignment Decisions in Peacetime and Wartime* (Paper presented at the International Studies Association Convention, San Diego, California, April 1996).
4. Small states in many cases 'borrow' security from great powers or alliances and this leads to a certain loss of autonomy. This passive balancing (reliance on the US and NATO) characterized Greek security policy from the end of the Second World War until the mid-1960s.

Since then, the reliance on the US and NATO decreased significantly, to be partially replaced by reliance on the EC/EU.

5. Although significant in a regional level, Greece's economic capabilities and political-military posture constitute no major (present or future) components of the European or global security system (D. Constas, 'Challenges to Greek Foreign Policy: Domestic and External Parameters' in D. Constas and N. Stavrou, *Greece Prepares*, p. 72.

6. Some analysts view Greece as a sensitive strategic outpost of the European Union and NATO in the troubled regions of the Balkans, the Black Sea and the Central–Eastern Mediterranean.

7. 'Of course, a country's strategic significance is not static. It is affected by the evolution of military technology and its impact on defence doctrine; by the constantly changing international and regional political environment; how influential states assess a country's strategic value and define policies to account for their strategic interests in that region; and finally by the willingness and ability of the states in that region to utilise their assets to advance their national interests' (Van Coufoudakis, *The Relative Strategic Significance of Greece and Turkey Before and After the Cold War*. Paper presented at a conference on 'The USA, Greece and Turkey in the Emerging International System', Athens, 19 June 1993, p. 1).

8. There is a long list of problems and threats to regional security and stability in the Mediterranean and the Middle East, such as the slow or negative economic growth, the demographic explosion in many countries, the spread of religious extremism (of special concern is Islamic radicalism), the proliferation of weapons of mass destruction and of sophisticated conventional weapons, the lack of democratization and of respect for human rights, the scarcity of water resources, the pollution of the Mediterranean as a potential threat to the economies of Mediterranean states and to the quality of life of their people and the large number of regional conflicts, the most important of which are the Kurdish problem, the occupation of Cyprus and the Greek–Turkish conflict and, of course, the apparently unending Arab–Israeli conflict. It should be mentioned that some of the above problems have a synergistic effect. See for instance, T. Dokos and P. Pierros, *The Mediterranean Towards the 21st Century* (in Greek), (Athens: Papazissis Publishers, 1996); T. Dokos, 'Sub-Regional Cooperation in the Mediterranean: Current Issues and Future Prospects' in A. Cottey (ed.) *Sub-Regional Cooperation in the New Europe: Current Issues and Future Prospects*, Institute for East-West Studies (London: Macmillan, 1999).

9. C. Arvanitopoulos, 'Greek Defence Policy and the Doctrine of Extended Deterrence', in A. Theophanous and V. Coufoudakis (eds) *Security and Cooperation in the Eastern Mediterranean* (Nicosia: Intercollege Press, 1997), p. 153.

10. From the very first days of the Cold War, Greece and Turkey were considered to be strategically interdependent. However, the US and NATO considered Turkey to be the more important of the two allies for a number of reasons. (Coufoudakis, *The Relative Strategic Significance*, p. 1).

11. I. Lesser et al., 'Greece's New Geopolitics', RAND-Kokkalis Foundation, Santa Monica, 2001, p.9.

12. T. Couloumbis and P. Yannas, 'Greek Security in a Post-Cold War Setting', *The Southeast European Yearbook 1992* (Athens: ELIAMEP, 1993), p. 52.

13. Stearns, p. 64.

14. T. Veremis, *Greek Security Considerations* (Athens: ELIAMEP, 1982), p. 79.

15. Coufoudakis, *The Relative Strategic Significance*, p.1. According to Professor D. Constas, 'Greece, along with most European World War II participants, made its fundamental decisions concerning bilateral and collective defence commitments in the period up to 1955. The legacy of the civil war and American direct involvement in this war left little room for a reconsideration of the future evolution of Greek security interests in a regional rather than a global context. External dependency and the resulting security perceptions, the banning of the Greek Communist Party (KKE), and the marginal role that other forces of the Left could play in the political process all but eclipsed domestic political debate over the terms and conditions of adherence to such arrangements, not to mention consideration of alternative collective security options. In turn, access to Western defence organizations and bilateral agreements with the US perpetuated Greece's introverted security orientation long after external and internal realities had shown a growing incompatibility between national and allied security needs' (Constas, 'Challenges to Greek Foreign Policy', p. 73).

16. Veremis, *Greek Security Considerations*, p. 79.

17. An abortive coup staged by the Greek dictatorship against the president of Cyprus, Archbishop Makarios, in 1974 offered Turkey a much sought-after pretext to invade the island (Constas, 'Challenges to Greek Foreign Policy', p. 73)

18. It is argued that the Turkish threat does not take the form of an imminent all-out war, but consists of a well-concerted strategy of intimidation manifested through a series of low level threats in a number of issue areas (Arvanitopoulos, p. 154).

19. *White Paper of the Hellenic Armed Forces 1996–1997*, Hellenic Ministry of National Defense, pp. 20, 22 and 27.

20. As a Carnegie Endowment Discussion Paper describes the situation, 'For Greeks and Turks, the past involves a pervasive underlying historical legacy of nationalistic, ethnic and religious emotions drawn from: A millennium of Muslim–Orthodox conflict; 400 years of Ottoman rule over Greece; and a century of bitter fighting and cruel atrocities from Greece's declaration of independence in 1821 through to the battles in Asia Minor in 1922. From the sweep of this history come stereotypes of alleged ethnic behaviours, Greeks and Turks locked in "age-old" enmity and the clash of their civilizations.' See *Carnegie Forum on the United States, Greece and Turkey*, p. 3.

21. Greek policy on the Kurdish issue consisted of a mixture of humanitarian concern and of acceptance of the logic that 'the enemy of my enemy is my friend'. In fact, this logic periodically prevailed in Greek and Turkish strategic thinking as both countries attempted, with very limited success, to develop relations with countries such as Armenia, Albania, Iran, Syria, FYROM, etc.

22. For many high officials and analysts in Turkey, the Greek involvement in the Ocalan issue was but a clear indication, if not proof, of Greece's plans to Turkey's dismemberment (in the general context of the so-called 'Sevres syndrome', which allegedly is haunting some Turkish policy makers).

23. It is rather early to say whether the *rapprochement* was facilitated by the personalities of the foreign ministers or by a 'paradigm shift' in Greek and Turkish foreign policy thinking. Both factors probably played a role.

24. Despite differences in style, both major parties (PASOK and New Democracy) showed remarkable continuity in handling core foreign policy questions.

25. The Byzantine/Greek–Ottoman/Turk relationship has been characterized by rivalry and military conflict since the eleventh century. Mainly as a result of the Ottoman occupation of Greece for four centuries, and the Cyprus problem, Greeks are highly suspicious of Turkish intentions. The same, to a lesser degree, is true of the Turks.

26. Y. Valinakis, *Greece's Security in the Post-Cold War Era*, SWP-S394, April 1994, p. 27.

27. Valinakis, *ibid.,* p. 30. See also, A. Platias, 'Greece's Strategic Doctrine: In search of Autonomy and Deterrence', in D. Constas (ed.) *The Greek Turkish Conflict in the 1990s* (London: Macmillan, 1991), p. 93.

28. Furthermore, the decision to produce such sophisticated equipment domestically in Turkey entails considerable financial sacrifices (the cost of the modernization programme for the period 1988–2001 would probably exceed $50 billion [in addition to 'regular' annual defence expenditures], which, according to many analysts, unambiguously reflects Turkey's priorities and potential intentions.

29. For the implications of the enormous defence expenditures on investment expenditure as a share of Greece's Gross Domestic Product, see C. Kollias and A. N. Refenes, 'Modelling the Effects of Defense Spending Relations Using Neural Networks: Evidence from Greece', *Peace Economics, Peace Science, and Public Policy*, 3, 2 (Winter 1996), pp. 1–12.

30. Since September 1994, and shortly before the entry into force of the 1982 Law of the Sea Convention, which calls for a territorial waters width up to 12 miles, the then Turkish Prime Minister Tansu Ciller and other senior government officials explicitly and repeatedly stated that such an extension by Greece would be considered a *casus belli*. This became official policy through a Resolution of the Turkish National Assembly.

31. According to official figures released by the Hellenic Ministry of Foreign Affairs.

32. Bulgaria's attitude towards its own Turkish minority (which is heavily concentrated close to the Greek–Bulgarian border) may prove to be an additional factor in this issue (see Valinakis, *Greece's Security*, pp. 39–40).

33. I. Lesser, *Mediterranean Security: New Perspectives and Implications for U.S. Policy* (Santa Monica, CA: RAND, 1992) p. 75.

34. The major breakthrough came in August 1987 when Greece terminated the state of war that had technically continued to be in effect since 1940, regardless of the establishment of diplomatic relations in 1971 (Constas, 'Challenges to Greek Foreign Policy', p. 87).
35. In July 1991, Athens issued a proposal for disarmament along the borders between Greece, Bulgaria and Turkey. Bulgaria expressed its support for the proposal which was, however, quickly rejected by Turkey primarily because it failed to embrace forces in the Aegean. The short-lived proposal was notable as a reflection of the Greek and Bulgarian concern that a more assertive Turkey might be tempted to use its military superiority in the Balkans as a pillar for its minority policy in the region. (Lesser, pp. 74–5).
36. Robert G. Kaufman, 'To Balance or to Bandwagon? Alliance Decisions in 1930s Europe', *Security Studies*, 1, 3 (Spring 1992) p. 420.
37. According to one analyst, 'the mistaken belief, shared by the Greek and Greek–Cypriot leadership, that diplomacy alone can moderate Turkish behavior and minimize as much as possible Turkey's political and military gains from the 1974 invasion, coupled with Turkey's intransigence, has eroded the credibility of Greek deterrence' (Arvanitopoulos, p. 157).
38. The credibility of the deterrent threat depends upon Greece being perceived as possessing: (a) the military capability to inflict a burdensome cost on Turkey and (b) the will to use those capabilities if necessary (Platias, p. 100)
39. White Paper of the Hellenic Armed Forces 1996–1997. Hellenic Ministry of National Defense.
40. The 2nd Army Corps is in the process of being transformed to a rapid-reaction force.
41. Because of various analyses of the alleged destabilizing consequences of the armament programme of the Republic of Cyprus, a brief reference should be made to the so-called Joint Defence Doctrine (JDD) between Greece and Cyprus. This has been a purely defensive initiative, with two main military objectives: (a) reduction of the vulnerability of Cyprus and increase the cost of any offensive move; (b) prevention of any territorial change by the use of force. The JDD and the modernization programme of the Cypriot National Guard are somewhat similar to the famous '*double-track*' decision by NATO to deploy Cruise and Pershing missiles in Europe in the early 1980s to counter the deployment of the Soviet SS-20s. The main difference is that the latter sought to neutralize an emerging threat, whereas the JDD seeks to balance the military superiority Turkey enjoys since the 1974 invasion. The Cypriot policy is a delayed response to the 'hostage situation' created by the Turkish invasion of 1974 and the deployment in the island of 35,000–40,000 heavily armed Turkish troops. The Greek-Cypriot message was rather straightforward: 'Both sides can build-down their arsenals and actually disarm or we will build-up in order to achieve not equality, but an equilibrium'.
42. Statement of Defence Minister A. Tsohatzopoulos to the Greek Parliament (November 1996).
43. For an illuminating analysis of the social and geographical background of the Greek officer corps, see P. Kassander, 'National Security', in R.S. Shinn (ed.), *Greece: A Country Study* (Washington, DC: The American University, 1986), pp. 292–3.
44. *Ibid.*
45. In fact, during the last years of the Cold War era Greece had ranked first among NATO countries in military expenditures in relation to GDP (6.6% in constant prices compared to a 5.6% figure for the US), and, as noted by a DPC report, 'its defence effort in terms of inputs, was "one of the best in the Alliance"' (*Enhancing Alliance Collective Security: Shared Roles, Risks, and Responsibilities in the Alliance*, A Report by NATO's Defence Planning Committee, Brussels, December 1988, pp. 13 and 50). V. Coufoudakis, 'The Essential Link-Greece in NATO', *Southeast European Yearbook 1988* (Athens: ELIAMEP, 1998)
p. 19.
46. This programme provided for the acquisition of AWACS, 60 third generation fighter aircraft (F-16 and M-2000-5), an initial order for 60 (with an option for an extra 30) fourth generation Eurofighter aircraft), the modernization of 39 F-4Es, medium transport aircraft, attack and transport helicopters, 250 third generation MBTs, MLRS, long-range SAMs (Patriot and S-300), SHORADS, frigates, corvettes, submarines, smart munitions, etc.
47. Approximately one third of Turkey's territory, in the southeast of the country, is excluded from numerical restrictions under the CFE Treaty.

48. This was one of the factors that led Greece, during the 1980s, to follow a 'solitary course' inside NATO, expressing its dissension on a number of issues.
49. Greece has offered to provide the HQ for the Multi-National Division-South (MND-S) in Thessaloniki.
50. Simitis also mentioned that '… It is also important to enhance the Mediterranean dimension of Euro-Atlantic security, always keeping in mind that the factors of stability and security in the region of the Mediterranean are not only military, but also social and economic', NATO 1949–1999, 50th Anniversary, Commemorative Edition, *NATO Review*.
51. WEU Charter, Article V, guarantees the security of its member states through collective action. Although a 19 June 1992 declaration of the heads of state and government of the WEU, issued at Saint Petersburg, imposed restrictions on that warranty when a member state's rival is a NATO member, Greek membership in WEU would nevertheless enhance the country's security posture (Constas, 'Challenges to Greek Foreign Policy', p. 79)
52. Greece has repeatedly expressed its willingness to actively participate in EUROFOR and EUROMARFOR.
53. T. Dokos, 'Greece', in H. Mueller (ed.), *European Non-Proliferation Policy* (Brussels: PRIF, 1996), pp. 213–22.
54. It should be noted that, although the US Congress established a 7 to 10 ratio for the annual provision of military assistance to Greece and Turkey in order to maintain the regional balance of power, it became standard practice for most US administrations to provide assistance to the two countries on a 5 to 10 ratio.
55. Greece contributed one destroyer/frigate to Operation Sharp Guard.
56. Greece has been quite active in the United Nations context in the past 1 to 2 years. Specific examples include its membership in the Executive Committees of UNICEF, UNESCO and the Coordinating Council HIV/AIDS, the Joint Greek–Turkish proposal on Dealing with Natural Disasters (1999) and, in a different context, the proposal for an Olympic Truce (2000).
57. In the post-Cold War period, NATO is no longer a shield against any particular threat, but rather the guarantor of stability in Europe (and in some surrounding regions). According to NATO's New Strategic Concept, the Mediterranean region has acquired increased importance and, some analysts argue, could even be the Alliance's new *raison d'être*. Therefore, there is an obvious need for a strong NATO Southern Flank.
58. T. Dokos, 'Amid the Turbulence: Greek Security Policy in the Eastern Mediterranean and the Balkans', *The Strategic Regional Report*, 6, 7 (October 2001), Western Policy Center, Washington DC, p. 1.

4

The United States and Greece in the Twentieth Century

JOHN O. IATRIDES

One of the more striking characteristics of the modern world order is the tremendous disparity in the power, actual or potential, of states and the apparent ability of the strong to dominate the weak. This was particularly evident during the years of the Cold War conflict when the two superpowers seemed to reign supreme in their respective camps. Yet a close examination of the actual record of interaction between so-called hegemons and their clients reveals that, more often than not, weak states in fact enjoy considerable freedom of action and are capable of initiatives which challenge the pre-eminence if not the actual strategic interests of the patron state. Relations between the United States and Greece, particularly during the Cold War, illustrate the limits of hegemonic control that could be exercised within the Western camp even at the height of that highly polarized and dangerous period.

EARLY BONDS

At the dawn of the twentieth century formal relations between Greece and the United States were fundamentally friendly but passive. Widespread admiration for the world of classical Greece dating back to Thomas Jefferson, and sympathy for fellow Christians struggling to free themselves from Ottoman rule, had fostered in America an active philhellenic movement. Beneath the façade of official neutrality Americans had supported the Greek war of independence with funds, supplies and volunteers and later assisted the infant state by establishing schools and hospitals. For many Greeks the far-away but benevolent land of Washington cited in Solomos' 'Ode to Liberty' became the symbol of personal freedom and self-aggrandizement, where hard work and ingenuity were rewarded and where humble origins were not an insurmountable barrier to success.

Formal diplomatic relations were established in 1833, and a commercial treaty was concluded four years later. In the late 1860s, during the Cretan revolt, the United States resisted urgent Greek pleas for help against the Turks but assisted in relief operations, establishing an important precedent for subsequent humanitarian activities in Greece. By the end of the nineteenth century, in addition to a resident minister in Athens, the American government maintained commercial agents in several Greek ports. However, for the time being Greece was beyond the sphere of significant American interests and concerns. The American presence in that small country was almost entirely confined to the work of private educational, religious and humanitarian groups. Across the Balkans the dominant influences continued to emanate from the capitals of the major European powers.

As a consequence of the First World War the United States took on a major role in Greek affairs. In 1918 the administration of President Woodrow Wilson joined Britain and France in providing a large loan to the insurgent government of Eleftherios Venizelos which brought Greece into the war against the Central Powers. The following year, at the Paris Peace Conference, the United States and the other Entente Powers endorsed Greek government plans to send an expeditionary force into Asia Minor. American warships paid frequent visits to Greek ports and American commercial activity in the area intensified. Without much fanfare the United States was establishing its presence in the Eastern Mediterranean and the Middle East, challenging the European powers' predominance in the region.

In November 1920, after the defeat of Venizelos at the polls and the return of King Constantine, the Wilson administration broke ranks with the major governments of Europe and established diplomatic relations with the new régime in Athens. In the process, Washington also secured a new commercial treaty and favourable agreements on American investments and on the Greek war debt.[1] As a result, by the time the forces of Kemal Attaturk had defeated the Greek expeditionary army in 1922, America's involvement in Greece and in the region had increased substantially. Accordingly, assisting the beleaguered state in its hour of crisis was dictated not merely by humanitarian sentiments but also by a measure of enlightened self-interest. In Smyrna, home of a significant number of American companies, United States officials tried without success to avert mass slaughter and American warships rescued some of the fleeing Greeks.[2]

The Greek crisis was complicated by developments in Athens where a military coup forced Constantine to abdicate in favour of his eldest son, George. Reluctant to take the lead in the matter, the United States withheld recognition of the new régime until Britain had done so.

Furthermore, when a number of prominent royalists were put on trial for causing the national 'catastrophe' in Asia Minor, the Department of State remained silent, unwilling to intervene formally. In Athens the American minister, acting largely on his own initiative, tried in vain to save the lives of the six among the condemned leaders who were executed. In the ensuing outburst of diplomatic outrage the United States expressed its disapproval of the executions and warned that if more death sentences were carried out American relief operations in Greece would be jeopardized.[3]

The magnitude of the disaster that had befallen Greece, a small and poor country suddenly compelled to absorb more than a million destitute and bewildered refugees, called for emergency measures of unprecedented proportions. As the major European governments appeared reluctant to assume the enormous burden, Greek appeals for assistance were directed primarily at America's government and philanthropic organizations. The response was prompt and generous. With the personal endorsement of President Warren G. Harding, the American Red Cross and the Near East Relief organization launched a highly successful fund-raising drive and soon the two institutions were operating a variety of projects designed to house, feed and provide medical care for the refugees. Energized by the plight of the motherland, the Greek American community supported the effort in many ways and emerged as a public advocate whose influence would grow in the decades to come. Following the signing of the Treaty of Lausanne, a League of Nations commission headed by Henry Morgenthau, an American, undertook the monumental task of permanently resettling the refugees and, in the process, making major improvements in the economic development of Greece through large-scale land reclamation and other public works projects. By all accounts, the success of the commission's operations was due to American organizational skills, co-ordination and generous support.[4]

In the 1930s, with the humanitarian mission accomplished, the American presence in Greece was once again reduced to commercial activities and the work of private educational and cultural institutions. From time to time the two governments addressed problems caused by Greece's failure to meet its foreign loan obligations. During 1932–34, the administration of President Franklin D. Roosevelt pressured the Greek government to secure the extradition of the Chicago financier Samuel Insull who, having been charged with embezzlement and larceny, had fled to Athens hoping to avoid prosecution. Otherwise, the United States displayed no special interest in Greece and the Balkan region, where the traditional influence of the major European powers continued to predominate.

Bilateral relations remained unaffected by the dictatorship of Ioannis

Metaxas (1936–41) which was careful not to interfere with American commercial interests and public works projects. The American minister in Athens, Lincoln MacVeagh, a friend of the Roosevelt family, developed a cordial relationship with King George and with a host of top-level government officials. He sent his superiors in Washington a steady stream of reports concerning Metaxas' efforts to avoid the approaching conflagration across Europe. Following Italy's attack on Greece in October 1940, Metaxas appealed to the United States for weapons of every kind and modern aircraft, arguing that Greece was fighting the battle of the democracies against the aggressive forces of Fascism. However, with Greece's meagre credits depleted and as the British government insisted that military supplies to Greece be handled through London, Metaxas' requests went unanswered.[5]

Indeed, throughout the Second World War, American officials were content to consign Greece to Britain's care. The government of Prime Minister Winston Churchill sent troops to Greece to fight the invading Germans and, when the front collapsed, evacuated King George and his government to Egypt where they were to remain under British protection. Whatever influence the Allies were able to exert on the large and fractious Greek resistance movement was channelled through British liaison officers who served with the various guerrilla bands and supplied them with weapons and gold sovereigns. Moreover, all Allied military operations in the Mediterranean were under British command. Consequently, the involvement of the United States in the affairs of enemy-occupied Greece was severely limited. Washington endorsed the lifting of the Allies' blockade so that the International Red Cross, with active American support, could bring food to the starving Greeks and prepared to provide relief through the United Nations Relief and Rehabilitation Administration (UNRRA) following liberation. Otherwise, there were no American policy initiatives affecting Greece.

This is not to suggest that American officials were indifferent to Greek issues or that they approved their management by the British authorities. On the contrary, during the war the Department of State viewed with alarm the rising level of violence between Greek resistance organizations, which it blamed in large measure on Britain's interventionist policies in support of the Greek monarchy and against the emerging communist-controlled powerful leftist movement. The department warned that the Allies 'should carefully avoid any action which could create the impression that they intend to impose the King on the Greek people under the protection of an Allied invading force or that the Greek people can secure the rewards of the common victory only at the price of accepting the return of the monarchy'. In a statement that would prove prophetic, American officials declared that the United States 'would regard it as a great tragedy should any civil disturbances arise in Greece as a result of internal opposition to the return of the King, in which it might be necessary for Allied troops to intervene'.[6]

However, the effectiveness of the American position concerning the growing Greek political crisis was undermined by a series of diplomatic moves dictated mostly (but not entirely) by higher wartime priorities and the need to avoid open friction with the Churchill government. In August 1943, at the First Quebec Conference, Roosevelt formally endorsed the British view that King George would be free to return to Greece 'as soon as possible', and would then be expected to submit the issue of the monarchy's future to a national referendum. A few months later, in December 1943, after the Foreign Office had modified its position and sought to convince the king to declare that he would remain abroad until invited to return by a national vote, Roosevelt met the king in Cairo and advised him to reject such a condition. Encouraged by this unexpected turn of events, King George refused to issue the declaration urged upon him by the British government and demanded by virtually all Greek political leaders. Finally, in the autumn of 1944, despite strong misgivings in the Department of State, Roosevelt gave his consent to Churchill to reach an understanding with Stalin which in effect divided the Balkans into British and Soviet zones, keeping Greece firmly in Britain's share of the spoils. Thus, the liberation of Greece and the return of the government-in-exile (under a coalition representing all major parties including the communists and headed by George Papandreou) took place under British auspices and with the assistance of British troops.

In Athens, Ambassador MacVeagh left little doubt that London's handling of Greek political problems did not enjoy the support of Washington. In December 1944, when serious fighting erupted in the Greek capital between the communist-controlled resistance bands and Papandreou's government (*Ta Dekemvriana*), the embassy and officials in Washington openly blamed the crisis on British mismanagement. In a thinly veiled reference to the situation in Greece Secretary of State Edward R. Stettinius Jr announced that 'the United States policy has always been to refrain from any interference in the internal affairs of other nations' and expressed American sympathy for 'the aspirations of the resistance movements and the anti-Fascist elements in liberated countries'.[7] American ships were ordered not to transport supplies to the British forces battling the insurgents in Athens and an angry Churchill had to call the White House before the order could be rescinded. In a personal letter to Roosevelt MacVeagh attributed the latest Greek upheaval to 'the handling of this fanatically freedom-loving country (which has never yet taken dictation quietly) as if it were composed of natives under the British Raj …'.[8]

Once again, however, the American position was confined to inef-

fective complaints and, after fierce fighting in Athens, British troops
were able to defeat the insurrection. While Ambassador MacVeagh kept
his distance, the British embassy supervised the truce talks which led to
the peace agreement of 12 February 1945, signed at Varkiza. In addition
to formally ending the hostilities the agreement called for the disarming
of the resistance bands, granted limited amnesty to the insurgents and
provided for national elections, to be followed by a plebiscite on the
thorny issue of the monarchy's return. A proposal for a US–British–
Soviet commission for Greece, with the participation of American civil
affairs troops, originally suggested by MacVeagh and endorsed by the
president (with lukewarm support from the Department of State), was
dropped when Churchill counter-proposed a purely Anglo–American
undertaking. Roosevelt did not wish to arouse Stalin's suspicion by
excluding the Soviets from an international effort to manage the problems of Greece. Instead, at Churchill's urging, Roosevelt supported
British pressure on King George to name Archbishop Damascinos
regent, thus defusing the monarchy issue pending a plebiscite. At a
stormy meeting of leaders of Greece's warring factions whom Churchill
lectured sternly about their misdeeds, MacVeagh's silent presence
perpetuated the prevailing impression that the British prime minister
was speaking for the American president as well.[9]

In the end, American frustration with Britain's high-handed policy in
Greece was manifested indirectly and in an unexpected forum. The
Declaration on Liberated Europe approved at the Yalta conference was
an American document drafted in large measure with Greece in mind
and designed to avert one-sided foreign interventions in the internal
affairs of countries recently freed from enemy occupation.[10] Moreover,
in March 1946, upholding the Yalta principles, the United States joined
Britain and France (the Soviet Union refused to participate) in supervis-
ing the first parliamentary elections in Greece since 1936, and of the
referendum which in September of the same year returned King George
to his throne. The United States also strongly supported the transfer of
the Dodecanese islands to Greece from Italy and was willing to consider
Greek government requests for small assistance loans. Otherwise, the
administration of President Harry Truman saw no reason to become
involved in the affairs of Greece where Britain's influence remained
strong.

THE INTERVENTIONISM OF CONTAINMENT

During 1944–45 Britain's military intervention and continued high
profile presence in Athens may have averted a communist victory, but
otherwise did little to end civil strife in Greece. On the contrary, it

emboldened the entrenched right-wing state authorities to persecute veterans of the wartime leftist resistance movement, many of whom fled to the mountains and formed armed bands. At the same time the government and its British advisers appeared incapable of moving the country forward on the road to genuine pacification, political stability and economic recovery. As for the communists, military defeat and the disarming of many of their followers had dealt a severe blow to their power and public image. Nevertheless, their leaders had not abandoned hope that they could achieve victory through a combination of mass mobilization, political agitation and armed force. By the spring of 1946 sporadic attacks by communist bands on isolated police stations and remote army posts, which gradually became bolder and more frequent, heralded the start of full-scale civil war. The following year a communist-controlled 'Democratic Army' was operating in much of rural Greece and was receiving substantial assistance from the neighbouring communist régimes. British efforts to boost the government's security forces appeared destined to produce a stand-off.

Initially the American embassy in Athens tended to attribute the rising level of violence to the reactionary tactics of the Greek authorities and the ineptitude of their British advisers. In his reports to Washington Ambassador MacVeagh repeatedly discounted charges that the Greek communists were launching an insurrection at the behest of Moscow.[11] However, in the early months of 1946, the Truman administration's attitude toward the Soviet Union underwent a dramatic change that was destined to affect Washington's view of developments in Greece. A series of disagreements with Moscow and escalating friction over Soviet behaviour along a wide front, extending from Germany and the Baltic states to Turkey and Iran, was eventually perceived in Washington as proof that the Soviet Union, with the active help of local communists everywhere, was on a campaign of world conquest. The central logic of this perception of Soviet strategy was provided by the now-famous 'long telegram' of 22 February 1946, which an American diplomat in Moscow, George F. Kennan, sent to his superiors in Washington. After a comprehensive analysis of the roots of Moscow's world view and resulting expansionist tendencies, Kennan advocated long-term American support for those free and independent states that might form a natural barrier to 'contain' the further spread of international communism and Soviet power.

For President Truman's advisers, who were already thinking along similar lines, Kennan's well argued message became the catalyst for high-level discussions and immediate action. Not coincidentally, within weeks of the telegram's arrival in Washington, an internal State Department document asserted that 'Greece fits into Russia's plans for expansion into the Middle East and toward the Mediterranean and the Indian

oceans' and that Greece and Turkey were the states where 'the Western
system has the opportunity of presenting the strongest front to the
outward and downward expansion of Soviet methods and influence'.[12]
As though timed to provide hard evidence to support such an analysis,
in August 1946 American intelligence sources in Athens reported that
the Greek communists were in fact secretly funded and controlled by the
Soviet authorities. A few weeks later Ambassador MacVeagh openly
blamed Moscow for the escalating political violence in Greece. In short,
the Greek civil war was now attributed to Moscow's expansionist
schemes and Greece was perceived as an important part of the wall that
would have to be built if Soviet communism were to be contained. The
stimulus for action was provided by Britain's decision to announce its
intention to end its programmes of assistance to Greece and Turkey,
secretly communicated to Washington on 21 February 1947 in two separate but nearly identical notes.[13]

Thus, from the outset, serious American preoccupation with post-
war Greece was motivated less by concern over developments in Greece
itself than by the dictates of an emerging regional strategy extending
from Western Europe to the Eastern Mediterranean and the Near East,
designed to deter further Soviet expansion. Moreover, within the framework of that strategy, the value of Greece as an ally of the United States
was directly linked to that of Turkey. As President Truman warned the
Congress in his historic speech of 12 March 1947: 'Should we fail to aid
Greece and Turkey in this fateful hour, the effect will be far reaching to
the West as well as to the East.' The Truman administration succeeded
in convincing the Republican-controlled Congress to inaugurate the
policy of containing Soviet expansionism by funding a programme of
assistance whose immediate goal was to keep Greece and Turkey from
being absorbed into Moscow's camp.

The carefully orchestrated campaign was highlighted by
Undersecretary of State Dean Acheson's assertion that a communist
victory in Greece would expose three continents to Soviet threats: 'like
apples in a barrel infected by one rotten one the corruption of Greece
would infect Iran and all to the east. It would also carry infection to Africa
through Asia Minor and Egypt, and to Europe through Italy and France,
already threatened by the strongest domestic Communist parties.'[14] As
already mentioned, President Truman repeated this argument in his speech
to the Congress. In order to leave no doubt about who, exactly, was to
blame, Ambassador MacVeagh testified before the Senate Foreign
Relations Committee that the causes of civil war in Greece were to be
traced to 'the fellow who controls the little countries to the north of
Greece ... right square back to the Moscow Government'.[15]

Britain's diplomatic move announcing the end of assistance to Greece
and Turkey, which could not have come as a surprise to American

officials, was particularly helpful for another reason. In addition to appearing to link the security problems confronting Greece and Turkey, it provided an element of urgency and created the impression that American decision-makers were faced with a crisis situation that called for quick and bold action. This despite the fact that, as Secretary of State, George C. Marshall observed to the British ambassador who delivered the two notes, 'the Russians had made no move with regard to Turkey for some time', a point that the British diplomat could not dispute.[16]

The first skirmishes of the Cold War involving Greece were fought in the newly created United Nations. During 1946 the United States played a leading role in the Security Council's rejection of Soviet charges that Britain's military presence in Greece and the policies of the Athens government threatened peace and security in the region. When Greece went on the diplomatic offensive and brought to the Security Council a complaint that its Balkan neighbours were aiding and abetting the communist insurgents, the Athens government received encouragement and advice from the Department of State. In October 1947 the United States brought the 'Greek Question' before the Security Council once again and orchestrated the council's decision to create a special UN commission to investigate the circumstances surrounding the Greek civil war. By then, however, American officials were already busy directing a massive assistance programme designed to ensure that the communist insurgency would be crushed. While the Truman Doctrine speech had carefully avoided naming the Soviet Union as its target, government documents intended for top-level officials were categorical on this crucial issue. A National Security Council report defining the American position concerning Greece stated the problem in stark and unequivocal terms:

> The Communists, under the leadership of the USSR [Union of Soviet Socialist Republics], seek world domination and to this end are making piecemeal advances, principally by aggression through indigenous Communist movements within other countries. In line with this strategy the Communist movement, operating through the Communist party of Greece and the Soviet satellite countries in the Balkans, is engaged in a forceful, energetic effort to overthrow the present Greek Government, and to achieve complete and dictatorial control of Greece ...

Accordingly,

> 13. The defeat of Soviet efforts to destroy the political independence and territorial integrity of Greece is necessary in

order to preserve the security of the whole Eastern
Mediterranean and the Middle East, which is vital to the
security of the United States.

14. The United States should, therefore, make full use of its
political, economic and, if necessary, military power in such
manner as may be found most effective to prevent Greece
from falling under the domination of the USSR, either
through external armed attack or through Soviet-dominated
Communist movements within Greece, so long as the legally
elected government of Greece evidences a determination to
oppose such Communist aggression.[17]

In the more apocalyptic words of a high level Department of State
official, Greece had become

... the test tube which the peoples of the world are watching
in order to ascertain whether the determination of the
Western powers to resist aggression equals that of international Communism to acquire new territory and new bases
for further aggression. We are convinced that if the United
States permits the conquest of Greece, the peoples particularly of Europe and of the Middle East will draw their own
conclusions and will be afflicted with a sense of uncertainty
and frustration similar to that found in Greece today.[18]

In practical terms, the American policy on Greece encompassed four
basic objectives. The first was to entrust government authority to a
broadly-based coalition of anti-communist political leaders that would
be able to establish legal order and create at least the semblance of
democratic rule. Such government would be expected to deprive the
communists of any popular appeal they still enjoyed and silence those
critics who accused the Truman administration of propping up a reactionary régime. This was not expected to be an easy task. As Ambassador
MacVeagh had reported in the fall of 1946, 'Small men, old men, and
men entirely lacking in the sense of realism which the situation requires,
are what we are having to deal with now. In addition, the king who has
been brought back as a "solution" for the problems which the politicians
will not tackle is the same old muddled indecisive figure that he always
was.'[19] Washington's prescription for strong and effective government in
Athens called for 'responsible Greek political leaders [who] would have
vision, restraint, and patriotism to form a political coalition which
would include those leftist, liberal and center groups sufficiently enlightened and loyal to refuse to have any further dealings or associations with

communists and those rightist groups which would be willing loyally to cooperate with all anti-Communist center and leftist groups'.[20]

Accordingly, in September 1947, under strong American pressure and with the cooperation of King Paul (younger brother of King George who died on 1 April 1947), Constantine Tsaldaris, leader of the right-wing Populist Party, turned the premiership over to Themistoclis Sofoulis, head of the centrist and one-time republican Liberal Party, while remaining in the cabinet as deputy prime minister and foreign minister. However, the ideal coalition American officials had hoped to assemble proved to be elusive and before long there were grumblings in American and Greek official circles that what was needed was a strong-man government. While such a radical solution was resisted, thanks to the firm stand taken on this issue by Ambassador Henry F. Grady, until the defeat of the insurrection in late 1949 the government consisted of prominent anti-communist personalities who continued their own quar-rels but were willing to carry out the dictates of the American embassy and various advisory groups and missions. In the name of anti-commu-nism and with American endorsement the Greek authorities intensified police controls, trade unions remained under close government supervi-sion and political intrigues continued among the military.

The second objective of the Truman administration was to turn the bloated, inefficient and thoroughly politicized state agencies into dynamic, efficient and impartial instruments of economic reconstruction and social progress. The first head of the US economic mission, Ambassador Paul A. Porter, characterized the existing Greek civil service as a 'depressing farce'.[21] Indeed, for many American civilian officials who served in Greece in various capacities, reforming the state bureau-cracy was their most daunting challenge and the only way to bring about a measure of economic development, modernization and higher stan-dards of living. In the pursuit of this ambitious undertaking Americans assumed direct control of virtually all key ministries, under terms care-fully stipulated in a number of bilateral agreements. The resulting 'pene-tration' of Greece, which was to plant the seeds of anti-Americanism in the years to come, brought about mixed results. Although the perfor-mance of state agencies generally improved, they remained politicized, rigid and insensitive to the needs of ordinary citizens. In fact, in Greece as elsewhere, Washington's experiment in 'social engineering' was less than successful and in later years would become the subject of much academic debate and bitter criticism. Yet in 1947, most Greeks, and not just the conservative élites, feared not only for their personal welfare but also for their nation's survival as an independent state. For them, the American involvement in their country's affairs brought welcome relief and the assurance that they would not share the fate of their communist-dominated Balkan neighbours. Having little faith in their own govern-

ment and national leaders they were not overly concerned that control
over key functions of the state would for a time be in American hands.
On this point they had no illusions. As the Greek ambassador in
Washington, Paul Economou-Gouras, pointed out to his superiors:

> Unquestionably the American plan will entail the limitation
> up to a point of our sovereign rights. But this must be consid-
> ered in the context of the tragic danger faced by our country
> to be swept under by Slavism. In view of England's weaken-
> ing power, [the American] intervention now appears as a life
> preserver and the only hope that Greece would not only
> survive as a country according to our liberal traditions but
> would be assured of its economic well-being. Accepting under
> the present circumstances the American intervention we may
> be certain that the Americans will depart on their own as
> soon as possible. On this we have guarantees based on
> America's past record and selfless sentiment of friendship of
> the American people for Greece. I believe that the only
> disturbing point would be the possibility that the Americans
> will withdraw prematurely, as happened in China. Such a
> possibility could be averted on the one hand by our willing
> and sincere co-operation and, on the other, by the American
> government's undertaking of the broadest possible activities
> [in Greece].[22]

The Americans' third objective was to provide the economic support
and technical guidance needed to repair the country's devastation and
build the foundation for long-term development. Beyond the assistance
programmes designed exclusively for Greece, the country was included
in the Marshall Plan, whose primary purpose was to restore Europe's
trade by providing the necessary working capital. In Greece, American
advisers paid particular attention to currency stabilization, control of
imports and exports and improving agricultural productivity. They also
sought to build the foundations for industrialization by repairing and
expanding the road and rail systems, introducing a country-wide
network of electrification, and strengthening the health services. By
1954, when programmes of purely economic assistance ended, Greece
had received more than two billion dollars in various forms of aid. To
be sure, during the years of civil war (1946–49) much of the assistance
had benefited first and foremost the government's military effort.
Nevertheless, the country's infrastructure was rebuilt and expanded and
basic living conditions rose above pre-war standards.

Despite impressive achievements, the impact of American policy on
Greece's economic and social development was not without its short-

falls. In particular, programmes designed to narrow the gap between the rich and the poor failed. Moreover, in subsequent years the modest success of industrialization gave rise to the charge that American planners had deliberately prevented Greece from maximizing its potential in industrial development.[23] While Washington's hopes for Greece did not in fact include building a heavily industrialized state, the deeper causes of the continuing social malaise could be found elsewhere, beyond the remedies the Americans could provide. According to a 1950 report of the head of the US economic mission,

> Economic and political leadership comes mainly from a small wealthy class which, with some notable exceptions, is indifferent to its social responsibilities, is resistant to reforms, and is motivated by a mercantilist and rentier philosophy rather than a production philosophy ...The tax structure is one of the most regressive in Europe, and tax evasion by many wealthy people adds to the inequality of burdens ... Many of the political leaders, supposing that the basic interests of the nation are safeguarded by American economic and military aid, indulge in the dangerous luxury of preoccupation with little things. Indeed, most ministers during the period of American aid have preferred to pass responsibility for difficult and unpopular decisions to the [American] Mission ... Local taxing authority has largely disappeared. The relationship of the people to their Government has become that of petitioners, and the Government has become a petitioner of the world.[24]

The Truman administration's fourth and most immediate objective was to improve the strength and fighting capabilities of the Greek armed forces so that they could go on the offensive and defeat the communist insurgency quickly and decisively. In this the Americans were entirely successful. Properly equipped and energized, the government's troops overpowered and crushed the so-called Democratic Army in less than two years. American advisers played an important role in the planning and execution of operations. On the other hand, although the matter was discussed at some length, no US combat troops were needed and the civil war was fought and won entirely by Greek soldiers.

The modernization and overall improvements the Americans introduced to all branches of the Greek armed forces was to prove lasting and was greatly enhanced by Greece's membership of NATO. At the same time, the Greek military's involvement in politics and their secret organizations continued and some among the officers came to regard themselves as a praetorian guard and arbiters of legitimacy of the nation's governing authority. It could thus be argued that the American influence over Greece's military failed to include one of the greatest pillars of American democracy: civilian rule over the military. However, if some Greek officers have periodically shown themselves capable of destroying their country's democracy one can hardly blame their American instructors.

In 1949, when the defeat of the insurgency appeared to be certain, the Truman administration announced its intention to curtail its involvement in Greece and to launch diplomatic initiatives largely within the framework of the United Nations in the hope of reducing Cold War tensions in the Balkans. The Greek government was advised to introduce conciliatory measures toward its domestic foes and to consider the legalization of the Communist Party, the repatriation of guerrillas, and the holding of national elections under international supervision with Soviet participation. In an abrupt abandonment of its earlier stand, the Department of State appeared willing to search for a political settlement of the Greek crisis through negotiations with Moscow. It also downplayed the strategic value of Greece and indicated that no American bases would be established in that country.[25]

While the Soviet government appeared puzzled by the new American position on Greece, British officials expressed concern that they had not been consulted and made no secret of their unwillingness to endorse what Washington proposed. As for Greece's political leaders, with the exception of the republican-liberal Nikolaos Plastiras and the conservative Speros Markezinis, they expressed alarm and dismay over what they saw as their abandonment by the United States. Military and security officials were particularly angered by proposed measures intended to promote reconciliation with the communist insurgents and their supporters. As a result, although the executions of condemned communists were stopped, Washington's recommendations were generally ignored.[26] Having co-opted the traditional politicians and the military against the communist threat, Washington could not make them toe its new line. In the end, the sudden outbreak of the Korean war in June 1950 and the red-baiting hysteria of McCarthyism prompted the Truman administration to abandon its modest 'peace initiative' for Greece and the Balkans.

In short, at the high point of American influence in Greece, Washington's ability to dictate and obtain satisfactory results was hardly limitless. For all their apparent subservience, Greek politicians were able to resist and subvert changes demanded by American advisers secure in the knowledge that they represented the only political elements the United States authorities were prepared to support. In their desire to avoid caving in to the Americans, Greek officials did not hesitate to exploit the public's growing resentment of what was perceived as crude foreign domination. Moreover, once the civil war had ended and emergency measures had been lifted, the highly personalized nature of politics returned with a vengeance, leading to renewed feuding and fragmentation and to weak coalition governments. Without firm leadership at the top, the implementation of reforms and programmes recommended by the Americans languished or was entirely derailed. To the dismay of American advisers, the elections of March 1950, in which more than 40 parties fielded candidates, produced an unstable coalition headed by Plastiras, hardly a favourite of the Truman administration. His successor, the centrist Sophocles Venizelos, was personally on good terms with American officials but his government remained shaky and inactive. Adding to the uncertainty, in May 1951, despite the strenuous efforts of Ambassador John Peurifoy, Marshall Alexandros Papagos resigned after a falling out with the king, leaving the armed forces without firm leadership. Nor was King Paul particularly receptive to American advice. In January 1952, when Ambassador Peurifoy suggested the need for a stronger government with the support of Papagos' newly formed Greek Rally party, the king reportedly replied that if the Americans wanted a new government, 'they could kick the present one out themselves'.[27] The following month, in the form of 'friendly advice', the king suggested that the embassy confine its interests to broad political issues and refrain from commenting on personalities.[28]

Undaunted by royal petulance, Peurifoy played what was always the embassy's strongest card – on 14 March 1952 he let it be known that American assistance to Greece, already considerably reduced from the previous year's level, might be further cut unless the approaching national elections were based on a simple majority system which was expected to greatly favour Papagos' Rally. Peurifoy's blunt warning prompted his British colleague in Athens to observe that, 'for good or ill the US Government have now committed themselves to a definite and overt interference in the internal affairs of the country'.[29] The Americans' open threat, which produced a storm of protests and criticism, prove effective. In November 1952 elections were held on a simple majority system and Papagos' Rally won a sweeping victory, receiving 247 of the parliament's 300 seats. Thereafter, with a strong conservative government eager to integrate Greece in the Western alliance and carry out the reconstruction and development plans prescribed by the Americans, Ambassador Peurifoy's persistent strong-arm tactics were no longer needed. Washington's influence could now be exerted through the more discreet methods of traditional diplomacy and through a network of clandestine personal contacts.[30]

Parenthetically, Peurifoy's tour in Athens, his first overseas assignment after many years in administration, represented the zenith of American intervention in Greek affairs and deserves brief comment. There is no question that, in general terms, Peurifoy carried out faithfully the instructions of his superiors which in turn reflected Washington's fears and anxieties precipitated by communist aggression in Korea; the Cold War suddenly intensified and became global. Yet he conducted himself in a manner that was uniquely his own. Determined to become the catalyst for producing a strong, broadly based and dynamic government that would cater to America's wishes, he inserted himself in the byzantine world of Greek politics with tenacity and self-confidence. He maintained a running dialogue, both publicly and in secret, with an assortment of politicians and government officials, as well as with the royal couple, Marshall Papagos and other senior military officers, all of whom regarded him as a major player in the game of political intrigue and self-promotion in which they were the grand masters. Like an amateur but supremely confident ringmaster, he struggled with only limited success to keep in line his high-spirited and undisciplined performers. His visibility and hyperactive diplomacy strengthened in the Greek public's perception the image of American domination that was to prove lasting. Needless to say, other American ambassadors would intervene in Greek affairs but none as frequently and conspicuously as Peurifoy.

The entry of Greece in NATO, formally secured in October 1951 thanks to Washington's efforts and implemented in the mid-1950s, and the dispatch of Greek troops to fight in the Korean war, strengthened further the bonds between the two governments and their security agencies. In 1953, a comprehensive 'status of forces' agreement granted the American military stationed in Greece and their families extensive rights and privileges including extraterritoriality. To highlight the close bilateral relations in November 1953 the Greek royal couple visited the United States and received an exceptionally warm welcome and much favourable publicity. At the same time the Eisenhower administration gave its cautious blessing to Greek diplomatic initiatives which resulted in the signing of a political and military pact between Greece, Yugoslavia and Turkey.[31]

Relations between Athens and Washington remained close following the death of Marshall Papagos in early October 1955. American officials had been following with interest and satisfaction the rise of Constantine Karamanlis in the ranks of the Rally party and in the Papagos cabinet. He had become known at home and abroad for his dynamic and tireless work ethic, his blunt language and organizational skills, and for his remarkable achievements as minister of public works. He was also staunchly anti-communist and fully committed to Greece's integration in the Western alliance. In short, he was clearly a man Washington hoped to see as the head of the Greek government and there is evidence that such a prospect was raised in discussions that Karamanlis and King Paul had with CIA agents or conduits.[32] Given the labyrinthine nature of contacts between Athens and Washington, which in addition to normal diplomatic exchanges included military, intelligence and private channels, it is impossible to assess with certainty the American 'factor' in this matter. In any event, when King Paul chose Karamanlis to succeed Papagos, bypassing the government's two senior leaders Stefanos Stefanopoulos and Panayiotis Kanellopoulos, the American embassy appeared to be taken by surprise and called the move 'bold and unexpected'.[33] Many years later Karamanlis would reject suggestions that his selection had been influenced by the Americans.[34] Perhaps one need not look beyond the simple explanation offered by the British ambassador who reported from Athens: '... King Paul with perhaps more daring than imagination decided to have done with the politicians of the old school and on (Papagos') death sent for Karamanlis, a more energetic and younger politician with a good record of achievement ...'.[35] On the other hand, foreign observers were anything but confident that Karamanlis could weather the storm which his appointment had unleashed in the ranks of the governing Rally party.

To clear the air and consolidate his power the new prime minister called for early elections. When the American bases agreement suddenly surfaced as a major campaign issue, Karamanlis demanded that the more controversial provisions be renegotiated. It was now Washington's turn to yield to Greek government demands. The Department of State advised the Pentagon to do everything possible to accommodate Karamanlis, who 'is anxious to subdue the anti-American emotions in Greece ...' and who 'deserves our full support'.[36]

All through the late 1950s Washington officials could count on a sympathetic hearing in Athens. In May 1957, ignoring criticism from pro-Arab circles, the Greek government endorsed the Eisenhower Doctrine which was designed to forestall Soviet penetration of the Middle East by promising American military assistance to victims of aggression in that region. In December 1959 President Dwight D. Eisenhower paid an official visit to Athens and praised the Karamanlis government as America's partner and dependable ally; he also promised economic and political support. In April 1960, in response to Soviet threats that Greece would be destroyed if it accepted nuclear weapons on its soil, Secretary of State Christian Herter travelled to Athens and publicly reaffirmed America's commitments to protect Greece. The following year President John F. Kennedy honoured Karamanlis at the White House and the Greek leader addressed the House of Representatives where he received a standing ovation. Relations between the two governments appeared to be closer than ever.

THE END OF HARMONY

However, appearances were deceptive. Despite formal manifestations of harmony and mutual goodwill, Athens and Washington were in fact on a dangerous course of mounting disagreement and friction. In part, the problem was caused by persistent anti-Americanism resulting from a variety of perceptions and misperceptions by the Greek public and by an international climate that was increasingly opposed to Cold War divisions and the dangerous nuclear arms race. The single most important issue was the Cyprus controversy which had contributed to mounting tension first in Greece's relations with Britain and Turkey, but which soon engulfed US–Greek relations as well.[37]

At first the Papagos government had hoped that, in addressing the Cyprus problem, it could count on Washington's sympathetic understanding and support. After all, self-determination, which formed the basis for the Greek position, was a concept borrowed from America's traditional foreign policy ideals. Rebuffed by the British, who dismissed Greek feelers concerning the future of Cyprus as the product of Papagos' 'personal vanity' and intellectual deficiencies,[38] in August 1953 the Greek government approached Washington and requested its help in dissuading Archbishop Makarios from raising the Cyprus issue in the United Nations on the grounds that only the communist world would benefit from such a rift in the Western camp. The American embassy in Athens endorsed the Greek appeal and warned that 'unless Makarios can be restrained, Papagos may feel that his posture as Paladin of Greek nationalism obliges him to take over leadership of this campaign. Certainly there are few issues on which the opposition could cause more embarrassment to the government than that of "betrayal of Cyprus"'. Despite the warning and the modest nature of the Greek request, the Department of State refused to intercede, taking the position that the United States was not a party to the dispute and that any American approach to Makarios would be undesirable and ineffective.[39] Not surprisingly, Greek hopes that Washington might try to persuade the British to be more flexible on the Cyprus issue were similarly dashed.[40] Thus, as the American embassy had forewarned in 1953, Papagos and his successors felt compelled to make Cyprus the centrepiece of Greek foreign policy, with predictably dire consequences for all concerned, but especially for Greece.

The effects of Greece's disillusionment with its western allies were soon all too evident, especially following the anti-Greek riots in Turkey in September 1955. The Greek government, which was aware that the violence had been orchestrated by the Turkish authorities, was especially embittered by Washington's attitude of blaming both sides equally for the outrage.[41] By the end of that year the British embassy in Athens reported that 'the decline in Greece's friendliness to us was reflected in a worsening of her relations with the United States and all her North Atlantic Treaty Organization allies (amounting, in the case of Turkey, almost to a suspension of relations)'.[42] Two years later the American embassy observed that 'We can no longer be as certain as we have been in the past that we shall have Greece's support in foreign policy matters that are critical to us ... In the Cyprus issue most of all we have failed in Greek eyes to support the Greek position, and to the Greeks there is no more important problem in this decade.'[43] In November 1959, even as a solution to the Cyprus problem appeared to be imminent, an embattled Karamanlis bitterly complained to the American ambassador, Ellis O. Briggs, that 'NATO allies have done little to show sympathy or understanding. Cyprus settlement was unpalatable to large segments of the Greek public and his government was correspondingly vulnerable'.[44]

Karamanlis' complaint reflected the fact that his had been Greece's most genuinely pro-American and pro-NATO government. He and his principal foreign policy advisers, including Foreign Minister Evangelos Averoff and Minister to the Prime Minister Constantine Tsatsos, were staunch supporters of America's leadership role in the free world and of its containment policy. Since Papagos' days of conservative government, the Greek armed forces had depended on the United States for their weapons, supplies, training, and even for their salaries. Many Greek officers had attended American military schools and held strongly anti-communist views. The Central Intelligence Service (KYP), another bastion of right-wing politics, was a virtual creation of the CIA and the ties between the two agencies had become so close as to border on the conspiratorial.

Karamanlis and his colleagues had no wish to improve relations with the Soviet bloc and resisted with equal determination Moscow's crude threats and peace offensives. They viewed with alarm the growing influence of domestic pro-communist elements which, under the façade of the Greek Democratic Left party (EDA), threatened to challenge Greece's pro-western orientation. EDA's popularity reflected the declining fear of communism and the growing anti-American and anti-NATO feelings of many Greeks. Especially in the aftermath of the October 1956 Suez crisis, which severely damaged the appearance of solidarity among the principal western powers and sparked threats of nuclear war, anti-government movements for peace and disarmament acquired momentum, particularly among Greek workers and students.

Beyond narrow politics, the country's chronic economic problems, including a heavy foreign debt, general backwardness and low productivity, threatened to undo whatever progress had been achieved in earlier post-war years thanks largely to American assistance. Any hope for further economic development and industrialization would prove

fruitless if US–Greek relations suffered a serious setback. Even the realization of Karamanlis' greatest dream, Greece's entry into the European
Economic Community, seemed to depend on Washington's support. In
March 1960 Ambassador Briggs was pleased to inform Karamanlis that
'the Department had been immediately responsive to his request that we
appeal to common market countries to facilitate Greece's entry and had
made representations in the various capitals'.[45]

Finally, on a personal level, Karamanlis appeared to have a genuine
admiration for America's role in world affairs, a sentiment that was
sometimes expressed in rather oblique ways. Thus, in May 1960,
following the shooting down by the Soviets of an American U-2 plane
and President Eisenhower's subsequent admission that the plane had
been on a spying mission, Karamanlis remarked to Ambassador Briggs:
'As [a] Greek, I was baffled; as [a] politician I thought admission damaging to allied cause. Maybe history will applaud you but in today's world,
as seen from Greece, only a great power could afford luxury of honesty
in those circumstances ...' Claiming that, as a result of Khrushchev's
bellicose rhetoric, the 'gangster face of communism is again exposed for
world to see', he added: 'Détente is revealed for phony tactic it always
was ... [W]hatever be [the] tide, Greece stands with US'.[46] Indeed,
Karamanlis was prepared to do everything within his power to avoid
friction with Washington. Ironically, although his downfall was precipitated by domestic factors, his determination to keep Greece close to the
United States and NATO also played heavily into the hands of his adversaries. It may not be unfair to say that the warm reception and high
praise he received on his official visit to America in April 1961 was in
no small measure his reward for remaining Washington's loyal friend
through extraordinarily difficult times. Unfortunately for him, foreign
accolades could not prevent the downward spiral of his political career.
His last major foreign policy gesture, made not long before his resignation and self-imposed exile in 1963, was to support the Kennedy administration's handling of the Cuban missile crisis.

In April 1963, during the political crisis that preceded Karamanlis'
resignation, the US military attaché in Athens learned that a group of
army officers led by Brigadier General Odesseus Angelis, Colonel
Alexandros Hatzipetros and Lieutenant Colonel George Papadopoulos
(the attaché characterized the last of the three named as 'not known to
this office') was preparing to seize power. Acting on his own,
Ambassador Henry R. Labouisse communicated to the conspirators his
strong disapproval of the proposed coup. A few days later, endorsing the
ambassador's initiative, the Department of State commented: 'In view of
our long involvement and large investment in Greece, we could not
stand idly by and witness the creation of a Latin America type of totalitarian government in Greece, nor do we want to return to the Metaxas

kind of tyranny. We are therefore unalterably opposed to such a "solution" in Greece.' In addition, the conspirators were to be warned that 'the use of United States equipment to achieve such a "solution" would be regarded with grave misgiving and disappointment by the United States', and that military assistance to Greece might be curtailed as a result.[47] At the same time the Department sent Prime Minister Karamanlis strong assurances of continued American support.

The fall of Karamanlis, the collapse of the conservatives' Radical Union (ERE) which he had led, and the electoral victory of the Centre Union under George Papandreou in 1964 signalled the dawn of a new era in Greek–American relations. Soon the new government was openly battling all of Washington's traditional allies in Greece: the conservatives, the palace and the military hierarchy. Moreover, the constitutional impasse in Cyprus (independent since 1960) and the renewed ethnic violence were certain to aggravate Greece's relations with Turkey and fuel once again anti-NATO and anti-American feelings in Greece. The presence in Greece of American bases, electronic surveillance facilities, radio stations and nuclear weapons was bound to make matters worse. Nevertheless, at first American officials chose to keep an open mind about the Papandreou government, whose victory had at least frustrated the hopes of the leftists that they might enter the cabinet. In Athens the embassy sought to cultivate the Centre Union's leaders, including the prime minister's son Andreas, a respected economist and US citizen with friends in the Kennedy and Johnson administrations. For its part, the new government appeared eager to assure Washington that its members were 'pro-West in orientation and great friends of the United States'; it also hoped that the United States would assist Greece in removing the sources of new friction in Cyprus.[48]

Adhering to the position of its predecessors the Johnson administration refused to be drawn into the morass of the Cyprus conflict. President Johnson was particularly irritated by British attempts to pressure him to send American troops to stop the violence in Cyprus. In January 1964 he considered dispatching to Cyprus a prominent American for an 'all-out diplomatic effort', together with perhaps one or two aircraft carriers, 'and say to those people, "Now we're going to make preparations and we're ready for a quick entry and we're not going to support you Turks if you pull anything like this [threatened invasion]" ... Tell the Greeks the same thing ... but just not let these damned British run us in there ...'.[49] The idea of sending a US naval force to the area was kept alive for several months and on 11 March Secretary of State Dean Rusk informed the President: 'Cyprus is very touchy and explosive. This is the big one at the moment, but I think we'll be able to get some forces moving fairly soon now that we've been able to put up some money. Now it looks as though the Turks themselves on the island are trying to create a situation where Turkey would have to come in. So both sides are at fault there at the moment. But we're working on it.'[50] In June 1964, in a move that obviously benefited the Greek side, Washington restrained Turkey from invading Cyprus when Johnson warned Prime Minister Ismet Inonu that such a move would have dire consequences for Turkey. The President's letter was characterized by a veteran American diplomat as 'the most brutal diplomatic note I have ever seen ... the diplomatic equivalent of an atomic bomb'.[51] Anxious to produce a settlement without further delay the administration's attention was soon focused on the 'Acheson plan' for the partitioning of Cyprus and there was no more talk of sending American forces to the area.

In Athens, as the prime minister fought to curb the influence of the palace over the military, Andreas Papandreou was implicated in left-wing conspiratorial activities in the armed forces, including those serving in Cyprus. Before long Washington became convinced that the two Papandreous were undermining American and NATO interests in Greece and were particularly irritated by Andreas' persistent attacks on the United States. In June 1964, following Johnson's stern warning to Inonu, George Papandreou visited Washington and was lectured on the need to end the Cyprus conflict without delay; otherwise, American assistance to Greece would be cut off. In case he was counting on Washington's protection, he was warned that if the Turks resorted to war, Greece would be defeated. The Johnson administration's stated preference was for the Greek and Turkish governments to settle the Cyprus controversy in direct bilateral negotiations. The only stipulations, the president told Ambassador Alexander Matsas, were that the settlement must be permanent, and it must not be humiliating to either party. Given the dangers created by 'two of our close allies ... growling at each other', as well as Makarios' own agenda and Moscow's desire to meddle in the affair, the president insisted that 'the Greeks must show some statesmanship and get moving toward agreement'. Having prevented Turkish military action in Cyprus in the past the United States believed that 'Greece should take the initiative'.[52]

However, the Greek government was unwilling to negotiate with Ankara under the continued threat of a Turkish invasion of Cyprus. Accordingly, Matsas suggested to Johnson that tensions would be reduced and Greece would end its military support to Makarios if the United States could get Turkey to promise not to invade. To this Johnson replied that 'we could not get the Turks to turn off [their threat of invasion] until there was some basis on which to argue with them'.[53] And since the Greek and Turkish governments could not agree on their own to engage in bilateral negotiations the Johnson administration attempted to cut the Gordian knot with a drastic scheme of its own.

The solution proposed by the Americans, the 'Acheson plan', might have been acceptable to the Greek side a few years earlier: most of Cyprus was to be given to Greece, while Turkey was to receive the rest of the island, a military presence and other compensation. Now it was too late for such Solomonic schemes. Following brief Greek–Turkish talks, Papandreou turned down the plan largely at the insistence of Cyprus President Archbishop Makarios who was by now determined to preserve the republic as an independent state. In the wake of the failed diplomatic efforts tensions grew and Greece refused to participate in NATO exercises. In March 1967 two officers of the American embassy in Athens walked out of a formal public gathering at which Andreas was analysing Greek foreign policy in strongly anti-American terms. Nevertheless, in November, when Turkey renewed its threat to invade Cyprus, once again Washington stepped in. Turkey was prevailed upon to forgo military action and the Greek government agreed to withdraw most of the troops it had sent to Cyprus.[54] However, by then Greece was under military dictatorship and US–Greek relations had entered yet another phase.

Having won a decisive electoral victory in February 1964, Papandreou's popularity continued to grow across a broad political spectrum, thanks in large measure to his anti-business reforms, improved relations with Soviet bloc countries, and his refusal to yield to American and NATO pressures for a new settlement for Cyprus. In the spring of 1965, in a bold move to strengthen his hold over the security forces, he attempted to fire his minister of defence and replace the army's top commanders, traditionally the favourites of the palace and right-wing politicians, with officers loyal to his Centre Union government. This at a time when his son Andreas, whose anti-American and anti-NATO rhetoric was becoming increasingly more shrill, was accused of involvement in leftist conspiracies in the army. When King Constantine refused to dismiss the minister of defence, Papandreou resigned, confident that he could get his way through another electoral triumph. In this he miscalculated badly. Anxious to prevent another Papandreou victory, the king tried to manage the situation through a succession of weak caretaker governments and the country descended into a protracted period of strikes, demonstrations, turmoil and uncertainty.

THE JUNTA YEARS

Even before Papandreou's resignation in July 1965, most American officials handling Greek affairs had become convinced that another Papandreou success at the polls would demoralize the armed forces and spell disaster for American interests in Greece. The few who continued to believe that it was still possible to work harmoniously with Papandreou's Centre Union were silenced at the embassy level.[55] However, there was no agreement on a proper course of action. When embassy and CIA officers persuaded Ambassador Phillip Talbot to recommend a 'modest covert operation' to avert a Papandreou comeback, the Department demurred, fearing exposure and a backlash. When King Constantine solicited the embassy's reaction to an 'extra-parliamentary' initiative he was contemplating – most probably a generals' coup acting with royal consent – the response was truly delphic: Washington's position 'would depend on the circumstances'.[56] However, when the coup finally came on 21 April 1967, it was hardly the one contemplated by King Constantine or anticipated by Ambassador Talbot.

Members of the military mission and the CIA station in Athens were in close professional and social contact with several officers plotting to seize power and very probably suspected that unlawful action of some kind was imminent. Whether they also knew of the actual coup before it was carried out remains uncertain. Colonel George Papadopoulos and his fellow conspirators were certainly capable of deceiving their American contacts as well as everyone else. Similarly, embassy personnel may have anticipated correctly the course of events.[57] Nevertheless, there is no evidence of American complicity in the coup. On the contrary, the embassy's initial reaction suggested not only surprise but contempt for the colonels, as well as the hope that the king and his generals might somehow regain control of the situation.[58] Washington's official stance was also one of surprise and 'ambivalence', coupled with expressions of hope that democratic government might soon be restored. The Department of State suspended 'full' diplomatic relations with the new régime and the embassy kept its distance until January 1968, when Washington officials apparently decided that they had no choice but to restore normal relations with Athens; on the other hand, they were in no hurry to replace Ambassador Talbot who had been reassigned to the department.[59] Except for the brief and largely symbolic suspension of deliveries of heavy weapons, most military assistance programmes continued virtually undisturbed. In the 1968 presidential elections, won by the Republicans under Richard M. Nixon, neither party mentioned Greece in its campaign platform.[60]

Despite its passivity, the Johnson administration viewed developments in Athens with considerable embarrassment and would have been happy to see the junta somehow eased out of power, perhaps by a group of prominent political leaders led by Karamanlis, who since 1963 lived in self-imposed exile in Paris. However, given the junta's ruthless determination not to yield, a 'Karamanlis solution', which at times King Constantine and even Andreas Papandreou (released from prison following the intercession of his friends in Washington and living abroad) claimed to favour, remained a totally unrealistic prospect.[61] In the end, fearing that the collapse of the junta would be followed by political chaos and even civil war, and being hopelessly bogged down in Vietnam, the president and his key advisers reduced themselves to the role of passive observers. In March 1968, when the junta produced a draft constitution, the Department of State expressed its satisfaction, prompting *The New York Times* to comment: 'This blessing, bestowed with such unseemly haste, is simply the latest in a series of moves that point to one conclusion: Washington has decided to do everything it can to provide the Athens junta with the prestige and respectability it has hungered after since its putsch of last April.'[62]

If under President Johnson Washington managed to suppress its disdain for the colonels' dictatorship, the Nixon administration became its principal supporter and defender. To be sure, there were the occasional expressions of pious hope that democracy might be restored in Greece and feelers to politicians, including Karamanlis in Paris, to solicit their views on the subject. In reality, ignoring opposition in Congress and an increasingly vocal anti-junta sentiment in the United States and Europe (because of its dictatorship Greece was forced to withdraw from the Council of Europe) the Nixon cabinet treated the colonels' régime as a valued friend and important ally. Led by Vice President Spiro Agnew, who suddenly rediscovered his Greek roots, a procession of high-level officials travelled to Athens and heaped praise on Papadopoulos and his government. On one such visit Secretary of Commerce Maurice Stans reportedly extolled the 'wonderfully close relations' between the two states and conveyed President Nixon's 'warm love' to the government and people of Greece. Subsequently the embassy quietly changed the wording to 'warmth and confidence'.[63]

The junta's well-publicized violations of human rights, including the torture of political prisoners, sparked repeated attempts in Congress to cut off military aid. However, the administration argued successfully that American strategic interests in the Eastern Mediterranean and the Middle East necessitated close military cooperation with Greece. At the same time, American involvement in Greek domestic affairs all but disappeared. Ambassador Henry Tasca was under strict instructions to steer clear of the junta's internal matters. For its part, the Papadopoulos government was prepared to go to great lengths to endear itself to its patrons in Washington. A far-reaching home-porting agreement granted the US Sixth Fleet enormous permanent facilities on Greek soil. American companies received lucrative contracts on unusually attractive terms. There is also reason to believe that the junta contributed generously to President Nixon's secret slush-fund used to pay the Watergate burglars in an attempt to buy their silence. Finally, for its own reasons the régime in Athens sought to undermine and topple the President of Cyprus, Archbishop Makarios, whom officials in Washington had taken to calling 'the Castro of the Mediterranean'. In and out of NATO councils Greek policy toward Turkey saw noticeable improvement.

To be sure, there were occasional signs that the Nixon administration regarded the colonels' régime as expendable, if a proper substitute could be found. In 1971, Ambassador Tasca's meetings with King Constantine (in Rome) and Karamanlis (in Paris) led to speculation that a change in American policy was under consideration, especially since, in his public comments, Tasca praised the exiled politician and expressed veiled hope that Greece might once again benefit from his leadership.[64] However Washington, and particularly the Pentagon, was much too comfortable with the existing situation to wish to change it. As for the junta's misdeeds, one could always rationalize that, in the words of one senior Pentagon official, 'we have a better chance to influence the [Greek] government to change if we continue to work with them than if we turn our back to them'.[65] Moreover, as they struggled to extricate themselves from Vietnam and pursue the all-important parallel dialogues with the Soviet Union and China (and, later, to deal with the Watergate 'cancer') the administration's top decision-makers could hardly focus much attention on Greece and Cyprus. Ironically, Washington's inattention greatly intensified the anti-American feelings of Greeks, many of whom found it convenient to blame the dictatorship on the United States. In the end, while American officials watched and temporized, the junta precipitated a new and violent eruption in Cyprus which unseated Makarios (who barely escaped with his life) and gave Turkey the opportunity to launch a full-scale invasion and cripple the island republic, in the process causing the junta in Athens to self-destruct.

In May 1974 the head of the Department of State's Cyprus desk, Thomas D. Boyatt, advised his superiors that the junta, now under Colonel Dimitris Ioannidis, was preparing a coup against Makarios; a CIA report from Athens apparently made a similar prediction. Boyatt's recommendation, that Ioannidis be given a clear and personal warning not to undertake such a move in Cyprus, was approved and instructions were sent to the embassy in Athens. Initially Ambassador Tasca refused to deliver the message claiming that it would inflame rather than restrain Ioannidis. Finally, pressured by his superiors, Tasca gave the warning not to Ioannidis but to the junta's puppet prime minister and foreign minister; he subsequently declared that an ambassador does not deal with a policeman (Ioannidis had been the head of military police). The Cyprus coup was carried out as predicted.

Dr Henry Kissinger, who in his memoirs of his years as secretary of state devotes a lengthy chapter to Cyprus, seeks to minimize the significance of Tasca's failure to follow specific instructions and attributes the ensuing crisis to Makarios, 'who was once again testing his dexterity on the high wire – this time with disastrous results'. Denying that he had been eager to see Makarios removed, he writes: 'I considered Makarios more a nuisance than a menace. At no time during my period in office did we take any measure to reduce his hold on power. We maintained an aloof, respectful and wary relationship with him.'[66] Few students of the Nixon administration's handling of the Cyprus problem are likely to feel comfortable with Dr Kissinger's account and explanations. In any event, following the coup and Makarios' flight to safety, Undersecretary of State Joseph Sisco hurried to Athens and Ankara and urged caution and restraint to anyone he could talk to in the two capitals. However, without a strong explicit message of warning from his government Sisco found himself armed, as he characterized it, with a 'virtually empty attaché case, a smile and a shoeshine'.[67] Convinced that this time Washington would not act to stop it, Turkey invaded Cyprus and eventually occupied about 40% of the island's northern part, turning some 200,000 Greek Cypriots into destitute refugees. In Athens, the junta collapsed and disappeared; after much confusion, recrimination and hand-wringing, a message was sent to Karamanlis to return from Paris and rescue the country from its latest catastrophe.

THE RETURN OF DEMOCRACY – AND OF ACRIMONY

The tumultuous welcome from his compatriots and messages of congratulation from foreign leaders, including Nixon and Kissinger, did not make Karamanlis' task any less daunting. To restore order and democratic rule he had to dismantle the legal and bureaucratic handiwork of the junta's seven-year régime, punish the leaders of the dictatorship, bring the armed forces firmly under his government's authority, prepare a new constitution and settle the question of the monarchy. To protect him from the more recalcitrant supporters of the dictatorship special security measures had to be taken and secrecy surrounded his whereabouts and work schedule. More importantly, however, his efforts to tackle the domestic problems could not succeed until he had addressed effectively the continuing disaster in Cyprus, where the Turks appeared intent on expanding the area under their occupation. Recalling his first months in office, Karamanlis told President Gerald Ford (at the May 1975 NATO summit) that when the Turkish troops resumed their advance in Cyprus he felt that he had three choices: retire from politics, declare war on Turkey, or withdraw from NATO's military structure. He claimed that he chose the third option as the least damaging to the Western camp.[68]

In reality, considering the chaotic conditions in which the armed forces found themselves in 1974, military action against Turkey was not a serious option. When the prime minister inquired of his senior military advisers if Turkish targets in Cyprus could be attacked by submarines and from the air their response was negative. Karamanlis then asked Britain if its naval forces in the Eastern Mediterranean could protect the transfer of one army division from Crete to Cyprus – apparently he intended to accompany the troops together with his defence minister Evangelos Averoff – but Prime Minister Harold Wilson politely refused the request. Parenthetically, there is no reason to suspect that a similar request for assistance was addressed to the United States, whose Sixth Fleet might have played a decisive role in the unfolding drama.

On 15 August, as the Turkish forces were completing their advance, Secretary of State Kissinger telephoned Karamanlis and invited him to meet President Ford in Washington (Nixon resigned on 9 August) to discuss the crisis caused by the Turkish invasion. When Karamanlis replied that he could not possibly leave Greece at that moment, Kissinger asked what the United States could do to assist in the situation. Karamanlis responded that he was prepared to resume negotiations with Ankara (as the Americans were urging him to do) but only if the Turkish forces returned to the lines established by the cease-fire agreement of 30 July, arranged by British Foreign Secretary James Callaghan. The best that Dr Kissinger could do was to promise that Turkish hostilities would end in a few hours; in fact, the Turkish advance stopped on 16 August.[69] In his memoirs Kissinger maintains that a British proposal to use air strikes to stop the Turkish troops and force them back to the cease-fire line was unsupportable sabre-rattling; that at that moment 'my own emotions were focused on easing Nixon's travail and preparing for the transition to Ford', and that 'asking a president in the first 48 hours of his administration to consider supporting military action' was simply 'out of the question'.[70]

When the Turkish government refused to receive NATO Secretary General Joseph Luns, who was anxious to step in and avert further damage to the alliance, Karamanlis felt he had been left with no other practical choice but to remove Greek officers from NATO commands. At the NATO summit in May 1975 the Greek prime minister bitterly reminded his foreign colleagues that the purpose of the alliance was to preserve peace 'under conditions of justice and constructive cooperation among all nations, allied or not'.[71] In Athens Averoff solemnly announced in parliament the obvious: the country's only external threat was Turkish aggression.

Despite generous praise for his statesmanship and vague promises of support, the Nixon and Ford administrations would not give Karamanlis what he needed the most, and what only they could provide: leverage to compel Turkey to withdraw its troops from Cyprus. Washington's unwillingness to help him on this critical issue and a wave of anti-American demonstrations and vandalism compelled Karamanlis to deny the Sixth Fleet home-porting facilities and access to the Eleusis naval base. Actually, without informing the Greek government the Department of Defense had concluded that the political climate in Greece had rendered the home-porting agreement unworkable and was ready to abrogate it unilaterally. Negotiations to renew the existing bilateral agreement on defence and economic co-operation (DECA) bogged down and the Greek government announced its intention to demand that all US bases in the country be placed under Greek command. As if to dramatize the acrimony in bilateral relations the CIA chief of station in Athens, Richard S. Welch, whose diplomatic cover had been blown by Philip Agee's recently published *Inside the Company: CIA Diary*, was assassinated on 23 December 1975.

If the Nixon and Ford administrations were prepared to countenance Turkey's aggression in Cyprus, there were many in Congress who were not. In the fall of 1974 prominent critics of the Vietnam war, many liberal Democrats anxious to do battle with an 'imperial presidency', and legislators friendly to the Greek–American community combined forces and succeeded in imposing an embargo on military assistance and arms sales to Turkey. Although a victory for the Greek lobby and for those sympathetic to Greece, the embargo had little if any practical significance: its provisions were watered down almost immediately and military equipment continued to be sent to Turkey. Moreover, the Turkish government remained defiant and refused to negotiate on the Cyprus issue as long as the embargo was in place. In September 1978, after repeated promises to seek a 'just and durable' solution to the Cyprus problem, President Jimmy Carter yielded to pressure from the Pentagon and other supporters of Turkey and lifted the embargo without making any attempt to extract from Ankara any concessions concerning the military situation in Cyprus.[72]

For all its frustrations and the public's tendency to blame American policies for the national humiliation in Cyprus, Greece could not afford to distance itself too much from Washington for fear that to do so would tip the scales of power even further in Turkey's favour. Nor could it allow itself to fall further behind in the arms race with its adversary across the Aegean. In January 1975 the government informed parliament that it was asking the Ford administration to restore programmes of military assistance which had been suspended or curtailed during the junta years. It also requested the postponement of plans to remove from Greece ageing American nuclear weapons lest their withdrawal be perceived as favouring the Turks. In 1977 it was announced that under the new four-year DECA, four of the seven major American bases in Greece would remain in operation; in return, Greece was to receive

$700 million in military assistance which would enable the government to rebuild and improve its armed forces. Nevertheless, until the end of 1981, when Karamanlis' New Democracy Party was defeated at the polls, relations between Athens and Washington remained correct but cool, clearly dominated by the continuing Greek–Turkish conflict. And although in his determination to bring Greece into the European Community Karamanlis was motivated by fundamental political, economic and social considerations, there is no doubt that he also wished to reduce the country's unhealthy dependence on the United States. Given Washington's preferential attitude toward Turkey, Greece would have to look elsewhere for understanding and support against its adversary.

In October 1981, the victory of the socialists (Pan-hellenic Socialist Movement – PASOK) led by Andreas Papandreou was in no small measure the result of frustration with the country's weakness at the international level and the government's failure to secure a favourable settlement of Greek–Turkish disputes. It also appeared to usher in a new era of friction and open confrontation with the United States. In addition to his well known neo-Marxist ideas, virulent anti-American rhetoric and combative style, in his campaign speeches Papandreou had revealed an ambitious vision that was bound to irritate Washington officials, many of whom had developed an intense dislike for him long before he became the head of government in Athens. In the spring of 1966, one such official had circulated a classified memorandum which characterized Andreas Papandreou as a man of 'overweening ambition, political ineptness, and conspiratorial nature', who had proven himself to be 'unscrupulous and amoral, prepared to go to almost any limits to achieve his objectives'. The memo claimed that in 1964 Andreas had manipulated his father to reject his cabinet's decision to accept the Acheson plan for Cyprus. It concluded with the warning that 'Andreas would try to move Greece toward a non-aligned, neutralist stance', which would 'obviously have serious implications for Greece's ties with NATO and especially with the United States, whose rights to military and other special facilities would be jeopardized'.[73]

Indeed, following his electoral victory Papandreou charged that previous governments in Athens had been the willing tools of capitalist-imperialist expansionism led by the United States. He promised to liberate Greece from foreign exploitation and advance it toward socialist development. The Cold War, which he blamed largely on Washington, was over and NATO was either irrelevant or dangerous. He believed that the destiny of Greece in the international arena was to serve as the bridge connecting East and West, Europe, the Arab world and Africa, and its initiatives would be 'the starting point of rapprochement among the nations'.[74]

Papandreou's message was not merely for the benefit of his domestic admirers. At the December 1981 meeting of NATO's defence ministers the Greek government demanded that the organization provide formal guarantees for the security of the borders of member-states against 'every threat, from whatever side it emanates'. When the Turkish representative vetoed the proposal Greece blocked the release of the council's final joint communiqué. Subsequently Papandreou declared that his government was no longer interested in NATO's guarantees, 'which are easily forgotten'. Instead, 'the greatest guarantee is our armed forces'.[75] Accordingly, his intention was 'to disengage ourselves from NATO's military wing ... Our problem lies in the east, not in the north. And NATO cannot help us. Therefore, Greece's national strategy is clearly different from that of NATO.'[76] Making it clear that Greece was not withdrawing from the Western alliance, he asserted that its membership in the organization was now 'inactive' and that its representatives would attend only those meetings whose agenda was of special concern to Athens.[77]

A particularly thorny issue in Greek–NATO relations involved the island of Leros where NATO planners, with the enthusiastic support of successive Greek governments since 1954, wished to establish a NATO naval base. Such an arrangement would have enabled Greece to station its troops on the island, albeit under NATO authority. However, insisting that the island had been demilitarized by international agreement, Turkey vetoed the plan, while Washington refused to support NATO's experts (and Greece) on this issue.[78] Charging that in failing to approve a base on Leros NATO 'not only takes sides against Greece in a Greek–Turkish dispute but is even fomenting a conflict between the two countries', the Papandreou government would not permit its forces to participate in NATO exercises in the Aegean and denied the use of Greek territorial waters and airspace for NATO exercises.[79] Furthermore, in 1985 the government announced a new national defence doctrine and a 'total popular defence' programme.[80] In essence, the plans provided for the redeployment of the bulk of the country's armed forces so as to protect the Aegean islands. In addition, a new treaty with Bulgaria and military consultations with Yugoslavia and Romania focused on the problems of defending Greek Thrace against a Turkish attack. In the event of war there were secret preparations to launch large-scale raids on the Turkish coast facing the Greek islands.

As was to be expected, the Greek government's negative stance toward the Western alliance was fully reflected in its relations with Washington. As openly conceded by a government spokesman, Greek relations with both Washington and NATO 'pass through Ankara', and 'we always assess our various political moves *vis-à-vis* NATO and the United States on the basis of their repercussions on Greek-Turkish relations'.[81] Publicly Papandreou continued to irritate the American government at every opportunity. In September 1983 he vetoed a formal European Community statement of condemnation of the Soviet government for shooting down KAL Flight 007 and asserted that the Korean airliner had been spying for the United States: 'if such a plane came into Greece', Papandreou asserted, 'we would have downed it'.[82] The following year he expressed support for the Polish government over its crackdown on the anti-communist Solidarity movement. When US planes bombed Libya's capital in retaliation for Colonel Quaddafi's suspected support of international terrorism a PASOK statement accused the Reagan administration of having 'dynamited peace and at the same time destroyed the independence of a nation in the name of imposing its hegemonic presence in the area'.[83]

Yet in the realm of foreign policy in general and US–Greek relations in particular Papandreou's bark was far worse than his bite. He and his aides could not fail to realize that their anti-NATO pyrotechnics and persistent needling of the American government were not strengthening Greece's position in its dangerous conflict with Turkey and was not solving the Cyprus problem. On the contrary, its role as NATO's loose cannon was rendering Greece more isolated and vulnerable. Therefore, below the level of public pronouncements and posturing they were careful not to push matters to breaking point. In this they were assisted by two US ambassadors who had previously served in the Athens embassy and had developed lasting ties with Greece: Monteagle Stearns and Robert Keeley. Having developed a good working relationship with Papandreou they ignored his bluster and concentrated on the essence of the bilateral relationship, which by the 1980s was focused on the question of the American bases.

It was not an easy task. PASOK's platform had included the categorical promise to close down the American bases and cut off military ties to Washington. Even as talks on a new DECA were quietly underway, Papandreou proclaimed that 'For us, the idea of having foreign bases on our soil is unacceptable, since we do not believe in the competition between the two superpowers and Europe's division'.[84] In the negotiations the PASOK government tried but failed to secure guarantees against possible Turkish aggression and support of Greek demands regarding NATO's proposed new command structure in the region, operational plans and exercises. But the twin core issues that had to be settled were the future of the American bases and the level of military and economic assistance to Greece. In the end, the new DECA announced in September 1983 called for the four existing main bases to remain in operation for five more years and there were symbolic concessions by the American side regarding base commanders and status of forces jurisdiction. In addition to the annual payments for the bases, the

United States pledged that, in providing future military assistance to Greece and Turkey, it would be 'guided by the principle ... that calls for preserving the balance of military strength in the region' (the so-called 7:10 formula). The more sensitive issues, including the precise language of the agreement, were settled by Papandreou in personal conversations with Ambassador Stearns. Whereas according to the English text the new DECA was 'terminable after five years', and thus renewable, in the equally authentic Greek text the key word was 'terminate', enabling the PASOK government to announce in triumph that the bases would be shut down in five years.[85]

Even before the conclusion of the 1983 DECA, and as its relations with Turkey continued to deteriorate, the Papandreou government toned down its criticism of the United States. A number of high-level American officials, including General Alexander Haig, Secretary of Defense Caspar Weinberger and Secretary of State George Shultz, visited Athens and their meetings with Greek officials and especially with Papandreou were generally productive and free of rancour. To be sure, a number of secondary issues remained unresolved. Negotiations concerning the status of Voice of America relay stations failed to produce an agreement; the Reagan administration complained of allegedly lax anti-terrorist measures in Greece, while an US 'travel advisory' in July 1985 damaged Greece's tourist trade and prompted angry responses in Athens. There were also charges that the PASOK government discriminated against American firms interested in building ships for the Greek navy and planes for Olympic Airways. Other American businesses operating in Greece complained of corruption and extortion by government officials. For its part, the Greek government charged that US warships visiting Greek ports carried nuclear weapons and that NATO exercises in which American units participated routinely violated Greek airspace.

Despite its widely publicized statements since 1983 that the American bases would be finally closed at the expiration of the latest DECA, during 1987-88 the PASOK government quietly entered into negotiations for a new agreement. However, due to the uncertainties created by national elections in 1988 and again in 1990, the talks were suspended and the current agreement remained in force. In January 1990, as part of a general reduction of overseas American military facilities made possible by the end of the Cold War, the Pentagon unilaterally closed down the Hellenicon airbase and the naval communications base in Nea Makri. The remaining two bases, the enormous Souda Bay complex which serves both naval and air components of the Sixth Fleet, and the electronic surveillance facility at Gournes, both in relatively remote locations in Crete, are less visible to the general public and thus less controversial. Suddenly, PASOK's campaign promises to get rid of the bases lost their appeal, while some Greeks began to worry about the possibility that the United States might decide to remove its military presence altogether.

In July 1990, with PASOK briefly out of power, the New Democracy government of Constantine Mitsotakis signed a new eight-year DECA which provided for the retention of the two American bases in Crete as well as the 7:10 ratio in US military assistance to Greece and Turkey. The new government was also eager to restore its position in NATO and Greek units took part in exercises intended to protect and control the Eastern Mediterranean. While the situation in Cyprus remained volatile and Aegean disputes continued to fester, the Mitsotakis government was increasingly anxious to lower the level of tension in Greek–Turkish relations. In part this was because dark clouds were now gathering in the north, where Yugoslavia's violent break-up had created the conditions for open-ended conflict, and Albania, Bulgaria and Romania were going through severe post-communist convulsions. Suddenly, in its confrontation with Turkey, Greece could not count on a stable and relatively sympathetic Balkan neighbourhood.

Mitsotakis was pleased to be invited to Washington, where he signed a number of trade and economic agreements. Despite strong domestic opposition, his government formally supported the US-inspired and UN-mandated war against Iraq and after much debate in parliament a Greek frigate joined the multinational naval force in the Red Sea. In a show of appreciation the administration of President George Bush agreed in principle to sell to Greece Patriot missiles and repeated the by now familiar assurances concerning that country's security. In July 1991 President Bush visited Athens and, speaking in parliament, paid tribute to the Greek nation for its dedication to the ideals of Western democracy and to the Atlantic alliance. The president's generous praise and friendly tone did little to placate Greek public opinion, that was greatly irritated by the Department of State's latest report on human rights which referred to a 'Slavo-Macedonian' minority in northern Greece. Viewed against the background of Yugoslav Macedonia's emergence as an independent state in 1991, to many Greeks the American report seemed to bolster the new state's apparent irredentist aspirations. Thus, Athens and Washington found themselves on opposite sides of a new controversy.

Having failed to prevent the break-up of Yugoslavia and fearing that ethnic conflict would spread across the Balkans, Washington sought to facilitate Yugoslav Macedonia's peaceful transition to statehood and urged the international community to support the government in Skopje. The United States recognized the new republic in February 1994 but, to placate Athens and the Greek–Americans, diplomatic relations were kept below the ambassadorial level. On the other hand, Greeks professed to find in the new state's constitution, flag, maps and currency proof of irredentism aimed at Greek Macedonia. Pressured by an aroused public and the inflammatory rhetoric of church and political personalities, the government attempted to prevent the recognition of the new state by the international community under the name of Republic of Macedonia; it also imposed on its neighbour a comprehensive embargo that threatened to cripple its small and weak economy. As a result, Greece found itself waging a hopeless war of words in the United Nations and in the European Union.

The return of PASOK to power in 1993 did not at first improve Greece's position in the international arena. Prime Minister Papandreou, still outwardly combative, was in reality politically chastened, in poor health and distracted by family problems. His official visit to the United States in April 1994, an event for which he had angled for years, was newsworthy because of his haggard appearance and subdued demeanour, but for little else. The Clinton administration offered once again the all-too-familiar promises to pursue new mediation initiatives in the hope of settling Greece's disputes with its neighbours, but there were no serious talks and no major breakthroughs. Nevertheless, Washington's influence continued to be felt and on several occasions proved to be helpful. In September 1995 quiet American diplomacy led to an interim agreement under which Yugoslav Macedonia pledged to remove from its flag the sun of Vergina and from its constitution passages which might be interpreted as hidden claims on Greek Macedonia; in return, Greece lifted its embargo. Negotiations concerning the new state's formal name were to continue without fanfare through normal diplomatic channels and soon that particular controversy no longer attracted much attention. Washington's envoys were also actively involved in negotiations that enabled Greece and Albania to diffuse a number of thorny issues that had severely strained their relations. Indeed, American mediation paved the way for the visit to Albania of President Constantine Stephanopoulos in March 1996, and the signing of a comprehensive bilateral agreement on friendship and co-operation.

Similarly, in January 1996, when Greece and Turkey suddenly found themselves in a new and dangerous military stand-off over uninhabited islets in the Aegean (the Imia crisis), friendly but firm telephone calls to Athens and Ankara from President Bill Clinton and senior American military and diplomatic officials averted disaster. Fortunately, by the time of this latest confrontation, in which Greek territorial sovereignty was publicly challenged by Turkey, the terminally ill Papandreou had been replaced by Costas Simitis, an uncharismatic but highly competent technocrat and influential member of PASOK's inner circle. The new leader's deft and pragmatic handling of the Imia episode gave reason for hope that Greek foreign policy, and particularly relations with the United States, would in the future be pursued in a more positive and constructive spirit. In April Prime Minister Simitis visited Washington for a series of high-level talks and this was followed by a very successful if essentially ceremonial visit to the United States of President Stephanopoulos.

The improved climate in which US–Greek relations were now conducted could not, of course, conceal episodes of irritation and friction. The situation was periodically aggravated by the tendency of Greek government officials to speak their mind in public on sensitive matters. Thus, in July 1998, Foreign Minister Theodoros Pangalos told reporters that President Clinton's pre-election statements concerning an American initiative to settle the Cyprus problem was a 'grand lie' and hinted that in future elections the Greek–American community might switch its support to other candidates, presumably Republican. Washington's reaction was swift and sharp. The White House spokesman characterized Pangalos' remarks as 'unbecoming a senior official of a close ally … and … inconsistent with what are otherwise close and warm bilateral relations'. In Athens, Ambassador R. Nicholas Burns delivered a verbal protest to the foreign minister.[86] Pangalos' mercurial style ceased to be an irritant in February 1999 when the Kurdish rebel leader, Abdullah Ocalan, whom the foreign ministry and security agencies had attempted to shelter in the Greek embassy in Nairobi, was captured by Turkish agents, apparently with American help. The fiasco precipitated a government crisis and several ministers, including Pangalos, had to resign. Under his successor, George Papandreou, the style and tone of Greek diplomacy, and possibly its substance as well, became noticeably more low-key and constructive.

Almost simultaneously with the Ocalan affair another squabble between Athens and Ankara involving Cyprus caused Washington to step in to prevent an open clash. In the summer of 1998 the Republic of Cyprus prepared to receive and deploy anti-aircraft missiles it had purchased from Russia. The obvious purpose of the new weapons was to strengthen the republic's defence against possible Turkish aggression in the future. Ankara responded with threats to destroy the missiles if they ever reached the island, and to deploy its own missiles in the Turkish-controlled region. As the Greek government was bound to support the Greek Cypriots' right to defend themselves – particularly under the doctrine of 'integrated defence' which Athens had adopted in the mid-1980s – the controversy over the Russian missiles had the makings of a dangerous stand-off between Greece and Turkey. The Clinton administration decided that the new missiles represented a destabilizing element in an already dangerous situation; they might also give Moscow the opportunity to claim an interest in the Cyprus

problem. Accordingly, Washington pressured the Cyprus government
and Athens to have the Russian missiles shipped to Crete instead. But if
the arrangement defused the latest controversy, American diplomacy
continued to have nothing to show for its much talked-about initiatives.
President Clinton's latest special emissary for Cyprus, Richard
Holbrooke, architect of the Dayton accords which stopped the civil war
in Yugoslavia, visited the island twice and also held meetings in Athens
and Ankara. But as other American diplomats had already discovered,
the impasse had come to rest on an insurmountable obstacle: the Turkish
Cypriot leader, Rauf Denktash, would resume negotiations only if the
Turkish-controlled part of the island was recognized as an independent
state. Holbrooke soon gave up and assumed his new duties as US ambassador to the United Nations. The deadlock on the Cyprus controversy
would continue into the new century.

All through the 1990s the gradual disintegration of Yugoslavia and
the Bosnian crisis represented for Greece the disturbing sound of
distant thunder. Traditional sympathies for the Serbs and a vague fear
that the empowerment of the region's Moslems would open the
Balkans to Turkish influence fuelled the Greek public's resentment of
the growing American involvement in the region. There was speculation in the press and elsewhere that Washington's ultimate objective
was to establish its hegemony over Southeastern Europe, perhaps in
collaboration with Berlin. The Greek government's attitude toward
international efforts to establish Bosnia as an independent state was
cool but correct and Greek troops joined peacekeeping operations,
motivated in part by the desire to match Turkey's active support of the
project. In the Kosovo crisis that followed, Athens again was steadfast
in its support of NATO's bombing operations despite strong opposition
from an overwhelming majority of the Greek public. The situation
became particularly sensitive when, with the consent and cooperation
of the Simitis government, NATO troops and equipment disembarked
at the port of Thessaloniki on their way to their destinations. The only
exception was the banning of Turkish warplanes from crossing over
Greek airspace as they flew to German and Italian bases to participate
in NATO raids on Yugoslav targets. As reported in the *Baltimore Sun*
(24, 28 April 1999), with NATO's approval the Greek government sent
tons of food and medicine to Serb and Albanian refugees in Kosovo. At
NATO's fiftieth anniversary ceremonies in Washington in late April
1999 Prime Minister Simitis dutifully endorsed the alliance's self-
congratulatory statements but cautioned that the prolonged bombing of
Yugoslavia could turn his compatriots against NATO as well as the
United States.[87] As everyone knew, Simitis' publicly expressed concern
reflected a serious domestic problem confronting his government.

Appropriately, the century closed with President Clinton's visit to

Athens, an event which revealed in high relief the ambivalence in the relationship. In the closing months of 1999 there was nothing of substance and urgency that necessitated a summit meeting in the Greek capital. The visit was part of a whirlwind tour intended to show the interest of the peripatetic president in the Balkan region. It was also a gesture of Washington's appreciation for the support the Greek government had provided in Bosnia and Kosovo, although for the hosts the event was to prove anything but a happy occasion. Despite predictions that the visit would cause large demonstrations and even violence, the tour had to include Greece. Otherwise, there was bound to be speculation about a rift between the two governments and the equally unwarranted suspicion that fear of terrorism had forced them to cancel the visit. As a result, in the months before the event the authorities found themselves engaged in 'damage control'. The visit was rescheduled so as not to coincide with 17 November (the name of a Greek terrorist group whose victims over a period of many years had included Americans), and drastically shortened, with the president's appearances confined to locations in the capital where adequate security could be guaranteed and the noisy demonstrators could not disrupt the ceremonies.

The Athenians' reaction to the event ranged from mild annoyance to open hostility. The demonstrators succeeded in capturing the attention of the news media in both countries while the invective hurled at the American president was reminiscent of the language of Iranian revolutionaries. One might have thought that, rather than the leader of the Western world and head of a friendly and allied state, the visitor represented Greece's worst enemy. Decades of anti-Americanism, frustration with Washington's stand on Greek–Turkish disputes and resentment of American involvement in recent Balkan crises had combined to create a public atmosphere that marred what should have been a routine and pleasant diplomatic event. The contrast to the warm receptions Clinton received in Turkey, Bulgaria, Former Yugoslav Republic of Macedonia (FYROM) and Kosovo could not have been more striking.

While the demonstrators and security troops had turned the heart of Athens into a battle zone, the two governments handled the affair as an exercise in cordiality and positive thinking. Prime Minister Simitis welcomed the president as 'the leader of a great country with which we are linked with traditional ties', and as 'a friend with whom we have already been able to discuss openly and sincerely all issues without any commitment'. Addressing his countrymen as much as his guest, Simitis stressed that 'economic weakness, recession [and] underdevelopment are linked to dependence and submission. We have realized successfully the challenge of [having] our destiny be determined by ourselves and no one else.' In turn, President Clinton heaped praise on Greeks for their achievements at home and abroad and, stealing a page from President

Kennedy's famous declaration in Berlin in June 1963 ('Ich bin ein Berliner'), quoted Shelley's line 'Eimaste oloi Ellines'. In what to most Greeks appeared to be a public apology, he acknowledged that, in supporting the junta, the United States allowed its interests in prosecuting the Cold War to prevail over its interests (it could be said its obligation) to support democracy, which was, after all, the cause for which we fought the Cold War. He defended NATO action in Bosnia and Kosovo and carefully touched on Greek–Turkish problems. Giving his audience a much-needed reason to applaud him, Clinton emphasized that Turkey has much to gain by 'making progress on issues like Cyprus and the Aegean matters', and that Ankara 'cannot be fully integrated successfully into Europe without solving its difficulties with Greece'.[88] Having failed to extract concessions from the Turkish side, this was the best he could offer his Greek hosts. During a visit to the Acropolis he mused for the benefit of the minister of culture that if it were up to him, the Elgin marbles would be returned to Greece. The few and rather anaemic bilateral agreements announced during the visit included annual high-level consultations on a broad range of topics, a joint initiative for technology co-operation in the Balkans, and Washington's promise for an early resolution of its case before the World Trade Organization charging Greece with violations of television copyright laws.

CONCLUSION

At the start of the new millennium relations between Greece and the United States are free of the poisonous effects of the Cold War decades. On the Greek side, the ruling socialists have lost their revolutionary zeal, there is no longer a domestic communist threat, and courting Washington's adversaries on the world stage is no longer an option. The palace's divisive role is gone, civilian authority over the military is firmly established, and becoming a favourite of the American embassy is no longer politically advantageous. The United States continues to be Greece's principal weapons supplier and attracting American investment is a major goal of any Greek government. On the American side, Greece is no longer a Cold War outpost to be held secure at all costs, and the US ambassador in Athens has no wish to involve himself in domestic partisan feuds or threaten that aid to Greece might be cut off. Terrorism, especially the November 17 group, threatens Greeks and Americans equally and thus serves to unite the two governments in a collaborative effort to stamp it out. In September 2000, after years of procrastination, a bilateral agreement was signed in Washington providing for cooperation between the intelligence agencies of the United States and Greece in combating terrorism, organized crime, Internet espionage and drug smuggling.

Although bilateral co-operation continues to serve the interests of both countries, the relationship is no longer intense and vital to either side. The expanding Atlantic alliance serves as a practical link between the two governments; it also represents proof that in the major military conflicts of the twentieth century Greece and America fought on the same side. The Greek American community is a vital cultural link between the two nations and, despite periodic flare-ups of anti-Americanism, the traditional reservoir of mutual goodwill is still intact. Above all else, both sides have become more realistic about the strengths and limitations of their relationship and the demands they make upon each other have become much more modest. In particular, the Greek government appears to have concluded that in its continuing disputes with Turkey and in other problems of the Balkan region Greece must rely much more on its own resources and on the European Union than on American support. To be sure, if Greece's security is threatened the United States can be counted on to play a decisive role. Otherwise, relations between the two states can be expected to remain friendly, stable, and on an even keel, even as their respective vital interests and concerns continue to drive them in different directions.

NOTES

1. Louis P. Cassimatis, *American Influence in Greece, 1917–1929* (Kent, OH: The Kent State University Press, 1988) p. 60.
2. G. Horton, *Report on Turkey: USA Consular Documents* (Athens: Journalists' Union of the Athens Daily Newspapers, 1985) pp. 149–51.
3. Cassimatis, *American Influence*, pp. 82–90.
4. *Ibid.*, pp. 135–50.
5. J. O. Iatrides (ed.) *Ambassador MacVeagh Reports: Greece, 1933–1947* (Princeton, NJ: Princeton University Press, 1980) pp. 236–90.
6. Foreign Relations of the United States, *FRUS*, IV, 1943, pp. 133–4.
7. FRUS, V, 1944, p. 148.
8. Iatrides, *Ambassador MacVeagh*, p. 660.
9. J. O. Iatrides, *United States' Attitudes toward Greece during World War II: Essays in Memory of Basil Laourdas* (Thessaloniki: Institute of Balkan Studies, 1975) pp. 625–6.
10. L. Henderson, letter to MacVeagh, 17 February 1945.
11. J. O. Iatrides, 'Perceptions of Soviet Involvement in the Greek Civil War, 1945–1949', in L. Baerentzen, J. O. Iatrides and O. L. Smith, *Studies in the History of the Greek Civil War, 1945–1949* (Copenhagen: Museum Tusculanum Press, 1987) p. 231.
12. *Ibid.*, p. 229.
13. J. Jones, *The Fifteen Weeks* (New York: The Viking Press, 1955) pp. 3–13; and D. Acheson, *Present at the Creation: My Years in the State Department* (New York: W.W. Norton, 1969) pp. 217–19.
14. *Ibid.*, p. 219.
15. US Senate, Committee on Foreign Relations. Legislative Origins of the Truman Doctrine (Executive Hearing, March April 1947) (Washington DC: Government Printing Office, 1973) p. 40.
16. Foreign Relations of the United States, Serial Publication of the Department of State (Washington DC: Government Printing Office, V, 1947) pp. 43–4.

17. FRUS, IV, 1948, pp. 4–5.
18. FRUS, IV, 1948, p. 12.
19. J. O. Iatrides, 'American Attitudes toward the Political System of Postwar Greece', in T. Couloumbis and J. O. Iatrides (eds) *Greek American Relations: A Critical Review* (New York: Pella, 1980) p. 59.
20. Iatrides, *Ambassador MacVeagh*, p. 59.
21. Iatrides, 'American Attitudes', p. 64.
22. Archive of the Greek Ministry of Foreign Affairs, Gouras tele. 1313, 1 March 1947.
23. J. Kofas, *Intervention and Underdevelopment. Greece During the Cold War* (University Park: The Pennsylvania University Press, 1989).
24. J. Warren, 'Origins of the "Greek Economic Miracle". The Truman Doctrine and Marshall Plan Developments and Stabilization Programs', in E. Rossides (ed.) *The Truman Doctrine of Aid to Greece: A Fifty-year Retrospective* (New York: The Academy of Political Science, 1998), pp.79–80.
25. Y. Staphanidis, *From Civil War to Cold War: Greece and the Allied Factor, 1949–52* (Athens: Proskinio, 1999) pp. 32–7 [in Greek].
26. Stephanidis, *From Civil War*, pp. 32–7; FRUS, IV, 1949, pp. 404–14.
27. Foreign Office Archives, Public Record Office, Kew, Surrey, United Kingdom, FO 371/101799.
28. FO371/101799; WG1017/3.
29. FO371/101799, WG1017/12.
30. Stephanidis, *From Civil War*, pp. 159–82.
31. J. O. Iatrides, *Balkan Triangle: Birth and Decline of an Alliance Across Ideological Boundaries* (The Hague: Mouton, 1968).
32. A. Papahelas, *The Rape of Greek Democracy: The American Factor, 1947–1967* (Athens: Estia, 1997) pp. 44–54 [in Greek].
33. FRUS, XXIV, 1955–57, p. 547.
34. C. Svolopoulos (ed.) *Karamanlis Archive, 1992–1997*, I, p.263, Constantine Karamanlis Archive. Events and Documents, Athens: Constantine G. Karamanlis Foundation.
35. FO 371/123844, RG1011/1.
36. FRUS, XXIV, 1955–57, p. 558.
37. M. Stearns, *Entangled Allies: US Policy Toward Greece, Turkey and Cyprus* (New York: Council on Foreign Relations, 1992) pp. 8–39.
38. FO 371/117612, RG1011/1.
39. FRUS, VIII, 1952–54, pp. 676–8.
40. FRUS, XXIV, 1955, p. 533.
41. Sterns, *Entangled Allies*, pp. 25–35.
42. FO 371/123844, RG1011/1.
43. FRUS, XXIV, 1955–57, p. 598.
44. FRUS, X, 1958–60, p. 686.
45. FRUS, V, 1958–60, p. 703.
46. FRUS, X, 1958–60, p. 720.
47. FRUS, XVI, 1961–63, pp. 664–8.
48. FRUS, XVI, 1961–63, pp. 686–7.
49. M. Bescholss (ed.) *Taking Charge: The Johnson White House Tapes, 1963–1964* (New York: Simon & Schuster, 1997) p. 191.
50. *Ibid.*, p. 282.
51. T. Schoenbaum, *Waging Peace and War: Dean Rusk in the Truman, Kennedy and Johnson Years* (New York: Simon & Schuster, 1988) p. 419.
52. Department of State Records (DSR) CYPS 9/1–9/5, 11 June 1964.
53. *Ibid.*
54. T. Couloumbis, *The United States, Greece and Turkey: The Troubled Triangle* (New York: Praeger, 1983) p. 63.
55. L. Stern, *The Wrong Horse: The Politics of Intervention and the Failure of American Diplomacy* (New York: Times Books, 1977) pp. 36–8.
56. *Ibid.*, pp. 38–9.
57. Papahelas, *The Rape*, pp. 237–90.
58. M. Goldbloom, 'United States Policy in Post-War Greece', in R.Clogg and G. Yannopoulos

(eds) *Greece Under Military Rule* (New York: Basic Books, 1972) pp. 240–1.
59. Papahelas, *The Rape*, pp. 363–71.
60. Goldbloom, 'United States', p. 245.
61. Karamanlis Archive, VII, pp. 28–59.
62. Goldbloom, 'United States Policy', p. 244.
63. *Ibid.*, p. 252.
64. Karamanlis Archive, VII, pp. 142–4.
65. Couloumbis, *The United States*, p. 53.
66. H. Kissinger, *Years of Renewal* (New York: Simon & Schuster, 1999) p. 199.
67. Couloumbis, *The United States*, p. 91.
68. Karamanlis Archive, VIII, 1996, p. 413.
69. C. M. Woodhouse, *Karamanlis. The Restorer of Greek Democracy* (Oxford: Clarendon Press, 1982) p. 218.
70. Kissinger, *Years of Renewal*, pp. 227–32.
71. Karamanlis Archive, VIII, 1996, p. 409.
72. Couloumbis, *The United States*, pp.103–8.
73. DSR NEA/GTI:RWBarham, 4/25/66.
74. Athens News Agency (ANA), 19 October 1983.
75. J. C. Loulis, 'Papandreou's Foreign Policy', *Foreign Affairs*, 63, 2 (Winter 1984/85) p. 386.
76. ANA, 5 November 1982.
77. ANA, 1 October, 15 November 1983.
78. J. O. Iatrides, 'NATO and Aegean Disputes: The Cold War and After', in A. Chircop *et al.* (eds) *The Aegean Sea After the Cold War: Security and Law of the Sea Issues* (New York: St Martin's Press, 2000) pp. 42–3.
79. ANA 28, 30 September 1983.
80. G. Tsoumis, 'The Defense Policies of PASOK', in N. Stavrou (ed.) *Greece Under Socialism: A NATO Ally Adrift* (New Rochelle, NY: Caratzas, 1988) pp. 102–11.
81. ANA, 14 October 1983.
82. J. G. Pyrros, 'PASOK and the Greek Americans: Origins and Development', in Stavrou, *Greece Under Socialism*, p. 247.
83. C. McCaskill, 'PASOK's Third World/Non-aligned Relations', in Stavrou, *Greece Under Socialism*, p. 324.
84. ANA, 1 July 1983.
85. ANA, 10 September 1983.
86. ANA, 25 July 1998.
87. *New York Times*, 26 April 1999.
88. US Embassy Release, 23 November 1999.

5

The Cyprus Question: International Politics and the Failure of Peacemaking

VAN COUFOUDAKIS

Located in the crossroads of civilizations and in one of the most strategic regions of the world, the fate of Cyprus has been affected by the actions of the power that dominated the Eastern Mediterranean. Because of its rich history and important strategic location, Cyprus has also been the object of study by a wide range of authors.[1] Studies ranging from literature to archaeology, from ecology to strategy, and most recently nationalism and ethnic conflict provide an unusually lengthy bibliography for a small country. This chapter will focus primarily on the post-Second World War international dimensions of the Cyprus problem and on the impact of international politics on the evolution of the Cyprus problem.

A BRIEF HISTORICAL BACKGROUND

The Ottoman conquest of Cyprus in 1572 permanently altered Cypriot culture, society and political developments. Cyprus attained a bicommunal character with two distinct ethnic communities, languages and religions. Even though the Ottoman Turks who settled in Cyprus were and remained a minority of the island's population, they were in control of the island until 1878 when Britain took over the island as part of its imperial expansion in the Middle East. Under the *Milliyet* system of Ottoman administration, the Orthodox Church of Cyprus assumed important secular administrative powers and became the ultimate spokesman of the Greek Cypriot community. Peaceful bicommunal coexistence marked most of the period of Ottoman and British rule. Many common links developed among the two communities despite separatist policies that became the hallmark of British administration. At the end, Britain's unwillingness to address the political demands of the

Greek Cypriot community for union to Greece,[2] Britain's failure to provide for self-government recognizing majoritarian interests and its reliance on 'divide and rule' politics, limited the political options of the Greek Cypriots and led them to the armed struggle against Britain starting in 1955.

The two communities were on separate political development paths. Whereas the Greek Cypriot political consciousness had been moulded by the last quarter of the nineteenth century and was expressed by various political movements, the Turkish Cypriot political renaissance did not come about until the late 1920s. The Turkish Cypriots considered the maintenance of the colonial *status quo* as the preferable alternative to the Greek Cypriot calls for *enosis* (union) to Greece. Cyprus, however, did not feature in Turkey's policy priorities until the early 1950s and the start of the Greek Cypriot armed struggle against British colonial rule.[3]

Initially, Britain drew Turkey into the Cyprus problem in an attempt to defuse the political demands emanating from Athens and Nicosia. However, as Robert Holland aptly documents,[4] by 1957 British policy on Cyprus was controlled by Turkey. Britain also drew the United States into the Cyprus dispute by framing the problem within the Cold War parameters of American policy in Southeastern Europe and the Eastern Mediterranean. This struck a responsive chord in the Eisenhower/Dulles administration, and set the tone of the American response to the Cyprus problem over the last half century. Washington's policy responses have focused on the impact of the problem on Greco–Turkish relations and on the politics of Greece and Turkey, on the effectiveness and cohesion of NATO's southeast flank and on Russia's possible involvement in an intra-NATO dispute. For these reasons Washington looked with disfavour at the United Nations involvement in the dispute, preferring instead consultations within NATO's framework, Greco–Turkish talks or other direct mediation attempts that limited the role of outside parties and especially of the former Soviet Union. Thus, for the United States, the involvement of the United Nations was acceptable only in the absence of other alternatives, or when it legitimized American initiatives. In such instances, Washington attempted to control the role of the United Nations and/or to influence the wording of UN resolutions[5] so that they did not contradict American objectives. This has been another constant of American policy since the early 1950s.

Faced with the threat of the implementation of Britain's partition plan and under considerable pressure from Athens, the Greek Cypriots reluctantly accepted an independence plan negotiated between Greece and Turkey in Zurich, and in London between Britain, Greece and Turkey in the spring of 1959. The Greek Cypriot fear of the partition of Cyprus has been another constant in the Cyprus problem that has affected Greek Cypriot negotiating positions since then.

FROM INDEPENDENCE TO THE 1974 TURKISH INVASION – ELEMENTS OF POLICY CONTINUITY

The London and Zurich agreements on Cyprus provided the rigid framework on which the constitution of the Republic of Cyprus was based. Eminent foreign constitutional experts characterized the Cypriot constitution as unique and unprecedented[6] because of the unusual veto powers reserved for the Turkish Cypriot minority and the difficulty of amending the constitution. Even though the United States hailed the conclusion of this agreement, confidential American diplomatic assessments[7] accurately pointed to the likelihood of deadlock and long-term instability in the new Republic because of these complicated agreements. This was indeed the case. Minority obstructionism[8] led President Makarios of Cyprus to propose 13 constitutional amendments late in 1963, which were rejected outright first by the government of Turkey and then by the Turkish Cypriots, who promptly withdrew from the government. By December 1963, intercommunal violence had erupted on Cyprus threatening the stability of Southeastern Europe and NATO's cohesion, and opening the door to possible Soviet involvement.

In view of the limitations imposed on the Cypriot Republic by its guarantor powers, the government of Cyprus sought to consolidate its independence and sovereignty through its participation in international organizations and by actively maintaining diplomatic relations around the world. The government of Cyprus even made quiet soundings about membership in NATO, soon after independence.[9] This was not seen with favour either in Ankara or in London, while the Kennedy administration encouraged Cyprus to play a moderating role within the non-aligned movement. This position, however, was soon abandoned by the Johnson administration that came to view President Makarios' policies as a threat to Western interests, especially with the presence of a strong Communist Party on Cyprus, the post-1964 expansion of the Soviet 5th Eskadra in the Eastern Mediterranean,[10] and the impact of the Cyprus problem on Greco–Turkish relations and on the cohesion of NATO's southeastern flank.

Thus, the crisis that erupted on Cyprus in December 1963 set in motion a number of policies whose fundamental assumptions are still affecting the evolution of this perpetuated dispute. One such policy is that of the internationalization of the Cyprus dispute. The government of Cyprus saw the United Nations and other regional organizations as a means of upholding the legitimacy of the Cypriot Republic and its government and of safeguarding its sovereignty and territorial integrity, especially in the aftermath of the withdrawal of the Turkish Cypriots from the government of the Republic, and Turkey's military threats against Cyprus. In contrast, de-internationalization was the policy thrust of the United States, whose preference was for quiet diplomacy through NATO or through a Greco–Turkish dialogue. As indicated earlier, the United States considered the United Nations to be a means of last resort, especially in the absence of other viable alternatives. The United Nations could also be used to legitimize American policies (e.g. the Acheson initiatives in 1964), while, by influencing the content of UN resolutions on Cyprus, Washington could introduce its policy agenda in this dispute. In the latter case, Washington sought to protect and promote American and Turkish interests in the dispute,[11] because Washington valued Turkey's strategic importance in the region. Washington was also concerned about Turkey's volatile politics in addition to Turkey's independent foreign policy. Washington and other influential actors viewed the Cyprus problem through the prism of international and regional politics, thus distorting the internal dimensions of the dispute. This has been another constant in the evolution of the Cyprus problem.

Turning to a second policy issue, Cyprus obtained its independence in August 1960. Since then, successive Cypriot governments, against overwhelming odds, have had as their primary policy priority the maintenance of the sovereignty and territorial integrity of the republic and the recognition of its government. Thus the issue of the continuity of the Republic of Cyprus has been another constant in the evolution of this dispute. From December 1963 to the 1974 Turkish invasion, the Republic survived despite threats to its existence which included the threat of a Turkish invasion, Turkish Cypriot secessionist activities and the destabilization of the Cypriot government by the Greek junta. There were also diplomatic initiatives by the United States, NATO, Greece and Turkey that sought the limitation, if not the termination, of the independence of Cyprus. These initiatives were justified as serving Western strategic interests in the region. A few examples will suffice.

In the aftermath of the intercommunal violence that erupted in Cyprus following the Turkish Cypriot withdrawal from the government of Cyprus in December 1963, Washington and London considered various peacekeeping and peacemaking options through NATO and through the replacement of President Makarios, who was seen as the chief obstacle to Western interests on the island. The chief architect of both policies was George Ball.[12] The NATO plan in particular sought the limitation of the independence of Cyprus through the placement of a NATO peacekeeping force, with significant American participation, whose commander would have powers above those of the government of the Republic.[13]

Ball failed in both attempts. Under the urgency of the situation a UN peacekeeping force (UNFICYP) was placed on the island in March 1964, under the control of the Security Council. Although significantly reduced in size, UNFICYP remains on Cyprus to this day. Peacemaking complemented the UN's peacekeeping activities under the good offices of the Secretary-General. However, UN peacemaking initiatives were systematically rejected or undermined when they contradicted Washington's objectives.[14] Washington's preference was for the de-internationalization of the Cyprus problem and for a solution through a secret Greco–Turkish understanding, with or without Cypriot consent. The Acheson/Geneva initiatives in the summer of 1964, and the Greco–Turkish 'Lisbon consensus' of June 1971, which was reached during a meeting of the NATO foreign ministers, are classic examples. In the former case, the UN provided a mantle of legitimacy for the secret American initiatives. In both cases a shared objective was the termination of the independence of the Republic of Cyprus, essentially through what amounted to a Greco-Turkish partition of the island.

In attaining these objectives three other tactics were utilized. One was the destabilization of the government of Cyprus by the junta ruling Greece (1967–74). The second included Turkish Cypriot secessionist activities in Cyprus. The formation of Turkish Cypriot enclaves, funded and armed by Turkey, became a fact of life prior to the 1974 Turkish invasion. The threat of force against Cyprus was the third tactic utilized against Cyprus. This included the bombing of Cyprus by the Turkish Air Force in the summer of 1964, and the threat of a Turkish invasion in June 1964 and November 1967. Washington was instrumental in stopping the two invasions. In 1964, Lyndon B. Johnson is credited for doing so through the 'ultimatum' sent to Prime Minister Inonu. Washington's response was affected by a Russian warning to Turkey, and Johnson's reluctance to face another crisis with the USSR in the aftermath of the Cuban Missile Crisis. It should be noted, however, that as Acheson's 1964 Geneva initiatives showed, Washington did not disagree with Turkey's objectives in Cyprus but only with its tactics, which risked broader American security interests. The 1967 American intervention also took place at a time of regional instability, following a devastating Arab–Israeli war. Moreover, the concessions made by the Greek junta to Cyrus Vance appeared to satisfy Turkey. As recent evidence suggests,[15] Washington and London had considered and planned, prior to 1974, for the possibility of a 'disciplined' (i.e. limited) Turkish military action in Cyprus that would safeguard minimum Turkish objectives without risking a Greco–Turkish war.

Why then did Washington and NATO allow Turkey to invade Cyprus in 1974? While the coup from Athens provided the rationalizations for the invasion, the absence of a Russian threat gave Kissinger the opportunity to permanently change the negotiating balance of power in Cyprus and to satisfy Turkey's long-standing demands on the island. The post-1972 détente with the Soviet Union and the Kissinger–Gromyko understandings about regional superpower interests made Soviet–

American relations very different from those of 1964. Kissinger assessed the role of the Soviet Union during the 1974 crisis in terms of what the Russians did not do. Moreover, contrary to Kissinger's attribution of the 1974 crisis to the Watergate paralysis,[16] he had far greater opportunity to manipulate events without White House supervision.

With nearly 38% of its territory under foreign occupation and its legitimate president in virtual exile, Cyprus had reached another fork on its tortuous road to independence. The Greek sponsored coup of 15 July 1974 not only gave Turkey the opportunity to attain a long-standing goal, it also destroyed the agreement reached between the two communities on 13 July 1974, on the issues dividing them since 1963. Needless to say that Mr Denktash had consented to virtually all the '13-points' that had triggered the 1963 constitutional crisis. In the aftermath of the Turkish invasion Cypriot diplomats, with support from various foreign countries, the support of the US Congress and the Greek–American community, were able to gain Washington's reluctant acknowledgement of the continuity of the Republic of Cyprus and its government since the 1963 constitutional crisis. Even though Cyprus won this diplomatic battle, with all the important consequences it has for the long term settlement of the dispute, this issue remains a major lever in the hands of American diplomats. This is especially true in the aftermath of the 1983 Turkish Cypriot UDI and the creation of the so-called 'Turkish Republic of Northern Cyprus' in the occupied areas. I will return to this point later in this essay.

A third area of continuity involves the relations between Athens and Nicosia. Cyprus, since the last quarter of the nineteenth century, has been an issue affecting popular sentiment in Greece and consequently in Greek politics. Cypriots consider themselves culturally and historically to be part of the Greek nation despite the physical distance from the Greek mainland and the unique elements characteristic of Cypriot culture. Both Greece and Cyprus experienced Ottoman rule. Britain, in turn, governed Cyprus from 1878–1960 while, prior to the 1947 Truman Doctrine, Britain exercised significant influence over Greek politics and foreign policy. Caught between the demands emanating from Cyprus, the impact of these demands on Greek public opinion and dependence on British support, successive Greek governments placed the interests of mainland Greece above those of Cyprus. This was true during the First World War, and during the 1931 uprising in Cyprus.[17]

Prime Minister Papagos was instrumental in bringing the Cyprus issue to the United Nations in the early 1950s. The international consequences of the 'Cyprus Question', American Cold War pressures and the consequences of the Greek inability to promote its goals at the United Nations on Greek politics and foreign policy, led Greece to the 1959 Zurich compromise with Turkey and to the imposition of the 1959

London agreement on a reluctant Archbishop Makarios.[18] In the aftermath of Cypriot independence the tension between Athens and Nicosia increased. Cyprus in the 1960s and 1970s had a level of economic development higher than that of Greece. It also had a vibrant and legal Communist Party (AKEL) at a time when communist activities were banned in Greece, while the non-aligned and independent foreign policy of President Makarios did not satisfy the conservative pro-American government that ruled Athens. The 1963 constitutional crisis on the island risked once more a Greco–Turkish confrontation. Thus, successive Greek governments confronted the dilemma of the domestic political pressures created by the new crisis on Cyprus, opportunities for political exploitation of the issue by the opposition parties, and the conflicts Cyprus created to a pro-Western Greek foreign and security policy. When forced to choose, Cyprus became a secondary priority of Greek foreign and security policy. This trend continues to this day,[19] providing another source of policy continuity.

The Cyprus problem became the downfall of many Greek governments. Thus, in contrast to the total dependence of the Turkish Cypriots on Turkey, especially prior to the last decade of the twentieth century, Greek Cypriots were able to influence and affect Greek policies and politics, despite their dependence on Greece. In turn, Greece, often acting as the *Ethnikon Kentron* (the national centre of Hellenism), attempted to impose its policies on the Cypriots. This reached a climax when the junta ruling Greece (1967–74) destabilized and eventually overthrew the government of Cyprus by a coup that provided Turkey with the pretext to invade Cyprus. The bitter aftermath of the invasion and the inability of the newly restored democratic Greek government to stop the second phase of the Turkish invasion in August 1974 brought the relations of Greece and Cyprus to a new level of maturity. Both sides had a better understanding of the other's limitations and commitments. Political élites in both countries viewed the invasion and occupation of Cyprus not as an isolated event but part of the broader threat posed by Turkey's revisionist policies in the Aegean and in Thrace. This required coordination, consultation and cooperation between the two countries in diplomatic, economic and military matters. Athens, publicly at least, defined its role as a supportive one, while policy decision-making centred on Nicosia.

A final element of continuity characteristic of the Cyprus problem has been the consistency of Turkish policy and its adaptation to the evolving international environment. The 1959 Zurich and London agreements formalized Turkey's position as a party of equal interest in Cyprus. Turkey viewed its new neighbour with suspicion. While it adopted a strict constructionist view of the constitution and of the degree of the independence of the new republic, it liberally interpreted its role as a guarantor power, especially following the December 1963 constitutional crisis. Turkey argued that the right of intervention under the Treaty of Guarantee included the right of unilateral military inter-vention in Cyprus, even though such an interpretation was in conflict with the UN Charter. In the aftermath of the 1964 and 1967 crises on Cyprus, Turkey embarked on a programme to develop amphibious capa-bilities which intensified in the aftermath of 1974 and the growing Greco–Turkish confrontation. Thus, by the 1980s, Turkey possessed the second largest fleet of landing craft among NATO countries. These craft were deployed in bases along Turkey's Aegean and Southern Mediterranean coasts.

Turkey also maintained that the Turkish Cypriots were one of the two co-founder communities and not a minority in the Republic of Cyprus. This is why it promoted their maximum autonomy and opposed any limitation of the veto powers granted to the Turkish Cypriots by the Zurich and London agreements. Following the 1963 constitutional crisis, Turkey continued financing, arming and training Turkish Cypriot militias, directing Turkish Cypriot politics and managing the movement of Turkish Cypriots into enclaves not under government control. These actions, along with the various schemes for the partition of Cyprus, enhanced the suspicions of the government of Cyprus as to Turkey's motivations and those of its surrogates on the island. The issue of the degree of Turkish Cypriot autonomy confounded the intercommunal negotiations from 1968–74, because these demands were seen as a step towards the partition of the island. As mentioned earlier, the fear of partition affected Greek Cypriot negotiating behaviour even prior to independence.

Partition was not an imaginary issue in the post-Second World War history of the problem. First raised in 1955 in discussions between Greece and Turkey and endorsed by the United States, the threat of partition became a reality under the Macmillan Plan proposed by the British in the closing days of colonial rule. The idea reappeared after the 1963 constitutional crisis in schemes such as the 1964 Acheson Plan, the December 1966 Toumbas–Caglayangil Protocol, and the Greco–Turkish talks at the Lisbon NATO meeting 3–4 June 1971.[20]

These schemes provided for various forms of union of a substantial portion of Cyprus to Greece and would have resulted in the termination of the independent Republic of Cyprus. In the aftermath of the Turkish invasion of Cyprus, and the escalating Greco–Turkish confrontation, Turkey lost interest in a traditional-type partition of Cyprus as this would have extended Greece's border to Turkey's southern coast. Instead, Turkey shifted its position in favour of a loose confederation that would maintain a weakened Republic of Cyprus under Turkey's hegemonial control. To attain these goals Turkey, especially after 1965, capitalized on its strategic position and its proclaimed independent foreign policy to promote its interests in the region with the toleration and support of both superpowers.

THE AFTERMATH OF THE INVASION – CONTINUITIES AND THE SEARCH FOR A SOLUTION

Turkey's 1974 invasion of Cyprus, the ethnic cleansing that was carried out by the Turkish army, and the occupation of nearly 38% of the Republic's territory, changed not only the negotiating balance between the two communities, but also drastically altered the demographic make-up of the island. The organized influx of Turkish mainland settlers, who now appear to outnumber the Turkish Cypriot population, added a new dimension to the problem.

The search for a comprehensive solution started in 1975 in Vienna and has continued to this day. While peacekeeping has succeeded, with the exception of the 1974 invasion which UNFICYP had neither the authority nor the capability to stop, peacemaking has not. After 26 years, some 100 UN resolutions on Cyprus, and the involvement of special emissaries, representatives of the Secretary-General, and other international mediators, the problem remains unresolved. At least four reasons account for the perpetuation of the Cyprus problem. These include (a) the failure to implement the United Nations Security Council resolutions on Cyprus; (b) the prevalence of strategic, economic and political considerations over a functional and viable solution; (c) the intransigent policies of successive Turkish governments, and (d) the political conditions existing in each Cypriot community.

As indicated earlier in this essay, Washington's approach, in contrast to that of Nicosia, emphasized the de-internationalization of the Cyprus problem. All UN Security Council resolutions on Cyprus were adopted unanimously. They contain the fundamental principles for a viable solution of the problem. However, Washington has succeeded in protecting Turkey from any effective sanctions for its violations of international law; it has watered down the wording of many resolutions, while introducing terminology compatible with American and Turkish goals; and has opposed the implementation of these resolutions. The issue of the implementation of the Security Council resolutions gained prominence following the 1990 Iraqi invasion of Kuwait and the determined American response which emphasized Iraq's compliance with all Security Council resolutions. Washington rejected all comparisons of its response to the Iraqi and Turkish actions. It rationalized its stand on the non-implementation of the resolutions in Cyprus with the spurious argument that they were adopted under Chapter VI, rather than

Chapter VII of the Charter. However, as international law authorities have indicated, article 25 of the Charter obligates members to carry out Security Council resolutions. This obligation is not confined to cases under Chapter VII. Otherwise this obligation would be served by articles 48 and 49.[21]

President Ford, under considerable domestic and international pressure, continued the American recognition of the restored democratic government of Cyprus as the government of the Republic despite the Turkish occupation of nearly 38% of the Republic's territory. That recognition was continued by President Carter in the aftermath of President Makarios' death in August 1977 and his succession by former Foreign Minister Spyros Kyprianou. As indicated earlier, the issue of the recognition of the government of Cyprus as the government of all of Cyprus and of the continuity of the Republic remained a consistent and primary Greek Cypriot goal. This goal attained even greater urgency in the aftermath of the 1974 Turkish invasion and occupation, and the unilateral declaration of independence of the occupied areas in 1983, when the so-called 'Turkish Republic of Northern Cyprus' was established under Turkish auspices. Even though the 'TRNC' has been recognized only by Turkey, the mere threat of its recognition by other states, and American pressures during the last five years in particular for an 'acknowledgement' of the existence of a 'political entity' in the occupied areas, has become a new source of diplomatic pressure on the Greek Cypriots.

Washington's post-1974 Cyprus policy attempted to limit the consequences of the Turkish invasion on Greek-Turkish relations,[22] while engaging in peacemaking efforts on Cyprus without undermining America's strategic and economic ties to Turkey. While this balancing act has included the recognition of the government of Cyprus and the continuity of the Republic, it has also reflected traditional American attitudes on the strategic and economic importance of Turkey resulting in the avoidance of any American or international sanctions on Turkey.[23] Washington, therefore, focused its attention on obtaining concessions from the Greek Cypriots in order to get movement on the peacemaking front. This was recognized by Turkey and the Turkish Cypriots who anticipated that their goals would be met through a long-term, consistent and intransigent policy which anticipated Greek Cypriot acceptance of the reality created by the 1974 invasion and occupation. American policy statements and peacemaking initiatives in the 1974–78 period reflect this balancing act. In the aftermath of the second phase of the Turkish invasion, Washington criticized Turkey's actions, advanced the territory/constitutional trade-off argument, but also opposed the early Turkish troop withdrawal from Cyprus and Congressional attempts to impose an arms embargo on Turkey for its violations of American and international law.

The first formal policy statement on Cyprus was Kissinger's 22 September 1975 statement at the UN General Assembly. His 'Five Points' on a Cyprus settlement included acceptance of the independence, sovereignty and territorial integrity of Cyprus. He emphasized the need for a territorial allocation that accounted for the economic and security interests of both communities and for Turkish Cypriot autonomy. Since then, for the Greek Cypriots, the challenge has been getting Washington to fulfil promises included in policy statements that appear to contain basic Cypriot objectives. The stalemate in the Vienna rounds of talks brought Clark Clifford, President Carter's emissary, to Cyprus in February 1977. His primary purpose was to express Washington's support for substantive talks on Cyprus reflecting constitutional trade-offs for territory. He therefore sought from the Cypriot government unilateral concessions that would bring the Turks and the Turkish Cypriots back to the negotiating table with more flexible positions.[24] This included the fulfilment of the Makarios–Denktash agreement on a bicommunal federation, which constituted a major shift in Greek Cypriot policy. Clifford employed a negotiating tactic that I describe as the 'salamisation' of the Cyprus problem. This involved getting a unilateral concession from the Greek Cypriots, without anything in return from the Turkish Cypriots, in order to re-start stalemated negotiations. Negotiations would end in a new stalemate due to Turkish Cypriot/Turkish intransigence, and the cycle would repeat itself. Clifford represented President Carter, whose principled stand on the Cyprus problem during the 1976 American presidential campaign had raised high hopes for an early, just and viable solution of the Cyprus problem both in Cyprus and in the Greek-American community. This is why influential Cypriot leaders feel bitter to this day about the sincerity and credibility of American emissaries. They simply feel that 'they were taken' by Clifford.

Clifford's visit followed days after a UN sponsored meeting between President Makarios and Turkish Cypriot leader Rauf Denktash that produced a set of broad guidelines for the solution of the Cyprus problem.[25] A couple of years later, Makarios' successor attempted to refine these guidelines in another meeting with Denktash.

However, the Markarios–Denktash agreement, which was based on the constitutional principle of a bicommunal federation, changed the nature of the peacemaking efforts on Cyprus and opened the way to constitutional schemes akin to confederation demanded by the Turkish Cypriots and Turkey, especially in the aftermath of the establishment of the so-called 'Turkish Republic of Northern Cyprus' in the occupied areas in 1983.

In the spring and summer of 1978 the Carter administration, contrary to its pre-electoral promises, intensified its efforts for the lifting of the Congressionally mandated arms embargo on Turkey. This, once more, reflected Washington's opposition to any sanctions on Turkey with the rationalization that sanctions only strengthened Turkey's intransigence. The embargo had become a symbolic act because the executive branch systematically undermined the Congressional embargo through NATO and other sources of weapons. Turkey, much as in the aftermath of President Johnson's 1964 'ultimatum', exploited the Congressional action by questioning Washington's commitment. President Carter narrowly succeeded in lifting the arms embargo late in the summer of 1978 by promising to redouble Washington's peacemaking efforts in addition to providing the Congress with bimonthly reports on the progress made towards a resolution of the Cyprus problem. These symbolic and rather meaningless reports present sanitized accounts of 'progress' while failing to criticize Turkey for its actions. Turkey's astute diplomacy has not failed to notice the fundamental assumptions of American policy.

Warren Christopher (later US Secretary of State), speaking at the Senate Foreign Relations Committee on 2 May 1978, repeated Washington's commitment to the independence and sovereignty of Cyprus, found the partition of Cyprus to be 'unacceptable', supported the idea of the constitutional transformation of Cyprus to a bizonal federation, and repeated the established American position of a reduction of the territory under Turkish Cypriot control with consideration of their economic and security interests. Some three months after the lifting of the arms embargo on Turkey, Washington presented its first comprehensive plan for the resolution of the Cyprus problem. Known as the 'ABC' plan because of its co-sponsorship by Britain and Canada, the plan was the brainchild of Matthew Nimetz, legal adviser at the US Department of State. The plan presented on 10 November 1978, on the eve of the discussion of the Cyprus problem at the United Nations,[26] included detailed constitutional proposals indicating Washington's preference for a loose federation/confederation. The plan tempered its acceptance of the UN resolutions with 'other agreements' (i.e. the 1977 Makarios/Denktash agreement), and left open to negotiation issues critical to the Greek Cypriots such as those of territory, security, the withdrawal of the occupation forces, etc. Even though the 'Nimetz Plan' failed to break the deadlock in the intercommunal talks, it is fair to say that it has become the foundation of subsequent American and UN initiatives on Cyprus. For this reason, the first substantive American plan is an important landmark in the post-1974 history of Cyprus.

The 1983 unilateral declaration of independence by the Turkish Cypriots was the culmination of Turkey's long-standing plans on Cyprus, despite Turkish arguments that Turkish Cypriot leader Denktash acted unilaterally. Even though Rauf Denktash was slowly gaining stature in the Turkish political world, his dependence on Turkish economic and military support made virtually impossible such a move without a 'green light' from Turkey's nationalist military establishment. Even though a rudimentary Turkish Cypriot 'administration' attempted to control the Turkish Cypriot enclaves that were established in the aftermath of the 1963 constitutional crisis, and a successor 'administration' was set up in the aftermath of the invasion, the 1983 UDI was a turning point in the evolution of the Cyprus problem. The so-called 'TRNC' remains unrecognized by all states except Turkey. It has also been condemned by all international and regional organizations,[27] while states have been called upon not to recognize this entity. Moreover, national and regional courts have refused to give validity to acts of the so-called 'TRNC'. However, Turkey has held steadfast in its actions hoping that time will bring about an acknowledgement of the post-1974 realities, first by the international community and eventually by the government of Cyprus. At the time of writing, Turkey's long-term strategy appears to be working, while the government of Cyprus is fighting rearguard actions at the United Nations and elsewhere attempting to stem Turkey's attempts to upgrade the standing of Mr Denktash and that of his régime. The creation of the so-called 'TRNC' has also given impetus to the Turkish Cypriot calls for a confederation of two equal, sovereign and recognized states.

Washington's diplomatic efforts face a number of dilemmas – how to keep the parties talking even though the gap separating their positions has increased, and how to get the Greek Cypriots to make the ultimate concession (i.e. the acknowledgment of the 'TRNC' in what amounts to a constitutional confederation).

SEARCHING FOR A SETTLEMENT – THE LAST DECADE

The last decade of the twentieth century brought significant changes in the international dimension of the Cyprus problem. The end of the Cold War left the United States as the dominant power in the international system. The collapse of the former Soviet Union reduced even further Russia's limited influence in this dispute. The ensuing collapse of Yugoslavia restored legitimacy to partition and ethnic cleansing as solutions to ethnic problems, creating a bad precedent for Cyprus. Finally, an invigorated European Union set a new framework for expansion in post-Cold War Europe.

Cyprus concluded an association agreement with the European Community in 1972. In 1990 the government of Cyprus applied formally for membership in the European Community, and in the fall of 1993 the Council of Ministers of the European Union accepted the

Cypriot application, despite concerns expressed by the Commission over the lack of a political settlement. Integration talks with Cyprus commenced on schedule in March 1998. By the mid-1990s membership in the EU became a Cypriot foreign policy priority. The European Union recognized the continuity of the Republic of Cyprus and its government, and this was reflected in actions of European courts and other EU organizations. The prospect of membership and the application of the *acquis communautaire* offered new options for resolving intractable issues such as those of human rights, borders and security. The United States, until the Clinton administration, had not looked favourably at the involvement of the EU in the Cyprus problem. The change in American policy served a number of objectives. It provided a new source of pressure on the Cypriot government to resolve the problem. Working in cooperation with Britain, Germany and other EU members, Washington promoted the idea of a solution prior to the entry of Cyprus to the EU. This was done despite public statements at the highest level of the EU that even though a political settlement was desirable prior to membership the lack of a settlement would not stop the integration of Cyprus. Washington's advocacy of a solution prior to entry gave Turkey an indirect veto over the membership of Cyprus, a power that Turkey did not formally have. Further, a solution prior to integration would legitimize derogations from recognized human rights[28] that normally would be protected under the *acquis* and other European legislation. Washing-ton's policy change also served another objective. By pressing the Europeans to grant candidate status to Turkey,[29] Washington gained political credit in Ankara by being Turkey's sole promoter among the reluctant Europeans.

The diplomatic activism of the 1990s carried into the new millennium. UN Security Council resolutions on Cyprus called on the Secretary-General to utilize his 'good offices' in the peacemaking process. He was therefore primarily responsible for maintaining the dialogue between the government of Cyprus and the Turkish Cypriots. In this task the Secretary-General has been assisted by his own special representatives, in addition to the special representatives of the United States, Great Britain and other foreign countries, initiatives by Secretaries of State and Foreign Secretaries, and the usual embassy level contacts. The involvement of so many foreign diplomats under the guise of supporting the Secretary-General raised questions about the coordination of their efforts, their commitment to a substantive process, their knowledge of the issues and of the players involved in these talks.[30] There were also questions about the aims and the tactics employed by these negotiators.

The Americans in particular expressed their frustration with the inconclusive negotiations. They attributed the lack of progress to the

two parties and their 'lack of political will' to make necessary concessions. However, Washington did not question its assumptions about
Turkey and its foreign policy, and its unwillingness to support the implementation of UN resolutions on Cyprus. Instead, Washington focused its
pressures on the victim of aggression so as to bring the Cypriot positions
closer to the confederation ideas demanded by Turkey and the Turkish
Cypriots. Working under the mantle of the UN American negotiators,
like Richard Holbrooke, the US engaged selectively in the talks. Failure
to resolve this perpetuated problem could then be assigned to the parties
or to the Secretary-General's office without risking the negotiators'
personal reputation or their political/diplomatic ambitions.

The American approach appeared to be along the lines of 'keep them
talking', even though the gap separating the two sides was growing
larger each year with new Turkish/Turkish Cypriot demands. The negotiating initiatives fluctuated between attempts at a comprehensive solution through a framework agreement arrived at high level meetings, to
limited confidence building measures that could open the way to a
comprehensive solution. Some of these meetings involved face to face
negotiations between the president of Cyprus and Turkish Cypriot
leader Rauf Denktash,[31] proximity talks (such as those in the current
phase of negotiations in Geneva), or even informal exploratory talks
among foreign representatives and representatives of the two sides.[32]

These meetings often produced documents such as the 1992 Boutros
Ghali 'set of ideas' which reflected commonalities in the positions of the
two sides and identified areas in need of further negotiation, or the
1993/94 proposals for confidence building measures (CBMs). These
documents could not break the deadlock because the Turkish Cypriots
used them as stepping stones to promote their separatist policies. The
fate of the 1993 package of confidence building measures (CBMs),
which had been accepted by the government of Cyprus, is a classic
example of the Turkish/Turkish Cypriot and American collusion. In
secret talks in Vienna in the spring of 1994, that excluded the Cypriot
government, 'clarifications' were added to the 1993 CBM package to
bring it closer to Turkish Cypriot positions which compromised the
unity and sovereignty of the Republic of Cyprus. As Turkish Cypriot
positions kept shifting closer to a confederation of two separate sovereign states, the Secretary-General was forced to issue critical statements
about the Turkish Cypriot negotiating behaviour in reports and statements to the Security Council both in 1993 and 1994. This, however,
had no effect on American, Turkish or Turkish Cypriot policies. On
29 August 1994, the so-called Turkish Cypriot 'Assembly' endorsed
Denktash's negotiating position by dropping federation as the aim of the
comprehensive settlement in favour of a confederation. Needless to say
the formal shift violated the 1977 and 1979 high level agreements and

the UN resolution that endorsed the principle of a bizonal-bicommunal federation. While the Turkish Cypriots and Turkey continued with their unilateral actions – the 1983 Turkish Cypriot UDI, the formal abandonment of federation in 1994, etc. – the government of Cyprus negotiated along lines agreed upon since 1977. Successive Cypriot governments never had the political courage to force the negotiations back to a zero base to counter Turkish Cypriot unilateral actions. By proving that they negotiated in good faith, the Greek Cypriots were forced into continuous concessions in order to keep the negotiations alive without any reciprocity from the other side.

In a series on 'non-papers' the Secretary-General's representatives in the 1997 face to face talks in Troutbeck, NY and in Glion, Switzerland, attempted to 'bridge the gap' in the position of the two sides by attempting to force the Cyprus government closer to the idea of confederation and of an acceptance of Turkish Cypriot sovereignty. The government of Cyprus, however, did take some bold initiatives in an attempt to break the deadlock on security issues by presenting on 17 December 1993, a detailed demilitarization proposal. Turkey and the Turkish Cypriots rejected this proposal and insisted on a continued Turkish military presence and intervention rights. The United States in turn has used this proposal to push for Greek Cypriot demilitarization, while maintaining a smaller Turkish military presence in the occupied areas with limited intervention rights in a reconstituted international force preferably under NATO command.

Thus, by the end of the Clinton administration, the Cyprus problem was treated not as a problem of invasion and occupation but as an intercommunal dispute. The break-up of Yugoslavia had given new legitimacy to confederation schemes and to ethnic separation. Turkey maintained that the Cyprus problem had been solved in 1974, and that the purpose of any negotiations was to legitimize the condition created since 1974, while clarifying issues of borders and property compensation. Turkey's long-term strategy on Cyprus was finally paying off. Aware of American attitudes on the importance of Turkey, it considered that the de facto recognition of the political entity in the occupied areas was a matter of time, and that international mediators would force the Cyprus government to acknowledge that reality.

In the second term of the Clinton administration the resolution of the Cyprus problem and the improvement of Greco–Turkish relations became a higher priority of American foreign policy. Greco–Turkish relations entered a new phase of instability in the aftermath of the January 1996 crisis over the Imia islets. Cyprus, since 1974, burdened Greek–Turkish relations even though implicitly it was not a Greco–Turkish issue. A resolution of the Cyprus problem was expected to have a positive effect on Greek–Turkish relations, while an improvement in Greek–Turkish relations would create a more positive climate for the resolution of the Cyprus dispute.

In addition to the movement in the relations of Cyprus with the EU, there were three other developments that directly impacted on the negotiations over Cyprus. First was the European Court of Human Rights ruling on the Loizidou case on 18 December 1996, which upheld not only the continuity of the Republic of Cyprus but once more held Turkey accountable for its control of the occupied areas and the consequent loss of Loizidou's enjoyment of her property rights.[33] This ruling directly impacted on the American and Turkish attempt to resolve property issues through compensation and by limiting the rights of settlement and property ownership in the occupied areas by Greek Cypriots. The second development related to the killing in cold blood of unarmed Greek Cypriot demonstrators along the dividing line near Dehrynia in October 1996 by Turkish Cypriot security forces and members of Turkey's right wing terrorist group, the 'Grey Wolves'.

Faced with Turkey's military threat both from the occupied areas and from bases on the southern coast of Turkey (these bases were exempt from CFE limitations), the last government of Andreas Papandreou, in cooperation with the government of Cyprus, proclaimed a 'unified defense dogma',[34] which incorporated Cyprus in the Greek defence space. Even though doubts were expressed early on about Greece's ability and willingness to meet such a commitment, especially in view of other defence priorities in the Balkans, in Thrace and the Aegean, Greece and Cyprus proceeded with plans for common defence planning, coordination of military procurement, military training, etc. Towards the end of 1996 Cyprus, with advice from Greece, ordered the S-300 anti-aircraft missile system from Russia. This decision was exploited for domestic purposes in Greece and Cyprus. It was condemned by the United States as a destabilizing action, while Turkey threatened to destroy these antiaircraft missiles if they were deployed on the island. Washington remained remarkably silent in view of Turkey's threats, and it was not until the autumn of 1998 that it issued lukewarm warnings about the use of force in the region. Washington, however, did not allow the sale of American defensive weapons to Cyprus, while supplying Turkey with massive amounts of sophisticated weapons[35] that posed a clear and present danger to both Cyprus and to Greece's Aegean islands. Turkey's threat against Cyprus was not surprising, but the American response was, as it confirmed that Washington considered Turkey as a hegemonic regional power.[36] The Clinton administration focused its pressures on both Nicosia and Athens. In December 1998, the government of Cyprus announced that the S-300s would not be deployed in Cyprus but, instead, they would be sent to Greece for deployment on the island of Crete. This decision effectively destroyed the myth of the

unified defence dogma between Greece and Cyprus. Turkey had threatened the use of force, and Greece and Cyprus blinked. For Turkey, this
was a significant victory as it proved that its diplomats could rely on
their country's military strength to achieve their objectives.

Greco–Turkish relations reached a low point with the arrest of
Kurdish leader Abdullah Ocalan in Kenya in the spring of 1999.[37] The
Ocalan affair caused a shake-up in the Greek Foreign Ministry. George
Papandreou, son of the late Prime Minister of Greece Andreas
Papandreou, assumed command of Greek foreign policy. The impact of
the Ocalan affair and a summer of devastating earthquakes in Turkey
and Greece gave Papandreou the opportunity to take bold initiatives
vis-à-vis Turkey. These initiatives, and especially the support Greece
extended at the Helsinki EU meeting to Turkey's EU candidacy in
December 1999,[38] improved the image of Greek foreign policy in
Europe and in the US. The conditions imposed at Helsinki on Turkey's
candidacy placed the ball in Turkey's court as well as in the court of the
EU, as the lack of progress in Turkey's European vocation up until then
had been conveniently blamed on Greece. The improvement in Greek–
Turkish relations in the last year of the twentieth century has not had a
positive effect on the Cyprus negotiations, as the next section will show.

THE UNITED STATES, THE G-8 FORMULA AND THE
2000 ROUND OF PROXIMITY TALKS

Washington, capitalizing on the euphoria of the improved climate in
Greco–Turkish relations, embarked on a campaign to make the governments of Greece and Cyprus more responsive to Turkey's regional
concerns. It also lobbied for Turkey's EU candidacy, without linking
Turkey's compliance to any of the conditions set by the EU and expected
of members and candidates of the EU. At the United Nations
Washington attempted to quietly upgrade the status of the régime in the
occupied areas of Cyprus during the discussions on the renewal of the
UN peacekeeping force.

UN Secretary-General Kofi Annan, in a letter to the president of the
UN Security Council dated 20 April 1998, concluded that Turkey
defined its Cyprus policy in the context of 'two states and three problems'. This included the recognition of Turkish Cypriot statehood as the
prerequisite for a solution. In turn, the three problems in need of resolution were those of security, settlement of property claims and the
delineation of borders. Further, they demanded the acknowledgement
of the legitimacy of Denktash's government and its political procedures,
the lifting of the economic embargo, the continuation of Turkey's military guarantee, and the acknowledgement of the political equality of the

two sides in all aspects of the negotiations. Mr Denktash also demanded the withdrawal of the Cypriot application to the EU, and that the UN and all external mediators accept this 'new political reality'. The Secretary-General described these points as Denktash's 'new positions' as a result of which the Turkish Cypriots rejected the intercommunal framework of all previous rounds of negotiations. Turkish and Turkish Cypriot officials blatantly argued that the Cyprus problem had been solved with Turkey's 1974 intervention and with the 'population exchange' that followed. Turkey, in order to facilitate its EU aspirations, agreed, late in 1999, to re-open talks on Cyprus and to seek a peaceful resolution of its differences with Greece. However, having attained candidacy status, it became clear that Turkey sought the de facto recognition of the occupied areas and the formation of a confederation of two, independent, sovereign and recognized states on Cyprus. It was in this context that they were willing to address issues of property compensation, security and limited border adjustments.

Turkey was fully aware of Washington's progressive support of most of these ideas, especially because, in his mission to Nicosia in May 1998, Richard Holbrooke promoted the idea of an 'acknowledgement' of the Turkish Cypriot political entity by the Greek Cypriots. That 'acknowledgement' included the legitimacy of the laws and institutions established there since 1974, and the fact that the Cyprus government did not speak on behalf of the Turkish Cypriot community. Instead, the Turkish Cypriots were represented by leaders elected through legitimate procedures. Sir David Hannay, the British representative on Cyprus, shared similar views. Both argued that such an 'acknowledgement' would provide the needed momentum in a new round of talks, as they both expected the Turkish Cypriot and Turkish sides to negotiate in good faith. This, of course, had been the history of the Cyprus negotiations since 1974.

Washington once more took steps to undermine the United Nations by bringing the Cyprus problem to the meeting of the G-8 in Cologne, Germany, on 20 June 1999. The attempt to minimize the role of the United Nations has been a constant element of American policy since the 1950s. The G-8 adopted the following formula[39] on Cyprus, which was later endorsed by UN Security Council resolutions 1250 and 1251 of 1999. The two sides were called to a new round of talks based on the following four principles: talks without preconditions; discussion of all issues; sustained talks in good faith and until a solution is found, and full consideration of relevant UN resolutions and treaties.

The G-8 formula contained both 'good' and 'bad' news. The reference to the UN resolutions implied an endorsement of a bizonal-bicommunal federation, with single sovereignty, international personality and citizenship. Further, earlier resolutions condemned the pseudo-state created by the Turkish army in the occupied areas, and called for its non-recognition. The 'bad news', however, was that 'the parties' could put on the table all issues without preconditions. This meant that Mr Denktash could present himself as president of a sovereign and independent state, and that he could present his proposal for a confederation of two sovereign states. The reference to the 'other' international agreements implied discussion of the Treaty of Guarantee and Turkey's intervention rights, in addition to the 1977 and 1979 high level agreements. Secretary-General Kofi Annan in his report to the Security Council on 22 June 1999, closely reflected the American and British ideas by noting that the political status of the Turkish Cypriots needed to be addressed. He attempted to do this in an addendum on the status of UNFICYP in December of 1999, but his attempt to do the same in June 2000 failed after repeated warnings by the Cyprus government. This was the reality facing the Cyprus government as it entered inconclusive rounds of UN-sponsored proximity talks with the Turkish Cypriots in the spring and summer of 2000. The proximity talks were also attended by American and British negotiators.

What advice did Washington offer the 'two sides' as they entered this latest phase of proximity talks?

1. Look to the future and not to the past.
2. Do not debate whether the events of 1974 were an invasion or an intervention.
3. Do not debate abstract notions of federation/confederation, or the nature of sovereignty. Arrive at a constitutional solution first, and name it later.
4. Leave out of the negotiations 'humanitarian' issues. These issues, in addition to the missing, included the 90,000+ Turkish settlers.
5. The government of Cyprus should commit to confidence building measures including the gradual lifting of sanctions against the so-called 'TRNC'.
6. President Clerides and Mr Denktash were urged to show political courage and imagination so as to close their careers with an agreement, because they have the moral authority over their respective publics, and can unburden their successors from politically costly choices.

The irony and cynicism of American policy is that while publicly American officials endorse a settlement based on a bizonal, bicommunal federation, privately they have given their full support to a confederation of two independent, sovereign states. American officials promote the 'land for constitutional concessions' principle. The greater the territorial compromise, the looser the confederation becomes. In 1992 the

United States had presented some 92 map variations which were rejected by the Turkish Cypriots. These territorial concessions ranged from 25%+ to almost 32% of the territory for the Turkish Cypriot 'state'. Alternative scenaria have also been prepared on the structure of the executive branch, while selective provision from the Swiss, German, Belgian and the Canadian constitutions have provided justifications as to how sovereignty can be divided in a two-state confederation, despite the UN resolutions calling for a state with a single sovereignty.

The following ten points offer insights as to how Washington has attempted to address the Turkish and Turkish Cypriot demand for recognition of the so-called 'TRNC' as a pre-condition for substantive talks.

1. The US will not support recognition as a precondition for the talks, but will assist the Turkish Cypriots to attain recognition as an outcome of the talks.
2. The US is interested in having continuous negotiations between the two parties to keep the momentum created by American initiatives and by the recent improvement in Greek–Turkish relations.
3. Meaningful talks require that the Greek Cypriots need to come to terms with the reality that has been created since 1974, and to be sensitive to Turkish Cypriot needs and concerns. For Washington the problem is one of intercommunal power sharing and not one of invasion and occupation.
4. It is up to the parties to decide what relationship they will have. They need to show flexibility, realism and political courage. The US will offer constructive suggestions and alternative scenarios to guide the talks.
5. Even though federation may be desirable, it must be wanted by both sides. The reality, however, is that the new constitutional arrangement requires an acceptance of elements of 'legitimized partition' reflecting the conditions existing since 1974. A stable partition will be better than the current unstable *status quo*.
6. The two sides need to negotiate the core issues, and not to debate issues like federation or confederation, invasion or occupation. The core issues involve: boundaries, property exchanges, resettlement of displaced persons, three freedoms, and compensation. Therefore, in these talks, it is the substance that counts, not the form! Once a settlement is reached, then constitutional experts and politicians can name it whatever they may!
7. Rauf Denktash and the Turks are realists and will come to the talks with something less than the *de jure* recognition of the 'TRNC' as an independent and sovereign state. Rauf Denktash will accept an 'acknowledgment' by the government of Cyprus that he and his administration represent the Turkish Cypriots and speak on their

behalf. Once granted such an acknowledgment he will negotiate in good faith. The US Department of State, Britain and Australia, suggest that the September 1993 exchange of letters between the government of Israel and the Palestinians be used as a precedent.

8. An 'acknowledgement' by the government of Cyprus does not have to be disclosed publicly until negotiations have reached a satisfactory stage.

9. Even though 'acknowledgement' amounts to recognition of the Denktash administration as the de facto government of the territory under its control, it will not have other legal consequences. Assurances will be offered to the Greek Cypriots that the international community, with the exception of Turkey, will not recognize *de jure* a Turkish Cypriot state.

10. When a full agreement has been reached, the international community will allow 'a brief moment of sovereignty' to the Turkish Cypriots, so that both sides can form a new partnership on Cyprus based on the political equality of the two constituent states.

By the end of July 2000 the gap separating the two sides was growing and this created a serious dilemma for the government of Cyprus. Abandoning the talks would have serious political consequences, especially on the progress of the talks with the EU. Remaining in the talks exposed the government of Cyprus to American, British and UN pressures for an acknowledgement of the Turkish Cypriot 'state' and for the formation of a confederation of two independent, recognized and sovereign states. Aware of these conditions, Turkey and the Turkish Cypriots held fast to their position on confederation as shown in the paper submitted by Mr Denktash to Mr Alvaro De Soto, the representative of the Secretary-General in Geneva during the July phase of the talks.[40] What was even more insidious was that De Soto's 'non-paper' was dictated to the parties. This UN 'non-paper', to which the parties were asked to respond, altered the terminology that had been included in UN Security Council resolutions on Cyprus. It was one more attempt to undermine the moral authority of the UN. This 'non-paper' adopted positions advocated by Turkey and the Turkish Cypriots. It included references to the 'common state' instead of the federal state on Cyprus; it spoke of the component states joining in a 50/50 partnership, terms used by Mr Denktash; it abandoned the concepts of a 'just and viable' solution in favour of an 'equitable' solution; it addressed the 'two sides' instead of the 'two communities', thus moving away from the principle of intercommunal talks; it provided for freedom of movement, but called for 'equity' in property compensation, effectively overruling the Loizidou ruling of the European Court of human rights; and called for a significant reduction in the number of Turkish troops on Cyprus and their presence in a new international force.

Two other critical points were also addressed by De Soto. The new state would have three constitutions with distinct definitions on citizenship. While earlier UN resolutions spoke of a sovereign Cyprus Republic with a single citizenship and international personality, De Soto proposed the distinction between separate internal citizenship and nationality. Finally, De Soto extended an indirect veto to the Turkish Cypriots on the issue of the EU, something denied to them by the EU, by indicating that EU integration must account for the 'legitimate concerns of both sides'.

These negative developments in the Cyprus talks were accompanied by other discouraging political developments. During the summer of 2000, the occupied areas entered a new phase of economic and political instability opening the way to more direct rule from Ankara. Moreover, in total disregard of the United Nations, the occupation forces violated the neutral zone and brought under their control the hamlet of Strovilia, causing only the verbal expression of 'concern' by the United States, Britain and the Secretary-General. Meanwhile, Ankara continued its campaign against Greece by formally repeating its known positions on Thrace, the Aegean and the Greek islands of the Aegean. These actions indicated that what had changed since the summer of 1999 was the tone, not the substance or the objectives of Turkish policy.[41]

This essay has shown how the Cyprus problem has been addressed by policies focusing on economic and strategic concerns of external powers that had little to do with the essence of the Cyprus problem. In the process the rights of all Cypriots were violated, along with the rules of international and American law, while the stature of the UN was further undermined. The prospect of EU membership for Cyprus continues to provide new opportunities for resolving this perpetuated problem. A solution based on the implementation of UN resolutions on Cyprus and of the principles of the *acquis* can restore stability and justice in the Eastern Mediterranean. Meanwhile, in the first year of the new millennium, Cyprus remains the last divided and occupied country of Europe.

NOTES

1. P. M Kitromilides and M. L. Euriviades, *Cyprus* (Oxford, Santa Barbara, Denver: Clio Press, 1995).
2. G. S. Georgalides, *Cyprus and the Governorship of Sir Ronald Storrs: The Causes of the 1931 Crisis* (Nicosia: Cyprus Research Centre, 1985).
3. Sir A. Eden, *The Eden Memoirs* (London: Cassell, 1960–65).
4. R. Holland, *Britain and the Revolt on Cyprus 1954–1959* (Oxford, New York: Clarendon Press/Oxford, 1998).
5. S. G. Xydis, *Cyprus–Reluctant Republic* (The Hague, Paris: Mouton, 1973).
6. T. Ehrlich, *Cyprus, the Warlike Isle: Origins and Elements of the Current Crisis* (Stanford Law Review, XVIII, May 1966) pp. 1021–98; S. A. de Smith, *The New Commonwealth and its Constitutions* (London: Stevens and Sons, 1964).

7. US Dept of State, Bureau of Intelligence and Research, *Analysis of the Cyprus Agreements* (Intelligence Report No 8047, 14 July 1959).

8. S. Kyriakides, *Cyprus: Constitutionalism and Crisis Government* (Philadelphia: University of Pensylvania Press, 1968).

9. M. Christodoulou, *H Poreia Mias Epochis* (The Direction of an Era) (Athens: I. Floros, 1987) pp. 318–21.

10. J. W. Lewis Jr, *The Strategic Balance in the Mediterranean* (Washington DC: The American Enterprise Institute, 1976).

11. A classic example is the rejection of the 1965 report by the UN mediator Galo Plaza. This report is one of the most perceptive documents on the Cyprus problem.

12. V. Coufoudakis, 'US Foreign Policy and the Cyprus Question: An Interpretation', *Millennium-Journal of International Studies*, 5, 3 (Winter 1976–77) pp. 45–68.

13. This precedent seems to have been applied in partitions implemented in the 1990s. See the role and powers of the international forces in Bosnia and Kosovo.

14. As in the case of the 1965 Galo Plaza Report in the mediation initiative by the Secretary General, U-Thant, in 1971.

15. B. O'Malley and I. Craig, *The Cyprus Conspiracy* (London and New York: I.B. Tauris Publishers, 1999).

16. H. Kissinger, *Years of Renewal* (New York: Simon & Schuster, 1999) pp. 192–239 and 330–43.

17. Y. P. Pikros, *O Venizelos Kai to Kypriako* (Venizelos and the Cyprus Issue) (Athina: Philippotis, 1980).

18. E. Averoff-Tossizza, *Lost Opportunities – The Cyprus Question 1950–1963* (New Rochelle, NY: Caratzas Publishing Co., 1986); Christodoulou, *The Path* and Xydis, *Cyprus*.

19. The latest examples being the decisions surrounding the deployment of the S-300 anti-aircraft missile system in December 1998 and the impact of the Greek–Turkish *rapprochement* on the current phase of negotiations on Cyprus.

20. Xanthopoulos, Ch. Palamas, *Diplomatiko Triptycho* (Diplomatic Tryptich) (Athens: Ekdoseis Filon, 1978).

21. F. L. Kirgis Jr, *International Organizations in Their Legal Setting: Documents, Comments and Questions* (St Paul, MN: West Publishing Co.) p. 404.

22. The possibility of a Greco–Turkish conflict, the reintegration of Greece in NATO's military wing, etc.

23. As in the case of the Congressionally-imposed arms embargo (1975–78), and in actions at the Council of Europe in cases involving Turkey under the European Convention on Human Rights.

24. M. Christodoulou, *Kypros: He Dichotomisi-Mia Poreia Choris Anakopi* (Nikosia: Proodos, 1996) [in Greek].

25. See Cyprus Intercommunal Talks 1979, p. 23.

26. An old American tactic intended to pre-empt discussion at the UN that could 'negatively impact' a new round of talks on Cyprus.

27. See UN Security Council Resolution 541, 18 November 1983.

28. In particular, the implementation of the 'three freedoms', i.e. movement, settlement and property ownership.

29. Candidate status was granted to Turkey at the Helsinki meeting of the EU in December 1999. Turkey was expected to meet a number of conditions by 2004 prior to the commencement of integration talks.

30. For example, President Clerides and Mr Denktash have been involved in the Cyprus problem since its colonial days.

31. Such as those between President Vassiliou and Mr Denktash in New York July and October 1992; the May 1993 meeting in New York between President Clerides and Mr Denktash, and those of 1997 at Troutbeck, New York, Glion, Switzerland and Nicosia.

32. Informal talks held in London during the spring 1995.

33. The Loizidou ruling, along with the US Federal District Court ruling on the Kanakaria mosaics, had significant political and legal implications. The European Court of Human Rights ruling on the Loizidou case remains unimplemented at this time, despite calls by the Council of Ministers of the Council of Europe for Turkey's compliance.

34. See EAX: Arvanitopoulos 'Greek', pp. 163–4.

35. These anti-aircraft missiles had a range of 150 miles. They were capable of shooting down aircraft flying out of bases in southern Turkey. Given the geographic location of Cyprus, Turkey elicited American and Israeli help on this issue by arguing that these missiles could also affect their security interests as well.
36. T. Gabelnick, W. Hartung and J. Washburn, *Arming Repression: US Arms Sales to Turkey During the Clinton Administration* (New York: World Policy Institute, 1999).
37. Abdullah Ocalan, the leader of the Kurdish rebellion against Turkey, had been evicted from Syria in October 1988 after Turkey threatened military action against Syria. In his quest for asylum Ocalan received clandestine support from members of the Greek government. He was arrested in Kenya in the spring of 1999 in a joint operation between the US and Turkey.
38. See Helsinki European Council, 10–11 December 1999.
39. See G-8 Statement on Regional Issues, p. 3.
40. *Cyprus Weekly*, 14–20 July 2000, p. 5.
41. *La Stampa*, 2 August 2000, article by Turkish Foreign Minister Cem.

6

Greece and the Balkans in the Twentieth Century

ARISTOTLE TZIAMPIRIS

INTRODUCTION

Greek history in the Balkans during the twentieth century is traumatic and tumultuous, as well as integrally linked to the Macedonian Question, 'the unyielding philosopher's stone of Balkan nationalism'.[1] In the first half of the century, Greek actions were associated with war and expansion, whereas the latter half was characterized by a process of consolidation and relative stability.

During the period 1900 to 1908 a fierce struggle was fought in Ottoman Macedonia by Greek irregular forces primarily against the Bulgarians, eventually succeeding in halting their ascendancy in the region. The result of the subsequent two Balkan Wars (1912–13) that took place almost exclusively in Macedonia, was the doubling of Greece's territory through the incorporation of more than half of the contested region. Some of these lands were briefly lost to Bulgaria during the First World War. Ultimately, though, a much more dynamic danger was posed to Greece by what can be called 'the communist factor'.

Beginning in the 1920s, Greek and Balkan communists attempted to transform the territorial, political and military arrangements in South Eastern Europe (SEE). As regards Greece, the Macedonian Question was again key to developments. Having allied with the Nazis, Bulgaria conquered part of the region. However, it was the communist guerrillas that became the most important force, threatening the loss of national territory in Northern Greece and eventually contesting (but failing) to attain power during the Greek Civil War (1944–49).

The victorious government of Greece thus averted any change of borders or of the régime in Athens, although the quality of the country's democratic arrangements remained unsatisfactory for many years. In terms of foreign policy and regional international relations, what ensued was a long period of peace, stability and limited cooperation among Greece and most Balkan states. In effect, the Cold War 'froze' History in the Balkans.

The end of the Cold War and Yugoslavia's violent dissolution marked the return of History in the region. A passionate dispute broke out between Greece and the Former Yugoslav Republic of Macedonia (FYROM). Arguably, it represented the most recent manifestation of the Macedonia Question. For a period, Greek diplomacy and domestic politics centred around the issue of the new republic's exact name. A tentative resolution of the dispute was only reached in September 1995. More importantly, it appears that Greeks learned some valuable lessons from this 'adventure'.

In the first years of the twenty-first century, Greece views its position and role in the Balkans with confidence. The recent Kosovo conflict and its aftermath demonstrated the positive ways in which the country can contribute towards stability. Prosperous, democratic and a member of the European Union (EU), it can play the role of (one of many) regional leaders, with the intention of assisting all efforts aiming to produce economic development, democratic reforms, respect for human rights and long-term security in SEE.

THE GREEK STRUGGLE IN MACEDONIA

At the turn of the nineteenth century, and despite the defeat in the 1897 war with Turkey, the dominant foreign policy ideology of Greece continued to be that of the *Megali Idea*.[2] Fuelled by feelings of nationalism, and envisioning the incorporation of Ottoman territories within the Greek state, the goal was to unite most of the Hellenes in their own, expanded, nation state. However, similar aspirations prevailed among all Balkan nations. The primary target and focus of these competing nationalisms was Ottoman Macedonia.

Bulgaria in particular seemed to enjoy particular advantages in this contest. In the forefront of the Bulgarian effort was the Macedonian Revolutionary Organisation (IMRO).[3] Founded in Thessaloniki on 3 October 1893, its goal was to 'further Bulgarian plans in Macedonia'.[4] Following increased guerrilla activities in 1902, IMRO decided to organize an uprising, which was declared on 2 August 1903 on Saint Elijah's day (Ilinden).[5] The initially successful Bulgarians captured the town of Krusevo, and proclaimed the short-lived 'Krusevo Republic'.[6] Faced by superior Ottoman forces, it became impossible to maintain military momentum and the uprising began to falter after just three weeks.

IMRO's leaders were aware that it was not feasible to overthrow the

Ottoman rule in Macedonia by military means. Rather, their strategy was based on the expectation that it would provoke Turkish atrocities and thus produce a European public outcry, and a direct Great Power intervention in the region.[7] The uprising ended on 3 November at a significant cost, and with no outside intervention.[8]

Ilinden represented a turning point for Bulgarian efforts in Ottoman Macedonia. It demonstrated their strength and vitality, but also weakened them, not least because it provoked Hellenism's ultimately successful counter-attack.

> Hellenism, in the widest sense of the term [was] a force which in Macedonia was not to be identified solely with the Greek language or race. Hellenism derived largely from the Patriarchal Church; from the flourishing Greek schools; and from a class which enjoyed in some measure an economic superiority, a class which was conservative, which had everything to lose ... Hellenism was a way of life, of which the outward manifestation was the acceptance of the Greek Orthodox Church.[9]

Far-sighted Greeks were able to understand that the Bulgarians represented their most serious and long-term adversaries in Macedonia. So the fact that they aided the Turks in their attempt to quell the Ilinden uprising is understandable.[10] The struggle of Hellenism was carried out by small armed bands, which initially received almost no aid from the Greek government and only limited assistance from private sources. Pavlos Melas, an army officer and a prominent citizen, was the leading organizer of such guerrilla activities in Macedonia. In a letter sent to the Patriarchal Metropolitan of Kastoria Germanos Karavangelis, he poignantly asserted that the Greek Ministry of Foreign Affairs is 'asleep'.[11]

This situation began to change after the killing of Pavlos Melas.[12] News of his fate had a profound effect on public opinion.[13] In conjunction with the shock produced by the Ilinden uprising, the result was a more determined, organized, and better funded Hellenic effort in Macedonia, aimed at weakening Bulgarian military activities. The Greeks also attempted to persuade (or force) villages to abandon the Bulgarian Orthodox Church (*Exarchate*), as well as 'protect and support Greeks who were not afraid to claim a Greek *national* identity and to inculcate it into those who felt only a Greek *Orthodox* identity'.[14] By 1908 these activities had succeeded, at least to the extent that they had 'prevented what later became Greek Macedonia from being lost'.[15]

THE BALKAN WARS AND THE FIRST WORLD WAR

In July 1908 the Young Turk revolution took place. Carried out by army officers in Thessaloniki, it achieved the securing of a constitution for the Ottoman Empire. This development produced a wave of optimism and much rejoicing in Macedonia. Significantly, the various guerrilla groups ceased their activities, though hopes were soon met with disappointment. The Young Turk revolution turned out to be essentially nationalist in character, since its ultimate goal was not only to modernize the Empire, but also to 'Ottomanize' it 'through the complete abolition of the rights and privileges of the different ethnic groups'.[16] Soon after, guerrilla activities resumed.

At the same time, Greece was about to enter a period of national 'renewal'.[17] In 1909, the military intervened in the country's political life, in what is referred to as the 'Goudi "revolution"'.[18] The end result was that the Cretan statesman Eleftherios Venizelos became Prime Minister, and embarked upon a programme of economic, social and military reforms. Characterized by Winston S. Churchill, a contemporary, as 'one of the greatest of men'.[19] Venizelos also took charge of Greece's foreign and security policies with spectacular results.

As regards the Young Turk 'revolution, far from arresting the disintegration of the Empire ... [it] at once accelerated it'.[20] Eventually, the Balkan states agreed upon a series of bilateral alliances. Serbia and Bulgaria signed one in March 1912, while Greece and Bulgaria followed in May.[21] Finally, Montenegro joined in alliances with Serbia and Bulgaria in October.[22] Montenegro also started the First Balkan War by initiating armed hostilities in Macedonia, in which Ottoman forces were outnumbered and, eventually, almost completely thrown out from the Peninsula. Greece managed to capture Thessaloniki, and Bulgaria was consoled with Adrianople. The May 1913 London Conference formalised the new *status quo*.

The victorious Balkan alliances were made possible because a unifying common goal existed: the overthrow of the Ottomans from the Peninsula. Nevertheless, there was considerable uncertainty and vagueness regarding the ways in which the newly liberated territories would be divided among the victors. Thus, despite the military successes in the First Balkan War and subsequent negotiations, 'the great problem of the division of Macedonia remained'.[23]

Desiring a favourable resolution of this contentious issue, Bulgaria decided to attack its former allies and initiated the 1913 Second Balkan War. Without the support of any Great Power, and facing a variety of problems, Bulgaria had actually committed one of the greatest political and military blunders in modern history, and was thus soundly defeated.[24] The August 1913 Treaty of Bucharest gave Greece and Serbia

51.5% and 38.4% of Macedonia respectively; Bulgaria received only
10.1%.[25] Greece had thus managed to almost double its size. Before the
Balkan wars it had a population of 2,631,952 and a territory of 63,211
square kilometres. After 1913, both increased to 4,718,221 and
120,308 respectively.[26]

However, despite this success, a great national schism and division
followed, related to the issue of the country's participation in the First
World War. Both Venizelos and King Konstantine realized that the
Central Powers were more favourably disposed towards Turkey and
Bulgaria. The monarch was convinced that they would emerge victori-
ous, and thus advocated a policy of strict neutrality. On the other hand,
Venizelos believed that the *Entente* would win, and that it was further-
more in Greece's national interest to ally with the great naval power of
the British empire. A struggle between the two leaders was inevitable,
leading to a separate Venizelos government based in Thessaloniki, the
King's abdication, and Greece entering the war in accordance with the
Cretan statesman's wishes. During the First World War, Bulgaria had
succeeded in regaining parts of Greek and Serbian Macedonia, as well as
Western Thrace.[27]

> The Bulgarian occupation authorities in Greek eastern
> Macedonia ... behaved towards the Greek population with
> brutality singularly inappropriate in supposed liberators ...
> 30,000 people ... died of hunger, blows, and disease during
> the occupation ... 42,000 [were] deported to Bulgaria, and ...
> 16,000 ... fled to Greece.[28]

After the defeat of the Central Powers, Bulgaria was once again forced
to abandon its Greek conquests – a development confirmed by the
November 1919 Treaty of Neuilly.[29] Crucially, Venizelos lost the 1920
national election, and the royalist forces pursued unsuccessfully Greece's
military campaign in Asia Minor.[30] Following the conclusion of the 1922
Greek–Turkish War, and the signing of the 1923 Treaty of Lausanne,
more than one million Greeks were forced to leave their ancestral homes
in Asia Minor. Almost half of the refugees were relocated in Greek
Macedonia.[31] As a result of this population transfer, 'Greece [became]
the most homogeneous state in the Balkans, if not of the entire Eastern
Europe'.[32]

THE COMMUNIST FACTOR AND THE SECOND WORLD WAR

The interwar years saw the rise in importance of communist forces,
which quickly moved to exploit national antagonisms and tensions,

especially in Macedonia.[33] The Balkan Communist Federation's position on the region was endorsed and clarified at the May–June 1924 Fifth Comintern Congress:

> The Communist Parties and the Balkan Federation must support to the utmost the national-revolutionary movement of the oppressed nationalities of Macedonia and Thrace *for the creation of independent republics.*[34]

In other words, the territorial settlements reached in the Treaty of Bucharest were being directly challenged, which in turn helps to explain the Bulgarian communist's attempt to persuade the Comintern to accept such a revisionist (and of course revolutionary) policy.[35] Importantly, the Greek Communist Party's (KKE) agreement with the Comintern's position on Macedonia was tantamount to accepting the loss of national territory.

During the period prior to the Second World War, politics in Greece was characterized by turmoil, frequent military interventions and instability. In 1928, Venizelos returned as Prime Minister, and until 1932 pursued a programme of economic modernization[36] and brilliant foreign policy consolidation.[37] His loss of the 1932 elections and death paved the way for Ioannis Metaxas to eventually establish a dictatorship on 4 August 1936.[38]

In 1940, Metaxas refused to accommodate Mussolini's demands, thus precipitating the Greek–Italian War. Greece's army conducted a successful campaign on Albanian soil, briefly liberating the Greek minority residing in the region of Northern Epirus.[39] However, on 6 April 1941 Nazi Germany invaded and occupied Greece.[40] Following the Nazi conquest, Bulgaria (which had joined the Axis Powers), was awarded parts of Greek Macedonia and Thrace. Bulgaria's King Boris III declared triumphantly:

> Thanks to this cooperation [with the Germans and the Italians] Macedonia and Thrace, these lands which have been so loyal to Bulgaria, which have been unjustly detached from her, and for which Bulgaria has been compelled to make innumerous sacrifices in the span of three generations, have now returned to the fold of the Bulgarian Motherland.[41]

Importantly, Bulgaria's occupation forces again exhibited tremendous brutality. 'A German report of the time described the Bulgarian occupation as "a regime of terror which can only be described as Balkan".'[42]

In occupied Greece, a resistance movement was soon organized. Some groups were right-wing (most notably the National Democratic

Greek League – EDES), though it was the KKE that became the major resistance force. The party took advantage of the political vacuum, utilized its experience from operating in a clandestine way and succeeded in setting up EAM (National Liberation Front) and its military wing ELAS (National Popular Liberation Army). Although not everyone associated with EAM was a communist, the organization was ultimately controlled by the KKE.[43]

Within EAM/ELAS, as Evangelos Kofos has explained, there were also Slavophones, not only of the Greek faction, but also persons who distanced themselves both from the Greek and the Bulgarian factions. [Thus] the traditional dichotomy of Slavophones [pro-Greek and pro-Bulgarian] gradually grew into a trichotomy.[44]

In order to exploit this situation, the KKE established the Slav Macedonian Popular Liberation Front (SNOF) in November 1943.[45] Its creation was in accordance with the wishes of the leadership of Yugoslavia's communist partisans, who under the guidance of Josip Broz (*nom de guerre* Tito), had at that point become the most powerful communist force in the Balkans.

As regards Macedonia, Tito aimed at the very least to maintain the part that belonged to Yugoslavia. He also entertained thoughts of uniting parts of Bulgarian and Greek Macedonia 'under his own aegis',[46] a fact that once again demonstrates the importance Macedonia has played in the international politics of the Balkans during this period.

Tito's intentions were partly expressed in the 2 August 1943 creation of the Anti-Fascist Assembly of the National Liberation of Macedonia (ASNOM).[47] On that day, ASNOM declared: 'Macedonians under Bulgaria and Greece! The unification of the entire Macedonian people depends on your participation in the gigantic anti-Fascist front.'[48] ASNOM's declarations form part of the basis on which the Socialist Republic of Macedonia (and subsequently FYROM), were founded. Significantly, they clearly reveal ASNOM's irredentist character and goals. For example, on 4 August 1944 ASNOM proclaimed the following:

> People of Macedonia!
>
> In the course of three years of combat you have achieved your unity … With the participation of the entire Macedonian nation against the Fascist occupiers of Yugoslavia, Bulgaria and Greece you will achieve unification of all parts of Macedonia, divided in 1915 and 1918 by Balkan imperialists.[49]

These irredentist goals represent a significant aspect of the historical background to the dispute between Greece and FYROM that broke out in the 1990s. Suspected adherence to these goals also caused friction between ELAS and SNOF during the final stages of the Second World War. As a result, ELAS and SNOF clashed militarily, and the latter's forces were expelled from Greece in October 1944. By November, the Germans had also left the country.

THE GREEK CIVIL WAR

In December 1940 there were bloody clashes in Athens between communist and government supporters.[50] The KKE was defeated, primarily because of the intervention of British forces. A rather tense situation existed until the February 1945 Varkiza agreement provided for the demobilization of all armed units. Despite this, however, the country did not manage to avoid the descent into civil war.[51]

As was the case with the two Balkan and World Wars, the Macedonian Question also proved of central significance to the Greek Civil War. Greece's relations with the Balkan states (and particularly with Yugoslavia) during these years were primarily connected to this issue. Its importance was initially linked to the creation by Tito in April 1945 of the National Liberation Front (NOF).[52] Composed primarily of former SNOF members, it 'acted as the instrument of the Yugoslav plans in Greek Macedonia'.[53] NOF did not honour the Varkiza agreement and engaged in periodic guerrilla activities in Greek Macedonia. In November 1946, NOF's forces were integrated with those of the KKE's military wing – the Democratic Army of Greece (DSE).

During the Civil War, the DSE managed to control various villages and mountainous regions, although almost all cities and towns remained under constant government control. Despite Tito's backing of the KKE, government forces received substantially more aid from the US.[54] By the 1948/49 winter, communist activities were essentially confined to parts of Western Greek Macedonia.

Facing an acute recruitment problem, the DSE was forced to rely heavily upon Slav-Macedonians. It has been estimated that they represented some 14,000 out of the DSE's total of 20,000 soldiers.[55] Given their important role, the KKE's General Secretary Nikos Zachariades proceeded to change his party's policy on Greek Macedonia. At the KKE's Fifth Plenum on 31 January 1949, the following resolution was passed:

> The Macedonian people are distinguishing themselves, and there must be no doubt that after the liberation, they will find their national restoration as they wish it. Various elements which are trying to break the unity between the Slav-Macedonia and Greek peoples should be guarded against.

This unity should be preserved as 'the pupil of the eye' and should be reinforced and strengthened firmly and continuously.[56]

Any ambiguity was clarified in a statement that was broadcast by the KKE's radio station 'Free Greece':

The Second Conference of the NOF ... will declare the union of Macedonia into a complete, independent, and equal Macedonian nation within the Popular Democratic Federation of the Balkan peoples.[57]

This policy advocated the secession of national Greek territory, and was thus viewed by government forces as treasonous.[58] However, it was never implemented, since in August 1949 the DSE was soundly defeated in the mountainous battlefields of Grammos and Vitsi.

THE 'LONG PEACE' AND THE 'SKOPJE ADVENTURE'

After the end of the Civil War, and with the onset of the Cold War, Greece and its Balkan neighbours found themselves belonging to different and opposing sides. Paradoxically though, it was precisely the Cold War that necessitated a halt in irredentist aspirations. Given the international politics of the era regional military actions were not contemplated, not least because they could potentially escalate into a Superpower confrontation. Thus, the period of 1950–89 can aptly be characterised as the 'Long Peace', since it represents a continuous and almost unprecedented time of relative stability and absence of war in the Balkans.

These peaceful years witnessed a gradual, limited improvement in bilateral and multilateral relations among the states of South Eastern Europe. Particularly impressive (especially given the history of the previous five decades), were the cooperative agreements that were signed between Greece and Bulgaria.[59] Bulgarian nationalism thus seemed to be entering a period of hibernation, since almost no irredentist claims were made against Greece and Yugoslavia, even on the level of rhetoric.

Greece also cooperated with Tito's Yugoslavia, the latter often being instrumental in securing the UN votes of non-aligned states in favour of the Hellenic side on the Cyprus issue. However, a point of dispute (albeit low key), remained that of irredentist propaganda often related to the existence of a 'Macedonian' minority in Greece.[60]

Relations with Albania were somewhat more problematic but of rather peripheral importance, given the country's extreme isolationist policies.

The fate of the Greek minority residing in Northern Epirus remained an emotional and sensitive issue, contributing to the continuous existence of a legal state of war between the two countries until 1988.

Greece's Balkan relations improved even more after the collapse of the Greek Junta (1967–74).[61] The subsequent Greek Prime Ministers Konstantinos Karamanlis and Andreas Papandreou explored new areas of cooperation especially on economic and technical issues, and appeared determined to maintain a stable and positive situation in SEE.[62] However, the Cold War was approaching its end. After the events of 1989, and the dissolution of the USSR in 1991, it became apparent that the forces of nationalism and violence would be unleashed in Yugoslavia.

The dissolution of Yugoslavia accelerated in the summer of 1991, when the republics of Croatia and Slovenia declared their independence. The Yugoslav Republic of Macedonia followed suit on 8 September, eventually eliciting a strong and at times furious Greek reaction. Given Greece's dramatic twentieth century history, it can perhaps be better understood that 'Greek attitudes toward Macedonian developments are so emotional that Greeks tend to magnify well out of proportion events or situations ... or keep a discreet silence'.[63] In the case of the 1990s dispute with FYROM, the people and most of the country's political leadership adopted a particularly vocal stance.

On 15 December 1991, the European Community's Foreign Ministers met and decided upon the criteria that would be utilized in recognizing the various new republics. As regards FYROM, there was agreement that it should:

> adopt constitutional and political guarantees ensuring that it has no territorial claims towards a neighbouring Community State and that it will conduct no hostile propaganda activities versus a neighbouring Community State, *including the use of a denomination which implies territorial claims* (EPC Press Release P. 128/91 16 December 1991; emphasis added).[64]

The latter of these three conditions proved particularly controversial and consequential. On 14 February 1992 one million people demonstrated in Thessaloniki, endorsing a resolution that contained the following passage:

> The Greek government is called upon to stand by the spirit and message of [this] resolution and demonstration. The people of Macedonia and Thessaloniki request from the Foreign minister that he continues to fight, and not accept the recognition of the state of Skopje [FYROM] with a name or designation that will include the name Macedonia.[65]

The Thessaloniki demonstration linked the issue of FYROM's name with the passions of almost a tenth of the country's population. After 14 February the people became active actors in Greece's diplomatic efforts on a specific issue, thus initiating a period of conflation between foreign policy, domestic politics and nationalism.[66]

Popular opinion was expressed by Greek Foreign Minister Antonis Samaras who pressured his government, which had only a slim majority in Parliament, to adopt a restrictive interpretation of the third condition. According to such an interpretation (consistent with the Thessaloniki resolution) the word Macedonia could not be included in any way in the new republic's name. This became Greece's official and near-unanimous position following a meeting of the leaders of the political parties on 13 April 1992.[67]

As a result, Greek foreign policy towards all issues emanating from the dissolution of Yugoslavia became subordinate to the issue of FYROM's name.[68] Furthermore, all subsequent mediation efforts were rejected by Greece for not conforming to the strict understanding of the third condition.[69] More specifically, Portugal's Foreign Minister Pinheiro proposed a package deal that included the name 'New Macedonia', while retired British Ambassador O'Neil suggested 'Macedonia (Skopje)'. Under the auspices of the United Nations, Cyrus Vance and David Owen attempted to strike a compromise on the basis of the name 'Nova Makedonija', again to no avail.

In the October 1993 general elections the conservative government of Konstantinos Mitsotakis was defeated. The new socialist Prime Minister Andreas Papandreou upheld the official policy towards FYROM's name, and also imposed an embargo on the intransigent young republic. A world outcry against Greece and a weakened FYROM created conditions for a compromise. An Interim Agreement was signed by the two states in September 1995 covering all areas of dispute with the exception of that of the name.[70] Bilateral relations subsequently improved, especially in the realms of trade and investment.

Greece's adventure with FYROM – or Skopje as it was popularly called – provided a series of important lessons. First, the country's diplomacy paid a high price because it was perceived by the international community as being part of the problem in the Balkans. It thus became evident that Greece not only benefits from regional stability, but must also strive to achieve and retain a reputation as a state effectively contributing towards stability in SEE.

It also became apparent that in the pursuit of foreign policy objectives, a hierarchy of goals and threats ought to be clearly defined. The '*skopjenization*' of Greece's foreign policy had the effect of diverting scarce resources and attention from other important and pressing issues. The 1996 Imia crisis demonstrated that Turkey and not FYROM represented a far more significant danger to national security.

Finally, the dangers of conflating partisan politics, personal animosities and popular passions behind specific foreign policy positions were widely recognized. At the very least, such a development limits the flexibility that is required in the effective pursuit of diplomacy. As will be shown next, all of these lessons were utilized during the 1999 Kosovo conflict, and seem to be guiding Greece's contemporary actions and policies towards the Balkans.

GREECE AND THE BALKANS IN THE TWENTY-FIRST CENTURY

Today, Greece is the only state in SEE that is a member of both the EU and North Atlantic Treaty Organisation (NATO), as well as of all the other major international organizations. It possesses the most dynamic and prosperous economy in the region, and has also secured a functioning and stable democratic system. Based on the realization of this situation, and having incorporated the lessons of the 1991–95 'Skopje adventure', a more positive outlook and strategy towards the Balkans has ensued.

Greece is not a revisionist state, and does not entertain any territorial ambitions of any kind. Furthermore, it has no illusion (or desire) to become the Balkan's hegemon. Greek goals are realistic and measured. The country aims to be one of many leaders in SEE, trying to encourage reform, stability and economic development. In the pursuit of this role, Greece enjoys certain advantages compared to other states and international actors. Of particular importance is that it possesses a more sophisticated and intimate knowledge of Balkan history. Also, it shares common interests and often common perspectives with other SEE countries. In this sense, Greece could on occasion represent the regional point of view more effectively and accurately in various international fora.

Greece's new Balkan outlook and strategy was exhibited during the Kosovo conflict. Despite popular passions overwhelmingly opposed to NATO's bombing campaign, both the government and the major opposition party exhibited realistic and mature attitudes. Both advocated a political solution to the dispute, which in the long run is the only viable and stable option. To the opposition's great credit, no efforts were made to 'score' partisan or personal points by exploiting popular views of developments in Kosovo; nor was there an attempt to incite the populace into violent demonstrations.

Despite the upheaval in the Balkans, the Greek government entertained absolutely no thoughts of advocating or trying to achieve changes in borders. Also, although there was no direct military participation in the bombings, Greece (correctly assessing its power and hierarchy of needs) did not veto NATO's actions, thus avoiding the potential 'wrath' of the United States and other powerful states.[71]

When the Kosovo conflict ended, Greece stressed the region's need for help, reform and reconstruction in areas such as infrastructure, crime, security, public administration, civil society, human rights and ethnic toleration. The Stability Pact for South Eastern Europe was thus supported as the framework organization that could organize international efforts to aid the Balkans. Recently, Greece's Foreign Minister George Papandreou explained that 'the Stability Pact can be the incubator of a new contract for the Balkans ... we need to empower [SEE] ... [the] Balkanization of the region ... must be replaced by coordination of international efforts...[and by] cooperation within the region'.[72]

Based on the above, it can be argued that during the Kosovo conflict and its aftermath, Greece behaved in an almost exemplary manner. The lessons of the 'Skopje adventure' were put into practice. Partisan and personal disputes did not seriously affect or determine the country's foreign policy. Actions were based upon a realistic assessment of the extent of Greece's influence and power. Furthermore, Greece successfully managed to be perceived by the international community as contributing towards the solution of the crisis, and not as a cause of it. Most significantly though, Greece eschewed any opportunism and focused upon the importance of stability in the Balkans, advocating and assisting in the implementation of international aid programmes for the entire region.

After a century that included costly wars, dramatic disputes and traumatic struggles, Greece is actively pursuing a new role in the Balkans. The country's ultimate goal is to be perceived as a beacon of reform, and as a confident, prosperous, democratic 'stabilizer'. Although the historical record stands against such a prospect, the Kosovo conflict and recent developments strongly suggest that we are witnessing a thoroughly transformed situation. Greece's history and role in the Balkans during the twenty-first century will most likely be entirely different in quality, intensity and outcome from that of the previous one hundred years.

NOTES

1.   M. Glenny, *The Balkans 1804–1999: Nationalism, War and the Great Powers* (London: Granta Books, 1999) p. 156.
2.   K. R. Legg and J. M. Roberts, *Modern Greece* (Boulder, CO: Westview Press, 1997) p. 18.
3.   For IMRO's subsequent history and mutations, see V. Vlasidis, 'The Autonomy of Macedonia: From Theory to Action', in V. Gounaris *et al.*, *Identities in Macedonia* (Athens: Papazisis, 1997).
4.   Vasidis, 'The Autonomy', pp. 65–6.

5. The decision to organize the Ilinden uprising was taken on 17 January 1903. See D. Perry, *The Politics of Terror* (Durham: Duke University Press, 1988) pp. 121–4; for a discussion of this fateful meeting. For accounts of the Ilinden uprising, see H. N. Brailsford, 'The Macedonian Revolt', *Fortnightly Review*, 74, 1903, pp. 428–44 and H. N. Brailsford, **Macedonia: Its Races and Their Future** (1906) pp. 111–71; D. Daikin, *The Greek Struggle in Macedonia 1897–1913* (Thessaloniki: Institute for Balkan Studies, 1966) pp. 92–107; E. Kofos, *Nationalism and Communism in Macedonia* (Thessaloniki: Institute for Balkan Studies,1964) pp. 33–6; and Perry, *The Politics*, pp. 127–40. It should also be noted that the diaries that Ion Dragoumis kept during the Ilinden uprising were recently published and make fascinating reading. See I. Dragoumis, *The Ilinden Notebooks* (Athens: Petziva, 2000).

6. Whether the Ilinden uprising was the work of Bulgarians or Slavs with a national 'Macedonian' consciousness has been disputed. Significantly, H. N. Brailsford, who eyewitnessed the events, devoted a chapter in his book *Macedonia Its Races and Their Future* to the Ilinden uprising, that was titled 'The Bulgarian Movement'. See H. N. Brailsford, *Macedonia*, p. 111.

7. I. Dragoumis, *Martyr's and Hero's Blood* (Athens: Nea Thesis, 1907/1992) p. 22; and Perry, *The Politics*, pp. 124–5 and 138. Particularly noteworthy are the striking historical parallels and similarities between IMRO's Ilinden strategy, and that pursued by the Kosovo Liberation Army (KLA) in Kosovo, almost a century later.

8. For the destructive results of the Ilinden uprising, see Daikin, *The Greek Struggle*, p. 104; Gounaris *et al.*, *The Events*, pp. 185–97; and Perry, *The Politics*, p. 140.

9. Daikin, *The Greek Struggle*, pp. 117–18.

10. Brailsford, *Macedonia*, pp. 129–30; and Perry, *The Politics*, pp. 137–8.

11. G. Karavangelis, n.d., *Memoirs* (Thessaloniki: Barbounakis) p. 42.

12. For an account of Melas' death and funeral, see *ibid.*, pp. 60–71.

13. Daikin, *The Greek Struggle*, p. 191; and Dragoumis, *Martyr's*, p. 9.

14. Emphasis in the original, see I. Koliopoulos, 'Brigandage and Irredentism in Nineteenth-Century Greece', *European History Quarterly*, 19, p. 209.

15. Daikin, *The Greek Struggle*, p. 475.

16. Carnegie Endownment, *The Other Balkan Wars* (Washington DC: Carnegie Endownment, 1914/1993) p. 35.

17. B. Theodoropoulos, *Review: The Foreign Policy of Modern Greece* (Athens: Sideris, 1996) p. 72 [in Greek].

18. See, V. Papacosmas, *The Army in the Politial Life of Greece* (Athens: Vivliopolion its Estias, 1981). The army's involvement in Greek politics remained of often extreme importance until 1974. For a classic study, see T. Veremis, *The Military in Greek Politics: From Independence to Democracy* (London: Hurst and Co, 1997).

19. W. S. Churchill, *The Aftermath* (Norwalk: The Easton Press, 1929/1991) p. 379.

20.

21. Significantly, the agreement between Greece and Bulgaria did not cover post-victory territorial settlements.

22. B. Jelavich, *History of the Balkans: Twentieth Century* (Cambridge: Cambridge University Press, 1983) p. 97; and K. Vacalopoulos, *The Macedonian Question* (Thessaloniki: Paratiritis, 1992) p. 347.

23. See, Jelavich, *History*, p. 99. It should be noted that 'by the end of May [1913] the Greeks and Serbs had signed a secret agreement to divide Macedonia west of the Vardar and to allow the fate of the areas east of that river to be determined by the principle of effective occupation'. J. R. Crampton, *A Short History of Modern Bulgaria* (Cambridge: Cambridge University Press, 1987) p. 61.

24. Crampton, *A Short History*, pp. 61–2; and Jelavich, *History*, p. 99.

25. Kofos, *Nationalism*, p. 44.

26. *History of the Greek Nation, Modern Hellenism From 1881 to 1913*, 14 (Athens: Ekdotiki Athinon, 1977) p. 354 [in Greek].

27. For an account of the events and consequences of the First World War in the Balkans, see Jelavich, *History*, pp. 106–33. For an excellent analysis of Bulgaria's foreign policy concerning Western Thrace during the years 1919–23, see M. Stavrinou-Paximadopoulou, *Western Thrace in Bulgaria's Foreign* Policy (Athens: Gutenberg, 1997) [in Greek].

28. E. Barker, *Macedonia: Its Place in Balkan Power Politics* (London: Royal Institute of

International Affairs, 1950) pp. 29–30.
29. A Greek–Bulgarian Convention was also signed, which allowed for the voluntary exchange of populations between Greece and Bulgaria. As a result, according to the League of Nations, by 1926 only some 77,000 Bulgarians were left residing in Greek. Other scholars put the number to 200,000 or even 240,000. See respectively, D. H. Close and T. Veremis, 'The Military Struggle', in D. H. Close (ed.) *The Greek Civil* War (London: Routledge, 1993) p. 98; and A. Rossos, 'Document: The Macedonians of Aegean Macedonia: A British Officer's Report 1994', *Slavonic and East European Review*, 69 (1991) p. 285.
30. L. M. Smith, *Ionian Vision: Greece in Asia Minor 1919–1922* (London: Hurst and Company, 1998).
31. A. Karakasidou, *Fields of Wheat, Hills of Blood* (Chicago: Chicago University Press, 1997) p. 145; and I. Koliopoulos, 'The War Over the Identity and Numbers of Greece's Slav Macedonians', in P. Mackridge and E. Yannakakis (eds) *Ourselves and Others* (Oxford: Berg, 1997) p. 51.
32. Kofos, *Nationalism*, p. 47.
33. The interwar years also witnessed IMRO's decline. See Barker, *Macedonia*, p. 45.
34. *Ibid.*, p. 58. Emphasis added.
35. Bulgaria's revisionism was also highlighted by the fact that the country was excluded by Romania, Yugoslavia and Greece who were the signatories of the 1934 Balkan Pact, as well as *status quo* powers. See C. Svolopoulos, 'Cooperation and Confrontation in the Balkans: An Historical Overview', in Van Coufoudakis *et al.*, *Greece and the New Balkans: Challenges and Opportunities* (New York: Pella, 1999) pp. 21–2.
36. See, Y. Mavrogordatos and C. Hadjiiosif, *Venizelismos and Middle Class Modernization* (Irakleio: Panepistimiakes Ekdoseis Kritis, 1989) [in Greek].
37. See, K. Karamanlis, *Eleftherios Venizelos and Our International Relations 1928–1932* (Athens: Elliniki Ethnoekdotiki, 1986).
38. R. Higham and T. Veremis (eds) *Aspects of Greece 1936–40: The Metaxas Dictatorship* (Athens: ELIAMEP and the Vryonis Center, 1993); and P. J. Vatikiotis, *Popular Autocracy in Greece 1936–41* (London: Frank Cass, 1998).
39. For Mussolini's decision to conquer Greece, see E. Averof-Tositsa, *Fire and Axe* (Athens: Vivliopolion tis Estias, 1996) p. 52 and Jelavich, *History*, pp. 227–8 (in Greek). For an analysis of Metaxas' statesmanship during this period that culminated with the rejection of Italia's ultimatum on 28 October 1940, see I. Koliopoulos, *Metaxas' Dictatorship and the War of '40* (Thessaloniki: Vanias , 1994) pp. 137–245.
40. Some parts of Greece were also occupied by Italy. For an excellent study of occupied Greece, see M. Mazower, *Inside Hitler's Greece* (London: Yale University Press, 1993).
41. Kofos, *Nationalism*, p. 100.
42. H. Poulton, *The Balkans* (London: Minority Right's Publications, 1991/93) p. 177.
43. EAM did not openly espouse or promote a Marxist revolutionary agenda.
44. E. Kofos, *The Impact of the Macedonian Question on Civil Conflict in Greece (1943–1949)* (Athens: Hellenic Foundation for Defence and Foreign Policy, 1989) p. 7.
45. On the SNOF, see Barker, *Macedonia*, pp. 110–12; Kofos, *Nationalism*, pp. 123–7; and I. Koliopoulos, *Pillage of Beliefs* I (Thessaloniki: Vanias, 1995) pp. 113–38 [in Greek].
46. Barker, *Macedonia*, p. 53.
47. The date was significant, since 2 August is Ilinden.
48. H. Poulton, *Who are the Macedonians?* (London: Hurst and Company, 1995) pp. 105–6.
49. *Ibid.*, p. 106.
50. L. Baerentzen and D. H. Close, 'The British Defeat of EAM, 1944–5', in D. H. Close (ed.) *The Greek Civil War* (London: Routledge, 1993) pp. 84–92; and D. H. Close, *The Origins of the Greek Civil War* (London: Routledge, 1995) pp. 137–49.
51. Numerous books have been written on the Greek Civil War. Of particular merit are Close, *The Greek*, 1993; J. O. Iatrides (ed.) *Greece in the 1940's* (Hanover: University Press of New England, 1981); and C. M. Woodhouse, *The Struggle for Greece, 1941–9* (London: Hart-Davis and MacBibbon, 1976) p. 262. .
52. Barker, *Macedonia*, pp. 118–28; Kofos, *The Impact*, pp. 17–21; I. S. Koliopoulos, *Pillage of Beliefs II* (Thessaloniki: Vanias, 1995) pp. 25 and 31 and 146–69 [in Greek].
53. Kofos, *Nationalism*, p. 107.
54. Close and Veremis, 'The Military', p.108.

55. Woodhouse, *The Struggle,* p. 262.
56. Barker, *Macedonia,* p. 119.
57. *Ibid.,* p. 120.
58. The KKE eventually abandoned and condemned this policy. See Kofos, *Nationalism,* pp. 221–3.
59. For an incisive analysis of the common national interests between Bulgaria and Greece during this period, see Y. Valinakis, *With Vision and Program: Foreign Policy for A Confident Greece* (Thessaloniki: Paratiritis and ELIAMEP, 1997) p. 158.
60. For example, see N. I. Mertzos, *We the Macedonians* (Athens: Sideris, 1992) pp. 403–46.
61. C. M. Woodhouse, *The Rise and Fall of the Greek Colonels* (London: Hart-Davis and MacGibbon, 1985).
62. Svolopoulos, 'Cooperation', pp. 25–6.
63. E. Kofos, 'The Macedonian Question: The Politics of Mutation', *Balkan Studies,* 27, p. 162.
64. EPC (European Political Cooperation) Press Release P. 128/91, 16 December 1991; emphasis added.
65. *Makedonia,* 15 February 1992.
66. A huge demonstration was held in Athens in December 1992; and there were again gigantic demonstrations in both Athens and Thessaloniki in 1994.
67. Only the KKE's General Secretary Aleka Papariga did not endorse the meeting's conclusions. For an account, see A. Tziampiris, *Greece, European Political Cooperation and the Macedonian Question* (Aldershot: Ashgate Press, 2000) pp. 122–5.
68. *Ibid.*
69. E. Kofos, 'Greek Foreign Policy Considerations Over FYROM Independence and Recognition', *The New Macedonian Question* (London: Macmillan, 1999).
70. C. Rozakis, *Political and Legal Dimensions of the New York Interim Agreement Between Greece and FYROM* (Athens: Sideris, 1996) [in Greek].
71. In addition, some unusually well informed and perceptive commentaries and analyses of the conflict originated in Greece. See especially T. Veremis, *Kosovo: The Long-Dawn Crisis* (Athens: Sideris, 2000).
72. *International Herald Tribune,* 21 October 2000.

PART III

The Political Scene:
Consolidating Democracy*

FOTINI BELLOU

Contemporary democracy, as a form of political system and governance, finds its roots in modern European Liberalism, yet in Greece it went through several turbulent decades in the twentieth century before being consolidated in the 1970s. In the early part of the twentieth century Greece was experiencing a cyclical period with intervals of democratic rule periodically interrupted by frequent military interventions.[1] The country entered a comprehensive democratization process only after 1974, in the wake of the colonels' junta (1967–74). As this article suggests, the process that started in 1974 demonstrated its sustainability almost a decade later, in 1981, through the peaceful and consensual political transition from conservative to socialist governance. Additional elements bolstering democratic consolidation gradually were embedded in Greece's political system as a result of the country's membership (1981) in the European Communities (EC), later the European Union, (EU).[2] By the end of the century, Greece managed to have attained a belated yet quickly evolving civil society, even if its full formation is yet to be accomplished. The main purpose of this chapter is to give the broader picture of the consolidation of democracy in Greece coupled by an examination of the elements that supported this process.

This chapter begins with an examination of the transition of the Greek polity from authoritarianism to democratic governance and continues with an analysis of the democratization process that was augmented after 1974. A presentation of the strengthening of the Greek democratic institutions as a result of the country's membership in the EC/EU will follow. It is argued that democratic consolidation in Greece resulted from a combination of factors the most important of which were the role and qualities of political leaderships (both conservative and socialist) in pursuing mainly a 'top-down' democratization process. Indeed, as Couloumbis has advocated, both leaders (Constantine

Karamanlis and Andreas Papandreou) demonstrated strong transform-
ing leadership in moving Greece's rudimentary society towards a stable
and democratic society, notwithstanding their differences in ideological
orientation and political statesmanship.[3]

However, as it will be shown, the fact that this process was by and
large incorporated into the struggle of the ruling parties to accumulate
power, through their efforts to patronize and control interest groups
and associations, may explain the considerable delays and at times fragmentation in the establishment of a comprehensive civil society in
Greece. In addition, Greece's membership into the EC/EU played a
profound role, again in a clear 'top-down' fashion, in consolidating
important aspects of democratic practice in Greek political life and
society.

DEMOCRACY IN TURMOIL:
AUTHORITARIANISM VERSUS PARLIAMENTARISM

The parliamentary political system of the nineteenth century had
become fully operational in Greece years before it was to be experienced
in other Western European countries. Yet, the 'monolithic' (top-down)
mode according to which it was established reflects a differentiated
nuance in the tradition of democratic governance. According to some
critics, parliamentarianism developed as the result of a power struggle
between élites rather than out of a social contract between the rulers and
the ruled.[4] Thus, although electorate rights had been largely proclaimed
for all male citizens since 1843 and were substantiated by the constitution of 1864,[5] parliamentary institutions were based on 'top-down'
power politics that was stripping democracy in Greece from its interac-
tive, reciprocal dimension between the political élite, on the one hand,
and the urge for political accountability on the other, as this was
supposed to be demanded by the grassroots.[6]

Since its inception, in the early 1830s, the modern Greek state was
characterized by the struggle of political parties (parties of notables
rather than of principle) to prevail against their opponents. The prime
objective of the political leaders was less to serve public interest in the
universalist sense of the term than to acquire the prerogative to allocate
patronage, namely to provide their constituents (in this case clients)
with the prospect of being recruited in the civil service (or state bureaucracy), which was regarded as the only source of employment in the
largely underdeveloped economy of the time.[7] Political parties suffered
not only from a lack of organizational and ideological bases but also
from high levels of clientelism in a Constitutional Monarchy setting
since the early 1830s. Both constitutions of 1844 and 1864 provided for

extended royal powers including the right to dissolve parliament, to dismiss or appoint ministers, to contract treaties and to declare war. The practice of the monarchy (after 1863 King George I – a Danish prince of the Glücksburg dynasty) to bless governments formed by leaders of minority parties of its liking had compounded an already unstable and personalistic political system which hardly resembled the second half of its denomination as 'Crowned Democracy' (*Vasilevomeni Dimocratia*). An important step in the direction of majoritarian rule was the decision by King George to accept the principle of the *dedilomeni* in 1875, meaning the obligation of the King to call the leader of the party that enjoyed the *declared* support of the majority in Parliament to form a government.[8]

Compared to the nineteenth century when Greece's parliamentary institutions were just about on a par with those functioning in advanced countries like Britain and France, the first seventy-four years of the twentieth century brought about a serious setback. Following the Balkan Wars (1912–13), the First World War, and the disastrous (for Greece), Greek–Turkish war (1921–22) the country entered a period of political instability or what Elias Nicolacopoulos has referred to as κακεκτική δημοκρατία (stunted democracy).[9]

One of the major destabilizing factors was the influx of 1.5 million refugees from Asia Minor following Greece's defeat by the forces of Kemal Ataturk's Turkey. In the period of 1922–36 (prior to the imposition of Ioannis Metaxas' dictatorship in 1936), there were over twenty attempts (coups and attempted coups) by a divided military along royalist versus republican lines. The monarchy, like an accordion, was in and out of Greece depending on the prevailing side, and the plebiscites on the fate of the monarchy in the 1920s and 1930s were notoriously tampered with. The Second World War visited Greece with a new and more pernicious schism (separating Greeks into communists and nationalists), adding to the vulnerability of Greece's polity.

FROM THE SECOND WORLD WAR POLITICS TO THE COLONELS' DICTATORSHIP

Following the Second World War, the Axis occupation and a destructive civil war, which had plagued Greek politics for more than a decade, the country started to experience astonishing levels of development. It took place in almost all key aspects of life. In other words, there was a virtual *metamorphosis* of Greece, which from a position of a quasi-underdeveloped country with a highly traditional society, it crossed the threshold of modernity. In the early 1950s, Greece achieved economic growth rates averaging around 6.6 while moving fast toward light forms of industrialization. Although in this period (1950–70) the economic performance and societal development of the country was remarkable,[10] political stability was not analogous and the role of the military, as has been already discussed, was frequently instrumental in determining political developments. Hence, one could argue that whereas a great economic, social and demographic transformation of the country was taking place during the 1950s and 1960s, it was only in the post-dictatorship years (1974 onwards) that Greece experienced a deep democratization process. As Sotiropoulos rightly observes:

> From the end of the Second World War until the advent of the colonels' régime (1967) the Greek state was more of a tool than an arena. It was the organizational tool of the conservative political class, which having defeated the Left in the Civil War, used the state to keep the Centre and the Left parties out of power and to intervene heavily in the rapid and uneven economic development of Greece in the post-war era.[11]

Indeed, one could observe three major structural weaknesses that constrained the process of democratization in Greek politics. The first weakness was political discrimination against Left and leftist segments thus reinforcing a 'particularistic' state policy. Specifically, the anti-communist state that was formed in the wake of the civil war was characterized by its constant efforts to exclude those social groups and political associations which might have had even an indirect affiliation with the defeated Left. Thus, the vanquished side in the civil war was totally excluded from positions in the armed forces and civil service. This also meant that clientelism continued to flourish to the extent that people with strong political connections with the ruling right-wing political élite were systematically appointed to influential state positions irrespective of their qualifications. In this context, irrationality, ineffectiveness and restricted access of the citizens to civil service structures usually encouraged ineptitude and corruption. The state sector started to expand dramatically and as a consequence the state became the mass employer in Greek society while, at the same time, suffering from low productivity.

A second structural weakness in that period was the 'particularistic' rationale in the way in which different social groups were integrated in the country's development. The social and economic benefits of the country's development were distributed unequally among the elements of society. The state enjoyed the wherewithal to satisfy primarily (frequently exclusively) the needs of particular interest groups. This approach functioned at the expense of a more rational and inclusive policy that could render the state apparatus as a reliable and accountable political structure in Greece. Importantly, this resulted in the division of the society between the satisfied Right and the excluded Left. This governmental attitude afflicted Greek society in several respects; it dimmed any prospect for establishing civil society, it marginalized state accountability, it created a growing number of political acolytes who supported the maintenance of the established political situation and, finally, it created a strong perception of exclusion among a large segment of society which continued well into the democratization years (1974 onwards).

As a consequence of the above, a final structural weakness was that the state evolved into a paternalistic, protective and inflexible set of institutions. Progressively small entrepreneurial units developed which were characterized by meagre and non-competitive production while being dependent on state interference and control. These processes became more acute during the dictatorial rule but were manifesting themselves also in its aftermath.[12]

DEMOCRACY IN POST-AUTHORITARIAN GREECE

In order to comprehend the degree to which democracy in Greece is fully consolidated, this analysis will follow the framework offered by Gunther *et al.*[13] In their view, 'in order to conclude that democratic consolidation has succeeded in a particular case, it is necessary first to ascertain whether the régime is fully democratic and then to determine if that régime is consolidated'.[14] Accordingly, the elements that manifest the democratic nature of the régime that assumed power following the fall of the junta in 1974 should be presented. Reference to some historical data is necessary at this point in order to place the decisions of the Greek political leadership on democratization in perspective. Constantine Karamanlis was appointed Prime Minister on 24 July 1974 to head a government of national unity after being called on from his self-imposed exile in Paris. This followed the fall of the Colonels' junta which took place in the wake of the junta-managed coup against Archbishop Makarios and the Turkish invasion of Cyprus. These events generated political chaos in Greece and brought the country to the brink of war with Turkey. On 26 September Karamanlis declared the formation of a new party, *Nea Dimocratia* (New Democracy–ND), which was described as an inclusive party covering the centre right political space. A few days later he announced (October 1974) that four months after his return to Greece, free and fully democratic elections would take place in Greece (17 November), the result of which would be fully respected by all parties while a referendum would follow in order to determine the status of the monarchy.[15]

An evolution in a number of parameters comprised the ingredients of the democratization process that was taking place in the Greek political system of the time. In particular, there was a distancing from power of persons or groupings not politically accountable to democratic principles. It meant in practice the end of the monarchy as it had been practised in Greece (especially in the 1963–67 period), the abolition of the erstwhile military interference in politics and the reduction of a hitherto almost institutionalized, international tutelage of the country (mainly by the United States after the Second World War). This was the context in which democratization in Greece was experienced.

It has been proposed that democratization of Greek political life involved five elements which can be regarded as the basic characteristics of the period between 1974–81.[16] The first was the establishment of democratically accountable institutions, especially a democratically elected parliament, guaranteeing the values of legitimacy, inclusiveness and accountability. The second characteristic was the widening of the country's political spectrum by the appearance of the *Panellinio Socialistiko Kinima* (PASOK), led by Andreas Papandreou, which introduced a Left, non-communist dimension in Greek politics. The third element of the democratization process was the modernization *per se* of the Greek Right, by abandoning its traditional anti-communism and its past tendency to tolerate military intervention in politics moved towards a new, more moderate political profile, this time around the centre.[17] Its new name, *Nea Dimocratia*, reflected the climate of the time and manifested an unprecedented inclusiveness in its partisan orientation.[18] The fourth element, of course, was the legalization of Greek communist parties that had been forbidden to function legally prior to 1974.

One could argue that the modernization of the Right did not materialize solely out of a political/strategic expediency. Rather, it indicated the political maturity of the new Right (and perhaps more than anything else its leader, Constantine Karamanlis) to appear flexible and adaptive to the new political environment so as not to exclude the rising forces of the Left, which undoubtedly had played a critical but not exclusive role in the campaign against the Greek junta. Indeed, the appearance of mass parties (Right and Left) which were able to organize segments of the public in favour of or against the political predilections of the government was the fifth important characteristic of democratization in Greece. As Diamandouros has advocated, these were the characteristics that marked the restoration of democracy in Greece.[19] In addition, they signalled the efforts of the state to move in parallel with other Western political systems.

The newly established *Nea Democratia*, led by Constantine Karamanlis, after a landslide victory in the November 1974 elections, proceeded towards a mode of governance that marked the dawn of an era known as *metapolitefsi*.[20] As was mentioned above, one of the most important ingredients in the democratization process that was set forth by the newly established government was its decision to legitimize the inclusion of communist parties within the Greek political system. This stance sowed the seeds of the learning process towards the consolidation of democracy in the Greek polity by bridging the gap, in fact the real political schism, between the hitherto excluded Left and the privileged Right, which had afflicted Greek political life since the 1930s. According to Juan Linz, a system can be regarded as democratic

> when it allows the free formulation of political preferences, through the use of basic freedoms of association, information, and communication, for the purpose of free competition between leaders to validate at regular intervals by nonviolent means their claim to rule, ... without excluding any effective political office from that competition or prohibiting any members of the political community from expressing their preference.[21]

Hence, political plurarism, expressed by the inclusion of different political perspectives in the Greek political system, enhanced the democratization process that was also encouraged by the ruling centre-right government of Constantine Karamanlis. There should be no doubt that this move was initiated in a 'top-down' fashion. In particular, it was the decision of the Karamanlis government to legalize in August 1974 the *Kommounistiko Komma Elladas* (Communist Party of Greece, KKE) which had been declared as illegal since 1947.[22] Certainly, the political juncture of the time was favouring rather than discouraging the inclusion of the Left in politics. However, it is particularly important that inclusion of the Left did not provoke what in the past would have been vociferous opposition.

The fair and democratic plebiscite that was conducted (8 December 1974) resolved another political debate, namely the political schism between those who supported parliamentary democracy and those loyal to a form of constitutional monarchy. The clear preference of the public, expressed by almost 70% of the electorate voting against restoration of the monarchy, put the final nail in the Greek monarchy's coffin. The country's political evolution and its democratic transition rested thereafter on the political parties which appeared as the primary means of motivating the public in this direction.

Civil society was particularly weak while the public, suppressed and weak until then, was unable to articulate initiatives towards democratization in a 'bottom-up' mode. Hence, the leverage that political parties gained, and most importantly those with considerable majorities, at times functioned at the expense of the creation of a strong civil society. In spite of the implementation of democratic principles, the intention of major party leaders to control key aspects of political life and to avoid losing the prerogatives that had accompanied a weak civil society, led to the creation of a political structure in which an all-powerful state executive prevailed and was underpinned by strong party structures. The state's omnipotence over the country's economy and social welfare afforded fertile ground for the political parties to strengthen their positions. The patron–client framework was sustained in the relations between parties and the public, whereas, while in power, leaders of political parties further strengthened their status through bureaucratic clientelism.

The obvious consequence was that a relatively small segment of the public appeared in a much more favourable situation in their ability to be appointed in the civil service, depending on which party was in power at a given time. This has been a practice that was observed regardless of party orientation. The commitment of the Karamanlis government following the elections of 1974 to consolidate democracy in Greece and move the country to its Western destiny was realized. In 1981 Greece became a member of the European Community (later the European Union). However, clientelism remained 'alive and well' at the expense of bolstering a context of civil society in Greece.

CONSOLIDATION OF DEMOCRACY

This analysis accepts the definition proposed by Gunther *et al.* regarding the meaning of a consolidated democracy. Accordingly, a democratic régime is considered to be consolidated

> when all politically significant groups regard its key political institutions as the only legitimate framework for political contestation, and adhere to its democratic rules of the game. This definition thus includes an attitudinal dimension, wherein existing political institutions are regarded as acceptable and without legitimate alternatives, as well as a behavioral criterion, according to which a specific set of norms is respected and adhered to by all politically significant groups.[23]

In this respect, the time when democracy was consolidated in Greece, in the sense of being fully tested, was the year (1981) in which the transition of Greek political life from conservative to socialist rule took place in an orderly and consensual fashion. Essentially, this marked the end of almost 45 years of uninterrupted rule by the Greek Right, 'whether in its parliamentary or its authoritarian manifestations'.[24] It is worth stressing that there is an essential difference between the democratization process that has been augmented since 1974 and the advent of PASOK in power in 1981 which offers a key dimension to the consolidation process. In the first occasion, democratization proceeded with the incorporation of the hitherto excluded social and political groups (rural and working class masses) into the Greek political system, whereas in the second occasion, in 1981, the party representing the interests of this segment of the Greek polity essentially came to power.

This was an unprecedented development in Greek political life in two respects: firstly, a left-of-centre government legitimately came and remained in power for a long time, thus marking the 'openness' of the Greek democracy. Secondly, the smoothness with which this transition took place manifested the maturity of the Greek democracy. Indeed, maturity and political rationality were demonstrated not only by the defeated political parties or the military, which had already abandoned any aspirations for assuming a role in politics, but also by the newly established socialist government, which was careful in avoiding practices, especially in the foreign policy area, that could provoke either the conservative opposition or the military.

Indeed, the new socialist government was particularly cautious with the military. Although all initiatives regarding the military aimed at eliminating past practices of military interference in politics, at the same time the Papandreou government tried not to challenge the corporate interests of the military and raised their salaries as soon as PASOK came to power.[25] In fact, Papandreou had moderated his tone and public rhetoric regarding the role of the military during the junta years and insisted that only a small number of arrant officers were responsible for the years of dictatorship. Another tactical step launched by Papandreou was his constant praising of the demonstrated devotion of the Greek military to defend the territorial integrity of the country, a stance that left little room for misunderstandings regarding the margins within which the military leadership could move.

Moreover, the salience of 'prudent military' in the reconstruction of the post-authoritarian political system in Greece was frequently noted.[26] In other words, there was a firm but not provocative stance by the Papandreou government aiming at preventing any concerns by the military that either their image or their prerogatives (mainly financial) would be challenged. The reality was that the previously flawed image of the military gradually improved in the eyes of the public, which had unhappy memories from previous decades.

Papandreou, equally pragmatically, moved to mend fences with the US and NATO, reassuring those in Washington who – judging from

PASOK's utterances in the mid 1970s – considered Andreas Papandreou something of a cross between Castro and Kerensky. The pragmatic adjustment of PASOK's foreign policy to the imperatives of geopolitics and geoeconomics is treated in depth elsewhere in this volume. A number of additional factors contributed to the constructive handling of civil-military relations by the PASOK government leading to a balanced professional army functioning in a modern, democratic society. It should be noted that Karamanslis had been elected by Parliament as President of the Hellenic Republic (May 1980) almost a year before Papandreou took office and enjoyed the military's undisputed respect.[27]

The PASOK government encouraged Karamanlis to become more involved in terms of statesmanship thus capitalizing on the latter's good relations with the military. This was a development that played a key role in preventing strong grievances by the military. In general, civil-military relations have adopted a clear democratic profile in the last two decades of the twentieth century. The legislation that was enacted in 1995 regarding the armed forces and which replaced that of 1977 maintains that the Minister of Defence has the final word in all military matters.[28] The military leadership is entirely accountable to the government and the defence minister, whose advisors also include a growing number of civilians. In addition, the Governmental Council for Foreign Policy and Defence (KYSEA), is the main decision making body regarding issues of national defence and is responsible for defence policy planning.[29] It is chaired by the Prime Minister and its members are the Ministers of Foreign Affairs, National Defence, National Economy, Interior-Administration-Decentralization, Public Order and the Chief Hellenic National Defence General Staff (HNDGS).[30] It can be advocated that at times there has been a strong civilian control over the military, as was the case in the Imia crisis in 1996 whereby the government used its prerogatives offered by the 1995 legislation and dismissed in a expedient fashion the Chief HNDGS, who was removed for mismanagement of the crisis.[31]

THE EUROPEAN FACTOR IN GALVANIZING THE CONSOLIDATION OF DEMOCRACY

A vital factor in the consolidation of key democratic elements in the Greek political system and society in the last two decades of the twentieth century has been the country's membership in the EU. Greece's statutory obligations to meet EU standards not only in harmonizing its legal and normative apparatus but mainly in adopting policies towards the promotion of civil society, fostered the strengthening of forces, which have started to function as intermediateries between the state and society, mostly in favour of the latter. This process became more apparent in the 1990s insofar as the EC/EU began to regulate policies favouring civil society. In particular, following the provisions of the Maastricht Treaty (article 8), which established the notion of citizenship of the Union, the idea of the 'Europe of citizens', valid since 1984, started to attract particular attention. In addition, the efforts and pressures by social groups of the EU member states aiming at gaining greater participation of the European citizens in the integration process than the Inter-Governmental Conference (ICG) of 1996 envisioned played an important role. It resulted in the inclusion of a number of provisions in the Treaty of the European Union which established a greater role for the European citizen within the mechanisms for an effective European Union.[32]

The strengthening of civil society in Greece in the late 1990s has received particular attention, in contrast to previous decades.[33] This by no means implies that the level of civil society which has developed in Greece resembles the conditions that can be observed in other Western European countries. As Mouzelis has argued in 1997, the key weakness of Greek democracy is a rudimentary civil society, which largely for historical reasons has taken the form of an arbitrary, despotic state and a party-controlled political system within which narrow bureaucratic interests prevail over the comprehensive interests of the Greek citizens.[34] Indeed, the idea of comprehensive interests of the citizens takes the form of a 'public good', the key characteristics of which involve universal and non-exclusive applicability. However, in recent years important steps have been taken towards building an effective civil society. Greek membership in the EU has contributed to a substantial degree in this direction. This contribution can been seen in at least three respects.

First, membership in the EU has provided regulatory mechanisms that function in a civil society context. This, in turn, has strengthened public awareness of citizens' rights and prerogatives. Specifically, there has been a broader inclusion of social, economic or political groups which directly interact with European authorities through Common European policies and initiatives. This direct relationship excludes decisive interference by political or economic élites, which in the past equated national interests with their own. In this light, a number of aspects of public policy are being implemented according to 'universalistic' modes of action and not 'particularistic' as had been previously the case in the Greek political system.[35] As a result, public confidence about the prerogatives of civil society is encouraged, a key aspect of which is the non-exclusion of the citizens from the benefits of public (and European) policies.

Second, the creation of new social structures and groups which are directly linked to or a result of European policies have also reduced in several respects the role of the state as well as the role of those interest groups that had in the past strong affiliations and dependencies with the state and the political parties. Therefore, there exists a greater autonomy and accountability of new social groupings and structures (i.e. citizens movements, environmental groups, non-governmental organizations). In addition, the role of these entities has been enhanced by the EU's structural policies, leading to the creation of broader European networks which transcend member state frontiers. Importantly, their participation in the decision making processes as important partners in the establishment or implementation of European policies has offered additional weight to the Greek experience of civil society building.

Finally, the creation by the EU of new rights for European citizens could not exclude Greece from the urge to adapt itself to the new realities that work largely in the direction of strengthening civil society. As a member state, by adopting the legal structure of the European Union, *the acquis communautaire*, Greece has promoted a number of additional rights for its citizens, while the notion of state accountability, as Ioakimidis notes, is to be fully developed.[36] The ability of the Greek citizens to protect their rights through European judicial and political structures (the European Court, the European Arbitrator, the European Parliament or even the Commission) is a matter of record.[37] Further, the introduction of a new legal framework in Greece aiming at establishing the constitutional protection of minorities (the laws passed in 1997 regarding the protection of personal data were a step in this direction) and other legal norms aiming at the protection of the rights of the European citizens, have contributed profoundly towards the consolidation of an effective civil society in Greece.

The establishment of the Ombudsman's Office in October 1998 has also been an important step in the direction of bolstering civil society in Greece. This independent state agency aims at safeguarding citizens' rights, alleviating the effects of malfunction by the state bureaucracy at the expense of the public, and working towards the maintenance of the rule of law in the civil service. It is worth mentioning that from October 1998 until the end of 1999, the Ombudsman in Greece had received 8,714 applications regarding the examination of an equal number of cases that affect explicitly or implicitly citizens' rights. In 1999, the Ombudsman worked on 8,223 cases which were classified according to the four issue areas the independent authority has been focusing.[38] In particular, the Human Rights division administered 1,212 cases (14.74% of total); the Social Protection division administered 2,260 cases (27.48%); the Quality of Life division administered 2,068 cases (25.15%); and the division of State-Citizen Relations administered 2,683 cases (32.63%).[39] The role of Ombudsman in Greek society has started to gain ground. Its independent character in mediating between the public and the Greek bureaucracy (judicial, economic, political and social) tends to establish a greater public confidence of citizens' ability to safeguard their rights in the face of an often inflexible and at times irrational state bureaucracy.

To conclude, consolidation of democracy in Greece has followed a difficult path since the fall of the Colonels' régime in 1974. The political tradition that included practices of clientelism and patronage, making the state appear as a despotic, 'particularistic' and inflexible giant started to change hesitantly, mainly as a result of the fashion in which charismatic political leaders started to employ democratic practices and principles into the Greek political system.

One can assume that despite the consolidation of democracy in Greece and the recent decisive steps that have been taken in the direction of bolstering civil society, state bureaucracy still retains strong aspects of clientelism and partisanship.[40] This appears to be the most serious impediment obstructing the comprehensive realization of a fully accountable civil society.

In order for Greece to attain a vigorous democratic political system in which the state can function as a rational and effective coordinator interfering in a fashion that can bolster private entrepreneurial initiatives as well as the mechanisms of an open market, a number of tasks have to be accomplished. First, there should be the political will by the Greek political leadership at least (bipartisan involving the major parties) to assume the political cost of a dramatic rationalization of the Greek civil service and the state bureaucracy in general. Second, a transition regarding the power relationship between state and government. As soon as the state structures are liberated from partisan politics and patronage, then there would be space for further modernization and democratization of both the economy and society.

NOTES

*The author would like to thank Dimitris Sotiropoulos for his useful and constructive comments. However, responsibility for errors of omission or commission rests with the author.

1. Dictatorships in Greece lasted only 12 years in the whole of the twentieth century (Pangalos' rule 1925–26, Metaxas's rule 1936–40, and the Colonels' régime 1967–74).
2. Hereinafter the EU.
3. T. Couloumbis, 'Karamanlis and Papandreou: Form and Substance of Leadership', *International Law and International Politics*, 16 (1987) pp. 9–10.
4. D. Charalambis, *Pelateiakes Sheseis & Laikismos: I Eksothesimiki Sinenaisi sto Elliniko Politiko Systima (Clientelistic Consensus and Populism: The Extra-Structural Consensus in the Greek Political System)* (Athens: Exantas, 1989) pp. 24–5.
5. Women for the first time exercised the right to vote in the general elections in 1956 and municipal elections (1952).
6. In a way, this dimension was not entirely removed even from the 'Third Greek Republic',

as some analysts like to name the democratization period which followed the Colonels' junta (1967–74).

7. R. Clogg, *Parties and Elections in Greece: The Search for Legitimacy* (London: Hurst & Co, 1987) p. 4.

8. This had resulted from a public uproar galvanized by a strong campaign led by Charilaos Trikoupis, a politician who had already begun his efforts against political corruption, instability and underdevelopment.

9. Elias Nicolacopoulos, *H. Kakektiki, Dimocratia, Kommata kai Ekloges 1949–1967* (*The Stunted Democracy, Parties and Elections 1946–1967*) (Athens: Patakis, 2001) [in Greek].

10. Some of the aspects that comprised this development included: the reconstruction of the infrastructure that had been damaged by the Second World War and the ensuing civil wars; the successful modernization of agricultural production; the move of great numbers of the populace from rural to urban areas providing a considerable labour force; the increase of industrial production; the substantial process against illiteracy; and the gradual establishment of modern principles and norms within society reflecting the progress of the country and its international new standing.

11. D. Sotiropoulos, 'State and Party: The Greek State Bureaucracy and the Panhellenic Socialist Movement (PASOK), 1981–1989' (PhD Dissertation, Yale University, 1991) p. 37.

12. N. P. Diamandouros, 'Transitions to, and Consolidation of, Democratic Politics in Greece, 1974–1983: A Tentative Assessment', *West European Politics*, 7, 2 (1984) pp. 50–71.

13. R. Gunther, N. P. Diamandouros and H. J. Puhle (eds) *The Politics of Democratic Consolidation. Southern Europe in Comparative Perspective* (Baltimore and London: The Johns Hopkins University Press, 1995) p. 5.

14. *Ibid.*

15. Literature on this issue is quite extensive; see G. Pridham and P. Lewis (eds) *Stabilising Fragile Democracies* (London: Routledge, 1996); S. Jr. Vryonis (ed.) *Greece on the Road to Democracy: From the Junta to PASOK, 1974–1986* (New Rochelle: A.D. Caratzas, 1991); Th. Couloumbis and P. Yannas, 'The Stability Quotient of Greece's Post-1974 Democratic Institutions', *Journal of Modern Greek Studies*, 1, 2 (1983) pp. 359–72; H. J. Psomiades, 'Greece: From the Colonels' Rule to Democracy', in J. H. Herz, *From Dictatorship to Democracy: Coping with the Legacies of Authoritarianism and Totalitarianism* (Westport, CT: Greenwood, 1982) pp. 251–73; and N. P. Diamandouros, 'Transition to and Consolidation of, Democratic Politics in Greece, 1974–1983', in G. Pridham (ed.) *The New Mediterranean Democracies* (London: Frank Cass, 1984) pp. 50–71.

16. Diamandouros, 'Greek Politics and Society in the 1990s', in G. T. Allison and K. Nicolaidis (eds) *The Greek Paradox, Promises vs Performance* (Cambridge, MA: The Massachussetts Institute of Technology Press, 1997) pp. 58–9.

17. *Ibid.*, p. 59

18. Diamandouros, 'Transitions', pp. 54–5.

19. Diamandouros, 'Greek Politics', p. 58.

20. *Metapolitefsis*, meaning the change of régime, denotes not only the post-dictatorial era (1974 onwards) but also the democratization process that was augmented at the time with its credentials being enjoyed today.

21. J. J. Linz, 'Totalitarian and Authoritarian Régimes', in F. I. Greenstein and N. W. Polsby (eds) *Handbook of Political Science*, Vol. 3 (Reading, MA: Addison Wesley, 1975) pp. 182–3.

22. The Communist Party of Greece had split into the Moscow-leaning KKE and the *Kommounistiko Komma Elladas-esoterikou* (Communist Party of Greece-Interior-KKE-es). See Glogg, *Parties and Elections*, p. 61.

23. Gunther *et al.*, *The Politics*, p. 8.

24. *Ibid.*, p. 29.

25. T. Veremis, 'Defence and Security Policies under PASOK', in R. Clogg (ed.) *Greece, 1981–89: The Populist Decade* (London: Macmillan Press, 1993) pp. 181–8.

26. See also C. Lyrintizis, 'Political Parties in Post Junta Greece: A Case of "Bureaucratic Clientelism?"', *West European Politics*, 7, 2 (1984).

27. For a presentation of the different political parties and elections in the Greek political system see Clogg, *Parties and Elections*, passim.

28. In contrast to Act 660/1977, according to which in cases of emergency, the military could assume direct responsibility in policy making regarding the defence of the country, Act 2292/1995 provided for the supremacy of civilian authorities, the Minister of Defence, in all defence decision making. For a concise work on this issue see N. Alivizatos, *E Syntagmatike These ton Enoplon Dynameon: E Arche tou Politicou Eleghou (The Constitutional Status of the Armed Forces: The Begining of Civilian Control)* (Athens: Sakkoulas, 1987); and T. Veremis, *The Military in Greek Politics. From Independence to Democracy* (Athens: Courier Publications, 2000).

29. The most concise analysis on Greek civil military relations is offered in the work of Thanos Veremis (*The Military*). The publication of 2000 of this book in Greek is based on an earlier book published in 1997 by Frank Cass.

30. For a detailed presentation of the Organisation and Operation of the Armed Forces, see White Paper of the Hellenic Armed Forces 1998–1999 (Athens, Ministry of National Defence, 2000).

31. Veremis, *The Military*, pp. 285–7.

32. There is an entire chapter in the Treaty of the European Union entitled 'The Union and the Citizen', which provides the ability of the European citizen to became fully aware of all the mechanisms and processes regarding the European Union. See Treaty on European Union, 1992, Part Two, Citizenship of the Union, Article 8.

33. Ioakimidis, 1998.

34. See N. Mouzelis, 'O Sinigoros tou Politi kai I Hameni Efkairia' ('The Ombudsman and the Missed Opportunity'), *To Vima,* 27 April 1997.

35. The author of this chapter employs the terms used by Diamandouros to distinguish between public policies that reflect the *universal*, non-exclusive interaction of the state with its citizens and those that serve the interests of *particular* political or economic groups. See, Diamandouros, 'Greek Politics', p. 37 (Greek version).

36. Ioakimidis 2000, p. 111.

37. Ioakimidis, 1998.

38. Although 8,714 applications were made since the end of 1999, the Ombudsman was able to examine 8,223 of the cases.

39. Ombudsman Annual Report 1999, p. 13.

40. N. Mouzelis, 'Greek Modernization', in *Greece in Transition* (Athens: Hermes) pp.33–8. [In Greek].

8

The Greek Media Landscape

INO AFENTOULI

INTRODUCTION

The development of the mass media in Greek society has followed the course of the development of the media in most Western societies. This is particularly true with regard to the preponderance of television as a consequence of economic growth and the introduction of the consumerism model. The effects of the dominant role of television in the media landscape are similar to those in other developed countries in Europe and in the US. Entertainment is gaining more and more ground and is influencing not only the proportion but also the content of information. Specialists call this phenomenon 'infotainment'. It should be noted however that the private electronic media are still immature in Greece, since they were permitted to operate only in the late 1980s. A long tradition of state control ended, giving birth to a great number of private radio and television stations, disproportionate to the audiences existing in Greece. The deregulation of the media landscape, following the 'Italian model', resulted in an explosion of radio and television stations functioning largely without rules. As a consequence a more complicated relationship has developed between the state, which still has the absolute right to allocate frequencies and operate licences for private radio, television stations and private media. These private entrepreneurs, through the coalitions they have developed amongst themselves, have gained a dominant position and great influence in public life. The evolution of this relationship and the changes which took place in the balance of power between the different components in the power game is perhaps the most interesting political development to have taken place in Greece during the last decade.

Thus, this chapter emphasizes the last period of Greek history, after the fall of the junta in 1974 and the so-called *metapolitefsi* (change of régime) describing the return of democratic rule in the country. In the last 25 years, the media landscape has changed radically in Greece following the pattern of the development of Western media.

POLITICS AND MEDIA AFTER 1974

During the years of the dictatorship (1967–74), freedom of the press was suppressed and many journalists were persecuted. Even prior to the dictatorship, the Greek press did not enjoy total freedom, due to the authoritative laws existing in the country following the Second World War. The experience of civil war and the deep division between right and left in the country had created a situation of semi-democracy which ended only after the fall of the junta.

With the fall of the military junta in July 1974, Greece, for the first time in its modern history, moved towards becoming a fully democratic state. The leader of this transition, Constantine Karamanlis, introduced a new Constitution in 1975 establishing parliamentary democracy and aiming at closing the gap between Greece and the Western European countries. Karamanlis' strategic goal was the admission of the country to the European Community, a goal achieved in 1981. During his seven years in office (1974–81), Karamanlis gave great emphasis to the consolidation of democratic institutions and the modernization of the country. Nevertheless, being a conservative leader, his actions and priorities had certain limitations. Karamanlis conducted public affairs in a paternalistic manner and in many respects was an authoritarian leader. This mentality was also reflected in his policy towards the media.

It might seem surprising to the external observer the degree to which developments in the media are linked to political developments. However, this was the case in Greece in the mid-1970s and it reflected the close relationship between political power and media power, as well as the dependence of the latter upon political decisions and often on economic subvertions and loans. On the other hand, political power was, at the time, preponderant in comparison with other powers; and priorities in public life were set mostly by the government. Over the next decade the distribution of power became more complicated and the dependence of politicians upon the media increased.

It is important to understand that the restoration of democracy in Greece led to a peculiar situation in the first post-dictatorship period, under the leadership of Karamanlis, who founded the New Democracy party in order to differentiate from the other parties of the right wing, which existed prior to the junta. However, political circumstances forced Karamanlis to reach a balance between the old guard of the right, including many representatives of the government who were not free of responsibility for the dictatorship, and a new generation of functionaries with progressive viewpoints. The latter wanted New Democracy to make itself known as a modern centre-right party, according to European prototypes. In spite of this tendency, as well as Karamanlis' reformist spirit, the Karamanlis period (1974–81) could be described as conservative. This juxtaposed with an intense progressive current in Greece which had begun to take shape during the dictatorship in the form of the resistance organizations and which took on new dimensions with the restoration of democracy. This current was political and social. It had characteristics of conflict with the political establishment and it could be compared to the protest movements in the USA and in Europe in 1968. Due to the previous suppression of dictatorship in Greece, this current was expressed in the *metapolitefsi*. In other words, the political expression of the *metapolitefsi* – with the coming to power of a competent but conservative leader such as Karamanlis – did not correspond to the changes which had in the meantime befallen Greek society. Later, this current found its political expression in the rise to power of PASOK and Andreas Papandreou.

This dimension was reflected in the mass media. It was expressed in the publication of a new newspaper, in July 1975, called *Eleftherotypia*, which could be characterized as a newspaper that embodied the spirit of the *metapolitefsi*. It was a newspaper of the left. It might be more accurate to say that it was a newspaper of the independent left since it expressed a broader anti-right front.

In the period from 1974–80, the line of separation between the right and the left remained very distinct, while party press blossomed. Another characteristic of this period was the existence of many political journals, an indication of the intense infusion of ideology into politics and the need for political expression following the dictatorship. The case of *ANTI* is a classic example. This was an innovative periodical published during the years of the dictatorship, soon banned by the junta. Later, with the restoration of democracy, it was published again constituting a vehicle of expression for all those forces that desired a renewal of the political system.

The circulation of newspapers increased significantly, as was to be expected with the *metapolitefsi*. In 1974, average daily circulation surpassed one million issues. However, as Zaoussis and Stratos observe, '... the abrupt increase was probably of a temporary nature. Gradually, circulation began to fall and in 1977, despite the holding of parliamentary elections, the level fell below 800,000 copies, where it remained until 1980'.[1]

RADIO AND TELEVISION

The polyphony and pluralism of the press was restored after 1974, but the same cannot be said for radio and television, which remained until 1987 under the suffocating control of the state. There was a state monopoly in Greece, as was the case in most other European countries until the 1970s. The radio and television stations belonged to the state and functioned in their news reporting capacity as promoters of government policies. As Alivizatos reports, 'Radio and television broadcasts were never recognized in Greece as individual liberties, as special dimensions of the intellectual expression of freedom, protected by the Constitution'.[2]

The result of this policy, that continued for decades, was a particularly insipid and frequently propagandistic coverage of current affairs, and was reflected in all the constitutions after 1952. The first experimental television show was broadcast in Greece in 1965. However, television functioned on a normal basis after 1967 within a completely oppressive environment, even providing a propagandistic weapon to the dictatorship.

The state monopoly was not abolished with the restoration of democracy in 1974. There were no more restrictions to the freedom of the written press. However, based on the provisions of the first constitution of the *metapolitefsi* – the constitution of 1975 – radio and television remained under the control of the state, and the monopoly was maintained and used by PASOK when it succeeded New Democracy in government in 1981. In addition to promoting government policies, state television would also be used as the basic lever of spreading and imposing the ideology which the party wanted to project as dominant.

The rise of influence of PASOK, the party which Andreas Papandreou founded, and its accession to power in 1981, had very significant consequences for the mass media. PASOK was not a traditional social democratic party of the European type.[3] It was a leader-oriented, personality-based, populist party, with a very intense anti-Western and anti-European character. The overwhelming personal stamp of its founder, Papandreou, did not leave room for the democratic functioning of the party. Moreover, Papandreou did not want the party to be identified with traditional social democracy. Rather, he was particularly attracted to the populist parties and movements outside Europe, such as the Baath type. On the one hand, he emphatically cultivated this dimension, while on the other hand, he promoted relations with countries of the Middle East and of the Third World, at the expense of relations with the natural counterparts and allies of Greece in NATO and the European Union. This political environment influenced the depiction of reality by the mass media, particularly in radio and television, which remained under the suffocating control of the state. Relics of that age are phenomena observed even today, such as nationalism, anti-Europeanism, distrust of institutions such as NATO and the European Union, from which Greece benefited enormously. However, the reversal of reality, and the deeply rooted distrust of the west and foreigners, has its origin in the expansion of the underdog culture during the first period of PASOK's governments (1981–88).

THE LANDSCAPE AFTER 1980:
THE INTRODUCTION OF NEW TECHNOLOGY AND TABLOIDS

The rise of PASOK coincided with a period of very important changes in the press. The most significant of these was the appearance of tabloids and the introduction of new technology into the publication process. In order to understand this phenomenon, we must explain that in Greece the tabloids do not have all the characteristics of newspapers of this category that are published in other countries, as for example in Britain or Germany.[4] In this sense, scandal sheets do not exist. There were always 'quality' and 'popular' newspapers. A distinction was made on the basis of the time of publication: morning papers stood for serious press, and afternoon papers stood for popular press, yet this distinction no longer exists. There are newspapers, which offer opinions that aim to shock, unrelated to the time of publication.

Greek popular newspapers do not have the same content as the British or German tabloids. That is to say, they do not follow the rules of the three S's (sex, scandals and sports). 'Voyeurist' journalism has not flourished in Greece, perhaps because the private life of public figures is not of interest to most people. Even when this was not the case, the reasons were political and not scandal-mongering. The case of Andreas Papandreou and his relationship with Dimitra Liani is a classic example. This relationship did not really stir public opinion, but rather it was connected with the political problems of PASOK during the 1988–89 period.

As a consequence, how can the 'popular' newspapers be distinguished from the 'quality' ones? Mainly through the way in which issues are presented on the front page, but also from the analogous political/social issues which are raised. As a rule, the 'popular' newspapers are small in format and set out their primary issues in banner headlines. In addition, they do not contain analyses and editorials and give a great deal of space to social issues. In contrast, the 'quality' newspapers emphasize current political events, analyses and opinion and their appearance is similar to that of quality newspapers in Europe and the USA.

At the same time, the basic difference between the Greek, the European and the American newspapers of quality is the limited space given to international issues, in contrast to current domestic political events. It is very rare for an international event to become the leading story in a Greek newspaper. This ranking is not unrelated to the nationalistic point of view that dominates Greek public opinion to a large degree and is reproduced – and often fed – by the mass media.

Another difference with regard to Europe and the USA is the absence of a regional press in Greece. When we speak of national newspapers, we are referring to newspapers which are published in Athens and circulate throughout the entire country. There is not a strong local or regional press. Even the newspapers of Thessaloniki, the second largest city in the country and an important economic centre, do not circulate on a national basis.

Returning to the changes in the press, we must point out that the 1980s was very important. Apart from the change in the form and the mode of printing of newspapers, a very significant increase in their circulation was observed. This was in contrast to the decade of the 1990s, during which time exactly the opposite happened.

In 1980, newspaper publishers clashed with the very strong Press Workers Union which reacted to the introduction of new technology and the abolition of the privileges of their members in the newspaper publishing process. The Press Workers strike lasted two months (June and July), but when it came to an end the workers had lost. The publishers won in this conflict and new technology was introduced into the field of the Greek press – photosynthesis. Today this has evolved into electronic publishing.

THE REPUBLICATION OF *ETHNOS*

The first tangible proof of the 'new age' for the Greek press arrives with the publication, in September 1981, of the first newspaper in small format with full colour pages. The title was old – *Ethnos*. This newspaper which had resisted the junta, had ceased publication during the dictatorship. The inability of its old owners (the Kyriazis family) to republish at the time of the *metapolitefsi* led to its sale, several years later, to the businessman G. Bobolas, who came from the construction and public works sector. This was the first transfer of the title of a newspaper to a non-traditional publisher, a tendency that would become common in the decade to follow with the introduction of business conglomerates into the mass media. Until the 1980s, traditional publishers dominated the Greek press and the publication of newspapers was a 'family matter'. Among the most important newspapers two of them –

To Vima and *Ta Nea* – belonged to Christos Lambrakis, *Kathimerini* to
Eleni Vlachos, *Apoyevmatini* to Nikos Botsis, and *Vradini* to George
Athanasiadis. Even *Eleftherotypia*, the newest title of the Greek press,
belonged to a traditional publisher, Christos Tegopoulos. Today, twenty
years later, only Lambrakis and Tegopoulos remain as traditional
publishers. The rest of the newspapers and the electronic mass media
belong to businessmen with other activities, and who often use several
means at their disposal to promote those activities.

According to the standards of the Greek press, the new *Ethnos* was a
newspaper completely different from the existing ones. It served to a
greater extent the visual needs of the reading public and the desire to
impress with banner headlines and short passages. Its great innovation
was the small tabloid format and its printing with photosynthesis technology, which until then had not been used overall. The multi-page
publication, the colours, the variety and the distinctiveness of the typo-
graphic data and, perhaps most importantly, the easy-to-use format,
became immediately accepted. Even though the tabloid's appearance
initially drew many critics, it was finally adopted by most of the afternoon newspapers. One should probably attribute the swift rise of circulation of *Ethnos* in Athens and in the rural areas to the appearance of
the tabloid, in combination with the shrewd choice of its publication
time, one month prior to the elections of October 1981.[5]

In this way, *Ethnos* introduced a new trend to the press and its circulation success gradually forced most newspapers to follow suit. Why did
this publication experiment succeed? It succeeded because it was the
first newspaper which responded to the new habits of the Greek readership (change in lifestyle, the uninterrupted eight-hour working day
and the introduction of television into the everyday life of the family).

PASOK AND THE PRESS

However, the big change during the 1980s was the political transition in
Greece. The mood of the majority for 'change' was expressed by the
success of PASOK under Andreas Papandreou. It was a genuine need, to
a large degree a natural continuation of the *metapolitefsi* of 1974,
driven by the fact that the fall of the junta had not been accompanied in
1974 by the predominance of a new political formation and the exhibi-
tion of new powers, but rather by the assumption of power by the
conservatives. For this reason the predominance of PASOK in 1981
reflected the major changes that had taken place in Greek society in the
previous years, the withdrawal of support for the right and the rise of
new social strata, which sought political expression. In other words the
catch-all nature of this party was also its strength.

This phenomenon could not leave the press unaffected. Most progressive newspapers supported PASOK during its rise to, and later its acquisition of, power. An initial consequence was an intensification of the dividing line between the newspapers of the 'right' and those which supported PASOK, as much during the strengthening of the party as after its subsuming of power. The latter were obviously more numerous and more dynamic than the former, expressing a broad central left majority in public opinion, if one judges from the significant rise in their circulation. According to the data presented by Zaoussis and Stratos, the Athenian press began from a level of 800,000 copies in 1981, reached 108,000 in 1985 and, following a slight decline, reached 110,000 copies sold in 1989, thus achieving the highest average yearly sales of all time.[6]

Students of this period connect the rise of circulation of the newspapers with the assumption of power by this party. As Psychoyios stresses, 'the increase in circulation of the press cannot be separated from the new political and social climate which the rise of PASOK created (primarily in the countryside)'.[7] Regardless of one's opinion concerning its long-term results, during the first four years of the premiership of Andreas Papandreou, a distributive economic policy was followed which strengthened the weaker strata and moved state resources to the countryside, while the Common Agricultural Policy steadily increased the incomes of farmers. The readers could see the increase in the selling price of the newspapers. The final remnants of the policing of ideas by the state was erased, the shadow of the policeman disappeared, the exchange of ideas was intense, the dictatorship had finally begun to belong to the distant rather than the recent past. The political intensity of the decade (1981 national elections, 1982 municipal elections. 1984 European elections, 1987 national elections, 1986 municipal elections) also boosted this rise. The newspapers constituted the basic means of obtaining information about politics and party conflict, since the electronic mass media, radio and television were under state, meaning governmental, control.[8]

Despite the broad support enjoyed by PASOK, not only during the first four years of its rule (1981–85) but also during the greater part of its second term (1985–89), it did not avoid the temptation to control the press.

AVRIANI AND AVRIANISM

The first attempt was made through a marginal newspaper which expressed the underdog culture of a large segment of the party supporters. This newspaper was called *Avriani*. It was first published in March 1980 and had a minimal circulation until the summer of the same year when it rocketed to 50,000 copies, exploiting the vacuum which existed due to the big strike of the press workers, which meant that no other newspapers were circulating. This newspaper was the first of the Greek press which could really be characterized as 'yellow' in the Anglo-Saxon sense of the term. Its main characteristics were slandering and attacks, often in the form of raw blackmail, against political figures.

Its first campaign of this kind began in September 1980 against the then Prime Minister George Rallis. As a result, its circulation reached 93,000 copies. It was later identified with the upcoming PASOK and within a few years it became the semi-official instrument of its expression. In 1984, its circulation reached 110,000 copies. Prior to the parliamentary elections of 1985, when it unleashed a frightening attack against the leader of the official opposition at that time, Constantinos Mitsotakis, it reached a circulation of 240,000 copies. As Zaoussis and Stratos observe, 'during this period, the newspaper was established as something like the conscience of the party. Even governmental officials started to use the characteristic language and the style of the newspaper and as a result the term 'avrianism' took political meaning.'[9]

THE COSKOTAS PHENOMENON

The second, and more serious, attempt to control the mass media took place after George Coskotas, a young businessman, entered this sector using the Bank of Crete, which he had already purchased, as his starting block. The augmentation of the mass media complex that he created through the purchasing of newspapers and the creation of journals and radio stations with the support of important functionaries of PASOK (the governing party), led to the upsetting of the equilibrium that had existed until then within the mass media.

A subsequent judicial inquiry proved that the funding of the mass media from the bank had taken place illegally and Coskotas fled abroad, where he was later arrested. This also led to the fall of Papandreou's government at the elections of June 1989. Later, the parliament sent the Prime Minister, and three other functionaries alleged to be involved in the scandal, to the Special Court, which finally found the former Prime Minister innocent.

This is one of the darkest pages of the *metapolitefsi* political history and resulted in a change in the balance of power between those with political power and the owners of the mass media.

THE END OF THE MONOPOLY IN RADIO AND TELEVISION

In 1986 there was a sentiment that the state monopoly in radio and television had reached its limits. This natural development, in market terms, took on a political dimension. PASOK, after five years in power, was showing the first signs of a serious crisis. It won the parliamentary elections of 1985 and imposed an economic stabilization programme in the spirit of the European Community at that time. However, a shift in economic policy aimed at satisfying the populist wing of the party, led the then Minister of Finance, Costas Simitis, to resign, disappointing Greece's partners in the European Community.

The largest opposition party, New Democracy, led by Constantinos Karamanlis, had recovered and now seriously threatened the party of Andreas Papandreou. In the municipal elections of 1986, New Democracy won in the three largest municipalities in the country – Athens, Piraeus and Thessaloniki. The newly elected mayors – Miltiades Evert, Andreas Andrianopoulos and Sotiris Couvelas, all prominent politicians of the conservative party – kept their promises and in 1987 founded municipal radio stations under the label of free radio. Compared with the state-controlled radio and television stations, they were an oasis in the media landscape and opened the way to private radio and television broadcast two years later.

Towards the end of 1989 two private television stations, Mega Channel and Antenna TV, began to broadcast. A law passed after the elections held in June 1989 provided the legal basis for this development. The political situation was very unstable during that period. The trial of Andreas Papandreou was going on and the New Democracy party had formed a coalition government with the left, since it did not have a clear majority in the parliament and could not therefore rule on its own. The weakness of the political system permitted the deregulation of the media landscape to the benefit of the coalition of publishers that had been formed some months before in order to address the threat of a newcomer (Coskotas). As Hairetakis notes:

> This wild deregulation brought to the fore a crass commercialization of advertising time and space (...) With a number of publishers owning sizable stakes in radio and TV stations, the expansion of media ownership and the increase in potential political pressure culminated in the formation of short and long-lived alliances among themselves, as well as with the newcomers in the media sector.[10]

TOWARDS TOTAL DEREGULATION

In the 1990s private radio, as well as private television, dominated the Greek media landscape. Some features elaborated by the Institute of Audiovisual Media are indicative (Institute of Audiovisual Media):

Radio

In 1996, 67% of adults were listening to the radio. In 1998, this had increased to 78%. In 1987 there were 4.1 million radios, in 1995 5.1 million and in 1999 5.7 million. Between 1988 and 1995, 1,734 private radio stations applied for a broadcast licence. As for advertisement, in 1988, radio advertisements covered 31.8 days. In 1998 they covered 113.4 days. Additionally, total advertising expenditures rose from three billion drachmas in 1988 to 22.4 billion in 1998.

Television

In 1992, 93% of adults watched TV. In 1998 this had increased to 98%. About 160 private television stations broadcast in Greece. Three channels are public (*NET*, *ET-1* and *ET-3*) and the rest are private. Among them the most important are: Mega Channel, Antenna TV, Star Channel, ALPHA TV, and Alter-5, all of which have national coverage. There are also three cable TV stations (Filmnet, Supersport and Kids TV). In 1987, there were 2.4 million TV sets in Greece. This figure rose up to 5.6 million in 1999. In 1992, 93% of the adult population watched TV for about three hours per week. By 1998 the figure had increased to 98% and to four hours per week. Advertising revenues have grown massively from the penetration of television into Greek households. In 1988, total advertising expenditures were 18.8 billion drachmas. In 1998, this figure was 205.8 billion.

Written Press

The predominance of television had serious consequences in the journal newspapers and journal market. Over recent years the circulation of newspapers registered a large decline, as Hairetakis reports (Institute of Audiovisual Media): '... according to the officially audited sales figures for the major Greek newspapers published by the Association of Athens Daily Newspaper Publishers, the total sales in millions of copies dropped from 314.7 in 1994 to 259.6 in 1998'.[11]

Political newspapers – made up of morning dailies, evening dailies, Sunday editions and weeklies – account for the greater share of total sales, although their share has been continually decreasing since 1990:

86.5% of total sales (1989), 82.6% (1992), 80.2% (1994), 78.% (1996), 73.4% (1998).

The number of newspaper copies sold per person annually has also dropped: from 43 copies per person in 1988; to 30.2 copies per person in 1994 and 1996; to 24.6 copies per person in 1998.

CONCLUSION

As reflected in statistics, private radio and television have dominated the media landscape in Greece since deregulation in 1987 and 1989. Despite the fact that the state still retains the right to allocate frequencies, the market has imposed its own rules concerning the content of information and entertainment provided by the private stations. Nevertheless, in comparative terms, the development of private radio and television stations in Western countries shows that the Greek case is not an exception. It would be utopian, and even undesirable, to return to a régime of tight control. What could counterbalance the anarchic deregulation of the Greek audio-visual sector? A public interest oriented television would be the easy answer. Greek public radio and television still bear the scars of their negative and static past. Despite past attempts to escape the stigma of a governmental mouthpiece, this has not succeeded yet. The public radio and television sector suffers from bad management, and as a result displays large deficits and finds it necessary to continually seek refuge in state subsidies. For this reason, it cannot be released from a clientelistic perception of relationships with the parties in power.

Only if a completely independent framework of functioning was formed, for radio and television, oriented to public interest philosophy, could it possibly acquire a significant part of the market directed to that segment of the public which rejects commercial radio and television. Even then, however, it is doubtful whether it could threaten the private sector, which has now acquired a dominant position in the Greek market. It would simply constitute the counterweight of quality which today is not offered by public radio and television, despite attempts at improvement.

The National Radio and Television Council has not managed to exercise effective control of the private mass media, although the institution was created in 1995 for this purpose. Again the relationship of the mass media with politics is at the heart of this problem. The National Radio and Television Council has, from time to time, made genuine efforts to limit the 'cannibalistic' tendencies of the private television stations. The penalties imposed are of two kinds: economic (fines), and a temporary cutting off of certain programmes that are judged to break the rules of ethics.

However, to date, no penalty has managed to influence seriously the quality of the programmes that are broadcast. Furthermore, with regard to monetary penalties, the Minister of the Press, who endorses them, has the final word. Often this does not happen so as not to disturb the relationship of the government with the strong radio and television media. As a result, only a really independent authority could impose substantive control over the quality of radio and television programmes.

The upgrading of the role of the National Radio and Television Council is particularly critical since the radio and television field finds itself once again on the verge of great changes. Other products are entering the market, such as subscriber or digital television. More specifically, since the possibility of state control over products such as the provision of information on the Internet is most uncertain, the introduction of an anti-trust law is now essential. This can be achieved provided that the application of the law does not depend on political power, but rather on an independent authority that can guarantee effective control on realistic terms.

NOTES

1. A. Zaousis and C. Stratos, *The Newspapers 1974–92* (Athens: Gnosis Publishers, 1993).
2. N. Alivizatos, *State and Radio-Television* (Athens: Sakkoulas, 1987).
3. R. Clogg, *Greece in the 1980s* (London: St Martin's Press, 1983); T. C. Kariotis, *The Greek Socialist Experiment: Papandreou's Greece* (New York: Pella Publishing, 1992); S Vryonis, *Greece on the Road to Democracy: From Junta to PASOK, 1974–1986* (New York: Aristides Caratzas, 1991); C. Lyrintzis,. 'Between Socialism and Populism: The Rise of the Panhellenic Socialist Movement', unpublished PhD Dissertation (London: London School of Economics and Political Science, 1983); P. Papasarantopoulos, *PASOK kai Exousia* (Thesssaloniki: Paratiritis, 1980); M. Spourdalakis, *The Rise of the Greek Socialist Party* (London: Routledge, 1988).
4. D. Psychogios, *The Uncertain Future of the Athenian Press* (Athens: Diaulos, 1992).
5. Zaousis and Stratos, *The Newspapers*.
6. *Ibid.*
7. Psychogios, *The Uncertain Future*.
8. *Ibid.*
9. Zaousis and Stratos, *The Newspapers*; Psychogios, *The Uncertain Future*.
10. E. Hairetakis, 'The Greek Media Landscape', in *The European Media Landscape*, European Journalism Centre (www.ecj.nl).
11. *Ibid.*

Science, Technology and the Environment

COSTAS B. KRIMBAS

During the Greek Enlightenment (1770–1820) Greek scholars, who were mainly priests or bishops, tried for the first time to infuse modern Greek thought with the 'new scientific worldview' and depart from the traditional education that focused on religious matters and as based on the commentaries of Aristotle. Scientific education in the new independent Greek state was closely linked to the foundation of the Othonian University of Athens (1937). Another institution of higher learning which preceded it was the Ionian Academy in Corfu, the capital of the Ionian islands, that was founded in 1817 by Lord Guilford, but only operated from the end of 1823 until 1864, when the Ionian islands were united to Greece, during which time it provided university level education in the sciences, in philosophy, in literature, as well as in medicine.

The Othonian University, which was renamed National and Capodistrian University of Athens after the expurgation of King Otto, was conceived as a German-style educational institution by the Bavarians who ruled Greece during the Regency. Few of the initial professors were German, instead the majority were Greeks, most of whom were educated abroad, in Germany and France. The proportion of those educated in Germany to those in France was 70% to 30% during all of the nineteenth century and the first half of the twentieth. The University started operating with four Faculties: Theology, Law, Medicine and Philosophy and the Sciences. This last Faculty was split in two in 1904: into the Faculty of Philosophy, and that of the Sciences. Sciences in Greece, during this period, were linked to the University, whose main concern was education and, to a much lesser degree, research. Another University level institution, the National Technical

University (Ethnikon Metsovion Polytechneion) developed in the late nineteenth, early twentieth century from the evolution of a lower level school for artisans which started operating in 1837. By 1887, it had already adopted a University level structure but it was only formally accepted as such in 1914, and was composed of Faculties of Engineering and Architecture. Another university level institution, the School of Fine Arts (Anotati Scholi Kalon Technon, 1910), derived from the same artisan school. At the National Technical University, mathematics, physics and chemistry were also taught.

In 1920 two new university level schools were founded – the Agricultural School of Athens (later Agricultural University) and the School for Economic and Commercial Studies (later Economic University). In 1925 the University of Thessaloniki was founded. This latter institution was supposed to represent a novel spirit and be a counterweight to the traditional Athens University. The University of Thessaloniki started with only the Faculties of Philosophy and of the Sciences, but it soon acquired Faculties of Agriculture and Forestry (1928), of Law and Economics (1930), of Theology and of Medicine (1942), and of Veterinary Studies. Later, it was provided with a Polytechnic School (1955), a Fine Arts Department and several other Faculties. Thus, it became the largest University in Greece both in numbers of professors and students. After the Second World War a new institution appeared, the Panteion University in Athens (which was originally founded as a private school in 1930, grew during the 1930s and in 1951 acquired the status of a higher learning institution educating administrators and managers, becoming a University in 1982).

In 1964, forty years after the establishment of the University of Thessaloniki, the planning of a new University in Patras generated greater debate regarding the structure of the country's universities. Until then, all these institutions in Greece were structured on the principle of Professorial Chairs, a tradition inherited from German and French universities. After the Second World War, in the 1960s, the number of scientists educated in English-speaking countries increased considerably. These scientists could not find positions in the old universities except as subalterns, the number of chairs being restricted. These young scientists were interested in research and were provisionally housed in two research institutions created in 1958, the Nuclear Research Centre 'Democritus' and the Royal (afterwards National) Research Foundation. The discussions on the structure of the new university were animated and, in opposition to the professors of the older universities, the young progressive Anglo-American educated scientists supported the idea that the new university should be restructured in departmental units, each department containing numerous professorial positions. However, the young scientists were defeated and Patras University was founded on the same principle and structure as the older universities. At the same time, the University of Thessaloniki created an annexe at Ioannina with two departments, that of Philosophy and that of the Sciences. Later, in 1970, this annexe evolved into the independent University of Ioannina. Somewhat earlier (in 1958) two schools were operating, one in Athens, another in Thessaloniki, which provided industrial, economic and managerial studies and evolved in the 1980s into universities (University of Piraeus, University of Macedonia).

After the fall of the dictatorship in 1974, two new universities that had previously been created came into operation: Thrace (1973, at Komotini and Xanthi) and Crete (1973 at Rethymnon and Herakleion); which was joined, in 1977, by a Technical University at Chania (Crete). In 1984 three more universities were founded, the University of Aegean (in four islands of East Aegean), the Ionian University (in Corfu), and the University of Thessaly (in three towns of this region). A school of home economics developed into a university in the 1990s (Haroko-peion Panepistimion). Recently planning started for a new university to be located in the central Peloponnese. In several of these institutions mathematics and the sciences are taught (Patras, Ioannina, Crete, Aegean), agriculture or environmental sciences (Thessaly, Aegean), engineering (Thrace, Crete, Patras), and medicine (Ioannina, Patras, Crete, Thrace, Thessaly). Thus, the number of teaching positions has increased greatly in the last quarter of the twentieth century. From 1982 onwards all universities, the old as well as the new, function under the provisions of a new law, which abolished the professorial chairs and established the department as the elementary organization unit.

SCIENCE: THE RESEARCH INSTITUTIONS

Along with the increase of higher level educational institutions, various research centres developed. As has already been indicated, the research tradition in Greece was not strong. Quite early in the nineteenth century (1846) a National Observatory operated as an institution partly linked to the National University of Athens. Before the Second World War the state founded several laboratories for agricultural research. At the beginning of the twentieth century (1901) a research institution on soil science, fertilizers and climate was created. Following it, the Ministry of Agriculture founded several other research units, which evolved later into institutions. Two were created in the 1920s, seven in the 1930s, along with a Plant Pathology Institute privately funded by the magnate, Emmanuel Benakis, and three more were founded after the war, two in the 1950s, and another in the 1960s. Agricultural research was important, Greece being at that time mainly an agricultural country. However, the research carried on in these institutions was of a simple, applied level.

We have already mentioned the creation, in the late 1950s, of two important institutions. The first of these was 'Democritus', a centre for nuclear research, which was under the authority of the Hellenic Atomic Energy Commission. This centre contained research departments in chemistry and biology besides those in physics, informatics and the management of the atomic reactor. For a short time, a postgraduate school in physics and philosophy also operated, but was soon closed down due to the hostility of the university professors. The second research institution was the Royal Research Foundation, housing research centres in the humanities, in biochemistry and in physical chemistry. At about the same time a State Centre for Geological Research and Prospecting was created (which repeatedly changed its name, the last being that of the Institute for Geological and Mineral Research, IGME). This institute made several discoveries of some economic importance. During the dictatorship of the military junta, an institute for marine research also started operating, which was later renamed the National Centre for Marine Research. In the 1970s and 1980s several other institutions were created, the most prominent of which was the research centre linked to the University of Crete, the Institute for Technology and Research (ITE). It houses several units focusing on molecular biology and biotechnology, on applied physics (lasers, etc.), informatics as well as parallel units covering the humanities. It also expanded with extra mural institutes, one of which is located in Patras and another in Thessaloniki. ITE is actually by far the most successful research institution in the country. It conducts research carried out in some areas that are in the forefront of international scientific endeavour (e.g. the discovery of a new mobile element, which permits genetic transformations in a more efficient way). As a companion to ITE, a marine research centre was created in Crete (Institute for Marine Biology of Crete, ITHABIK) specialising in fish culture. Both marine research centres have their own oceanographic boats. In addition, the Academy of Athens, among several research institutes, has institutes devoted to the sciences. Medical research is mainly confined to universities and hospitals but there are also a few research centres. In 1919, the Hellenic Pasteur Institute was created as an associate to the one in Paris. Three other institutions were or are currently being organized, one of them devoted to psychiatric research.

SCIENCE: HISTORY AND EVALUATION OF RESEARCH ACTIVITIES

During the nineteenth century the only original research dealt with issues concerning the natural history of Greece. Thus, in botany, Professor Th. Orphanides and his collaborator Th. von Heldreich (a

German naturalized Greek and educated in France) discovered and described more than 750 plant species. These botanists were internationally known for their achievements and mentioned in the works of their European colleagues. A similar study regarding insects was conducted by Th. Krueper (another German scientist working in Athens University). These endeavours continued in the twentieth century by Greek scientists and some amateurs on several animal groups (Lepidoptera, Hemiptera, Acarea, land snails, fishes of inland water, and many others). They were linked to the movement for the study of nature in Greece, a movement associated with ecology and the protection of nature. Similar work was carried out in geology and paleontology; and the German-educated scientists Professors K. Mitsopoulos and Th. Skoufos should be mentioned for their work at the end of the nineteenth century and the early twentieth. However, the studies of the flora and fauna of Greece as well as of its geological description were mostly carried out by German, French and British scientists (the names of J. Pitton de Tournefort, J. Sibthorp, J. B. G. M. Bory de Saint Vincent, M. Chaubard, E. Boissier, E. von Halacsy, A. von Hayek, K. H. Rechinger, W. Greuter and many others in botany, of numerous zoologists and of R. Lepsius, A. Philipson and C. Renz in geology substantiate this statement). However, their research work was generally descriptive and hardly of an innovative nature. The same applies to the enumeration and description of cultivars and local animal breeds made by several agronomists (e.g. vine cultivars by B. Krimbas).

The pattern differs for more sophisticated research activities. In physics, in the twentieth century, most of the achievements of importance should be credited to Greeks who were studying or working abroad. When these scientists returned to their home country they generally stopped working or performed less significant research. This is the case of D. Chondros, Professor of Physics at the University of Athens, Professor A. Papapetrou, who made important contributions working abroad after being obliged to leave Greece for political reasons, Professor A. (Tom) Ypsilantis, a Greek from the diaspora, whose contributions were made in the USA and Switzerland while his rather short stay in Greece was a traumatic experience, Professor J. Iliopoulos in France, G. Nicolis in Belgium, and others. However, there are exceptions to every rule: in cosmology Professor G. Kontopoulos and in physics Professor G. Gounaris made their valuable contributions while in Greece. The same pattern is encountered in chemistry, L. Zervas made his world-renowned contributions when in Germany, although he continued his research when he returned to Greece and formed a school of organic chemists. Some of the best mathematicians of the country made significant contributions when working in foreign institutions (Ch. Papakyriakopoulos, D. Christodoulou, N. Varopoulos, Athanase Phokas and T. Apostol to mention a few). The great C. Kartheodory, a Greek from the diaspora, was twice asked to come to Greece to help organize university level education, but after he encountered the hostility of the local scientific establishment, he left the country and his proposals were mostly ignored.

It has to be admitted that this pattern was greatly modified after the middle of the twentieth century. Scientists educated abroad were interested in research and continued their activities in Greece. Most of them functioned as foreign correspondents of the foreign research groups or of the schools to which they belonged. In this respect, the Greek scientific diaspora played a major role. Greeks who emigrated and acquired important scientific positions abroad played the role of intermediaries between the foreign scientific community and the indigenous one.

By the 1960s, Greeks occupied important positions in the US (the physicians G. Papanikolaou and G. Kotzias became known for their discoveries, the engineer Ilias Gyftopoulos held a position at MIT, K. Alexopoulos was a well-known mycologist among others). During the 1970s a younger generation of scientists appeared, a generation which was willing to play an important role in their home country (the molecular biologist F. Kafatos, the mathematician S. Negrepontis, the physicist E. Oikonomou and several others). Some of them were instrumental in establishing research centres and university institutions and played an important innovative role. The research centre ITE and the University of Crete were two institutions which benefited from such influence. On the other hand the old universities were mostly reluctant to apply innovative changes. The law for restructuring universities on departmental units and another law, which soon followed, regulating research activities, were mostly based on modern views and inspirations. On the other hand many Greek scientists from the diaspora tried to take advantage of the prestige conferred to them by their positions in universities abroad: they accepted professorial positions in Greek universities but hardly worked for the indigeneous institutions because they simultaneously kept their foreign professorships. The role played by the Greek scientific diaspora is in a sense parallel to that displayed by the Israeli one. However, in the field of science, the Greek diaspora has been somewhat less important than its Jewish counterpart.

Achievements made abroad have conferred greater prestige than any work done in Greece. This, combined with the devaluation of locally made contributions, has deep ideological roots in Greece, more than in any other country belonging to the scientific periphery or semiperiphery. Greeks tended to rate themselves according to the opinion of foreigners. Greeks expected support from the Western powers to gain freedom, when subject to the Ottoman occupation, protection of their state after the liberation, fulfilment of their national expectations, and assistance to sustain progress. Foreigners wanted to see in modern Greeks the descendants of the ancient Greeks. So Greeks valued everything to do with their attributed past and everything foreigners achieved (the real successors of ancient Greeks), while tending to devalue everything produced locally. This had a negative effect in efforts to establish a local scientific tradition, every generation bringing from abroad the scientific innovations and the new world view, thus inhibiting the development of any local tradition. This situation could have been changed by the formation of strong research groups starting in the 1970s. Local 'schools', worthy of their name, developed in only a few cases. Two examples should be mentioned – the Plant Pathology School formed by John Sarejanni and the School of Hematology by Phedon Fessas. The founding fathers of these schools shared some common characteristics. They possessed personalities characterized by the broadness of views, intellectual prowess and intellectual honesty. Their scientific agenda was the study of an important local problem (important for the well-being of the Greek population). Sarejanni abandoned theoretically inclined work and devoted his efforts to assembling all instances of local plant diseases and their vectors. Fessas focused his attention on genetically determined anemias, frequent in the country because their carriers exhibited a resistance to malaria which is endemic in Greece. To date these schools have produced three to four generations of research workers.

In the 1950s, most young Greek scientists were eager to follow a research career in physics (especially nuclear, high energy or theoretical physics). The structure of matter was the challenging issue which inspired them. This interest resulted from the recent military production and use of atomic bombs. Starting in the 1980s, this trend has greatly changed. Molecular biology on one hand and informatics on the other replaced the physics of elementary particles. Numerous Greek scientists are now devoting their energies successfully to the study of developmental biology at the molecular level and to biotechnology, while evolutionary studies attract them less. Informatics has also enjoyed great success among the young people and Greeks seem, by tradition, to be well adapted to an abstract way of thinking – a qualification that renders them successful in this area.

PROGRESS IN TECHNOLOGY AND TECHNOLOGICAL ACHIEVEMENTS

We will not follow the assessment of Professor A. Dimarongonas that the history of modern Greek technology starts in 1975 when A. G. Petzetakis invented the spiral plastic tube. It is a fact that Petzetakis' industry became prosperous from this invention. Neither should it be denied that very few such innovations were made by and used in Greek industries. On the other hand, it is a fact that the country changed during the second half of the nineteenth century and the first half of the twentieth. It moved from the level of traditional technology to that of an industrial and modern state: it moved from sailing boats to steamships; trains and a road system were developed, which changed the ways of travelling and trade; and ports were constructed in Piraeus and Thessaloniki as well as in smaller coastal cities. Starting from the end of the nineteenth century and until the end of the third decade of the twentieth, the country was provided with electrical power. In several provinces more than 50% of the houses had electrical power by 1930, this percentage in big towns reaching 65%, while in the area of Athens it was nearly 100%. Industry, and especially chemical industry, developed.

The technical know-how was provided first by the military schools, where engineering, mathematics and physics were taught. Later, the Technical University played the same role along with foreign experts and specialists. We should also not forget the presence, in the beginning of the twentieth century, of the Roussopoulos Academy, a private school of applied science studies, which focused mainly on chemical industries. This school contributed to the education of technicians equipped with scientific knowledge.

However, the contribution *in situ* of foreign experts was instrumental. French technicians and engineers played a significant role in directing great public works and in forming a local élite equipped with technical and managerial capacities. The French influence was thereafter succeeded by the English and American influence. Greeks, who studied abroad in France or at the Technical Universities of Switzerland (Zurich) and Germany (Munich), were those who created the first cement industries, as well as other chemical industries. They also played an important role as intermediaries between the foreigner and local technical communities.

In the short paragraph which follows, I shall only mention important technical and managerial achievements in Greece for which foreigners as well as Greek engineers and other scientists were responsible. The completion of these works shows also how a young country with an inexperienced group of technicians, with the help of foreign know-how, managed to solve urgent and complicated problems. The technological effort started in the 1870s, when the Hellenic Government decided to ask for French help. A French Commission for Public Works was formed in 1883, which planned, or approved plans of major works and supervised their implementation. In 1892 some Greek technicians already believed that their country was self-sufficient in technical expertise. In 1920 the chemists who studied at Athens University were more numerous than the positions to be filled. In 1925 a Chamber of Technicians was founded, grouping all kinds of engineers and architects.

However, Greece's delay in catching up with technical matters and in industrialisation is obvious. While trains started in 1830 in western Europe, in Greece the first train appeared forty years later. By 1886 several tracks were laid in Sterea Hellas, in Thessaly and in the Peloponnese. Efforts to construct a modern network of roads only started in earnest in 1927. Electrical generators appeared for the first time in the USA and in Britain in 1880, in Italy in 1883, in Hungary and Rumania in 1884, and in Greece in 1889. The construction of the modern port of Piraeus only started in 1923.

The most important achievement in the nineteenth century among the major public works was the cutting of the Corinth Canal. It was an important technical feat and a risky economic operation. The cutting of this isthmus was thought to provide opportunities for shortening sea travel from Piraeus to Patras. In the beginning of 1882, a French company started the work. After eight years, this sociétè had managed to remove about 9,300,000 cubic metres of earth but finally went bankrupt. A Greek company succeeded it and completed the task between 1890 and 1893 by removing the remaining 2,800,000 cubic metres of earth. However, this technical achievement did not prove to be a great economic success, as was initially thought. A second great work was the drainage of Lake Copais. In 1882 a French sociètè signed a contract and started working on it in 1886. After its bankruptcy, a British concern took over in 1892, but the complete drainage was only achieved in 1931. The surface of the lake drained was 250,000,000 square metres. A similar drainage in Italy of a lake of 300,000,000 square metres was achieved in twenty years (1854–75).

An important technical and managerial enterprise which exceeds the usual measures, is the settlement of some 1,500,000 immigrants coming mainly from Asia Minor, including urban as well as rural populations, after the defeat of Greece in the Greek–Turkish war of 1922 and the following agreed compulsory exchange of populations between Greece and Turkey. The settlement was achieved by an agency (the 'Commission for the Establishment of Refugees' under the authority of the League of Nations with a loan provided to this effect) with Greek personnel (engineers, agronomists and other experts) under the supervision of foreigners from 1923 to 1928. It was a complicated task but was nonetheless successfully completed.

Thus, before the Second World War, Greece was a state which achieved a level of modernisation despite the wars in which it had participated (from 1912 to 1922 without interruption). The Second World War, the German, Italian and Bulgarian occupation, and the civil war which followed, destroyed both the infrastructure to a great degree as well as some of the previous achievements, thus creating extremely precarious conditions. The Marshall Plan came to the rescue, but the reorganization was controlled by foreigners, this time Americans. Despite the fact that the Americans thought that Greece should be a simple agricultural country without important industries, the Greeks managed to rebuild the country, to organize a state electrical company (a monopoly) and to achieve the complete electrification of the country. In our time, Greece has achieved a status never reached before. The country before 1960 and its present state are, according to William Hardy McNeal, two completely different countries![1]

In several areas local expertise is even better than foreign. Two cases will be mentioned. First the expertise in construction in areas subjected to earthquakes. Greek experts, like Professors Th. Tassios and P. Karydis are consulted by countries which also suffer from seismic activity. Second, as already noted above, the Research Centre in Crete, ITE, has developed technical innovations in several areas (application of laser technology for cleaning valuable paintings, discovery and use of new efficient mobile elements, etc.) that exceed similar achievements made abroad. Although Greece is presently far from the level of the most advanced countries, it is advancing at a steady pace in an attempt to close this gap.

ENVIRONMENT

Greece is a heterogeneous country which is divided, to an extreme degree, into small geographic compartments. Mountain ranges divide the land into small plains. To these 9,835 islands, islets and isolated rocks in the sea should be added, about one hundred of which are inhabited. In the nineteenth century, when inland roads were undeveloped, the easiest way to travel in the mainland from one to another coastal place was not by land but by sea, because of the mountaineous landscape. The length of the coastal line is impressive, reaching 16,000 kilometres. These physiographic and geomorphological characteristics, as well as the geographic diversity of the climatic conditions, permit the presence of numerous and diversified biological communities, ranging from alpine to coastal. Mediterranean shrubs and maquis (macchia) are succeeded by forests, ravines by plains, semi-arid areas by waterlands and lagoons, rivers cross the plains and form deltas when reaching the sea. Lagoons, river deltas and marshes are rich in bird species. Bory de Saint Vincent, heading the French scientific expedition to the Morea in 1829–30, had already noted the extreme diversification of the terrain of the Peloponnese at that time.

The geographic position of Greece, situated among three continents (Europe, to which it belongs, Asia and Africa), its complicated geological history and its great ecological heterogeneity account for the richness in species of fauna and flora to be found in Greece. Species belonging to several biogeographic areas (European, Asian, African, Mediterranean and Pontic) are encountered. The number of species included in the fauna of Greece is estimated to be equal to about 700 Chordates (Vertebrates) and to 20,000–30,000 Invertebrates. About 6,000 plant species belong to the flora of Greece, of which more than 700 are endemic. At the end of the twentieth century it was estimated that 186 Chordate species, 10% of the invertebrate ones, and about 300 plant species were under threat of extinction.

Since Greece is considered to be one of the many centres of biological diversity (it is the richest in number of species per square kilometre among European countries, including Italy and Spain, which are also quite rich in this respect) a considerable effort has been made to counteract the causes of species depauperation. The most expedient way of achieving this is to minimise human interventions and activities in areas of great biological importance. Indeed, human activity is the main reason for ecological deterioration; it has led to deforestation (by tree cutting, by goat breeding, often by arson in order to use the land for housing), drainage of waterlands and lakes, and over-exploitation of natural resources (overfishing, overhunting). Further, the destruction of the natural environment by direct and indirect effects has been caused by urban development, by the growth of sea traffic and by the expansion of industrial and agricultural activities.

It seems that this deterioration is of ancient origin. Plato remarked that in his time the forest coverage was reduced in Attica in comparison to the conditions a few generations earlier. A scholar in forestry, the late Professor P. Kontos, insisted that the coverage of forests decreased dramatically from the time of the Greek Revolution (1821–28) to the middle of the nineteenth century, from 48% to 38% of the country's surface. There are strong reasons to doubt this claim. It seems that what was defined as forest has changed between the two estimates. However it seems that the forest coverage further declined: in 1898 it was 28%, in 1911 23.1%, in 1930 19.7% and in 1938 it had further diminished. According to recent estimates the forest coverage of the country amounts to approximately 20% and to this is usually added about a 26% of coverage of 'forest vegetation' (meaning land partially covered by forest trees – 24.7% and phrygana vegetation – 1.7%). In a later estimate the total forest covering is of 65 million *stremmata* (25,09 million square miles) of which 51% are public 'forest vegetation' and 30% are private 'forest vegetation'. In a recent (2001) statement the Minister of Agriculture claimed that forests plus forest vegetation amount to 49.3% of the total land area (that is, equal to 6,513,068 hectares.) Landscape drawings and paintings from the nineteenth century by foreign travellers, as well as by Greeks, indicate that several places now covered by forests were previously uncovered. A state effort at reforestation, at least in Attica, is evident. On the other hand several previously covered areas are now urban or denuded (the forest of plane trees covering Platania in the Prefecture of Chania, Crete, during the visit of the French traveller Claude Savary in 1779, is now covered by small hotels). Even before the Second World War, but mostly after it, several areas were declared protected by state decrees (areas of absolute protection of nature, areas of protection of nature, national parks, protection of natural formations, of landscapes and natural elements of landscapes, and finally areas of ecological development). The Greek state also signed several international treaties concerning the protection of the natural environment, such as Ramsar for waterlands protection, Berne for wild life protection, Bonne for the protection of wild migrating species, Barcelona for the protection of the Mediterranean sea environment, and the CITES forbidding the trade of species facing extinction. Eleven waterlands have been declared protected areas according to the Ramsar convention:

1) The delta of Evros river, at the frontier with Turkey, an especially rich place for avifauna
2) The delta of the rivers Louros and Arachtos at the Amvrakikos Gulf, a place of equal importance for the avifauna
3) The lake of Mikri Prespa (small Prespa), a rich place for several bird species and the only area in Europe where the Rose Pelican nests
4) The delta of the river Nestos
5) The deltas of the rivers Axios, Loudias and Aliakmon
6) The lake Ismaris (Mitrikou) and the lagoon of Mesi
7) The lake Vistonis-Porto Lago
8) The lakes Koronia and Volvi
9) The lake Kerkini
10) The lagoon of Messolonghi and the delta of Acheloos
11) The lagoon of Kotychi at the Ilia department.

However, these regions are only theoretically protected. Almost no steps have been taken for their actual protection. Furthermore, several other lakes are not declared protected areas, such as Pamvotis (the lake of Ioannina) and Kourna (in the Prefecture of Rethymnon, Crete). In total, 400 waterlands have been registered in Greece. It should be added that for reasons of sanitation several important waterlands have been drained and turned into cultivated land, in order to eradicate endemic malaria. The most famous examples are that of Lake Copais in Beotia and that of the marsh of Yannitsa in Macedonia. The most recent case was that of Lake Voiviis (Karla) in Thessaly. However, after drainage, Karla underwent soil saltification and plans are being made to reclaim it as a waterland. Even the non-drained lakes suffered, the extent of the water surface of the lakes in Aetoloakarnania and of Lake Kerkini were greatly reduced, as was plant coverage at the coasts of the lakes in Aetoloakarnania. Several other permanent, but also some temporary marshy places have been sanitized by proper draining, or through the shaping and arrangement of river beds. Thus, the locations and extent of waterlands have been greatly reduced by numerous efforts during the nineteenth and especially the twentieth century. This greatly reduced the avifauna, the amphibian and other water life as well as the flora. Ten national parks were declared in order to protect forests, ravines and their flora and fauna:

1) The valley of Vikos (Valia Calda) and Aoos river in Epirus
2) The Samaria gorge (ravine) in the Prefecture of Chania, Crete
3) The Ainos mountain in Cephallonia island, with its fir forest of Abies Cephallonica
4) The Oiti mountain in Phthiotis Department
5) The Olympus mountain in Thessaly
6) The Parnassus mountain in Phthiotis Department
7) Mount Parnes in Attica. All the above mountains are covered by firs of the same species as that of Ainos but also present an interesting collection of flowering plants
8) Sounion
9) Mount Pindos, the most important of the mountain ranges running from North to South, separating Epirus from Macedonia and Thessaly. Several species of forest trees are found in Pindos. Besides the forest, these areas have a wealth of flowering plants species and harbor populations of rare mammals, such as bears and wolves
10) The forests around the Lake Mikri Prespa.

The national parks are also theoretically protected but, as opposed to the waterlands, their area has been properly defined and thus they face fewer legal problems for adequate future protection.

There are also two national sea parks dedicated to saving sea animals facing extinction. One is the North Sporades national park for the protection of seals. Seals have a more extended area distribution, they are either sporadically or permanantly found around the coasts of the Ionian islands and of several islands of the East Aegean sea. However, the island park near Alonisos intends to be a sanctuary for them. The other is the Laganas coast in the island of Zakynthos, an oviposition site of the sea turtle *Caretta caretta*. This turtle also has other coastal sites of oviposition in western Peloponnese as well as other places, but the Zakynthos coast seems to be one of the most important. Nineteen forests of 'aesthetic quality' have also been declared under protection. They include orchards, such as the Almond orchard in Cavala. Fifty-one 'natural monuments' were also declared under protection. They include 36 single trees or clusters of trees, 10 forests – among them the virgin forest on central Rhodopi mountain, at the border with Bulgaria – one small island, one site of flowering plants, one site of *Sphagnum* vegetation, one site of water fountains, and the forest of fossil trees of Lesvos island.

A few other places rich in fossil depositions should be mentioned and protected, such as the Pikermi which was the first to be discovered and which is widely known for its mammal fossils, and Tilos island, where dwarf elephants and other mammals have been excavated. The natural environment of Greece has been subject to various and changing pressures from human intervention. During the Ottoman rule, an important part of the population withdrew to the mountains, where several villages and greater agglomerations became populous centres. Mountain populations, besides a restrained agriculture, were mainly occupied with goat and sheep breeding, and as a result mountain forests suffered from the presence of these animals. From the time of Greek independence the formation of urban centres in the plains and coasts has attracted rural populations. During the nineteenth century, but mainly after the reception of the exchanged orthodox population from Asia Minor following the 1922 defeat, the urban centres increased considerably in size. This increase continued at an accelerated pace after the end of the Second World War and especially during the civil war. From 1950 to the present, urban increase proceeded geometrically while the non-urban population severely declined. Thus, important urban centres were formed, such as the greater Athens zone (including the port of Piraeus and all suburb conglomerations), the Thessaloniki centre (with its suburbs), Patras, Herakleion (in Crete), that of Volos, that of Larissa and several others. The pressure to extend city limits and the consequent appropriation of land for human habitation has greatly transformed the environment around these urban concentrations. Pressures to extend tourism has also drastically modified the environment of coastal areas and islands, as have the pressures for secondary habitats. Yet, not all islands have experienced the same pressures. Concurrently, the pressure for land for housing is smaller in mountainous regions and their forests, especially in those places that are situated away from Attica and Thessaloniki.

In these urban regions the environmental deterioration has been greatest. In some locations the establishment of industries has had a deleterious effect. Official allocation of land use in different areas to preserve traditional activities or the natural environment (coastal as well as forest) has not proved to be efficient. Land use could be legally modified, by permitting post facto original illegal uses. The reason for this is that political influence on the government has been extremely effective in changing land use, and the state has been reluctant to demolish the illegally built houses. The absence of a cadastre facilitates the appropriation of lands owned by the state.

Political pressures were also crucial for the regulation of the hunting periods. Illegal hunting is still extremely prevalent and has been a major cause in the decline in numbers of several species now nearing extinction. Most significantly the period of legitimate hunting has not been regulated according to the European Community rules, which specify the suspension of hunting at times when species reproduce. The inefficient protection from illegal hunting adds to this sad situation. Mass harvesting of fish by illegal dynamite fishing is another cause for the depauperation of the sea environment.

There are several non-governmental organizations that have been pressing the government to implement effective measures for the protection of nature. The oldest is the Society for the Protection of Nature (Etaireia Prostasias tis Fyseos), which was created in the 1920s. The Hellenic Society, established during the junta régime, aimed to protect the natural, as well as the human environment, local traditions in urban centres and the preservation of those architectural monuments not included for protection by the archeological service. ERYEA, a society for the protection of land, air and water from pollution, was short-lived but nonetheless helped in drafting legal documents for these purposes. There are several other societies and organizations that engage in the protection of living organisms: the Hellenic Zoological Society (a scientific society), the Ornithological Society, and several groups aimed at the protection of specific animals (bears, seals, sea turtles). The Goulandris Museum of Natural History is both a depository of materials and a centre for educating children. It is also responsible for the Centre for Waterlands. WWF–Hellas, a filial society of the WWF in Switzerland, has also been actively engaged in several campaigns, the preservation of Laganas coast for sea turtle oviposition being the most important. Despite the useful efforts of these organizations, the future cannot be viewed optimistically. Only regulation from the European Union can act as an appropriate counterweight to the internal political pressures exercised on the Greek government and force it to implement efficient measures to preserve nature.

NOTE

1. W. H. McNeal, *The Metamorphosis of Greece since World War II* (Chicago: Chicago University Press, 1978).

10

Greek Education in the Twentieth Century: A Long Process Towards a Democratic European Society

ANNA FRANGOUDAKI

INTRODUCTION

The history of Greek education is full of characteristics and events described as disconcerting, and often interpreted through reference to the particularities or specificities of Greek society. Among such particularities is the predominance of the language issue, on which there is an extended bibliography. Another is the much lower social class selection in education in comparison to almost all other European countries, which has been explained by the 'tendency to education' of lower social strata in general and by the agricultural population in particular.[1] As is the case with most issues in Greek society, to understand the current problems it is necessary to refer to their historical roots. In this chapter it is suggested that the history of Greek education in the twentieth century has been a particularly long process that has resulted in an educational system based on the principle of equality of opportunity in education, that corresponds to the demands of economic development, and which responds to the factors necessary to make Greece a European society. Educational reforms, designed to create a modern educational system, have been pending for several decades, from the very beginning of the twentieth century and up to the mid-1970s.

The democratic right of all citizens to be educated appears very early in the writings of the Greek Enlightenment scholars, and their dream of an independent Greek state was gradually transformed into a political project that was realized in the early nineteenth century. During the first years of the war of independence the leaders of the revolt, referred to as the Peloponnesian Senate, envisaged schools where 'both males and females' would study 'free of charge'.[2]

However, up to the 1920s, this right of education for all was, understood in terms of social class and gender division. According to official documents, primary school was addressed to the 'lower class', 'middle school' to the 'middle class' and higher education to the 'upper social class'.[3] During the same period, gender inequality was perceived as 'natural' although the early feminist weekly review, *The Ladies' Gazette*, had argued since 1880 for the right of women to education and salaried work.[4] Until the First World War women's education was seen as a privilege accorded to 'girls' rather than a right, and it was limited to learning in order to efficiently exercise the 'duties of the female sex' as a wife,[5] and particularly the national duties of the Greek mother to educate her sons as patriots.[6] At the same time, higher education for women was seen not only as 'unnecessary', but even as 'harmful' to society, because of the 'nature' of women, who were seen as having 'fragile health' and a 'weak morality'.[7]

After the First World War this social class and gender taxonomy of education was gradually removed from institutional texts, leaving in its place a conception of educational equality seen as the right of all citizens to have access to all levels of school, regardless of differences, whether they be social, geographic, economic or gender based.

TOWARDS THE PRINCIPLE OF EDUCATION FOR ALL

As a result of the widespread acceptance of the principle of educational equality in the above sense, during that period, attention was focused between the wars on the slow access to education and on illiteracy, which became the main subjects in the public debate about schooling. In fact, in the 1910s, primary education enrolled only 12% of boys and 5% of the girls aged 5 to 12,[8] while during the 1930s almost 40% of the total population were illiterate, of which 60% were women (1928 Population Census). Illiteracy was violently denounced by the radical political discourse of the 1930s as 'intellectual slavery of the people' serving the 'interests of reactionary forces'.[9]

An educational policy that aimed at the creation of schools in a modern sense appeared early in Greek society. By the end of the nineteenth century, and most definitely around the 1910s, this policy had been formulated, carefully documented as to its necessity and supported by the liberal political forces. The main elements of the policy were as follows: the establishment of *Demotic* (or spoken) Greek as the language of schooling, the creation of an educational system that would combat illiteracy within one generation of compulsory schooling, that would serve the needs of economic development by introducing sciences and vocational material into the curricula, and form technical and vocational channels, including citizenship education, thus giving schools the function of forming responsible citizens.[10] This educational policy became a political project, part of the general social reform policy of the governments of Eleftherios Venizelos, after 1910. Nevertheless, it did not secure parliamentary support until the inter-war period. It reappeared again after the end of the 1950s, and it was finally enacted in 1976. As the main historian of Greek education puts it, there is a dire need for interpretation of why the 'educational reform did not take place' for almost a century, from the 1880s to 1976.[11]

In order to find an explanation of the above phenomenon, one should start with an issue that dominated the social conflict over education for a long time, namely the language question. In fact, every other issue concerning Greek education was for almost a century overshadowed by the so-called language 'problem', an understanding of which is necessary in order to explain all other education issues.

THE PREDOMINANCE OF THE LANGUAGE QUESTION IN EDUCATION

The language question is an old issue in Greek society. The conflict over language arose initially during the formation of the vision for an independent Greek state which led, in the early nineteenth century, to the revolution against the Ottoman Empire. The intellectuals, being the leading national figures of the time, were divided concerning the question of the national language. Some believed that the 'revival' of Ancient Greek was fundamentally connected to the dream of the formation of an independent nation, while others were strongly in favour of the adoption of spoken Greek as the language of the new state. The linguistic conflict was resolved at that time by the intervention of Enlightenment intellectuals who proposed a compromise in favour of the 'living language'. The adoption of a purified form of spoken Greek was proposed as the language of the new state. Thus, *Katharevoussa* (or pure) Greek was invented, and at the same time the proposal of resurrecting Ancient Greek was abandoned.

Since that time, *Katharevoussa* has coexisted in society with the spoken varieties; standardized and codified by linguists under the name of *Demotic* Greek. The linguistic reform, aimed at establishing *Demotic* Greek as the language of education, has had a long history of consecutive failures. The first such failure, and one of the most dramatic, was the inclusion in the Constitution of 1911 of a provision establishing *Katharevoussa* as 'the official language of the Greek state' and forbidding its 'falsification'.[12]

Inherent in this constitutional provision protecting *Katharevoussa* Greek was a significant contradiction that remained unresolved for many decades. Eleftherios Venizelos, at the head of the government when this provision was voted on, had acted against his own educational policy. The leaders of the movement in favour of *Demotic* Greek had interpreted this provision either as a 'betrayal' of the liberal ideas,[13] or as a a victory of the reactionary forces, albeit unclear and unintelligible as to its causes.[14] It should be noted here that the rationality of the Demoticist theorists' discourse, and the documentation they had accumulated on the necessity of establishing the spoken language in education, was for them self-evidently related to fundamental national interests. They documented *Demotic* Greek to be closely related to the implementation of compulsory attendance, to be unavoidable for the development of technical and vocational channels in education, and ultimately the only linguistic tool for the assimilation of linguistic minorities. Thus, they were unable to understand the true reasons for their defeat.

As we have elsewhere suggested,[15] Venizelos had subordinated his social and economic policy to the 'national question'. In the 1910s Venizelos, Greece's leading social reformer, was at the same time facing the priority of the national project. His government, representing the majority of Greek society at the time, was planning the acquisition of territories, first from the Ottoman Empire, but also from other neighbouring Balkan countries. The realization of the economic and social policy aiming at industrialization, agrarian reform and urbanization presupposed serious social and political pressures. On the other hand, the realization of 'national aspirations', that is, the acquisition of territories by war, necessarily involved 'national mobilization', through social unity and class coalition, and ultimately required political peace in order that all social forces should remain united to the service of the national objective. Consequently, Venizelos subordinated his social and economic policy to the 'national question'. He made two important symbolic compromises: postponing both language and agrarian reform. His policy in fact led to the Balkan Wars that, by 1913, almost doubled the territory of the Greek state.

To an extent, Venizelos' symbolic compromise over language has had a long-term effect, determined at the same time by the political situation which permits the language question to remain the focus of social concern. This was the case in 1917. After *a coup d'état* of army officials against the pro-German monarchy, Venizelos established in Thessaloniki a 'revolutionary government'. Thereafter, he imposed it on Athens under the military protection of the Allies, and forced the participation of Greece in the First World War on the side of the Entente. It was a law passed by the 'revolutionary' government of Thessaloniki that finally established the educational reform, considered to be one of the most important changes in the educational history of the country.[16] The 1917 reform introduced *Demotic* Greek as the language of primary education.

As for higher levels of education, it reserved the authority to rule on educational matters to the leaders of the Demoticist movement.[17]

The 1917 reform lasted only three years. It was swept away in 1921 after the fall of the Venizelos government. The Demoticist leaders were accused of various crimes 'against the nation', on the basis that their ideas endangered the nation through the 'falsification' of the 'ancestors' language'. *Demotic* Greek was condemned as 'peasant dialect' inappropriate for education, and when, in 1929, the then Venizelos government legislated the last pre-war educational reform, *Demotic* Greek remained the language taught in primary schools, while secondary education trained students mainly in Ancient Greek and *Katharevoussa* Greek. Additionally, *Katharevoussa* remained the language of public administration, law, science, the great majority of the academy, and the press.

It was not until 1964 that a progressive set of educational reforms was set in motion, requiring, among other things, Demotic Greek as the language of instruction at all levels of education. Abrogation of this law was to be one of the first actions of the junta, which imposed a dictatorship from 1967 to 1974. After the fall of the junta and the restoration of parliamentary government in 1974, the age-old 'language protection' provision was not included in the amended democratic Constitution of 1975, and language reform was unanimously voted in 1976 establishing *Demotic* Greek as the language of public administration, law and education.

In order to understand this long dominance of *Katharevoussa* or pure Greek, and the social conflict related to the language issue, one should refer to the social function of the two Greek languages. *Katharevoussa* Greek functioned as a 'high' language until the interwar period. Since the 1930s, and clearly after the 1950s, the Greek *diglossia* can be described as transitional, according to the term introduced by Joshua Fishman,[18] because of the gradual change of the social function of both *Demotic* and *Katharevoussa* Greek. Since the 1930s, and definitively since the 1950s, speakers used *Katharevoussa* in an effort to produce latent messages of educational status, higher ranking and seriousness.[19] Gradually, the preciosity and opacity of *Katharevoussa* was increasingly used by second-order intellectuals in order to hide tautology among resonant datives and to conceal the absence of information among incomprehensible ancient words. This gradual loss of legitimacy produced another function of *Katharevoussa* elements in the *Demotic* vernacular, used in order to produce messages of irony or sarcasm.[20] At the same time *Katharevoussa*, used by public authorities lacking consensus, became a major instrument for exercising power by the use of language. It increasingly became the chosen code used by public speakers who had no information to impart other than their right to be on the tribune and no other intention than to legitimize through speech their position in the social hierarchy.[21]

The connotations of *Demotic* Greek evolved correspondingly. The gradual loss of legitimacy of the purist code increased the usage of *Demotic* Greek in formal contexts. Such usage classified the speaker (according to the context) as a holder of radical positions and beliefs or, in the case of fluent users of formal *Demotic* varieties, as part of the pro-democratic opposition intellectual groups.

The social utility of the purist code, thus explaining its persistence, was related to the deep social crisis that Greek society entered at the end of the Second World War. This war, particularly destructive for the country because of the brutal Nazi occupation and a fierce resistance movement, was followed by a civil war which ended in 1949. By the beginning of the 1950s, the economic infrastructure was almost completely destroyed, the political institutions were in serious crisis, and the social equilibrium was sustained by overt foreign intervention. Thus, during the 1950s, social organization was determined by the 'Great Fear' of the civil war. The authorities in power, lacking legitimacy and feeling insecure, systematically produced messages that were empty of information. In this context, the use of *Demotic* Greek was seen as potentially subversive of the social order, while the grandiloquence and opacity of *Katharevoussa* Greek was deemed particularly valuable. Gradually, *Katharevoussa* came to be identified with governments that treated democratic values as dangerous for the social *status quo*, obstructed freedom of the press, and violated the rules of free parliamentarism. As a result, the use of *Katharevoussa* connoted, since that decade, acceptance of established hierarchies, respect for traditional values, resistance to change and support of the given order.

By the early 1960s, important political and economic changes were taking place, and the old demoticist arguments on the necessity of adopting *Demotic* Greek in education became once again the centre of public debate. Although the opposition of many established academics and representatives of other learned institutions was violent,[22] the argument on the necessity for a functional educational system, and its closer correspondence with economic development, led to the above-mentioned educational reform of 1964.

The misuse and abuse of the magical qualities of *Katharevoussa* Greek by the dictators (1967) and their supporters was the final *coup de grâce* to the already bruised and depreciated legitimacy of this purist code. After the fall of the junta and the restoration of parliamentary government in 1974, *Katharevoussa* had no other social function than to identify the speaker with pro-dictatorial positions. It had become a code without any social utility. For this reason, *Demotic* Greek was in 1976 unanimously and finally given the status of the state's language by the Parliament. It had been a long road to education for a democratic society.

Indeed as a result of economic difficulties, and the series of wars the Greek state was involved in from 1912 to 1922, and from 1940 to 1949, access to education had been quite slow. Thus illiteracy remained high, as mentioned above, until the end of the civil war (1949). Efforts to combat illiteracy during the 1929 educational reform had been neutralized by the social crisis, resulting in the dictatorship of 1936, and then had been completely abandoned during the Nazi occupation and the civil war. In the 1950s new efforts to rebuild the educational system, combat illiteracy and modernize schools were unsuccessful because of the serious crisis of political institutions that followed the civil war. Lacking legitimacy, in the Weberian sense, the authorities in power assigned to the educational institutions the sole function of ensuring the political and ideological control of the younger generations. Official pronouncements on education defended a school system based on the predominance of dead languages, and consistently stressing the dangers for the nation's morality inherent in modern, technological civilization. Technical education and the use of *Demotic* Greek in schools were seen as subversive.[23]

This situation started to change in the 1960s. Important economic transformations took place, reflecting the Greek economy's integration in the world market. At the same time, the active population in the agricultural sector decreased dramatically, while that in the industrial sector, construction and services, increased. These transformations posed the problem of government involvement in the formation of the labour force, and the improvement of labour productivity, a problem made more acute by the increased emigration of Greek workers to western Europe, which reached 80,000 to 100,000 a year during the 1960s (Ministry of Labour 1973).

As a result of the above, the necessity for a closer correspondence between the educational system and the needs of economic development became the centre of public debate in the 1960s. During this same period, the 'human capital' theory, stressing the use of a nation's intellectual resources for its development, was imported into Greek society from the country of its origin, the United States. This theory influenced a number of economists and intellectuals, thus converging and strengthening the fifty-year-old liberal reform efforts.[24] At the same time, the political slogan 'education for all', supported mainly by the so-called centrist political forces, had a great impact, as well as the socialist and communist left. Acceptance of *Demotic* Greek in the schools, the rationalization of the educational system, and the formation of a widespread technical educational sector, were the progressive demands of the opposition forces, and were largely supported by a popular majority.

The educational reform of 1964, in addition to introducing *Demotic* Greek as the language of education, made a strong effort to modernize schools, by extending compulsory education from six to nine years, and forming a technical and vocational channel, that intended to include the majority of the student population. During the same years, a parallel effort was undertaken for the reform of higher education. New universities (such as in Patras and Ioannina) were founded, university tuition fees were removed, and greater emphasis was placed on the natural sciences and engineering.

The above evolution was also cut short by the junta, in power from 1967 to 1974. The restoration of parliamentary government, in 1974, found the educational system in a situation often described as held back by almost a century.[25] Illiteracy in the total population over 14 years of age reached 22.2%, 14.6% for men and 29.1% for women (1980 Population Census). The drop-out rate from secondary education was high, resulting in around 60% of the total population entering the labour market with only a six-year primary school degree. Technical and vocational education was almost non-existent, and until 1980 university education was highly unequal as far as gender enrolment was concerned (60% versus 40%).

GREEK EDUCATION IN THE NEW EUROPEAN ERA

Since the mid 1970s, and following the restoration of parliamentary democracy, radical changes have taken place in Greek education. The reform passed by the Greek Parliament in 1976, besides establishing *Demotic* Greek as the language of education, extended compulsory schooling to nine years, and created the framework for the formation of a large technical secondary sector in education. This reform was further augmented, during the 1980s, when the Socialist Party (PASOK) took power, through a series of fundamental changes in the national curricula, and school textbooks.

Illiteracy disappeared in the younger generations. At the beginning of the 1990s, analphabetism for the age group 15 to 24 was 3% of the total age population (3.8 for men and 2.2 for women). The prevention of dropping-out was also targetted with a series of measures such as compulsory enrolment through nine years of education, and the introducion of the 'automatic progress' in primary school since June 1980, which prevented the repetition of the same class during the six years, thus permitting all pupils to finish primary school at the same age (while the ones evaluated as not performing well enough are offered supplementary education in 'special' classes). Furthermore, entrance examinations into higher secondary school (Lyceum), following the completion of the three-year gymnasium, were abolished in 1981. This absence of selective barriers has considerably increased enrolment in secondary education.

As a result of these measures, during the 1990s, kindergartens now enrol 55% of all children. The nine years compulsory school enrols close to 95% of the total age population, and enrolment in upper secondary education (the 3 years Lyceum) has doubled. At the same time, new universities have been established in various provinces and tertiary non-university education has also been established (as a result tertiary education graduates have quadrupled).

At the same time, there is no more gender inequality regarding school attendance, although there remains gender inequality in terms of educational access to disciplines traditionally addressed to men. There is also pronounced inequality in the way educational success is being actualized in university education. Women today comprise 56.9% of the total number of students (the evolution at university level being the following: 25.4% women in 1960–61, 30.4% in 1970–71, 40% in 1980–81 and 53% in 1990–91).

Beyond the above notable changes in the last 20 years, serious content improvement of school textbooks has been undertaken. School books, especially history books, in use until the fall of the dictatorship (1974), served the ideological triptych of nation-religion-family, contained falsifications, distortions and blunt political propaganda. In the current school textbooks there is an expressed intention of objectivity and a modern historical approach. History is no longer exclusively devoted to the narration of wars, treaties and actions of monarchs or state leaders. Textbooks now contain additional information on the economy and its development, on social groups, social life and culture. There is also an equally expressed intention of transmitting democratic values, both directly, by presenting them as principles to be defended, as well as indirectly, by looking objectively at authoritarian governments or the use of coercion, and by underlining the importance of democratic values. A last change is the intention of no longer presenting conflicts and wars as 'natural' incidents (as was the case in the books before 1974), but as a consequence of social and economic conditions, the result of inadequate social organization and ineffective political régimes. There are no more derogatory references to other nations, no negative evaluative attributions, no generally hostile statements. There are references to the necessity and the value of peace, as well as descriptions of the magnitudes of destruction, pain and grief caused by wars.[26]

Along with the rise in the general level of education, Greece is currently facing issues similar to those arising in other European countries, namely the growing numbers of graduates, from a range of areas, who have difficulties in finding work corresponding to their diplomas and, more generally, a growing number of an over-qualified workforce. At the same time, social class selection is becoming more and more pronounced as far as university education is concerned, and the correlation between school achievement and social origin is today clearly obvious. Thus Greek Society is no longer different from other European ones, as had been the case in the past.

Past efforts of the authorities to diminish demand for higher education through the expansion of a large technical and vocational channel, in order to make the educational system correspond to the needs of the labour market,[27] have been documented as being totally unsuccessful.[28] These have now been replaced by new policies offering second chances for education, as a soft measure for addressing youth unemployment.[28] Meanwhile the old emphasis on the urgent need to solve the social problem of huge numbers of young people 'slaughtered *ante portas* of the universities' by the entrance examinations and the *numerus clausus*,[29] is being replaced by the idea, proposed by the Minister of Education in 1999, to render university entrance accessible to all holders of secondary education diplomas.

The fact that school achievement is determined by social origin is clear in the rapidly increasing numbers of pupils classified as having 'learning difficulties', especially in the rural areas. In 1993–94, these pupils represented 10% of the total population in primary education, and 40% in the lower secondary Gymnasium, according the degree of compulsory school.[30]

As studies in the sociology of education have long documented,[31] the modern open door educational system reproduces social inequality, and school achievement is everywhere determined by social origin. This was not the case in Greece, where traditionally the university students of peasant origin represented 25% of the total student population (at least until the end of the 1970s); a very high percentage in comparison with other countries. This high percentage, together with the growing demand for higher education, was seen as pronounced evidence of the democratization of Greek education.[32] Nevertheless, the factor of social class selection in education had been functioning until the 1980s through the assignment of students to various kinds of disciplines. In fact, schools distributing diplomas with a high economic and symbolic value, such as the Athens School of Medicine or the Technical University of Athens, always had a much lower percentage of children of peasants than the national average.

According to the latest available data, 1996–97, students of peasant origin, a vocational category representing the 18% of active population, represent only 5.6% of the total national university student population, and only 2.1% at the Technical University of Athens.[33] The social selection phenomenon is quite apparent if we isolate the university students of the two higher social categories. They are over-represented within this educational level, and particularly at the more prestigious schools. For example, these higher categories, representing 10% of the active population, account for 26% of all university students, and make up 40% of the student body at the Technical University of Athens.[34] In fact, in the past 20 years, the presence of children of peasants in university education has been diminishing at a much faster rate than the decrease of this category in the active population. This despite the increase in the total number of students. In other words, the democratization of education has been accompanied by a definite increase of social selection in schools.

Taking into consideration all the changes mentioned above, we can conclude that the Greek educational system has evolved spectacularly over the last 20 years. Nevertheless, it still has a number of characteristics carried over from the past, such as school textbooks and teaching materials, religious education, school procedures and methods of teaching.

The Greek educational system remains highly centralized. There are no flexible teaching materials. School textbooks are intended to ensure the strict application of the curriculum, which is developed by the Ministry of Education and is equivalent to state legislation. Textbooks are commissioned from specific authors, who are mostly educationists and not necessarily specialized in a particular field, especially at the lower educational levels. Their drafts are monitored and approved by the Educational Institute, that is by representatives of the government in power. There is one single (approved) textbook for each course, which, in turn, is distributed to the children free of charge. A corresponding manual is made available to the teacher.

Religious education is compulsory in Greek schools. In addition to the relatively high religious homogeneity of Greek schoolchildren, there is no separation of Church and state. Thus, religious education in primary and secondary schools is addressed to all pupils, and religious practice (such as prayer before classes) is quite common. Non-Christian Orthodox children have the constitutional right not to attend these classes and practices, but there is evidence of intolerance in practice.[35] Such intolerance mainly centres on non-Christian religions, and on faiths considered by the official Church as 'sects' (e.g. Jehovah's Witnesses).

In general teachers have insufficient education. Moreover, lesson content, teaching methods and classroom organization are still traditional. This fact is also relevant to the understanding of how Greek teachers conceive of 'normal' school procedures and methods of teaching. Pupils are seated in rows starting at primary school. Teachers simply narrate the knowledge they are supposed to transmit, and then question the students to see if they have understood. The only source of knowledge is the school textbook. There is much emphasis on rote memory and less emphasis on comprehension, thus excluding a critical approach *vis-à-vis* the subject matter.

As a result of their initial (traditional) education, a large proportion of primary school teachers (40%) disagree with the current ideological goals of education, regretting the loss of the values of the triptych 'fatherland-religion-family', which they consider the foundation of all schooling. A majority (55%), nevertheless adheres to the new values and practices, and is open to reforms and modern teaching approaches.[36] In-service teacher training programmes, focusing on new teaching approaches and pedagogical methods, have been introduced on an experimental (pilot programme) basis since the 1990s.

The traditional traits of the Greek school are currently being challenged by new social phenomena, the most important being the growing presence of migrant populations in schools.

The problems regarding the migrant population are intimately connected to the novelty of this social phenomenon. Greece, for historical and social reasons, has been a country exporting human labour.[37] For the same social and economic reasons, Greece had never until now experienced the presence of non-Greek immigrants. Moreover, mainly after the exchanges of populations during the 1920s and 1930s, whereby the bigger part of Turkish and Slav minorities left Greece, and after the Nazi extermination of almost the entire Jewish population of northern Greece, there has been a relatively high cultural, linguistic and religious homogeneity within the country as a whole. The historically constructed homogeneity has been accompanied by a highly ethnocentric policy concerning ethnic and religious minorities. In the early twentieth century an assimilation policy was adopted regarding education. The only exception to this has been the Muslim minority, of mainly Turkish ethnic background, living in the province of Thrace, whose special bilingual (Greek and Turkish) education is regulated by bilateral and international agreements.

It is apparent from the above that Greek society is not adequately prepared to deal with the migrant phenomenon. According to semi-official and journalistic sources, the number of migrant workers who entered the country in the last two decades is estimated at between 600,000 to 700,000 people. The majority of the immigrants are Albanian, Polish, Turkish and Kurdish, with a smaller number of Egyptians, Philippinos, Yugoslavs and Romanians, and yet smaller numbers of Indians, Pakistanis, Latin-Americans, Vietnamese and other nationalities. Given past educational practices aimed at a homogeneous school population, Greek schools have been ill-prepared to deal with children of other languages and cultures.

Racist and xenophobic attitudes have been multiplying in schools and teachers often feel that they do not know how to handle the new situation. At the same time, the children of migrant parents are increasing in numbers, teaching in 1999–2000 close to 60,000 pupils in primary education, that is 10% of the total enrolled population.[38]

This difficult situation has, nevertheless, put in motion a number of significant transformations, the most important being the government's realization of the need for a new educational policy capable of facing the new challenge. A law on 'multicultural education' was voted in June 1996, and a special secretariat with the same name was created in the Greek Ministry of Education. Three sizable projects (using mainly European Union funding) were launched in 1997, aimed at dealing with the education of migrant students in Greek schools. Additionally, for the first time in Greek history, plans are being instituted to reform the education of the Muslim minority of Greek citizens in Thrace, mainly of Turkish ethnic identity and language, as well as to enrol the Roma children in school to illustrate the magnitude of this change of policy. We should note that when the projects were launched Greek society was generally, but also officially, considered monocultural, the existence of minorities was ignored (evidenced by the total lack of official statistics about minority populations) and minority parents whose children were refused registration in schools were met with traditional indifference by educational authorities. However, over the last three years, there have been important changes. An extended effort to integrate the children of migrants in schools has started, and there has been definite success regarding efforts to enrol Roma children in primary schools. Furthermore, there has been a visible amelioration of the Muslim minority students' achievement record, according to unpublished reports of the Secretariat of Multicultural Education of the Greek Ministry of Education (February 1998, June 1999, May 2000).

In addition to the above official changes in educational policy, the presence of a migrant population in Greek society has put in motion a process of self-examination regarding the xenophobia and racism. We should stress the importance of the acknowledgement of this phenomenon. Almost until the end of the 1980s, there reigned in Greek society an almost unanimous belief that *'Greek people are rather xenophile than xenophobe'*, as Greek authorities rather naïvely put it, in 1991, in an introduction to the report on *Greece*, in a publication of the European Parliament of a special committee reporting on 'racism and xenophobia in the European Union countries'. Another example of unawareness of xenophobic tendencies is offered by an empirical survey involving a representative sample of school teachers, which shows Greek teachers rejecting the adjective 'racist' as a trait among 'Greek people' by an overwhelming percentage of 98%.[39]

Research has now begun to document racism as a phenomenon characterizing Greek society, involving the violation of the constitutional rights and religious freedoms in practice, and the acute xenophobic attitude of school personnel (teachers, principals and associations of parents). The educational system has thus become the focus of investigation with regard to its relationship with the formation of xenophobic attitudes. An analysis of school textbooks,[40] on the presentation of the Greek national identity, revealed that in spite of the expressed intention of objectivity and a modern historical approach, current school text-books include a single definition of the Greek nation, presented as an almost 'natural' entity, comprising three main traits: an uninterrupted historical *continuity* since antiquity, a great ability to *conserve* the main cultural characteristics, and a high cultural *homogeneity*. This entity is systematically defined by the generic term 'Hellenism', thus the nation appears as an anthropomorphic being in a millenary march through history. The conservation of cultural characteristics for thousands of years requires documentation, at least for the latent denial of evolution and change it contains. Thus, the virtue of conservation is proven through a denial of almost any external influence ever affecting the Greek people, as well as through the emphasis on the homogeneity of Greek culture, proven by side-stepping the historical construction of homogeneity through assimilation, the exchanges of populations, and the Nazi extermination of the Greek Jews, as well as the present conditions of minority populations.

The most interesting conclusion, in the above analysis, was that the fictitious 'Greekness' narrated in schools results in an ambivalent and fragile national identity, incapable of coping with the current European realities.

In fact, the current national myth cultivated by schools is a product of both tradition and, paradoxically, the European Union.[41] The integration of Greece into the Union has had a powerful ideological effect on the national self-image. This is for many reasons, but mainly because of the dominant, even if continuously challenged in all countries, stereotype of the alleged superiority of the northern and western European zone. The Eurocentric stereotype includes a hierarchical taxonomy of peoples and cultures in which everything considered to belong to the 'south', as well as the 'east', of this imagined superior area is a misfortunate for those concerned. Moreover, it contains a great admiration for Greek antiquity, whose cultural products are considered of universal value, and an acknowledgement of this antiquity is seen as having shaped European civilization. This Eurocentric stereotype is present in Greek society and education, and it is currently being reproduced as an evident truth within every schoolbook. At the same time, it is a firm belief among Greek school teachers who, as a result, think that European integration could be a danger to Greek language and culture.[42]

We suggest that the acceptance of European taxonomy denigrates Greek culture that, in addition to its Ancient Greek and Byzantine influences, has also been shaped by Ottoman, Turkish, Middle Eastern, Sephardim, Arab and Slav influences. Instead of rejecting this taxonomy through the powerful argument that it is an ideology belonging to the age of colonialism, the Greek educational system accepts it. It, therefore, presents the Greek nation as a mythical entity. Greek culture is not described as a product of history and social evolution, it is not seen as the consequence of cultural counter-influences and inter-mixture. It is, instead, described directly as homogeneous and indirectly as pure. This image of Greek culture is contradictory to elementary historical knowledge, as well as to mere common experience, since several cultural influences are present in social reality. It is, therefore, harmful to Greek students. The Greek national identity is presented to them as of high value, by refusing to acknowledge part of its cultural traits. As a result, the Greek school constructs a national identity which is fragile and ambivalent.

CONCLUSION

Presenting the story of a whole century of Greek education has not been an easy task. If we summarize the contents of this chapter, the main trait appears to be a very long and difficult road towards a democratic society, and a corresponding educational system. The democratic principle of the right of all citizens to education appears very early in the history of the Greek state, despite the fact that for almost a century this excluded the lower social strata and women (as was the case in other European countries).

The political project that aimed to create an educational system that enrolled all those at the correct age in compulsory schooling, being adapted to the needs of economic development and forming responsible citizens, also appeared very early. It first took shape in the 1880s, and it was proposed in the form of a project of laws in Parliament in 1913. Part of this educational policy involved the language issue, that is, the demand to use spoken Greek in school instead of a purist, mainly written, code. A violent social conflict over language, parallel to the conflict over the dangers inherent in technology and the loss of the moral function of school, resulted in adjourning, then suspending, educational reform for several decades.

The reasons were mainly political, although very different, varying with each historical period. In the 1910s, the liberal social project of reforming education in order to adapt it to wider European trends was subordinated, by its political originator Eleftherios Venizelos, to the national policy that led to the Balkan wars, and the doubling of the territory of the Greek state. In the inter-war period, linguistic and educational reform was placed at the centre of public debate, but failed to materialize because of the deep social crisis that had been produced by serious economic problems, leading to social unrest, and to consecutive oppressive governance, up to and including the 1936 fascist dictatorship.

Greek schools in the 1950s could be described as transmitting the grammatical knowledge of dead languages and blunt political propaganda. These were the times of the 'Great Fear' of the civil war. The authorities in power lacked legitimacy, and felt insecure to the point of treating democratic values and freedom of the press as socially dangerous, and finding no better political means than concentration camps in order to neutralize the influence of the defeated communist left. During this period schools functioned in accordance with this profound crisis in all institutions.

Economic development in the 1960s, the successive integration of Greece's economy in the world market, and the opening of society to new ideas, led to a combination of the age-old liberal educational reform with the 'human capital theory' borrowed from the USA. The educational reform voted in 1964, albeit against violent opposition from traditionalist elements, was indicative of the beginning of a new era. The spoken language was established as the language of education, compulsory school was extended to nine years, new knowledge was introduced in schools, and the revision of school textbooks began being revised to reflect rational approaches to culture and society. The abrogation of the 1964 reform was the first act concerning education of the military dictatorship in August 1967.

Deadlocked for half a century, the open door school, functional to society and its economic needs, and basing the selection of transmitted knowledge on rationality and democratic principles, became a reality only after the fall of the junta and the restoration of Parliamentary government in 1974.

With the beginning of the 1980s, spectacular changes started taking place. Among these changes was the generalization of compulsory education, the doubling of the secondary level student population by the abolition of the selective barriers of entrance examinations, the quadrupling of the student population enrolled in tertiary education, and the definite modernization of school textbooks, adapted to European and democratic values.

Greek society and its education are today based on a European model. This means that they reflect the above positive traits but, at the same time, some negative ones. The most important among these negative traits are the following: (a) high social selection, rendering school an inefficient institution for children of lower social strata background, migrants and minorities; and (b) a high degree of ethnocentrism cultivated in schools.

These two negative traits, common to all European Union countries, are inter-related. In all European Union countries, pupils are evaluated and selected according to their acquaintance with the dominant culture, everywhere presented as 'the' national culture, a process through which school achievement is highly determined by social origin. The big economic differences, observed in European Union societies, have shaped ideologies of antagonism, disdain for some groups and violence. At the same time, Europe has a record of colonialism, expansionism and violent struggles leading to the formation of a multitude of independent nation states. This turbulent past has shaped ideologies that legitimize territorial claims, expansion and wars, as well as dominance over 'other' peoples. Educational systems in all European Union countries continue to transmit knowledge, which presents notions of nation, race and sex as natural taxonomies. There is an urgent need for the widespread understanding that this taxonomy is damaging to all children, in the sense that it is harmful not only to the victims of such discrimination, but to majorities as well. The idea of homogeneity and purity implied in the traditional terms of nation and national culture is harmful to everybody.

Greek education is today definitely European. It is, therefore, facing the new and significant challenge of how to find its way towards a tolerant society by restructuring the traits of national identity and efficiently fighting against the racist defence reaction, which many Greek intellectual groups and educators refuse to see in themselves in the 'underdeveloped' and 'levantine' image reflected in the European mirror.

NOTES

1. See C. Tsoukalas, *Exartisi kai Anaparagoghi: o koinonikos rolos ton ekpaideftikon michanismon stin Ellada (1830–1922)* [*Dependence and Reproduction: The Social Role of Educational Mechanisms in Greece (1830–1922)*] (Athens: Themelio, 1979).
2. See A. Dimaras, 'I Metarrythmisi pou den egine, 1821–1894' (Tekmiria Istorias), ['The Educational Reform that did not take place' (Historical Documents)], *Hermis*, Vol. A, (1973) pp.23, 27.
3. See *Nomoschedia Ekpaideftika*, National Printing Office, Athens (1899).
4. See E. Varica, 'I Exeghersi ton Kyrion. I gennissi mias feministikis sineidisis stin Hellada 1833–1907' ['The Revolt of the Ladies. The appearance of a feminist Consciousness in Greece 1833–1907'] *Idryma Erevnas kai Paideias tis Emborikis Trapezas tis Hellados* (1987).
5. See A. Balakaki and E. Elegmitou, 'I ekpaidefsis is ta tou oikou' ['Education of house wives'], *Historiko Archeio Hellinikis Neolaias*, Geniki Grammateia Neas Geneias (1987).
6. See Ziogou-S. Karastergiou, 'I Ekpaidefsi ton Koritsion stin Hellada (1830–1893)' ['Women's higher education in Greece 1830–1893)'], *Historiko Archeio Hellinikis Neolaias*, Geniki Grammateia Neas Geneias (1986).
7. See A. Balakaki and E. Elegmitou, 'I ekpaidefsis is ta tou oikou' ['Education of house wives'], *Historiko Archeio Hellinikis Neolaias*, Geniki Grammateia Neas Geneias (1987) pp. 20, 24.
8. See D. Glinos, *Enas Atafos Nekros. Meletes gia to Ekpaideftiko mas Systima* [*An unburied Dead. Studies of our Educational System*] (Athens: Rallis, 1925) p. 45.
9. See D. Glinos, 'Eklektes Selides', *Stochastis*, Vol. 4 (1981) p. 116.
10. See A. Frangoudaki, *Ekpaideftiki metarithmisi kai fileleftheroi dianooumenoi* [*Educational*

reform and liberal intellectuals] (Athens: Kedros, 1977) pp. 26–34.

11. See A. Dimaras, 'I Metarrythmisi pou den egine, 1821–1894' (Tekmiria Istorias), ['The Educational Reform that did not take place' (Historical Documents)], Vol. A, *Hermis* (1973) and A. Dimaras, 'I Metarrythmisi pou den egine, 1895–1967' (Tekmiria Istorias) ['The Educational Reform that did not take place' (Historical Documents)], Vol. B, *Hermis* (1974).

12. See Article 107 of the Constitutions of 1911, 1952 and 1968.

13. See articles of Yannis Psycharis, Arghyris Eftaliotis and others in the Demoticist Gazette *O Noumas*, respectively nos. 427 and 428, 13 and 23 March 1911.

14. See M. Triantafyllidis, 'Demotikismos'['Demoticism'], *Complete Works*, Vol. 5 (1926).

15. See A. Frangoudaki, 'O ekpaideftikos demoticismos kai o glossikos symvivasmos tou 1911' ['Educational reform and liberal intellectuals'], *University of Joannina Press* (1978) pp. 115–34.

16. A. Dimaras, 'I Metarrythmisi pou den egine, 1895–1967' (Tekmiria Istorias), [The Educational Reform that did not take place (Historical Documents)], Vol. B, *Hermis* (1974) pp. 120–34.

17. For documentation on this statement, see Frangoudaki 1977, pp. 27–48.

18. See J. Fishmann, *Sociolinguistics: A Brief Introduction* (Rowley, MA: Newbury House) pp. 73–90.

19. See M. Setatos, 'Phenomenologia tis Katharevoussas' ['Phenomenology of Katharevoussa Greek'], *Epistimoniki Epetirida Philosophikis Scholis*, University of Thessaloniki (1973) pp. 43–80.

20. See *ibid.*

21. See A. Fragoudaki, 'The metalinguistic prophecy on the decline of the Greek language: its social function as the expression of a crisis in Greek national identity', *International Journal of the Sociology of Language*, 126 (1997) pp. 63–82.

22. See A. Dimaras, 'I Metarrythmisi pou den egine, 1895–1967' (Tekmiria Istorias), ['The Educational Reform that did not take place' (Historical Documents)], Vol. B, *Hermis* (1974) pp. 275–80.

23. See *ibid.*, pp. 248–84.

24. See E. Papanoutsos, *Agones kai agonia gia tin paideia* [*Struggles and Apprehension for Education*] (Athens: Ikaros, 1965).

25. See 'Synchrona Themata', *Special Issue on Education*, B/1, 4 (Spring 1979).

26. See A. Fragoudaki and Th. Dragonas (eds) *Ti ein'I patrida mas?: Ethnokentrismos stin Ekpaidefsi* [*What is our country? Ethnocentrism in Education*] (Athens: Alexandria, 1997) pp. 344–400.

27. See E. Papanoutsos, *Agones kai agonia gia tin paideia* [*Struggles and Apprehension for Education*] (Athens: Ikaros, 1965).

28. See I. Panagiotopoulou, *I geografia ton ekpaideftikon diaforopoiiseon. I mesi epangelmatiki ekpaidefsi sti metapolemiki Hellada* [*Geography of educational differentiation. The secondary professional education in post war Greece*] (Athens: Odysseas, 1993).

29. See E. Papanoutsos, 'The slaughtering ante University portas', *Ta Nea* (4 November 1972).

30. See 'Scholiki Apotychia' ['School underachievement'], *Paidagogiko Instituto*, Greek Ministry of Education (1997) pp. 54–5.

31. See for example, Coleman 1966; Boudon 1973; Bowles and Gintis 1975; Bourdieu and Passeron 1964 and 1970.

32. See C. Tsoukalas, 'Some Aspects of "Over-Education" in Modern Greece', *Journal of the Hellenic Diaspora*, VII, nos. 1 and 2, Spring–Summer (1981) pp. 109–21.

33.   TABLE 1
Evolution of enrolment in University education: sons and daughters of parents working
in agriculture, representing today 18.8% of the active population

	1960/1	*1969/70*	*1984/5*	*1991/2*	*1996/7*
Total of Greece	25.0	25.5	13.5	9.0	5.6
Uni of Athens	19.8	17.8	12.2	7.2	4.5
Technic Uni Ath	6.2	10.5	4.5	3.1	2.1

Source: Combined data from the National Statistical Service of Greece on Education (1990–91) and
unpublished data from the Greek Ministry of Education (1997).

34.   TABLE 2
Evolution of enrolment in University education: sons and daughters of parents from the
two higher socio-professional categories (High Administration, Academy, Finance and
Liberal Professions), representing today the 10.1% of active population

	1960/1	*1969/70*	*1984/5*	*1991/2*	*1996/7*
Total of Greece	13.5	12.4	16.2	20.7	26.3
Uni of Athens	19.8	16.7	18.7	22.1	26.4
Technic Uni Ath	18.8	18.1	24.6	31.5	40.1

Source: Combined data from the National Statistical Service of Greece on Education (1990–91) and
unpublished data from the Greek Ministry of Education (1997).

35. See G. Sotirellis, *Thriskeia kai ekpaidefsi* [*Religion and Education*] (Athens: Sakkoulas, 1993).
36. See A. Fredericou and F. Folerou-Tserouli, *I daskaloi tou demotikou scholeiou: Mia koinoniologiki prosengisi* [*The teachers of primary education: A sociological approach*] (Athens: Ypsilon, 1991).
37. During the 1950s to the 1970s the country has experienced large population outflows (political refugees after the civil war, and migrants searching for work in other countries, as mentioned above).
38. In secondary education, the presence of students from migrant parents is smaller, they are close to 28 thousand teenagers, that is, almost 4% of the total student population (unpublished data of the Secretariat of Multicultural Education, Greek Ministry of Education, July 2000).
39. See A. Fragoudaki and Th. Dragonas (eds) *Ti ein'I patrida mas?: Ethnokentrismos stin Ekpaidefsi* [*What is our country? Ethnocentrism in Education*] (Athens: Alexandria, 1997) pp. 193, 495.
40. See *ibid.*, pp. 344–489.
41. *Ibid.*, pp. 143–98.
42. *Ibid.*, pp. 244–76 and 284–304.

11

The Salience of the Greek Language in the European Union Melting Pot

GEORGE BABINIOTIS

Greek happens to be a language spoken by a relatively small population, and yet it has a substantial cultural appeal at the international level. In the contemporary setting, the Greek language belongs to the cluster of 'less spoken languages' in Europe, belonging to countries with small populations and limited size, and perhaps also rather weak economies and relatively limited political influence. Needless to say, the terms 'less spoken languages' or 'small' languages are used by linguists solely in linguistically quantitative terms to signify the number of people who speak the language, how frequently these languages are used at the international level, in which countries these languages are taught, or how frequently they are translated into other languages.

However, there is another vital dimension to language, namely its *diachronia* (timelessness). In this case, what matters is the cultural and qualitative presence of a language throughout history. In this sense, Greek is one of the most important languages, not only because of its presence through time, but mainly because of its effect on other European languages. Basic concepts and key terms in European and Western thought, in general, are expressed and denoted through the use of key words from the Greek language. In this respect, one can argue that the presence and contribution of the Greek language is decisive, in terms of expressing and understanding the complex structures of communication (political rhetoric, scientific discourse, etc). The same also applies – perhaps in somewhat smaller scale and for certain conceptual areas – to another classic language, Latin. The difference is that several of the Latin terms or concepts are themselves transferred denotations or reflections of Greek prototypes.

The following hypothesis is being advanced without intent of provocation. Yet, it has become evident that we, the so-called intellectuals and all who are involved in human sciences, respecting what is currently called 'political correctness', avoid declaring publicly within and outside Greece that the Greek language happens to be exceptionally fertile in its expressional capacities, especially when employed by great minds of non-Greek thought. This, in a certain sense, renders the Greek language unique, in cultural and linguistic terms, and provides, even today, as Webster writes, 'an inexhaustible source in international scientific terminology'. Certainly, we should stress, such an observation by no means implies any linguistic racism or ideological discrimination through classifying languages in terms of 'higher' or 'lower' quality.

For analytical purposes, it might be useful to note the way in which the Greek language has contributed to French, as this is explained by Bouffartique and Delrieu.[1] The objective of their book, as the authors argue in their preface, was to demonstrate the suitability and transferability of the Greek language in scientific discourse across cultural and geographic frontiers. For Frenchmen, as the authors advocate, the importance of knowing the Greek roots of their vocabulary strengthens their capacity to re-discover its essence. For example, Greek roots provide the French language with its deepest bond with high levels of abstraction and deduction. In other words, as Bouffartique and Delrieu assert, Greece, a distant source of the French culture, is still alive and well in contemporary France; in fact, it blends with the French language every day.

Historically, the Greek language occupies a cardinal place in the thought and linguistic expression of Europe in most forms of the so-called 'demanding communication'. It is not only the word 'Europe' (in all probability stemming from the feminine of the adjective *europos* which means 'with wide open eyes', namely open-minded (*ανοικτομάτης*), which is a Greek word. But the ranges of organization and expression of European thought are heavily indebted to word-concepts, such as theory (*theoria-θεωρία*), and empirical (*empiriki-εμπειρική*) or practical (*praktiki-πρακτική*) knowledge, the system (*systima-σύστημα*) and the method (*methodos-μέθοδος*), logic (*logiki-λογική*) and the organization (*organosi-οργάνωση*), hypothesis (*hypothesis-υπόθεση*) and criteria (*kritiria-κριτήρια*), hierarchy (*hierarchia-ιεραρχία*), category (*catigoria-κατηγορία*), taxonomy (*taxinomisi-ταξινόμηση*), analysis (*analysi-ανάλυση*), synthesis (*synthesi-σύνθεση*), idea (*idees-ιδέες*), thesis (*theses-θέσεις*), themes (*themata-θέματα*), crisis, (*crisis-κρίση*), problems (*problimata-προβλήματα*), technology (*technologia-τεχνολογία*), machine (*mechani-μηχανή*), type (*typos-τύπος*), analogy (*analogia-αναλογία*), phase (*phasis-φάση*), programme (*programma-πρόγραμμα*), sphere (*sphera-σφαίρα*), atmosphere (*atmosphera-ατμόσφαιρα*), diagnosis (*diagnosi-διάγνωση*), symptoms (*symptomata-συμπτώματα*), therapy (*therapia-θεραπεία*), enthusiasm (*enthousiasmos-ενθουσιασμός*), mystery (*mystirio-μυστήριο*), magic (*mageia-μαγεία*), symmetry (*symmetria-συμμετρία*), rhythm (*rythmos-ρυθμός*), style (*style<stylus<στύλος*), period (*periodos-περίοδος*), epoch (*epochi-εποχή*), tone (*tonos-τόνος*), melody (*melodia-μελωδία*), democracy (*democratia-δημοκρατία*), politics (*politiki-πολιτική*), dialogue (*dialogos-διάλογος*), monologue (*monologos-μονόλογος*), energy (*energeia-ενέργεια*), passion (*pathos-πάθος*), poetry (*poiisi-ποίηση*), theatre (*theatro-θέατρο*), drama (*drama-δράμα*), economy (*oikonomia-οικονομία*), mathematics (*mathematika-μαθηματικά*), arithmetic (*arithmitiki-αριθμητική*), symphony (*symphonia-συμφωνία*), school (*scholio-σχολείο*), myth (*mythos-μύθος*), history (*historia-ιστορία*), automatic (*automatoi-αυτόματοι*), electronic (*ilektronikoi-ηλεκτρονικοί*), atomic (*atomiki-ατομικοί*), mechanisms (*mechanismoi-μηχανισμοί*), etc.

From a semiological perspective, these concepts function, in a way, as 'proto-concepts' or 'root-concepts' with advanced denotation. Indeed, the great physicist Werner Heisenberg has advocated that the period of time when he studied the ancient Greek language was the greatest mental exercise he undertook, 'given that in this language he found the most comprehensive juxtaposition between a word and its semantic content'. Precisely because the beginning of knowledge in all its forms is to understand the denomination, namely, the words that denote every unit of information – *archi epistimis onomaton episkepsis* (the beginning of science is to visit, to know, its terms), as ancient Greeks advocated – access to the Greek language is particularly fertile. For this reason, the knowledge of Greek, as well as Latin, has to acquire a special position in the context of a deeper and substantive conception of conscious and creative European education. If something stands out in what we call European thought, it is the creative discourse with great texts of human thought, applying not only to their context but also to their linguistic expression. In these texts, the Greek language and the (ancient) Greek texts occupy vital space.

Elaborating on the meaning and essence of the Greek language it is worth noting the following: precisely because the Greek language never ceased being used in Greece, in other words because it is characterized by a long and undisrupted continuity, everything that is being said about the Greek language in fact concerns the entirety of the medium as a diachronic expression of Greek thought. Hence, the Greek language cannot be reduced to either ancient or medieval or modern Greek, which reflect only methodological aspects of a unified Greek language.

THE GREEK LANGUAGE IN THE EUROPEAN UNION

A multinational and multicultural union of states, such as the European

Union, is by definition multilingual. Integration in post-Second World War Europe, resulting in the European Union, was based on a vision of uniting all countries of Europe in one commonwealth while sustaining mutual respect for culture, traditions, language and the national characteristics of every member-state. The idea aimed (and still does) at creating a structure that could function as a synthesis of the peoples and states of Europe – not as an amalgam. A fully amalgamated European Union, which ignores the peoples of its member-states, would simply be a political utopia. Equally, a European melting pot attempting to dilute the different cultural physiognomies of its members would culminate in a gigantic cultural fiasco.

Hence, as a matter of principle (institutional, Treaty of Rome; political, equal rights of citizens; and cultural, respect of cultural identity and heritage) a multilingual Europe should be considered as given. The fundamental right of all citizens in the European Union to express themselves in their mother tongues should be respected by all. For each of the languages used by European citizens represents their national and personal identity while reflecting their culture, traditions, education and ways of thinking.

One could argue that the real issue in the European Union – both as a policy and practice – should be the maintenance of multilingualism in all its facets. This can be attained through learning (and teaching) of more than one language in schools; the use of various languages in deliberations and communication; the translation of texts in all official European Union languages (this has to apply not only to official documents but also to works of science, literature, information, etc.). Certainly, multilingualism should also apply to the interpretation of the deliberations of the European organs wherein complex and delicate exchanges are taking place.

The call for multilingualism, which has been partially served by the European programme LINGUA, should evolve into a permanent and comprehensive European Union policy. There should be no doubt that the deepest and most genuine understanding among European citizens will be attained through knowledge of two or more European languages thus reflecting the character, culture and attitude of every European citizen. Above all, language is a value, and a cultural asset, and not simply an exchange of practical information or a means for superficial communication. For this reason every European language is indispensable. This does not imply by any means that everyone should be able to speak or understand all languages of the European Union. What can be sought and can be cultivated, however, is to have more people speaking more than one language, especially the young people who are being called to live in a civil society with no internal borders.

Putative policies or utilitarian attitudes that could torpedo European multilingualism threaten to jeopardize the essence of the union and Europe's civil society. If the spirit of tolerance toward each national language and the utilization of linguistic multiplicity in Europe does not prevail, then the pragmatism and their economic-political – not necessarily cultural – equivalents will surely lead either to monopolies or to oligarchies of one, two, or, at best, three languages.

The above pessimistic prognosis does not concern the language that individuals will speak in their own countries, since each people would find effective ways to protect and sustain their language. Instead, the issue is being raised with respect to the fashion with which European citizens will be communicating with one another across the rapidly enlarging European Union. At this point, it should be stressed that linguistic compellence of any form, either as a monopoly or a linguistic oligarchy, will pose a major contradiction in the face of multiculturalism and thus the multilingual character of the European Union. Importantly, an attempt to arbitrarily subdivide European languages into 'powerful' and 'weak' ones, discriminating in terms of 'first class' and 'second class' languages, will be the beginning of the end of the very idea of the European Union, as envisioned by its founders; namely, an entity ensuring equal participation and integration but not amalgamation of the citizens of its member-states.

With respect to the modern Greek language and other 'less spoken languages' in Europe, I would argue the following: firstly, any potential linguistic constraint or attempt of exclusion in the European Union might function at the expense of the very institutional essence of the European Union; secondly, multilingualism, even if – following enlargement – the languages of the European Union proliferate, constitutes a blessing for the cultural and national idiosyncrasy of Europe *per se*; and thirdly, the learning and usage of several European languages, 'large' or 'small', constitute the greatest cultural challenges facing European citizens. For this reason, the aforementioned variables should function as guiding lights for Europe's linguistic policy. It seems to me that European citizens will never acquiesce to the exclusion or the undermining of their mother tongues, which in many respects reflect their national conscience and identity.

In any event, the command and the use of several European languages (which presupposes the principle of multilingualism and the equality of European languages) has already begun to appear as an important dimension in the cooperation patterns of European citizens. Various motivations – economic, entrepreneurial, cultural, educational, touristic, etc. – have moved the younger Europeans, in a region that has abolished internal borders, to learn various languages not excluding those spoken by fewer people (Greek, Danish, Dutch and Portuguese). Interestingly, there has been an increase in 'demand' for the Greek language in second and third language programmes throughout Europe. For young people, multilingualism, when tangible motivations are offered, transcends the limitations of utilitarian scepticism of older generations and thus is more easily accepted.

For languages such as the Greek, however, which have an indisputable longevity and continuity, there is the added ingredient of interdependence with its ancient and Byzantine phases, which interact with and fortify its modern avatars. Finally, command of the Greek language in the European Union will change fundamentally if professional motivations could be created for the learning of the language; namely teaching Greek at schools, creating job opportunities in interpretation and translation, jobs in business with interests in the Greek market, and participation in common programmes for the promotion of European languages.

NOTE

1. J. Bouffartique and A. Delrieu, *Tresors des Racines Greques* (Paris: Belin, 1981).

12

The Legal Parameters of Church and State Relations in Greece

IOANNIS M. KONIDARIS

RELIGIOUS FREEDOM AND RELIGIOUS MINORITIES

The system of relations between Church and State in Greece is shaped by the 1975 Constitution in force as amended in 1986. In particular, there are two defining poles: Article 3 and Article 13.[1]

Article 13 safeguards religious freedom as an extension and complement of the right to individual freedom as the latter is provided by Article 5 par. 1 of the Greek Constitution.[2] This connotes a great deal more than mere religious tolerance; the foundations of which were laid in the initial Constitutions of the revolutionary period against Turks, and which were, in 1821, of great scope and of a more positive nature.[3]

Religious freedom establishes that the state should not intervene – neither by acting nor by failing to act – in the process of forming religious convictions (freedom of religious conscience) or in their manifestation (freedom of worship). Religious freedom is however rendered conditional in advance by setting boundaries to it by means of the self-same Article 13 of the Constitution: Freedom of worship is protected, provided that the religion in question is a 'known' religion, that the practice of it does not offend 'public order' or 'moral principles', and under the condition that no proselytism, which is generally prohibited, is perpetrated by its members.

On the other hand, according to Article 3 of the Constitution, the Eastern Orthodox Church is pronounced the prevailing religion in Greece. It is obvious that Article 3 imposes certain restrictions upon Article 13. The extended protection which is constitutionally provided through Article 13 to religious freedom is qualified by the fact that the Eastern Orthodox Church is pronounced to be the predominant religion.[4] Still, there is a crucial difference between these two Articles: only Article 3 can be a subject of a future constitutional review.[5]

Religious minorities are allowed to pursue their faith in 'known' religions, referring to religions whose doctrines are accessible to anybody providing the public practice of worship, not necessitating any initiation.[6] Furthermore, religions or cults should neither offend 'public order' nor the 'moral principles' of the Greek State.[7]

To be established and recognized, religious communities have to abide by the laws relevant to associations which are included in the Civil Code; under this Code these are considered private law entities.[8] In contrast, the Orthodox Church is a legal entity incorporated under public law; this affects the Orthodox Church as a whole as well as its separate entities (including Dioceses, parishes, monasteries and other ecclesiastical foundations).[9] As far as the minorities of Muslims and Jews are concerned, there is special legislation regulating the function of their communities, which are also public law entities.[10]

While most of the Orthodox Churches follow the New Calendar, a few continue to abide by the Old one. There thus exists a schismatic aspect that considers the introduction of the corrected Julian Calendar as an innovation which the Greek Orthodox Church canons forbid.

The legal problem, of course, lies not in the worship of God according to the so-called Old calendar, as is the case with other Orthodox Churches with which the Church of Greece has enjoyed regular communication such as, for example, the Patriarchate of Jerusalem or the Patriarchate of Russia or the Greek Orthodox Monasteries of Mount Athos. Instead the problem lies with the Old Calendarists who have formed separate administration mechanisms with Metropolitan Bishops, Archbishops and Synods in contradiction to the Constitution, pursuant to Article 3, which recognizes only one Orthodox Eastern Church and stipulates exactly how its administration is to function.[11]

As a result, Old Calendarists today have to depend on the statement by the Deputy Minister of National Education and Cults, during the parliamentary discussions on the 1975 Constitution, according to which 'the so-called Genuine Orthodox Christians [meaning Old Calendarists], may perform their religious duties unhindered'.[12]

RELATIONS BETWEEN THE STATE AND THE ORTHODOX CHURCH

The Orthodox Church of Greece has been closely related to the modern Greek State.[13] This has been especially so since practically the beginning of the struggle for freedom (1821), when it separated itself from the Patriarchate of Constantinople, declared itself Autocephalous in 1833, and was not sanctioned by the Ecumenical Patriarchate until 1850.

The existence of special bonds between the Orthodox Church of Greece and the State is explained by the fact that this Church helped the nation survive through 400 years of Ottoman occupation, by maintaining the faith, the language and the culture. When the Greek State was founded (1830), the Metropolitan, Episcopal and Archepiscopical Dioceses that were within its limits, belonged to the Ecumenical Patriarchate. These were formed in 1833 against Canon Law, meaning without the permission of the Mother Church, i.e. the Ecumenical Patriarchate, and then in 1850 canonically as the Autocephalous Church of Greece.[14]

From that time on, the gradual enlargement of the Greek State saw the corresponding growth of the Autocephalous Church of Greece, through the addition of the Metropolitan, Episcopal and Archepiscopal Dioceses of the Ecumenical Patriarchate in the districts annexed to the Greek State after the Balkan Wars (1912–13).

Thus when we speak of the Orthodox Church of Greece, we mean the Church formed from: *First* the Autocephalous Church of Greece as it was constituted canonically in 1850 and enlarged later through its union with the Dioceses of the Ionian islands in 1866, part of Epirus and Thessaly in 1882.[15] And *secondly* the Dioceses of the annexed New Territories, meaning the rest of Epirus, Macedonia, Thrace and the Aegean islands, which were formally ceded to it in 1928 by the Ecumenical Patriarchate. The latter, it should be noted, nevertheless reserved its spiritual control over them.[16]

All Greek Constitutions enacted '*in the name of the holy and consubstantial and indivisible Trinity*', including the Constitution of 1952, which was in force until 21 April 1967, included at their start an almost identically worded definition on the relations of State and Church in Greece.[17]

The current Constitution of 1975 treats the relation of Church and State in Article 3[18] of the Second Section entitled 'Relations of Church and State of the Constitution's first part on 'Basic Provisions'.

The Orthodox Church of Greece is recognized by the Constitution as having the same ecclesiology, that is the same dogma, as the Ecumenical Patriarchate and the other Churches of the same doctrine. Indeed, the Church of Greece is obliged to have the same ecclesiology as the other Orthodox Churches in order to be itself Orthodox and to be with them 'the One, Holy, Catholic and Apostolic Church', and without which it would otherwise be considered heretical.

A *prima facie* contemplation of the first paragraph of Article 3, which contains the guidelines of the relations between the State and the Church in today's Greece, could lead to the opinion that practically nothing has changed and that the same formulation as in previous Constitutions has been used. A closer examination of the individual provisions, however, shows that the intention of the constitutional legislators was a liberalization of the relations between State and Church.

The three items of the first paragraph of Article 3 name the three foundations of this relationship: that orthodoxy is the 'prevailing' religion, the observance of canons and traditions, and the Autocephalous character and self-government of the Church of Greece. These three components should be explained further:

Under the Constitution of 1952 – according to universal opinion – the prevailing religion occupied a privileged place.[19] This manifested itself among other things in that the King and the Crown Prince had to be members of the Orthodox Church (Articles 47, 50–52 of the Constitution of 1952); that the King had to solemnly swear before the Parliament and the Holy Synod of the Church of Greece 'to protect the prevailing religion of the Greeks' (Article 43 of the Constitution of 1952) and that proselytism was forbidden by the Constitution insofar as it was directed against the prevailing religion.[20]

According to the Constitution of 1975, the head of State, the President of the Republic, is neither required to be a Christian, nor swear, at the time of taking his oath before Parliament, to protect the established religion;[21] proselytism is in general prohibited, irrespective of the 'known' religion against which it is perpetrated;[22] the previous provision prohibiting all other interventions aimed against the prevailing religion is omitted;[23] confiscation of newspapers and other publications upon their distribution is allowed in cases where not only the Christian religion, but any known religion, is offended.[24]

Therefore, the concept of 'prevailing religion' is not to be construed as the right to dominate other religious communities; it now has no normative content. Instead it has a mainly declaratory sense namely,[25] it denotes that the overwhelming majority of Greeks belong to this Church and that State occasions are only celebrated according to the rites of this Church.

In addition, Apostolic and Synodal Canons and sacred traditions are to be understood as the Canons of the Ecumenical Synods and the Canons of the Apostles, which were ratified by Canon 2 of Trullanum (Quinisextum 691), the Canons of eight local Synods and the thirteen Fathers of the Church, as well as the sacred traditions not only the Sacred Tradition, but also the apostolic tradition.

These Canons and traditions are protected by the Constitution from the Church as well as from the State. Any deviation either by the Church or by the State from these constitutionally protected rules and traditions would have not only canonic but also constitutional consequences, as such behaviour would represent a violation of Article 3 of the Constitution.

Under the Constitution of 1952 the problem of whether Canons only referred to the dogmatic rules or also the administrative ones had divided jurisprudence in Greece. Through Article 3 par. 1 III, however, according to which the Church of Greece is administered in observance of the 1975 Constitution with the provisions of the Patriarchal and Synodal Acts of 1850 and 1928, the continuous questions of State intervention in the administration of the Church are practically solved. Accordingly, besides the dogmatic Canons, those administrative rules adopted by the Constitution are valid today. Nevertheless, a constitutional basis for the protection of the Holy Canons and the sacred traditions is also offered by Article 13 of the Constitution, and this argument has been adopted in the more recent decisions of the Greek Council of State.[26]

The Orthodox Church of Greece is (in part) Autocephalous, exercising its rights independently of any other Church, within the framework of the constitutional provisions and under the condition that its autocephaly does not endanger the unity of doctrine of the whole Orthodox Church. The self-administration of the Church of Greece was guaranteed under the Constitution of 1952, and confirmed by the legal precedents of the Supreme Administrative Court of Greece. Furthermore, Article 2 of this Constitution provided that the Church should be led by a Holy Synod of Bishops.[27] The Constitution of 1975/1986, which does not directly and expressly provide for the self-administration of the Church, does not limit itself to the abstract provision of the previous Constitution, but – and this is the novelty – describes the guidelines which have to be followed during the administration of the Church. Consequently, legislators are restricted in that the administrative organs of the Church have to be formed not uncontrolled, but in observance with the Patriarchal Tome of 29 June 1850 and the Synodal Act of 4 September 1928.[28]

In conclusion, on the basis of the innovations and differentiations between the 1952 and the 1975 Constitution, and perhaps as a result of an atmosphere of euphoria, some had asserted that the status of State–Church relations calls for co-existence under equal terms; that the regulation of the relations of State and Church fluctuates between the concept of a statutory precedence of the State and that of equivalence of State and Church (*ομοταξία*).[29]

On the other hand, in the Preamble of the Constitution, there appears again an invocation to the Holy Trinity,[30] which has also been included in the oath of the President of the Republic (Article 33 par. 2) and the Members of the Parliament (Article 59 par. 1). Additionally, one of the aims of education involves the development of a religious conscience (Article 16 par. 2); the Statutory Charter of the established Church must be passed by the Plenary Session of Parliament;[31] the holidays of the Greek Orthodox Church are acknowledged as official national holidays; the State pays the salaries of the clergy, the preachers and lay employees of the Orthodox Church; the Orthodox Church and the other ecclesiastical public law entities are exempted from paying taxes.[32]

Since the establishment of the 1975 Constitution, although the bond between the State and the Orthodox Church has become more relaxed, it has simultaneously become more tense.[33] At the same time the conditionality of religious freedom, introduced by means of Article 3 of the Constitution, has not been overturned or nullified, but rather it has become wider in scope and has taken on greater dimensions.[34] Characteristic examples of this situation are:

a) The constitutional opportunity of legislative intervention into the internal affairs of the Church.[35]
b) The repeated direct or indirect reformulations of the Statutory Charter of the Greek Orthodox Church made by each governmental majority.[36]
c) The restoration of the status of the 1952 Constitution, which establishes, with reference to elementary and secondary education, the primacy of specifically Orthodox teaching over broad teaching about Greek-Christian civilization (Law 1566/1985, Article 1).[37]
d) The acknowledgement of the religious wedding as equal to the civil (Law 1250/1982 and Decree 391/1982).
e) The total financial dependence of the Orthodox Church upon the Greek State, which does not accept church taxes but on the other hand has already appropriated the vast majority of the Church's property.[38]
f) The assimilation of the clergy of the established Church with the ranks of public servants.

All these examples illustrate vividly that the Eastern Orthodox Church has always been, and still remains, the official Church, the Church of the State.[39]

ORGANIZATION AND ADMINISTRATION OF THE CHURCH OF GREECE

The Orthodox Church of Greece is composed of the Dioceses (Metropoleis) of the Autocephalous Church of Greece according to the Patriarchal Tome of 29 June 1850 and the Patriarchal and Synodal Acts of July 1866 and May 1882 and those of the 'New Territories' based on the Patriarchal and Synodal Acts of 4 September 1928;[40] their members are all Orthodox Christians who inhabit these Dioceses.

Each of the Dioceses is divided into parishes, the centre of which is the parochial church (Statutory Charter, Article 11, par. 3). The Church of Greece, its Dioceses (Metropoleis) and the parishes are public law entities.[41]

The highest authority of the Church of Greece is represented by the Holy Synod of the Hierarchy located in Athens, consisting of the serving Bishops, i.e. of all Metropolitans,[42] under the chairmanship of the Archbishop of Athens and all Greece.[43] A regular assembly of this Synod is convened once a year, on the first of October, but under certain preconditions it may also be convened in extraordinary assembly.[44] The Statutory Charter of the Church describes in detail the legislative, organizational and jurisdictional powers of the Synod of the Hierarchy, to whose sole jurisdiction falls the election of the Archbishop of Athens as well as of all other Bishops.[45]

The representative of the Synod of the Hierarchy, except at the time of its convention, and the permanent administrative organ of the Greek Church is the Permanent Holy Synod of the Church of Greece, venued in Athens.[46] It consists of the Archbishop of Athens, who is also its chairman, and twelve members, who according to the above-mentioned Patriarchal and Synodal Acts of the Ecumenical Patriarchate of 1850 and 1928 assemble in a particular order. To be precise, six Bishops of the Autocephalous Church of Greece and six Bishops of the Dioceses of the so-called 'New Territories' (jurisdiction of the Ecumenical Patriarchate) respectively assemble in accordance to the particular sequence of their commencement of office.[47] The term of office of the twelve members, as well as the session of the Permanent Synod, lasts one year; it begins on 1 September of each year and lasts until the following 31 August.[48] The powers of this Permanent Synod are also determined by the Statutory Charter of the Church too (Article 9, par. 1).

To support the work of the Synod of the Hierarchy, as well as of the Permanent Synod, the Statutory Charter provides for twelve Synodal Committees.[49] Each of these Committees, comprising seven members, three of whom are always laymen (Article 10, par. 2), has a specific area of responsibility. The respective Committees' duties are the following: General Secretariat, ecclesiastical art and music, dogmatic and nomocanonic matters, service and pastoral matters, monasticism, Christian education of the youth, inter-orthodox and inter-christian relations, ecclesiastical education and further education of the clergy, press and public relations, sect problems, social welfare and Church finance (Article 10, par. 1 I–XII).

SPECIAL ECCLESIASTICAL REGIMES

There are, however, ecclesiastical districts in Greece that do not belong to the Church of Greece, that means neither to the Autocephalous Church of Greece nor to the Dioceses of the so called 'New Territories', which belong to the Ecumenical Patriarchate of Constantinople.

The Greek Constitution as well as the Statutory Charter of the Church of Greece contain identical provisions to the effect that the ecclesiastical régime existing in certain districts of the State shall not be deemed contrary to the provisions of the two Constitutions.[50] This refers to the ecclesiastical regimes of Crete, the Holy Mountain of Athos and the Dodecanese.

Crete

Since 1900, and based on an agreement between the Ecumenical Patriarchate of Constantinople and the former Cretan State, a semi-autonomous Orthodox Church exists on the Island of Crete.[51] After Crete and Greece united in 1913, the Orthodox Church of Crete retained its independence from the Greek Church. The above-mentioned agreement was later enshrined in a Greek State Law of 1961.[52]

The highest administrative organ of the Orthodox Church of Crete is the Provincial Holy Synod of Crete, consisting of all the Bishops of the eight Dioceses of the Church of Crete, under the chairmanship of the Archbishop of Crete, situated in Herakleion.[53]

The Bishops of the Church of Crete are elected by the Provincial Synod; the Archbishop, however, is elected by the Synod of the Patriarchate of Constantinople, upon a proposal from the Greek Government and of three Bishops of the Church of Crete.[54] The autonomy of the Church of Crete is thus limited through the intervention rights of the Ecumenical Patriarchate of Constantinople as well as the rights of the Greek State.

Athos

Greece took over *de facto* control of the Holy Mountain of Athos as a protectorate in 1912. In 1923 this control became *de jure*. According to the Statutory Charter of the Holy Mountain (Mount Athos),[55] and the Greek Constitution (Article 105) the Athos peninsula from Megali Vigla onwards, which contains the area of the Holy Mountain, is an autonomous region in the Greek State, while the sovereignty of the Greek State over the peninsula remains intact.[56]

The Holy Mountain, which in spiritual aspects comes under the immediate jurisdiction of the Ecumenical Patriarchate,[57] was in the nineteenth century literally flooded by monks coming from Russia and South East European countries. The stream of monks originating from these countries ebbed after the end of the Second World War. As a result of this influx since 1926, according to the Statutory Charter of the Holy Mountain and the Greek constitution, all those who live in Athos with their admission as novices or monks automatically acquire Greek citizenship.[58]

According to the Statutory Charter of the Holy Mountain, corresponding to its ancient régime, no female being (including female animals) may cross its border;[59] it is also prohibited for people of other religions or for schismatics to live there as monks.[60]

The monks live in twenty monasteries and in smaller monastic communities subordinated to these monasteries (Sketai, Kellia, Kalybai, Hesyshasteria, Kathismata).[61] All the monasteries are today cenobitic.

According to its régime, the Holy Mountain is administered by the twenty monasteries, among which the whole Athos peninsula is divided, the land of which must not be sold.[62] The régime of the Holy Mountain, and in particular the manner of its function, is provided in the Statutory Charter of the Holy Mountain, which is drafted and passed by the twenty monasteries in collaboration with a representative of the State, and is thereafter confirmed by the Ecumenical Patriarchate and the Greek Parliament.[63]

The administration of the entire Mount Athos is exercised by the *Holy Community*, which consists of twenty members, is seated in Karyes (capital of Mount Athos), and includes one representative from each of the twenty monasteries. These representatives are elected pursuant to each monastery's by-laws and hold office for one year. The executive authority is exercised by the four-member *Holy Epistasia*, that is, representatives chosen by rotation on the basis of a tetrad system. In effect, the twenty monasteries are divided into five tetrads, with one of the five senior Athonite monasteries as the first member of each tetrad. Each tetrad in turn constitutes the Holy Epistasia every year, headed by a member of the senior monastery of the tetrad as chief monk, the *Protepistates* (or *Protos*, i.e. first elder).[64]

The strict observance of the Holy Mountain régime as regards the spiritual element is under the broad supervision of the Ecumenical Patriarchate. As regards the administrative element, this is under the supervision of the Greek State, which is also solely responsibility for the public order and security (Article 105, par. 5 of the Constitution). These state powers are exercised by a Governor[65] who, together with a small number of public servants and police officers, is dispatched by the Greek government to Karyai. This has been the practice since 1923.

Dodecanese

After the Second World War Greece, through the 1947 Peace Treaty with Italy, took control of the Dodecanese.[66] However, the four Dioceses of the Dodecanese remained,[67] subordinate to the Patriarchate of Constantinople. The ecclesiastical law valid in the Dodecanese is that which is valid in the jurisdiction of the Ecumenical Patriarchate. Notwithstanding this arrangement, some laws of the Greek State are also valid in the area of ecclesiastical law, such as marriage law provisions.[68]

NOTES

1. I. Konidaris, *Egheiridio Ecclisiastikou Dikaiou* (Handbook of Ecclesiastical Law) (Athens: Komotini: Sakkoulas, 2000) pp. 45ff. and 65.
2. Article 13 of the Greek Constitution states: Par. 1. Freedom of religious conscience is inviolable. Enjoyment of individual and civil rights does not depend on the individual's religious beliefs. Par. 2. All known religions shall be free and their rites of worship shall be performed unhindered and under the protection of the law. The practice of rites of worship is not allowed to offend public order or moral principles. Proselytism is prohibited. Par. 3. Ministers of all known religions shall be subject to the same supervision by the State and to the same obligations toward it at those of the prevailing religion. Par. 4. No person shall be exempt from discharging his obligations to the State or may refuse to comply with the laws by reason of his religious convictions. Par. 5. No oath is enforced void law, which also defines its norm.
3. A. Manessis, *Syntagmatika Dikaiomata, A' Atomikes Eleftheries* (*Constitutional Rights, A' Individual Liberties*), 4th edn (Thessaloniki: Sakkoulas, 1982) p. 249.
4. Manessis, *Constitutional*, p. 256; and Konidaris, *Handbook*, p. 47.
5. Cf Article 110 par 1., Greek Constitution.
6. This is the definition used by the Greek Council of State: see judgements 2105 and 2106/1975 in A. Konidaris, *Nomiki Theoria an Praxi gia tous 'Martyres tou Jehova'* (Legal Theory an Practice for 'Jehova Witness'), 3rd edn (Athens: Sakkoulas, 1991) p. 83.
7. For the legal problems concerning the prohibition of proselytism and the establishment of places of worship, see A. Konidaris, 'Legal Status of Minority Churches and Religious Minorities in Greece', in European Consortium for Church-State Research: *The Legal Status of Religious Minorities in the Countries of the European Union* (Thessaloniki: Sakkoulas; Milano: Giuffrè, 1994) p. 171ff.; C. Papastathis, 'State and Church in Greece', in G. Robbers (ed.) *State and Church in the European Union* (Baden-Baden: Nomos Verlag, 1995) pp. 83–5; N. Alivisatos, 'A New Role for the Greek Church', *Journal of Modern Greek Studies*, 17 (1999) p. 28ff.; Konidaris, *Handbook*, pp. 54f and 61ff.
8. The Greek Catholic Church maintains that it is recognized as a public law entity; K. Vavouskos, *Handbook of Ecclesiastical Law*, 5th edn (Thessaloniki: Sakkoulas, 1989) pp. 99ff. and 103; I. Konidaris, 'Legal Status of Minority Churches and Religious Minorities in Greece', in European Consortium for Church-State Research, *The Legal Status of Religious Minorities in the Countries of the European Union* (Thessaloniki, Milano: Sakkoulas, Giuffrè, 1994) p.175.
9. See Law No 590/1977 'On the Statutory Charter of the Church of Greece', Art. 1, par 4 in I. Konidaris, *Fundamental Provisions in Church–State Relations* (Athens: Sakkoulas, 1999) p. 49) [in Greek].
10. See the Israelite communities Law 2456/1920 and the Emergency Law 367/1945 and for the Muslims, Law 1920/1991; the texts in *ibid.*, pp. 395ff. and 411ff.).
11. For the whole matter see Metropolitan Bishop of Dimitrias (Today: Archbishop of Athens 1998–) Christodoulos [Paraskevaidis], *Istoriki kai Kanonistiki Theorisis tou Palaioimerologitikou Zitimatos kata te thn Genesin kai tis Ekseliksin aftou en Elladi,*

(Historical and Canonal Perspective of the Old-Calentarists Issue: Genesis and Evolution in Greece) (Athens: 1982) pp. 230ff., 358ff.). Christodoulos [Paraskevaidis], Metropolitan Bishop of Dimitrias [Archbishop of Athens, since 1998].

12. See the minutes of the parliamentary discussions on the 1975 Constitution (Athens: Parliament of the Greeks, 1975) p. 421.

13. The Orthodox Church consists of several autonomous, i.e. mutually independent (Autocephalous) Churches, which through the unity of doctrine and cult are joined into a sort of Church-federation. These Autocephalous Churches have mutually equal rights, and the Ecumenical Patriarchate of Constantinople holds a position of *primus inter pares* (first among equals), i.e. it has no right to intervene in any way in the administration of the individual Autocephalous Churches. Each Autocephalous Church is divided into several Dioceses and each one of those into several parishes. All Bishops of each Autocephalous Church form the Synod of the Hierarchy, which is the highest administrative organ of each particular Church. In many Autocephalous Churches besides the Synod of the Hierarchy there exists a Permanent Synod, which consists of a limited number of Bishops, and represents the periodically assembling Synod of the Hierarchy. Of course, from Church to Church there are differences in organizational and administrative details which, however, do not alter the fundamental concepts of administration in any way, especially their democratic character, which is guaranteed for the whole Orthodox Church through the independence of each of its Autocephalous Churches as well as for each particular Church through the equal rights of the bishops among themselves.

14. See the text of the Patriarchal and Synodical *Tomos* of 1850 by Konidaris, *Fundamental*, pp. 31ff. Cf I. Konidaris, *The Debate Between Legality and Regulation and the Establishment of Integration* (Athens: Sakkoulas, 1994) p. 40ff. (in Greek); and Konidaris, *The Ecumenical*, p. 75ff.).

15. See the text of the Patriarchal and Synodical Acts of 1866 and 1882 in Konidaris, *Fundamental*, pp. 37ff. and 41ff.).

16. See the text of the Patriarchal and Synodical Act of 1928 in *ibid.* p. 44ff.; and Cf Konidaris, *The Debate*, p. 56ff. and Konidaris, *The Ecumenical*; p. 18ff.; Konidaris, *Handbook*, p. 80ff.).

17. Konidaris, *Handbook*, p. 94ff.

18. Article 3 of the Constitution states: Par. 1. The prevailing religion in Greece is that of the Eastern Orthodox Church. The Orthodox Church of Greece, acknowledging our Lord Jesus Christ as its head, is inseparably united in doctrine with the Great Church of Christ in Constantinople and with every other Church of Christ of the same doctrine, observing unwaveringly, as they do, the holy apostolic and synodal canons and sacred traditions. It is autocephalous and is administered by the Holy Synod of serving Bishops and the Permanent Holy Synod originating thereof and assembled by the Statutory Charter of the Church in compliance with the provisions of the Patriarchal Tome of 29 June 1850 and the Synodal Act of 4 September 1928, Par. 2. The ecclesiastical régime existing in certain districts of the State shall not be deemed contrary to the provisions of the preceding paragraph, Par. 3. The text of the Holy Scripture shall be maintained unaltered. Official translation of the text into any other form of language, without prior sanction by the Autocephalous Church of Greece and the Great Church of Christ in Constantinople, is prohibited.

19. A. Christophilopoulos, *Hellenic Ecclesiastical Law*, 2nd edn (Athens: 1965), p. 76ff.; S. Troianos, Courses on Ecclesiastical Law, 2nd edn (Athens: Komotini: Sakkoulas, 1984), p. 91ff.; C. Papastathis, 'State Financial Support for the Church in Greece', in Church and State in Europe. State Financial Support. Religion and the School (Proceedings of the meeting Milan-Parma, 20–21 October 1989) (Milano: Giuffrè, 1994), p. 57ff.; Konidaris, *Handbook*, p. 94ff.

20. Article 1, Par. 1 of the Constitution of 1952.

21. Article 31 and 33, Par. 2 of the Constitution.

22. Article 13, Par. 2, of the Constitution.

23. Cf. Article 1, Par. 1, of the Constitution of 1952.

24. Article 14, Par. 3 of the Constitution.

25. T. Tsatsos, 'Die verfassungsmässige Gewährleistung der Religionsfreiheit in Griechenland', in C. Schmitt, *Festgabe* (Berlin, 1959), pp. 221ff. and 229; Troianos, *Courses*, pp. 94–5.

26. Konidaris, 'The Debate', p. 219ff.; and Konidaris, *Handbook*, p. 100ff.

27. See judgement 1476/1975 of the Greek Council of State: *To Syntagma* (Constitution) *1975*, p. 887ff.
28. Article 3, Par. 1 III of the Constitution. Cf. Law No 590/1977 'On the Statutory Charter of the Church of Greece', Art. 1, Par. 2 text, see Konidaris, *Fundamental*, p. 49ff.
29. See A. Manesis and K. Vavouskos, 'State-Church Relations According to the New Constitution. Commentary', *Nomikon* Vima, 23 (1975) p. 1031ff.; Vavouskos, *Handbook*, pp. 246ff and 261. For relations between the Ecumenical Partiarchate of Constantinople and the Greek State see E. Venizelos, *State and Church Relations*, 5th edn (Thessaloniki: Sakkoulas, 2000) p. 73.
30. See G. Kassimatis, 'The Preamble of the Constitution', in Kassimatis and Mavrias, *Interpretation of the Constitution* (Athens: Sakkoulas, 1999 [in Greek].
31. Article 3, Par. 1 in conjunction with Article 72, Par. 1.
32. Papastathis, 'State', p. 9ff.; and Konidaris, *Handbook*.
33. I. Konidaris, *The Law 1700/1987 and the Recent Crisis in Church-State Relations*, 2nd edn (Athens: Sakkoulas, 1991) pp. 44–5.
34. I. Konidaris, 'Die Beziehungen zwischen Kirche und Staat im heutigen Griechenland', in *Österreichisches Archiv für Kirchenrecht* 40, 1991, p. 131ff.
35. Article 3, Par. 1 in conjunction with Article 72, Par. 1 of the Constitution.
36. See, for example, Laws 1041/1980, Article 8; 1351/1983, Article 15; 1811/1988; 1951/1991, Article 12 and 13; 2084/1992, Article 21; 2606/1998, Article 16; 2817/2000, Article 15, Par. 8 and 2819/2000, Article 19, Par. 5.
37. G. Sotirelis, *Religion and Education*, 2nd edn (Athens, Komotini: Sakkoulas, 1998) p. 35ff. [in Greek]; and I. Sotirelis, *Constitution and Democracy in the Era of Globalization* (Athens: Komotini, 2000) p. 292ff. [in Greek].
38. See Laws 1700/1987; 1811/1988 and 2413/1996, Article 55 in Konidaris, *Fundamental*, p. 119ff. For the Church's property see Konidaris, *The Law 1700/1987*, p. 101ff. and passim.
39. See Konidaris, 'Die Beziehungen', p. 131ff. and 137f.; Papastathis, 'State', p. 57ff.; and Alivisatos, 'A New Role', p. 25ff.
40. Law 590/1977 'On the Statutory Charter of the Church of Greece', Article 11 and Law 1951/1991, Article 12; see the texts in Konidaris, *Fundamental*, p. 49ff.
41. Statutory Charter, Article 1, Par. 4.
42. Statutory Charter, Article 3, Par. 1; and Konidaris, *Handbook*, p. 130ff.
43. With the election of Archbishop of Athens Christodoulos [Paraskevaidis] (28 April 1988) a new phase in the relations between the Greek Orthodox Church and the State appears to have started; see, Alivisatos, 'A New Role', p. 23.
44. Statutory Charter, Article 6, Par. 1.
45. Statutory Charter, Article 4, Par. 1.
46. Statutory Charter, Articles 3 and 7, Par. 1.
47. See Articles 3, Par. 1 of the Constitution and Article 7, Par. 1 of the Statutory Charter (Law 590/1977); see, Konidaris, *Handbook*, p. 134ff.
48. Statutory Charter, Article 8, Par. 1.
49. Article 10, Par. 1; see Konidaris, *Handbook*, p. 137ff.
50. See Articles 3, Par. 2 of the Constitution and Article 1, Par. 5 of the Statutory Charter (Law 590/1977).
51. Konidaris, *Fundamental*, p. 217ff.; and Konidaris, *Handbook*, p. 246ff.; and Christophilopoulos, *Hellenic*, p. 318ff.; Troianos, *Courses*, p. 522ff.; Vavouskos, *Handbook*, p. 136ff.
52. Law 4149/1961 'On the Statutory Charter of the Orthodox Church of Crete'; for the text see Konidaris, *Fundamental*, p. 220ff.
53. Statutory Charter of the Church of Crete, Article 2 in conjunction with Article 2 in conjunction with Article 2, Par. 1, of the Emergency Law No 137 of 1967.
54. Statutory Charter of the Church of Crete, Articles 19–22.
55. Statutory Charter of the Holy Mountain Athos of 10 May 1924 and Legislative Decree of 10/26 September 1926; see the texts by (Konidaris 1991, p. 285ff., 300ff.).
56. Konidaris, Handbook, p. 251f.; Christophilopoulos, *Hellenic Ecclesiastical*, p. 320f.; Troianos, *Courses*, p. 463ff.; Vavouskos, *Handbook*, p. 139.
57. Article 105, Par.1 II of the Constitution and Article 5 of the Statutory Charter of Athos.

58. Article 105, Par. 1III of the Constitution and Article 6 of the Statutory Charter of Athos.
59. Article 186 of the Statutory Charter of Athos in conjunction with Article 43b of the Legislative Decree of September 10/26, 1926. See also (Konidaris 2000c, p. 65ff.).
60. Article 105, par. 2 of the Constitution and Article 5, par. 2 of the Statutory Charter of Athos.
61. Statutory Charter of Athos, Articles 1 and 126–66.
62. Article 105, Par. 2, I of the Constitution.
63. Article 105, Par. 3 of the Consitution.
64. Article 105, Par. 2, I of the Constitution and Articles 14–40 of the Statutory Charter of Athos.
65. See, Article 105, Par. 5, I of the Constitution; Legislative Decree of September 10/26, 1926, Articles 3–5; and Law 2594 of 1998, Article 21.
66. Undersigned in Paris, on 10 February 1947.
67. The Dioceses of Rhodos, Karpathos, Kos, Leros, and Kalymnos.
68. Konidaris, *Handbook*, p. 258f.; Christophilopoulos, *Hellenic Ecclesiastical*, p. 325f.; Troianos, *Courses*, p. 538ff.; Vavouskos, *Handbook*, p. 139.

PART IV

13

The Economy:
Growth without Equity

THEODORE C. KARIOTIS

> I am absolutely convinced that no wealth in the world can help humanity forward, even in the hands of the most devoted worker in this cause. The example of great and pure individuals is the only thing that can lead us to noble thoughts and deeds. Money only appeals to selfishness and irresistibly invites abuse.
>   Can anyone imagine Moses, Jesus, or Gandhi armed with the money-bags of Carnegie?
>
> *Albert Einstein*

The most important economic issue that will face the world of the twenty-first century will be the unequal distribution of income and wealth within countries but also among countries and regions. The slogan 'the rich become richer and the poor become poorer' is the legacy of the twentieth century and it will torment the global citizens in the next century.

The issues of equity and economic justice that are so closely related to income distribution are concepts that are not easily defined. Economists, philosophers and theologians have grappled with the notion of justice for several millennia. The topic of economic justice and distributive justice deals with complex issues of equity, equality, fairness and opportunity. The ancient Greeks were the first to consider such issues. Their writings, particularly those of Aristotle, constitute the classical references in the literature of economic justice.

Aristotle was the first to make the distinction between, on the one hand, the household or simple market economy in which production and exchange were for use, and on the other hand a more advanced market economy in which exchange was initiated by the merchant using his money capital to buy in order to sell at a profit and thus to increase his wealth. He saw that his own society had moved well along the road from the simple to the advanced market economy. He made a strong

ethical case that the latter was destructive of the good life. He called it
unnatural, on three grounds: it makes acquisition the goal instead of
merely a means of the good life; the accumulation process is without
limit whereas the good life requires only limited material wealth; and it
is a means by which some men gain at the expense of others, which is
unjust.[1]

But the descendants of Aristotle, the present-day Greeks, as this essay
is going to demonstrate, have not paid proper attention to this issue in
the twentieth century. Today, in spite of the great and impressive
economic progress that Greek society has achieved the last 50 years of
the twentieth century, economic inequalities are greater than ever
before.

ECONOMIC DEVELOPMENT IN THE LAST 100 YEARS

Before we discuss the subject of the distribution of income of the Greek
people, we should summarize the developments of the Greek economy
in the twentieth century, in particular the developments after the Second
World War and the Civil War, which left the Greek people on the brink
of economic collapse. As we are going to see, what transpired from that
period until today represents one of the most fascinating examples of
economic progress in the history of the world.

In the beginning of the twentieth century, in 1901, Greece was a very
small nation trying desperately to survive in a very hostile environment
in the Balkans. Now in the year 2000, the last year of the century,
Greece is the economic leader of the Balkans, a vibrant member of the
European Union, with a very healthy political, social and economic
system and ready to get rid of its own currency, the Drachma.

In order to understand the great leap forward that Greece has accomplished we should quote two statements fifty years apart. The first is a
description of the conditions that prevailed in the country at the end of
the Second World War, which had literally crushed its economy:

> The losses of population exceeded half a million; for every
> second family, on an average, there was one war death. The
> level of public health dropped dangerously, with tuberculosis
> ravaging the masses. Of the children, 72% were seriously
> weakened. Thousands of villages were set on fire and several
> cities turned into ruins, with 23% of total housing demol-
> ished. The railway network, on account of war destruction,
> had stopped functioning ... The road network and other
> Communications were left in a lamentable condition.
> Merchant shipping was lost for 77%. Agricultural and live-

stock production dropped to 25%–40% of the prewar level. Industry was also damaged and its population decreased. The entire economic life of the country was dislocated.[2]

The second statement was made a half a century later and shows the incredible success of Greece's economic journey. At the end of the European Council meeting that took place in Santa Maria da Feira of Portugal in June 2000, the Presidency of the Council stated:

> The European Council congratulates Greece on the convergence achieved over recent years, based on sound economic and financial policies, and welcomes the decision that Greece will join the Euro area on 1 January 2001 which constitutes an additional positive step in the monetary integration of the Union.

Looking at the table below, we can easily see the tremendous economic progress that has taken place in Greece in the last 100 years. In fact this growth of the national income would have been more impressive if (excluding the tragic decade of the 1940s) the Greek economy did not perform so poorly in the last 20 years of the century.

TABLE 4: GREEK NATIONAL INCOME IN THE
TWENTIETH CENTURY, 1901–2000

Decade	Increase per decade	Average annual rate
1901–1910	29.0%	2.9%
1911–1920	104.3%	8.3%
1921–1930	14.7%	1.6%
1931–1940	37.6%	3.6%
1941–1950	5.7%	0.6%
1951–1960	65.0%	5.7%
1961–1970	87.0%	7.2%
1971–1980	54.0%	4.9%
1981–1990	7.0%	0.6%
1991–2000	17.05%	1.9%

Source: Bank of Greece and National Statistical Service, various bulletins and reports.

The three most important events that played a critical role in the future developments of the economy of Greece and the economic conditions of its people in the second half of the century were: the defeat of the communist forces during the Civil War at the end of 1940s, the economic penetration of the United States in every aspect of economic activity in the 1950s, and Greece becoming the tenth member of the then EEC in 1981.

From the table below we can clearly see what the future would have held for Greece if the other side had won the Civil War. The table compares the three most advanced communist countries of Eastern Europe with that of the four European capitalist countries that were least developed in the base year (1950). Not only did the GDP of the communist countries grow more slowly than that of the capitalist countries but, as shown in the last column, workers in the communist countries spend much longer in their place of work. Of course we should emphasize that of all the seven countries Greece had attained the highest GDP per capita for this period, an astounding 519.5%!

TABLE 5: GROWTH AND LABOUR INPUT (1950–89)

	GDP Per Capita		Annual No. of Hours Worked per Capita	
	In 1950	*In 1989*	*1989/1950* (%)	*1987*
Czechoslovakia	3, 465	8,538	246.4	936
Hungary	2,481	6,722	270.9	839
Soviet Union	2,647	6,970	263.3	933
Greece	1,456	7,564	519.5	657
Ireland	2,600	8,285	318.7	524
Portugal	1,608	7,383	459.1	738
Spain	2,405	10,081	419.2	591

Note: GDP per capita, reported in the first and second columns, is measured in US dollars at 1985 US relative prices.

Source: Janos Kornai, 'What the Change of System From Socialism to Capitalism Does and Does Not Mean', *The Journal of Economic Perspectives*, vol. 14, no. 1, Winter 2000, p. 39.

If we want to compare the economic performance of Greece in the twentieth century with the rest of the world, we can see from Table 6 opposite that Greece's per capita GDP was higher in both halves of the century. We can see that in the last half of the century the average growth of GDP per capita in every region of the world except Eastern Europe was higher than the first half of the century and still the living conditions of a large portion of human beings of our planet have not benefitted from economic growth.

From Table 7 we can get a clear indication that Greece has followed the classic case of all advanced countries, irrespective of their initial level of development. That is, an initial phase of development, in which labour moved out of agriculture and into industry, was followed by a second phase, in which the dominant trend was the growth of the services at the expense of both industry and agriculture.

TABLE 6: GROWTH OF GDP PER CAPITA

	Annual average percentage changes		
	1900–2000	*1900–1950*	*1950–2000*
OECD	2.0	1.3	2.6
Non-OECD	1.6	0.7	2.4
Eastern Europe	1.2	1.3	1.2
Latin America	1.6	1.7	1.5
Asia	1.8	0.1	3.5
Africa	1.0	1.0	1.0
World	1.9	1.1	2.5
Greece	3.7	3.4	4.0

Sources: Andrea Boltho and Gianni Toniolo, 'The Assessment: The Twentieth Century – Achievements, Failures, Lessons', *Oxford Review of Economic Policy*, vol. 15, no. 4, Winter 1999, p. 3. The calculations for Greece are from the National Statistical Service.

TABLE 7: GREEK CIVIL EMPLOYMENT

	Classified by sector in '000s			
	1900	*1950*	*1971*	*1998*
Agriculture	922	1,367	1,222	788
Industry	301	550	826	889
Services	636	922	1,095	2,207
Total	1,859	2,839	3,143	3,884

Source: Charles Feinstein, 'Structural Change in the Developed Countries during the Twentieth Century', *Oxford Review of Economic Policy*, Special Issue: The Twentieth Century, vol. 15, no. 4, pp. 52–4.

TABLE 8: DE-INDUSTRIALIZATION: THE FALL IN
THE PROPORTION OF CIVILIAN EMPLOYMENT IN INDUSTRY, 1955–98

	Peak year	*% in industry at peak*	*% in industry in 1998*	*Percentage fall: peak year to 1998*
UK	1955	47.9	26.6	44.5
Belgium	1957	47.0	26.1	44.5
USA	1966	36.0	23.6	34.4
FRG	1970	49.3	35.0	29.0
Japan	1973	37.2	32.0	14.0
Ireland	1974	32.6	28.3	13.2
Spain	1975	38.4	30.4	20.8
Greece	1980	30.2	22.9	24.2
Portugal	1982	37.5	36.4	2.9

Source: Charles Feinstein, 'Structural Change in the Developed Countries during the Twentieth Century', *Oxford Review of Economic Policy*, Special Issue: The Twentieth Century, vol. 15, no. 4, p. 39.

Table 8 shows the process of de-industrialization in the developed world that started in the late 1950s, in the United Kingdom and Belgium, which were the first industrialized nations in the nineteenth century and ending with Greece and Portugal in the early 1980s. By the end of the century the labour force occupied in the Greek industrial sector from its peak year in 1980 had declined by 25% and in some other more advanced nations by more than one third.

PHASES OF DEVELOPMENT

From the end of the German occupation to the end of the twentieth century, the economic history of Greece has gone through six fairly distinct phases. The years between 1944 and 1947 constitute the first phase, when the country slowly began to emerge from the wounds of the Second World War with the help of the British and the United Nations Relief and Rehabilitation Administration (UNREA). The second period began with the announcement of the Truman Doctrine in March 1947, and ended in November 1952 with the creation of the Papagos government. The third period, the so-called 'stable period' of the Greek economy, commenced in 1952 and continued to the coup d'état of 1967. The years of the dictatorship from 1967 to 1974 constitute the fourth phase. The fifth phase, from 1974 to 1980, was characterized by the movement toward integration with the EEC; and the last phase, from 1981 to 2000, was the unexpected domination by the socialist party (PASOK) that Andreas Papandreou had created in 1974.

Although it is not the purpose of this essay to review the economic development of Greece in the second half of the twentieth century, it is important to understand the latest developments and how the present economic system was established in order to understand where the country is heading in the next century. We will, therefore, provide a short description of the first and last phases of this development.

AMERICAN ECONOMIC PENETRATION

In order to understand how the present economic system was established we should go back to the end of the Second World War and see the crucial role the American factor played when the British decided they could not play an important role in the political and economic affairs of Greece.

The historical process of American economic penetration in Greece can be followed through the correspondence between the American Embassy in Athens and the State Department, and from different memoranda of conversations. In the late summer of 1946, a delegation (one of its junior members was Constantine Karamanlis) headed by Sophocles Venizelos, arrived in Washington to outline Greece's financial needs. The Americans agreed to send a team of experts to survey the economic situation in the country and Paul Porter was appointed head of the first mission from 18 January to 22 March 1947. Porter's description of economic conditions in Greece as he found them upon his arrival is interesting:

> There exists a wide disparity in the living standards and income throughout all Greece. Traders, speculators and black marketeers thrive in wealth and luxury, a problem with which no government has effectively dealt. At the same time, the masses of people live on a bare subsistence. There is a vast amount of concealed unemployment with some 20% of the population employed by or partially dependent upon the state. The sub-standard levels of existence of the civil servants, indigents, pensioners and other dependents is an important contributory factor to the political and social tension which characterizes Greece today. No government since Liberation has made any plans to provide useful work for the employables among this large group of the population.[3]

The Porter Report actually consisted of two reports; the first, classified as 'confidential', was entitled 'Tentative Report of the American Economic Mission to Greece', and reached Washington on 1 April 1947; the second, classified 'secret', was called 'Report of the American Economic Mission to Greece', and reached Washington on 30 April 1947. The confidential report was never seen by the Greek people, whereas the secret report was published in Greece. Although both documents were approximately 30 pages long and consisted of essentially the same analysis, major differences did exist. In the unpublished report, the Americans insinuated that the Greek leaders were incapable of developing any kind of economic policy and that their main concern was the maintenance of their own political power. The Americans came to believe that the political arena in Athens was corrupt and manipulative, and that the opportunity to control the political life and, more importantly, economic life of the country was theirs. Because the Greek state was confronted with a desperate economic crisis (one that it could not meet alone) the Greek leaders had little choice but to accept American aid. They did, however, become complacent to American demands, and, with minor exceptions, did not resist what became a crude intervention into every aspect of Greek life. In addition, the published report spoke of 'foreign' individuals who would advise the Greek Government, whereas the unpublished report clearly stated that

> The Greek Government should be induced to employ
> American citizens as individuals in key executive positions.
> These men who will be selected with the advice of the
> Mission will be in a position to see that official policy is
> carried through in the day-to-day operations of the govern-
> ment, thus permitting the Mission to avoid the burden of
> making routine decisions for the Greek Government.
> Conditions in Greece are such that many of the measures
> undertaken cannot be carried out by Greek personnel who
> will inevitably be charged with political ambition, corruption
> or favoritism.[4]

The American mission completed its assessment by stating, in the unpublished version of the report, that:

> The American Recovery Mission should have two sanctions
> to induce the acceptance of its advice. First, it should have the
> power to stop or curtail financial aid, not only in general but
> in the cast of any particular project or activity, upon the
> failure of the Greek Government to comply with the condi-
> tions on which the aid was granted; second, it should have
> the obligation to publish quarterly reports on the progress of
> Greek recovery for the benefit of the people and Government
> of the United States and of the people and Government of
> Greece. ... [A]t the first clear and unreasonable failure of
> performance, the sanctions should be applied in order to
> make it evident that the Mission's advisory powers are
> backed with strength.[5]

Top secret State Department memoranda of conversations show
clearly that the future of Greek economic development lay exclusively in
the hands of the American planners responsible not only for the reconstruction of the Greek economy but also for its future path. The subject
of one memorandum, dated 4 August 1949, was 'Capital Investment in
Greece for Economic Development'. The two major characteristics of
the State Department meeting referred to in this memorandum were
that none of the participants were Greek and that the conversations
indicated that seven Americans were planning the future path of
economic development and capital investment in Greece without the
consent or advice of the Greek authorities. Parts of the conversations are
highly illuminating. George C. McGhee, the Coordinator of Aid to
Greece and Turkey, remarked that

It would be necessary to bear constantly in mind the political consequences of negative decisions on Greek industrial development projects. It might be desirable to reduce the doses of American aid to Greece, so that the Greek standard of living would gradually be brought down to a level which the economy of the country could support. However, this process would have to be carried out gradually and very carefully to avoid violent or unfavorable political reaction in Greece. It would have to be accompanied by some plan for large-scale emigration ... [I]t would be pleasant for the Greeks to have more electricity for civilian consumption and convenience, but the question [is] whether there would be a productive industrial market for the additional electric power which would help raise the Greek standard of living.[6]

Further along in the memorandum, still another astonishing remark was made by another State Department official:

Mr Dort commented that Greece will achieve economic viability at some level, and that we do have to decide what that level will be.[7]

Comments of that nature were the ones that helped, more than 30 years later, Andreas Papandreou to use so successfully the slogan 'Greece belongs to the Greeks' and help bring into power his political progressive party without the blessing of the Americans. His progressive party (PASOK) was destined to be in power again when the time came for Greece to become the twelfth member of the Economic and Monetary Union of the European Union.

FROM THE DRACHMA TO THE EURO

After 2,700 years of existence the Greek Drachma was consigned to history on 1 January 2002. This was a historic event of major proportions for Greece and its economy because the fact that the Euro has become the currency of Greece is a clear indication of the economic progress Greece has achieved.

Greece was officially and unanimously accepted as the twelfth member of the EMU in June 2000, when a European Union summit, that took place in Portugal, endorsed Greece's long-awaited entry into the euro-zone, which officially occurred on 1 January 2001, at a central rate of 340.750 drachmas per euro. It was also a personal triumph and the finest moment for Prime Minister Costas Simitis who had led, for the previous four years, the effort to reach this great accomplishment. It was, therefore, very fitting for Simitis to declare with pride that day:

> Our country's accession to the Economic and Monetary Union opens up a new era of security and stability, development and prosperity. The image of a small and introverted Greece is finally leaving our horizon. Today, Greece is a strong and modern country, with a robust economy and international recognition.

This event was unthinkable a decade earlier, when inflation had reached 25% and the state debt was worth more than the country's GDP. It has been a remarkable shift in the country's fortunes. Four years after Mr Simitis came to power, Greece has achieved two ambitions that seemed so distant then; the defeat of inflation and membership in the single European currency. Also, at the end of the twentieth century public finances are under control for the first time in almost twenty years. With inflation close to 2%, long-term interest rates close to convergence levels, falling public debt and a declining budget deficit, Greece has shown a sustainable convergence. But the efforts of all Greek governments, since the time Greece became the tenth Member State of the then European Economic Community, has come with a high cost. Although the standard of living of Greeks has risen substantially, as we are going to see further down the road, it will also mean an increase in income inequalities that have risen slowly and, as a result, Greece is today the second most unequal Member State of the European Union.

In his last two years as a Prime Minister, Andreas Papandreou became more involved in the economic affairs of the country and changed his economic policies after he realized that although his populist economic policies were necessary in the 1980s, they could be very dangerous in the 1990s. Thus in 1993 the economist prime minister started a new course of economic policies and developments so that his country would not be left behind the other Member States of the European Union.

But today the present PASOK government, under the able leadership of Constantine Simitis, has given up its trust in the role that the public sector can play in the economic developments of the country. A strong private sector is necessary for achieving high growth rates but it has no concerns with issues of equity and fairness. We should, therefore, remind the Greek government of what one of its economists has put so well:

> The weaknesses and disadvantages of the Greek public sector come from not only actual economic imbalances (fiscal deficit, high public debt, inflation), but also from the shat-

tered reputation of the Greek state as an economic manager, regulator, and mediator of social processes. The correctives cannot come simply from net reductions in the role of the public sector, such as privatization policies. They must also come, and perhaps with higher priority, from a reform of the whole nexus of economic relations between state and society ... It is chimeric to think of any solution to Greece's economic and structural problems without the reinstatement of the public sector's reputation in the new competitive era. Reinstatement of reputation organized around a public investment core can also ease financing problems, since both additional EC funding and domestic tax revenues can be legitimized in an investment climate.[8]

We are certain that if Andreas Papandreou was amongst us today, he would have approved such a statement.

THE TWIN OBSTACLES: INFLATION AND UNEMPLOYMENT

If the condition of the Greek economy had not deteriorated in the last twenty years then we could have easily said that the economic performance of Greece was one of the ten best in the world in the twentieth century. Unfortunately, the low growth rates together with high rates of inflation and unemployment that prevailed during this period prevented the Greeks from making such a claim.

In fact one of the reasons that income inequality has risen in the last couple of decades is the poor performance of the economy in three critical areas. Global studies on income distribution has shown that low rates of GDP growth, high rates of inflation, and high rates of unemployment are major contributors to the worsening of the distribution of income and wealth within countries.

Of these three problems the most difficult to tame is that of unemployment. Figure 1 gives us a better picture of the problem. In 1999 the unemployment rate had reached an unprecedented 11.73%.

In the 1960s and early 1970s the unemployment rate was about 2% and then increased to an average of 8% in the 1980s and 10% in the 1990s. In any other period of time, a double digit rate of unemployment would have been the number one concern of any Greek government, but in the 1990s the obsession of the governments of Greece was meeting the Maastricht criteria in order for Greece to be completely integrated in the Economic and Monetary Union (EMU) of the European Union. The problem of unemployment could not be tackled while budget deficits and inflation rates were the major priority.

FIGURE 1: UNEMPLOYMENT IN GREECE (1977–99)

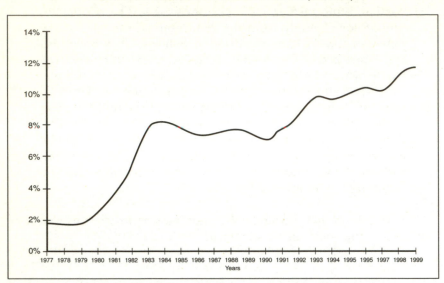

Source: Bank of Greece, various Annual Reports.

In all fairness to the Greeks, we should mention that high unemployment is not uniquely Greek. Similar unemployment rates have existed throughout the European Union in the last two decades of the twentieth century. For sometime now economists have been puzzled when attempting to understand and compare the high unemployment rates that persist in western Europe with the low unemployment rates that exist in the United States. One view holds that high unemployment rates in Europe are due to its generous social welfare system and 'rigid' wage structures, or in other words to the equality characteristic of social democracy. In contrast, low unemployment in the United States is credited to that country's 'flexibility' and therefore its willingness to tolerate high inequality in wages and incomes.

A new study shows that across Europe the relationship between income inequality and unemployment fails to fit the conventional view.[9] The authors of this study indicate that unemployment rates are systematically lower in the richer and more equal countries of Europe where wages are high and social welfare systems are strong. In the EU today unemployment is higher in countries like Spain and Greece which are not high income countries, and who have weak social welfare systems and the most inequality.

Their analysis suggests that the real rigidities of Europe are different from the conventional view:

Indeed they have nothing to do with supposed inflexibility of relative wages inside any particular country. Quite the contrary; increasing relative wage differentials would only cause even more low productivity people to abandon their present employments in favor of the job queue and the dole.[10]

The authors also believe that Europe's governments should be blamed for the current situation first because of their unwillingness to make the vast income transfers that would be required to make life in Spain and Greece as attractive as it is in Sweden, and secondly because of the unwillingness to develop macroeconomic policies that can effectively build Europe's peripheral economies through national programmes of full employment. They assert that:

European policy is designed to work in just the opposite direction, to restrict both the autonomy of both monetary and fiscal policies and to impede the achievement of full employment on the national scale. Meanwhile, barriers to migration and resettlement obstruct the citizens of the European periphery from taking full advantage of the more generous social welfare systems to the North. This concentrates unemployment in Spain, Italy and Greece and reduces the pressure on wealthier countries in Europe to pursue full employment policies.

This view has checkable implications. It implies, for instance, that unemployment is negatively associated with income levels between countries and positively with inequality within them. Lower incomes and more inequality should mean more unemployment. And as unemployment rose while European economic integration proceeded, it should be true that the rise in unemployment has been sharper in the lower-income, high inequality countries than in the higher-income, egalitarian countries.

The facts line up impressively with these predictions. Unemployment has long been higher in the poorer and more unequal countries of Europe. As overall unemployment has grown, the rise has been systematically greater in lower-income countries. The main exception is Portugal, which has low average income but also low inequality – and high emigration. High-wage employment for the Portuguese occurs, it would appear, mainly outside the country.

Europe therefore faces three choices. One of them is impossible, a second is unacceptable, and the third is necessary. Europe could, in principle but not in practice, restore

national means for the pursuit of full employment, in the
form of independent monetary, fiscal and trade policies,
alongside capital controls. Or, it could break down its
national and regional enclaves, establishing a unified labor
market from the Baltic to the Algarve, so that the poor populations relocate to the rich countries, like Mississippi's blacks
to Chicago. We do not think this would be well received.

And if not this, then Europe must establish, on a continental and international scale, the kind of social welfare transfer
and employment-subsidy mechanisms that have heretofore
existed only within the smallest, richest, and most resolutely
socialist nations of the continent – but that are entirely
routine in the United States.[11]

As the authors indicate, this third option is a necessary one but even
if the Greek government considers adopting it, it cannot be implemented since this type of decision is no longer taken in Athens but in
Brussels. Because of its important message, this was a necessary lengthy
quotation in order to show that the EU is not a panacea that will solve
all the economic problems of Greece. Nevertheless, the insistence of
Prime Minister Constantine Karamanlis to make Greece, in 1981, the
tenth member of the European Economic Community, and the obsession
of Prime Minister Costas Simitis to make Greece a member of the
Economic and Monetary Union, were not really alternative solutions to
other choices that they might have made.

We should also understand that the road ahead will be a road of
increased inequalities for the people of Greece, since the Greek government insists that the overall picture is more important. We cannot have
high rates of GDP growth, decrease of public debt, and decrease inflation and at the same time believe that we are capable of decreasing
income inequalities and unemployment rates. The target that the
ministry of National Economy has set for the next decade is a GDP
growth of 5% and if the rest of the EU growth rates do not exceed 3.5%,
then Greece can reach the economic level of its partners by the year
2015.

Although the present Greek government believes that social justice
should be an important ingredient of its economic goals, it cannot be
realized. The choice of growth without equity is necessary if the Greeks
are interested in catching up with their EU partners. As we leave the
twentieth century the goal is clear. The Greeks need, for mostly psycho-
logical reasons, to be part of the rich nations of Europe and it seems
that, in the long run, they will close the gap on their partners in the EU,
but that this type of economic development will increase the income gap
between the rich and poor segments of the Greek population.

Nevertheless, the objective of convergence with the EU levels of per capita income can be achieved if Greek economic growth is more rapid than that of the rest of its partners. This goal can be achieved by increasing the efficiency of the use of the factors of production, which means nothing else but an increase in the level of productivity. Labour productivity has been shown to be a major element in the level of GDP per capita. One of the reasons that we believe that Greece cannot succeed in its convergence effort and catch up with its partners in the next ten years in the GDP per capita, is the low level productivity that has existed throughout the last twenty years. As shown in Figure 2, among it EU partners, Greece has the second lowest level of labour productivity. In 1986 Greece's hourly productivity was 10.4 euro (in 1997 euro). By 1997 there had been a very modest increase to 11.9 euro per hour, which is half of the EU average.

FIGURE 2: LABOUR PRODUCTIVITY IN THE EUROPEAN UNION

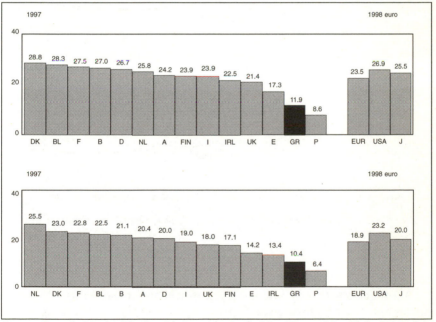

Source: Carmela Martin, *The Spanish Economy in the New Europe* (New York: St Martin's Press, 2000) p. 25.

In a study of the economy of Spain,[12] the author used a method for measuring total productivity by choosing the version of the Tornqvist-Theil index – known as the multilateral translogarithmic productivity index – which allows a comparison of productivity levels both over time and across countries. The author of the study wanted to compare the overall productivity of Spain with the most and least productive EU countries – Germany and Greece, respectively – standardized by the European average. As seen from Figure 3 the news on the Greek position is not good. However, a closer look indicates that this method shows that Greece's position relative to the EU average is better than that reflected in the labour productivity indicator (60% instead of 50% of the EU average).

FIGURE 3: TRENDS IN TOTAL FACTOR PRODUCTIVITY OF
VARIOUS EU COUNTRIES
(Index of multilateral translogarithmic productivity, EU = 100)

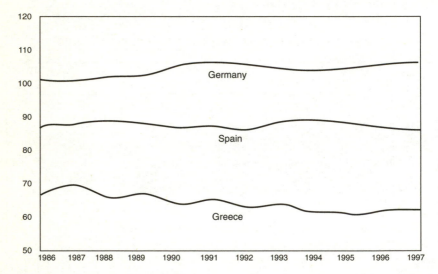

Source: Carmela Martin, *The Spanish Economy in the New Europe* (New York: St Martin's Press, 2000) p. 27.

Another issue that makes us very sceptical about the ability of Greece to catch up with its European partners is the fact that it is lagging in the field of technology. Recent growth models stress the essential role played by technology, although its measurement poses many problems. The study of the Spanish economy already mentioned has attempted to measure the technological capital ratio of the EU Member States and as Figure 4 indicates Greece stands last on this front. At the core of this enormous technological insufficiency lies the meagre research efforts on both the public and private fronts.

FIGURE 4: TECHNOLOGICAL CAPITAL
(Ratio of stock technological capital to GDP mp, EUR in 1986 = 100)

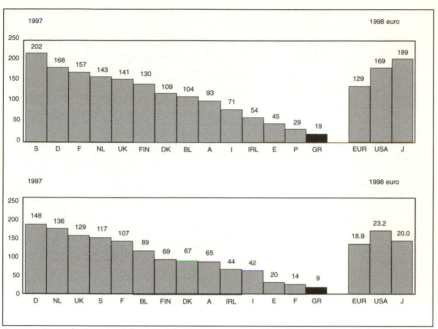

Source: Carmela Martin, *The Spanish Economy in the New Europe* (New York: St Martin's Press, 2000) p. 31.

As we turn our attention to the second of the twin obstacles, that of inflation, the news is no better. In Greece today inflation has been tamed and represents a major accomplishment of the PASOK government. Figure 5 speaks volumes.

As Figure 5 indicates double digit inflation had dominated the Greek economy since the 1970s and it was only after 1995 that inflation declined again to single digits. This of course was not the case in the 1960s where the average consumer price index was only 1.95%, while in the period from 1970 to 1998 it was eight times higher (15.9%). It is obvious that the main target of the macroeconomic policy of the Greek government since 1994 was the taming of inflation in order to meet the Maastricht criterion in order for the drachma to enter to the euro-zone, and their success was undoubtedly a great achievement for Greek economic planners. It should also be mentioned that Andreas Papandreou was the architect of this policy when he came to power for the second time in the early 1990s, and the present government continued this policy even more successfully.

FIGURE 5: INFLATION IN GREECE (1975–99)

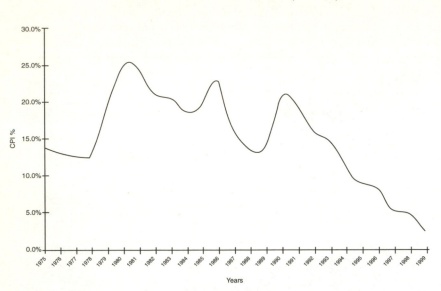

Source: Annual Report for the year 1999, Bank of Greece, Athens, 2000.

Thus, the inflation rate was lowered to 2.6% in 1999 and it was projected that it would be close to 2% in the year 2000. As we will see next, these high rates of inflation that Greece had experienced for almost three decades were also responsible for the worsening of the distribution of income.

THE UNDERGROUND ECONOMY

Before we discuss the distribution of income we should also mention here another problem that is facing the present and future Greek governments, that of the underground economy, since it has also distributional implications. One issue that fascinates economists around the world is that of the underground or shadow economy; is the name given to unreported income by individuals eager to avoid paying taxes or because their income is derived from illegal activities? This type of economic activity not only is a fact of life around the world but it seems to be rising. Creating accurate statistics and gathering information about underground economic activity is a difficult task, because the people who are participating in such activities do not want to be identified. But in order for governments to make effective economic policy decisions it is crucial to know the frequency and magnitude of such activities.

Over the last couple of decades a few Greek studies and some international ones have indicated that Greece has one of the largest underground economies in the world. The latest study[13] shows that Greece has the largest underground economy of all OECD countries. From Table 9 we can see that the southern European countries are the leaders in shadow economic activities.

TABLE 9: SHADOW ECONOMIES IN OECD COUNTRIES
(Size of Shadow Economy as % of GDP)

Country	Average 1990–93
Greece	27.2
Italy	20.4
Spain	16.1
Portugal	15.6
Belgium	15.3
USA	13.9
Australia	13.1
Netherlands	11.8

Source: Frederick Schneider and Dominik H. Enste, 'Shadow Economies: Size, Causes, and Consequences', *Journal of Economic Literature*, vol. xxxviii (March 2000) p. 102.

There are a few important reasons why the economic policy makers of the Greek government should be concerned with the rise of the underground economy. The most important ones are:

(i) A growing shadow economy can be seen as the reaction of individuals who feel overburdened by the state and who choose the 'exit option' rather than the 'voice option'. If the increase of the shadow economy is caused by a rise in the overall tax and social security burden together with 'institutional sclerosis', then the 'consecutive flight' into the shadow economy may erode the tax and social security bases. The result can be a vicious circle of a further increase in the budget deficit or tax rates, additional growth of the shadow economy, and gradual weakening of the economic and social basis of collective arrangements.

(ii) A prospering shadow economy may cause severe difficulties for politicians because official indicators – on unemployment, labour force, income, consumption – are unreliable. Policy based on erroneous official indicators is likely to be ineffective, or worse.

(iii) The effects of a growing shadow economy on the official one must also be considered. On the one hand, a prospering shadow economy may attract (domestic and foreign) workers away from the official economy and create competition for official firms. On the other hand, at least two-thirds of the income earned in the shadow economy is immediately spent in the official economy, thus having a positive effect in the official economy.[14]

This is an issue that will trouble the Greek economy for decades to come because the tendency of Greeks to hide their incomes is not only related to economic issues but also to sociological and cultural ones that are beyond the scope of this study. Nevertheless, such a large underground economy indicates that the Greeks are richer than the official statistics indicate and that the inequalities in the distribution of income are less than the official numbers, since various economic studies indicate that the poorer classes are more capable of hiding income than the rich.

THE GREEK DISTRIBUTION OF INCOME

In spite of the long-standing interest in the idea of economic equality, there has not been any long tradition of systematic work on the concept of income equality or on the personal distribution of income in Greece. Of course, systematic work on the distribution of income by size on a global scale, at different stages of development is of very recent origin – it could even be argued that it started only in 1955 with Kuznet's classic article on economic growth and income inequality.

In Greece the issue of economic equality has been neglected and serious studies on the subject have only appeared in the last twenty-five years. One of the first studies conducted on a global scale had included the following information about the distribution of income in Greece in the late 1950s:

TABLE 10: INCOME DISTRIBUTION IN GREECE (1957)

	Poor	Low Middle	Middle	Upper Middle	High	Highest
Percentage of population	0–20	20–40	40–60	60–80	80–100	95–100
Percentage of income	9.0	12.8	12.30	16.40	49.50	23.0

Source: Irma Adelman and Cynthia Morris, *Economic Growth and Social Equity* (Stanford: Stanford University Press, 1973) p. 152.

One of the foremost Greek economists of the second half of the twentieth century, Professor D. Karageorgas, was the first economist to pay attention to the issue of income distribution and its effects on the Greek economy. In the midst of the military dictatorship, and although he was injured as a result of his anti-junta activities, he published a brilliant article in 1973 in which he stated that:

> instead of improving the situation, the Greek tax structure increases the inequality of income distribution. This adverse distributional effect of taxation is shown by the fact that the Gini coefficient increases from 0.5884 before taxes and transfer payments to 0.6058 after the allocation of the tax burden. Among the reasons for such a distributional impact are the regressive effective tax rates of almost all consumption taxes, the extensive tax evasion located mainly in the high income levels, and the great number of special tax privileges to various persons and social groups.[15]

This finding was not very surprising because one of the most interesting results of the junta's economic policy was the fact that it gave many concessions to the Greek economic establishment. With the law that the junta created in 1967, the marginal rate of taxation for the very rich had been reduced from 60% to 49%. So people with incomes over one million drachmas had to pay less taxes than before.

After the fall of the dictatorship, issues of equity came in the forefront, especially with the creation of the Panhellenic Socialist Movement by Professor Andreas Papandreou who was very concerned as a politician and as an economist with the concept of economic justice. Since then many economists have tackled the issue of the distribution of income in Greece. We will not attempt to present the exact results of such studies here but instead present the latest and perhaps the best study so far on this subject, done by a team of economists of the Centre of Planning and Economic Research (KEPE) in Athens. Table 11 presents the results of this study.

The results of Table 11 are certainly disheartening: the poorest 20% of the population receives only 3.6% of total income, and the richest 20% receives almost half (48.4%) of the total income. And the news is getting worse. If we compare the income inequalities in Greece almost 40 years apart, we can see from the comparative Table 12 that the distribution of income has worsened between the late 1950s to the early 1990s. The picture is not pretty. Clearly the rich have become richer and the poor have become poorer. In the 1950s the poorest one-fifth of the families were receiving 9.0% and almost 40 years later they are receiving only 3.6% of total income.

One other issue that has contributed to the inequalities in the distribution of income is the stagnation of the real average disposable income

TABLE 11: INCOME DISTRIBUTION IN GREECE (1994)

Deciles*	% of income
1st	1.1
2nd	2.5
3rd	3.9
4th	5.4
5th	6.8
6th	8.5
7th	10.5
8th	12.9
9th	17.0
10th	31.4

* The order of the deciles is from the poorest one-tenth to the richest one-tenth of the population.

Source: K. Kanellopoulos *et al.*, *Distribution, Redistribution and Poverty* (Athens: Centre of Planning and Economic Research, 1999) p. 99.

TABLE 12: THE GREEK DISTRIBUTION OF INCOME IN
TWO DIFFERENT DECADES

Quintiles	1950s	1990s
Lowest 20%	3.6	9.0
Second 20%	9.3	12.8
Third 20%	15.3	12.3
Fourth 20%	23.4	16.4
Highest 20%	48.4	49.5

Source: KEPE, 1999 and Adelman and Morris, 1973.

of wage earners in the last 20 years. The latest Annual Report of the Bank of Greece indicates that for the last two decades of the twentieth century the real income of wage earners has remained the same! If we take as the base year (index: 100) the year 1980, then we can see that the real average disposable income of wage earners had shown a marginal increase of 101.2 for the year 1990 and then in 1999 had declines to 100.2, an amazing figure. What is still more amazing is the fact that a socialist government was in power for the majority of these years. Table 13 shows the results described above.

Another study of the poor in 38 countries, including Greece, reveals that the poor suffer more from inflation than the rich. This survey has been done by the Development Research Group of the World Bank[16] and the evidence supports the views that inflation is regarded as more of a problem by the poor than by the non-poor, and that inflation appears to reduce the relative income of the poor.

TABLE 13: DISPOSABLE INCOME AND INFLATION

	Average Disposable Income (Nominal)	*Average Disposable Income (Real)*	*Index*	*Consumer Prices*
1980	23.0	−1.4	100	24.8
1981	22.3	−1.8	98.2	24.5
1982	24.4	2.8	100.9	21.0
1983	15.8	−3.7	97.2	20.2
1984	22.2	3.1	100.2	18.5
1985	22.0	2.3	102.5	19.3
1986	11.3	−9.5	92.8	23.0
1987	11.6	−4.1	89.0	16.4
1989	22.0	7.3	100.5	3.7
1990	21.2	0.7	101.2	20.4
1991	15.2	−3.6	97.6	19.5
1992	15.8	−0.1	97.5	15.9
1993	6.3	−7.1	90.6	14.4
1994	11.5	0.5	91.0	10.9
1995	10.3	1.3	92.2	8.9
1996	9.7	1.4	93.5	8.2
1997	10.7	4.9	98.1	5.5
1998	5.9	1.0	99.1	4.8
1999	3.7	1.1	100.2	2.6

Source: Annual Report for the Year 1999, Bank of Greece, Athens, 2000, p. 133.

One of the questions of the survey was the following: *Do you strongly agree, mostly agree, mostly disagree, or strongly disagree with the following statement: 'In our society, the rich get richer and the poor get poorer'?* In Figure 6 we graph the percentage of respondents in each country who answer this question 'strongly agree' against the actual rate of inflation 1985–94. We see a positive association (which is highly statistically significant) but also we see that Greece figures prominently here since 70% of the Greeks perceive that in their country 'the rich get richer and the poor get poorer'.

The same World Bank study examined the impact of changes in inflation on direct measures of poverty and relate them to inflation. They found that high inflation tended to lower the share of the bottom quintile and the real minimum wage, while tending to increase poverty. This is another indicator that shows that the high rates of inflation that Greece has experienced from 1980 to 1995 have contributed to the increasing inequalities in the distribution of income during this period.

FIGURE 6: ASSOCIATION BETWEEN PERCEPTION THAT
'RICH GET RICHER AND POOR GET POORER' AND ACTUAL INFLATION

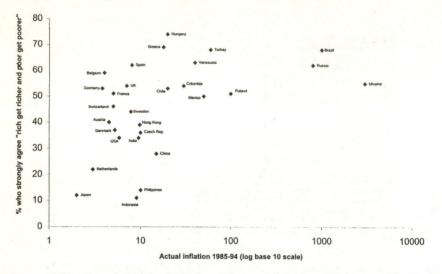

Source: William Easterly and Stanley Fisher, *Inflation and the Poor* (Washington: The World
Bank, 2000) p. 21.

INEQUALITIES IN THE EUROPEAN UNION

Although we have criticized the inequalities of income in Greece we
need in all fairness to compare them with other societies in order to get
a better perspective and a yardstick of comparative analysis. Further on
in this chapter some global inequalities will be explained, but in this
segment we should compare the inequalities that have more relevance
for Greece – the income inequalities that exist inside the European
Union.

In the latest study called 'Analysis of income distribution in 12 EU
Member States', that was done by Eurostat, the complex reality of
poverty and income disparity across the European Union was revealed.
The figures show that one out of six citizens and households live below
the poverty threshold and just over one-third of poor households are
working. The figures confirm that social exclusion leading to poverty
affects a great many people across the EU, in both affluent and less affluent Member States.

As Figure 7 indicates, the proportion of households below the
poverty line was 17% in the EU 12 as a whole. Portugal had the highest
rate of poverty with 29%, then came Greece with 24% and the United
Kingdom with 23%. At the other side, Denmark had the lowest poverty
rate with 9%, followed by German and Belgium each at 13%.

FIGURE 7
PROPORTION OF POOR HOUSEHOLDS IN THE EUROPEAN UNION (1993)

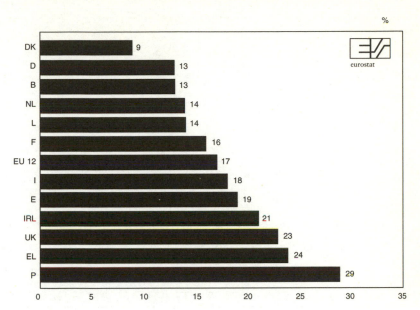

Source: Statistics in Focus: Analysis of income distribution in 13 EU Member States, Eurostat, no. 11, 1998, p. 6.

In the same study an analysis of income distribution among the EU 12 Member States for the year 1993 shows that Greece is the second most unequal country in the European Union after Portugal. As measured by the Gini coefficient, Portugal appeared to have the highest degree of inequality with a Gini coefficient of 0.42 followed by Greece (0.38) and then the United Kingdom and Italy (both at 0.37). At the other end of the spectrum, Denmark had the lowest degree of inequality with 0.25. The study did not include Austria, Finland and Sweden since they were not at the time of the study members of the EU. It is important to note that these three countries have an even better distribution of income than Denmark. As Table 14 indicates, the poorest 20% of the households received between 6% (Greece, Spain, Italy and Portugal) and 9% (Belgium, Denmark and Ireland) of total household net monetary income; whereas the richest 20% of households, received between 33% (Denmark) and 46% (Portugal).

Furthermore, in Figure 8 we present another study also done by Eurostat, which shows the percentage of the population under the low-income threshold in each country as well as the monetary value in PPS corresponding to the threshold and the Gini coefficients. The highest

TABLE 14: HOUSEHOLD NET INCOME DISTRIBUTION IN EU 12 (1993)

Decile	EU1	B	DK	D	EL	E	F	IRL	I	L	NL	P	UK
Shares	2												
Bottom 1	2	3	5	3	2	2	3	3	2	3	3	2	3
2	4	6	7	6	4	4	5	6	4	5	5	4	5
3	6	7	8	6	5	6	6	6	6	6	6	5	6
4	7	8	8	7	7	7	7	6	7	7	7	6	7
5	8	9	8	8	7	7	8	7	8	7	7	7	7
6	9	9	9	9	9	8	9	8	9	9	9	8	9
7	10	10	10	10	10	10	10	10	11	10	10	10	10
8	12	12	11	12	13	12	12	12	12	12	13	12	12
9	15	14	13	15	15	15	15	16	16	14	15	16	15
10	26	22	20	23	27	27	25	27	20	27	25	30	28
Gini	0.35	0.31	0.25	0.30	0.38	0.35	0.33	0.34	0.37	0.32	0.34	0.42	0.37

Numbers represent % of total household net monetary income.

Source: Statistics in Focus: Analysis of income distribution in 13 EU Member States, Eurostat, no. 11, 1998, p. 8.

FIGURE 8: THE LOW INCOME POPULATION (IN PPS AND %)
AND THE GINI COEFFICIENT (1994)

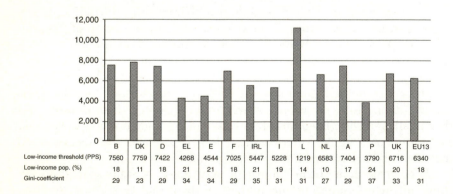

	B	DK	D	EL	E	F	IRL	I	L	NL	A	P	UK	EU13
Low-income threshold (PPS)	7560	7759	7422	4268	4544	7025	5447	5228	1219	6583	7404	3790	6716	6340
Low-income pop. (%)	18	11	18	21	21	18	21	19	14	10	17	24	20	18
Gini-coefficient	29	23	29	34	34	29	35	31	31	27	29	37	33	31

Source: Statistics in Focus: 'Social Exclusion in the EU Member States', Eurostat, Theme 3 – 1/2000.[17]

low income threshold by far is found in Luxembourg (11,219 PPS). At the other end, the low income threshold in Portugal is third of the threshold in Luxemburg at 3,790 PPS. From the point of view of low income population, the lowest (10%) belongs to the Netherlands and the highest one (24%) belongs to Portugal. Greece again has the second lowest level in both the low income level threshold of 4,268 PPS and the low income population (21%).

Finally, another way of looking at income distribution in the EU is the ratio of the top 20% to the bottom 20% where a lower figure indicates greater equality. Greece again has the second lowest ratio (6.6) and the poorest 10% of the population receives only 2.2% of income while the richest 10% receives 26.3% of total income (Table 15).

TABLE 15: THE DISTRIBUTION OF INCOME IN THE EUROPEAN UNION

	% of total income received by bottom 'poorest' 10% of population	% of total income received by top 'richest' 10% of population	Ratio of top 20% to bottom 20%
EU13	2.6	24.0	5.5
Belgium	2.9	22.5	4.8
Denmark	4.4	20.2	3.1
Germany	2.7	22.7	4.9
Greece	2.2	26.3	6.6
Spain	2.5	24.9	6.0
France	3.3	22.8	4.5
Ireland	3.0	26.6	5.9
Italy	2.4	22.9	5.4
Luxemburg	3.1	23.6	4.8
Netherlands	4.1	20.0	3.5
Austria	2.7	22.8	4.9
Portugal	2.2	27.7	7.1
UK	3.0	26.1	5.6

Source: Statistics in Focus: Population and social conditions, no. 11/98, Analysis of Income Distribution in 13 EU Member States, Eurostat, 1998.

The great and sustained effort that Greece has to make in the next ten to fifteen years, in order to catch up with its European partners, in the so called 'real convergence', requires an emphasis in concepts such as 'high growth rates', 'privatization', 'decreasing government deficits', that are capable of making the figures for the Greek economy look better both for domestic and international audiences. This approach will result in the continuation and perpetuation of the concept of 'growth without equity' and if, in fifteen years from now, Greece has reached the high level of income of its partners, it will have done so only at the expense of the poorest 20% of the Greek population. Therefore, Greece will remain well behind its EU partners in the levels of poverty and income inequalities.

INTERNATIONAL COMPARISONS

As we have already seen, income inequalities in Greece are quite high in comparison with almost all the Member States of the EU. However we need to get even a better perspective by making some international comparisons. Since the latest data on Greece is that of 1994 we can compare it to that of the United States and Brazil in the same year.

The first column of Table 16 indicates the percentage of population (from the poorest one fifth to the richest one fifth) and the other columns represent the percentage of income that corresponds to each of the quintiles.

TABLE 16: INTERNATIONAL COMPARISONS OF INCOME DISTRIBUTION
(Percentage share of income)

Quintiles	Austria	Greece	USA	Brazil
Lowest 20%	10.4	3.6	4.2	2.5
Second 20%	14.8	9.3	10.0	5.7
Third 20%	18.5	15.3	15.7	9.9
Fourth 20%	22.9	23.4	23.3	17.7
Highest 20%	33.3	48.4	46.9	64.2
Gini coefficient	0.231	0.436	0.426	0.601

Sources: KEPE, US Census Bureau, and World Bank.

Brazil is considered the country with the most unequal distribution of income in the world and clearly the distribution of income of Greece is better than that of Brazil. But what is disturbing about this table is the fact that Greece has a worse distribution of income than the United States. For a long time Greek public opinion, and supported by many politicians, has held a strong belief that although the United States is the richest country on earth, it is nevertheless a highly unequal society. They will, therefore, look with disbelief at the above figures that show that Greece has a worse distribution of income than the United States.

The table above also includes the distribution of income of Austria for comparison. This has been done as Austria has the best distribution of income of all the countries of the European Union. These inequality figures are from the early 1990s. Latest figures indicate that inequalities in the 1990s in the United States, which has experienced an unprecedented prosperity, have dramatically increased. Clearly the benefits from this prosperity in the wealthiest country in the world have not affected its poorest segment. According to the United States Census Bureau (US Census Bureau 2000) statistics, the income inequality has continuously increased since the 1960s. In the last decade of the twentieth century the inequalities in the US were higher than any other decade since the end of the Second World War. At the extremes of the distribution, family income fell at the bottom and grew at the top over the past quarter century. Most industrialized nations have also experienced growing income inequality, but in the United States, where the existing income disparity was greater, the rise has been more rapid.

Although statistics on Greek income inequalities do not exist for the last five years of the twentieth century we should not assume, although we could suspect, that these inequalities have also increased in Greece. This suspicion is likely to be confirmed as the country is attempting to emulate the Wall Street model of economic development that was responsible for 'the rich to become richer and the poor to become poorer' during this period in the United States. As already mentioned earlier, the only issue that perhaps has made these inequalities less pronounced in Greece is the successful combating of inflation during the last five years.

Finally, it is important for Greek society to comprehend that the phenomenal success of the so-called 'new economy' in the United States in the 1990s had benefited a small percentage of the families in the United States and that the 'American dream' is still unattainable for a large portion of American society. Figure 9 does not need any explanation at all. It is a shocking picture that shows that the top 1% of the families increased their wealth by 35% from 1983 to 1997, and for the same period of time the bottom 40% of the families had seen their wealth decline by 36.2%! Unfortunately, statistics on the distribution of wealth are not available in Greece and thus we cannot make any speculation and comparisons on this issue.

In a special issue on 'The Twentieth Century' by the Oxford Review of Economic Policy, it has been stated that:

> Perhaps the century's biggest failure has been the conspicuous absence of productivity and living standards convergence in the world. Despite much greater overall prosperity, much improved methods of communication and transportation, and much more widespread awareness of poverty across the globe, inter-country income gaps today are greater than 100 years ago.[18]

The ratio of average income of the richest country on the world to

FIGURE 9: THE GLOBAL DISTRIBUTION OF INCOME AND WEALTH

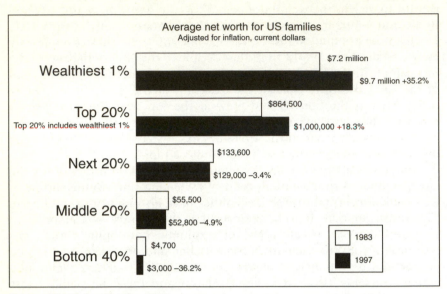

Source: *USA Today*, October 1999.

TABLE 17: RICH AND POOR PEOPLE IN THE WORLD

	1800	*1950*	*1995*
World GDP*	229,095,000,000	2,626,407,000,000	17,091,479,000,000
Rich	56%	83%	80%
Poor	44%	17%	20%
World Population	944,000,000	2,147,000,000	5,716,000,000
Rich	26%	33%	20%
Poor	74%	67%	80%

* Estimated GDP (in 1980 dollars).

Source: Nancy Birdsall, 'Life is Unfair: Inequality in the World', *Foreign Policy*, Summer 1998, no. 111, p. 79.

that of the poorest has risen from about 9:1 at the end of the nineteenth century to at least 60:1 today. Since 1950, the portion of the world's population living in poor countries grew by about 250%, while in rich countries the population increased by less than 50%. Today, as Table 17 shows, 80% of the world's population lives in countries that generate only 20% of the world's total income.

As Nancy Birdsall indicates:

> Ironically, inequality is growing at a time when the triumph of democracy and open markets was supposed to usher in a new age of freedom and opportunity. In fact, both developments seem to be having the opposite effect. At the end of the twentieth-century, Karl Marx's screed against capitalism has metamorphosed into post-Marxist angst about an integrated global market that creates a new divide between well-educated elite workers and their vulnerable unskilled counterparts, gives capital an apparent whip hand over labor, and pushes governments to unravel social safety nets. Meanwhile, the spread of democracy has made more visible the problem of income gaps, which can no longer be blamed on poor politics – not on communism in Eastern Europe and the former Soviet Union nor on military authoritarianism in Latin America. Regularly invoked as the handmaiden of open markets, democracy looks more and more like their accomplice in a vicious circle of inequality and injustice.[19]

A report by the United Nations has calculated that:

- The three richest persons on the planet own assets that exceed the combined GDP of the world's poorest 48 countries.
- The richest 225 people in the world have a net worth equivalent to the annual income of the poorest 2.5 billion people in the world.
- In 1985, the average income person in the richest country was 76 times as much as that in the poorest; in 1997, it was 288 times.
- Basic education for all would cost $6 billion a year; $8 billion is spent annually on cosmetics in the US alone.
- Installation of water and sanitation for all would cost $9 billion; $11 billion is spent annually for ice cream in Europe.
- Basic health care and nutrition would cost $13 billion; $17 billion a year is spent on pet food in Europe and the United States.

> This is a world that does not make any sense. This is the world that our children are inheriting from us. We hope that they realize that their role should not be to interpret this

world but to change it, since the salvation of mankind lies only in making everything the concern of all. If the twenty-first century follows the pattern of inequality of the previous century, then we cannot close our eyes to these numbers and continue talking about the great 'progress' that humans have made in the twentieth century. Clearly, the distribution of income and wealth among nations and within nations is going to be the most important and crucial issue that will be facing our planet in the next century. The inevitable movement towards globalization can make us very pessimistic since globalization by its nature is not conducive to a world of decreasing inequalities but rather the opposite.

Today global capitalism and its unparalleled dynamism represents the new economic system that dominates the world, but it would not have been a surprise to Marx and Engels, who in 1848 predicted that capitalism would spread to the entire world. They wrote:

> The bourgeoisie, by the rapid improvement of all instruments of production, by the immensely facilitated means of communication, draws all, even the most barbarian, nations into civilization. The cheap prices of its commodities are the heavy artillery with which it batters down all Chinese walls, with which it forces the barbarians' intensely obstinate hatred of foreigners to capitulate. It compels all nations, on pain of extinction, to adopt the bourgeois mode of production; it compels them to introduce what it calls civilization into their midst, i.e., to become bourgeois themselves. In one word, it creates a world after its own image.[20]

If Marx were around today, he would have probably explained that 'globalization' is the last, highest stage of capitalist development. Most economists, of course, believe that Marx's prediction of the demise of capitalism following the immiserization of the masses has been completely incorrect. Although, clearly, this prediction has not materialized, at least not in the Western industrialized countries, we should not be so certain about the mistaken prediction of Marx if the gap between the rich and poor citizens of our global village continues to widen. In fact Marx's interpretation that gaps in income between rich and poor are caused by exploitation rather than differences in productivity remains even today his most deadly legacy. The curse of inequality has spread like fire at the end of the century. At the same time, global capitalism has created more wealth than any preceeding centuries together.

PROSPECTS FOR THE FUTURE

A new book published in the United States, *Growing Prosperity*,[21] warns that the obsession of the US government with federal debt reduction and inflation control – the very essence of what the authors call the 'Wall Street model' – will in fact sabotage growth in the United States. We mention it here because the similarities with the present policies of the Greek government are striking – the obsession with public debt reduction and inflation control – and will not allow an equitable expansion in the next century. The authors of the book believe that a 'Main Street model' should replace the 'Wall Street model' that is presently dominating the economic system in the United States. In Table 18 these two different models are presented, since they can be of some interest to Greek policy-makers.

TABLE 18: WALL STREET POLICIES VERSUS MAIN STREET POLICIES

Wall Street Model	Main Street Model
Balance federal budget/build up surpluses.	Invest in R&D, infrastructure, and human capital.
Encourage unlimited free trade.	
Maintain downward pressure on wages.	Establish fair trade based on labour rights and standards.
Encourage employment insecurity.	
Deregulate domestic markets.	Foster rising wages.
Impose conservative Federal Reserve policy.	Improve employment security.
Deregulate global markets.	Create incentives for corporate best-practice policies.
	Allow expansionary Federal Reserve policy.
	Regulate global speculation.

Source: Barry Bluestone and Bennett Harrison, *Growing Prosperity* (Boston: Houghton Mifflin Co., 2000) p. 262.

Of course some of the Main Street Model recommendations are not applicable to the Greek economy and one of them – expansionary monetary policy – cannot even be considered since independent Greek monetary policy no longer exists. In the last decade of the century Greece together with many other countries not only discovered the Internet but also discovered the stock market. The stock market mania that has engulfed Greece represents a dangerous force since the majority of the people that invest have no idea what the stock market really is and what it represents. The mentality of getting rich quickly by playing the stock market will become, in the short run, an obstacle to the future development of the country until the thrill with the buying and trading of stocks subsides.

CONCLUSION: GROWTH WITH EQUITY

In Greece, as in most Western countries, economists and political leaders have embraced the private market as the answer to all our troubles and have put faith in the American model to bring us a new era of prosperity. But it should be understood that the American model, thanks to the revolution in computer and information technology, cannot be duplicated. Moreover it should be regarded as undesirable since it creates a more unequal society. The whole 'New Economy' thesis ignores the unique context of the US, which makes its recent success impossible to replicate. Few countries can borrow abroad in their own currency and so go on living above their means without deflating and defaulting. Why the world's 'most competitive economy' must import so much more than it exports is as much a mystery as why the world's richest economy cannot save.

In the United States:

> rather than equipping people with the means and the institutional supports for coping with a world of hyper-mobile capital and chronic uncertainty about the future, government has been promoting the low road of ever brutishly competitive capital and labor markets. The notion that this has contributed to prosperity rather than threatened its sustainability needs to be recognized for the illusion it is.[22]

The present Greek government understands this illusion and now that the goal of monetary union has been accomplished, an economic policy of growth with equity is the proper road to be followed for the prosperity of all Greeks in the twentieth century. If the present and future Greek governments believe that the 'new economy' paradigm of the United States, that has been glorified around the world, is the answer to the future path of Greek economic development, undoubtedly the country will prosper and the pattern of 'growth without equity' will continue at the expense of the weaker members of Greek society. A good society cannot be judged by the number of its winners but by the number of its losers. As Aristotle said: 'A state is not to be termed happy in regard to a portion of the citizens, but in regard to them all.' At the end of the twentieth century Greece is a more unequal society than at its beginning. We hope that future generations will not come to the same conclusion at the end of the twenty-first century.

NOTES

1. C. B. Macpherson, *The Rise and Fall of Economic Justice* (Oxford: Oxford University Press, 1987) p. 6.
2. A. J. Sbarounis, *Economic Development of Greece* (Athens: 1959) p. 15.
3. T. C. Kariotis, 'American Economic Penetration of Greece in the Late Nineteen Forties', *The Journal of the Hellenic Diaspora*, 6, 4 (1979) p. 87.
4. *Ibid.*, p. 88.
5. *Ibid.*
6. *Ibid.*, p. 92.
7. *Ibid.*
8. S. Thomadakis, 'European Economic Integration, the Greek State and the Challenges of the 1990s', in H. S. Psomiades and S. B. Thomadakis (eds) *Greece, The Europe and Changing International Order* (New York: Pella Publishing Company, 1993) p. 373.
9. P. Conceicao, P. Ferreira and J. K. Galbraith, *Inequality and Unemployment in Europe: The American Cure*, UTIP Working Paper, 11 (Austin, TX: LBJ School of Public Affairs, University of Texas at Austin, 1999).
10. *Ibid.*, p. 4.
11. *Ibid.*
12. C. Martin, *The Spanish Economy in the New Europe* (New York: St Martin's Press, 2000).
13. F. Schneider and D. H. Enste, 'Shadow Economies: Size, Causes and Consequences', *Journal of Economic Literature*, 38, 1 (2000).
14. *Ibid.*, pp. 77–8.
15. D. Karageorgas, 'The Distribution of Tax Burden by Income Groups in Greece', *The Economic Journal*, 83, 330 (1973), p. 447.
16. W. Easterly and S. Fisher, *Inflation and the Poor*, Policy Research Working Paper, 2335 (Washington, DC: World Bank and IMF, 2000) p. 21.
17. *Explanations of terminology:* the *low-income threshold* is set at 60% of the median equivalised income per person in each Member State. *Equivalised income*: in order to take into account differences in household size and composition in the comparison of income levels, the amounts given here are per 'equivalent adult'. The household's total income is divided by its 'equivalent size', using the modified OECD equivalence scale. This scale gives a weight of 1.0 to the first adult, 0.5 to the second and each subsequent person aged 14 and over, and 0.3 to each child under 14 in the household. *Purchasing Power Parities* (PPP): convert every national monetary unit into a common reference unit, the 'purchasing power standard' (PPS), of which every unit can buy the same amount of goods and services across the countries in a specific year.
18. A. Boltho, G. Toniolo, 'The Assessment: The Twentieth Century – Achievements, Failures, Lessons', *Oxford Review of Economic Policy*, 15, 4 (1999), pp. 1–17.
19. N. Birdsall, 'Life is Unfair: Inequality in the World', *Foreign Policy*, 111 (1998) p. 77.
20. K. Marx and F. Engels, *The Communist Manifesto* (Midddlesex, England: Penguin Books, 1967) p. 84.
21. B. Bluestone and B. Harrison, *Growing Prosperity* (Boston: Houghton Mifflin Co, 2000).
22. *Ibid.*, p. 260.

14

The Changing Role of Women in Greece

ANNA KARAMANOU

INTRODUCTION

The history of women's human rights in Greece is very recent. It was not until the beginning of the twentieth century that women started to emerge from the darkness and appear in the limelight of public life. The recognition of women's human and political rights, their massive participation in education and economic activities, changes in the roles of the two sexes as well as in family structures, are all factors that constitute the greatest peaceful social revolution in the age-long history of Greece. The twentieth century began with the demand by women for equal access to education, paid employment and politics, and ended with their claim for a fair and balanced gender participation in the democratic institutions and political decision-making process.

Evaluating the achievements of the twentieth century and the changes that have taken place within their lifetime, Greek women feel duly justified, despite the fact that their problems have by no means been adequately solved. Greece's entry into the European Community in 1981 encouraged the adoption of policies for the elimination of discrimination on grounds of gender, contributed to the development of a solid legal basis upon which equality could be sufficiently established and created an institutional framework which can be said to be one of the most progressive in the modern world.

Today Greek women are very proud of the fact that 57% of students in the Greek universities and 40% of the workforce are female, whilst at the same time we can easily observe women's dynamic breakthrough in all scientific and vocational fields. In the legal profession 75% of the newcomers are women, and the same applies to the public services. The position of Greek women is definitely improving. However, the apparent increase in women's participation in educational and economic life has neither been accompanied by a redistribution of family responsibilities nor by the representation of women in democratic institutions and the political decision-making process. In Greece, female participation in politics remains very low and does not match the progress achieved in other areas.

Political reality today denotes a serious deficit in terms of democracy, as the majority of the Greek electorate, that is 51.5% of the population, is either in a minority in or absent altogether from, the political decision-making centres. Greece ranks last among the 15 countries of the European Union in terms of gender empowerment and 66th worldwide, according to the classification of the UN.[1] The results of the 1998 local elections and the 2000 general elections in Greece indicate the democratic deficit in political life: 7% female participation in local councils, 10.3% in National Parliament and 11.6% in government.[2]

It is obvious that what the Greek historian Thucydides had written 2,500 years ago, namely 'The City Belongs to Men', still remains valid today and constitutes the basic principle of the structure and operation of the Greek political system. At the same time, continuing direct and indirect discrimination and inequality in the labour market, high unemployment rates, inadequate social infrastructure, unequal distribution of time and responsibilities between men and women, violence and sexual harassment, the portrayal of distorted stereotypes by the mass media and the double standards of sexual morality, are all problems that are dialectically connected to the low participation of women in economic and political power structures.

Quite paradoxically, the transition to democracy, which coincided with the industrial revolution and the Enlightenment in Europe, did not actually lead to the recognition of women as equal to men. During the French Revolution, Olymp de Gouz was beheaded after daring to ask for equal rights for women. It was only after many years of struggle that women, having overcome their traditional role, finally achieved, at least in legal terms, their full recognition as political players, equal to men, both in Europe and Greece.

It is a fact that the Aristotelian theory of the division into two spheres of life, that is the private and the public, has had a profound impact upon philosophical discourse, social structures, political thought and analyses of traditional issues and values such as freedom, equality and justice, throughout the centuries. Women are absent from the classical texts of political thought, whilst political analysts up until recently have made no reference to the inequalities between men and women in their studies. Even today in Greece, some remain completely silent on these issues; perhaps due to their total inability to sufficiently explain historical degradation, marginalization, deprivation of women from basic human rights and their confinement within the sphere of private life.

Feminism, as a social theory of the equality of the sexes, and as a movement fighting for the elimination of discrimination and the participation of women in economic, social and political life, emerged in Europe in the eighteenth century. Greece, located at the southern end of Europe, away from the central European political stage, was the late recipient of these trends, facing at the same time serious problems of social and economic development, as well as of national integration. In the early twentieth century international sociopolitical developments occurring in Europe reached Greece through the activities of educated people, mainly women, who travelled abroad and became familiar with developments outside Greece. These women made considerable efforts and contributed substantially towards the development of the women's movement in Greece, which became better organized after the First World War.[3]

The socialist and trade union movement played a protagonistic role in the demands for social emancipation in Greece in the twentieth century. However, as is well known, according to socialist theory, the division of society is examined mainly in economic terms and all other issues are of secondary importance. As a result, any discussion with regard to women's rights was regarded, as it still is today, as a threat to the unity of the movement and as a distraction from the main enemy, capitalism.

It was mainly Engel's work titled 'The Origins of the Family, Individual Property and the State' (1884) and Bebel's work titled 'Women in Socialism' upon which intellectuals, trade-unionists and progressive politicians of the twentieth century based their approach to the concept of inequality between the sexes. Both thinkers argued that 'The Woman Issue' could only be solved within a socialist society and, therefore, it was women's duty to combat capitalism. For the theorists of the time, women's emancipation was seen more as a pious hope or an accessory to socialism. As a result they never prepared the ground for the examination of patriarchy as an oppressive system. Gender oppression was basically missing from the socialist analyses and equality was not included in the agenda of the trade unions which actually failed, at least in the early years, to acknowledge the importance of gender equality and the fact that women deserve equal rights to men insofar as they constitute half of the population.

To conclude, progressive thinking and social movements of the twentieth century in Greece, initially acknowledged and ultimately ignored 'The Woman Issue', therefore encouraging outdated ideas to prevail. This resulted in delaying the recognition of women's rights, perpetuating segregation of labour by gender and reinforcing male monopoly over political and economic power.

Socialist International Women filled in the gaps in socialist theory and practice. When women founded this organization, many socialist theorists argued that women's problems could be solved later. Even today, many of those still attached to their original socialist theories view women's claims and pursuits with suspicion and enmity.

By emphasizing the need for social and economic justice and the need for a gender balanced participation in democratic institutions, modern European progressive and social democratic parties – PASOK and Synaspismos in Greece – have appeared to be quite open to feminist theory and feminist demands.[4]

Not without hindrance, and slowly but steadily, the recognition of equal rights and responsibilities for the sexes, *de jure* and *de facto*, is becoming a reality. The role of women is changing as a result of deeper socioeconomic changes and transformations taking place both inside and outside Greece. It is becoming obvious that globalization and new technologies require the mobilization of the whole population, not just half of it, and the new society of knowledge cannot be viable without the contribution, the creative imagination, the sensitivity and the abilities of women.

THE ROLE OF GREEK WOMEN: A BRIEF CHRONOLOGICAL ACCOUNT OF THE TWENTIETH CENTURY

The course of organized efforts made by women for the recognition of their rights and the promotion of their role in Greek society are closely connected to the economic and social developments of the time as well as to Greek history as a whole. These efforts have been, however, diversified depending on the type of target and special pursuits prevailing at the time. The following historical periods can be identified as evidence of the changing role of women according to the sociopolitical developments of the time.[5]

From the end of nineteenth century to the Balkan Wars and the First World War

In 1887–88 the motto 'voting rights for women' is first heard. It appears in the *Ladies' Newspaper*, which was published for 30 consecutive years by Kalliroi Parren, the most prominent figure in the women's movement in Greece. A teacher by profession, she was the first to become conscious of the oppression suffered by women, initiating the task of their familiarization with these problems. In 1911 she established the Greek Women's Lyceum, while at the same time a number of female publications were issued, with female authors and editors.[6]

In 1908 the National Council of Greek Women was founded, as was a federation consisting of 80 Greek and Cypriot women's organiza-tions.[7] Additionally a number of other organizations, frequently of a philanthropic or cultural nature, came into being without any feminist orientation. Many of these organizations were in close cooperation with similar organizations abroad. The Balkan Wars halted the activities of women's organizations and publications, but they were to reemerge after the First World War.

From 1920 to 1922 – The Period Between the Wars

This is the period in which the women's movement actually developed. The Minor Asia Disaster (1922), which led to the influx of 1.5 million Greek refugees, was the real catalyst.[8]

Women's organizations become very active in healthcare and welfare, in the education and employment of women, and proving their useful-ness and worth. Women from Asia Minor, many of whom were very well educated and bi-lingual, brought new standards of social behaviour, established new patterns of employment and gave an impetus to the economic development of the country. The number of Greek women in the workforce started rising. Thus, the first real female workforce was formed. However, this workforce was characterized by low wages and long hours. The first workers, both local and refugees, realized the exploitation of their employers quite soon, and as a result they decided, together with men, to mobilize themselves and participate in strikes.[9]

At the same time the first women's organizations were formed (Association for Women's Rights (1920), Youth Christian Association (YCA) (1922), Association of Greek Women Scientists (1924). YCA constitute a great achievement of those women who came to Greece after the Minor Asia defeat of the Greek armed forces. Such an achieve-ment also resulted in the establishment of several schools and the American College of Women. Issues of women's education and employ-ment now became matters of primary importance, and demands for participation in political life first appeared. At this time, the main demand was the right to vote.

In 1930 Greek women acquired the right to vote, although only in local elections, on condition they were over 30 years old and capable of writing and reading. In 1934 only around 240 women voted for the first time in local elections. This small number can be attributed to the fact that there were few literate women over 30. This period ended with Metaxa's dictatorship and the outbreak of the Second World War, when all progress and discussion about women's rights came to an end and the role of women changed to dedicating themselves exclusively to resisting the enemy. Their participation in the National Resistance was multifaceted and quite remarkable in all areas of anti-occupation activity ranging across towns, villages, and in the mountains. During the Second World War, Greek women showed an unequalled heroism in the history of anti-fascist resistance.[10]

From 1944 to 1974

After the Second World War Greek women became conscious of the necessity to continue the struggle for their rights in order to avoid returning to a position of dependence. A number of organizations were founded that no longer addressed highly educated women only, but had a popular base and welcomed women from all social strata. In 1946 the first Panhellenic Women's Conference took place in Greece leading to the establishment of Panhellenic Federation of Women was decided. Although this seemed to be more promising for the women's movement, it came to an end with the start of the civil war. Thereafter the demand for full political rights arose again in 1949, but was only in 1952 that Greek women acquired the right to elect and be elected in general elections. Despite this, only a very few women vote in the November elections due to late registration in the electoral catalogues. In compliance with Law 2620/1953, ratifying the International Convention of New York, all discriminations against women are abolished, certain regulations are put into effect which enable women to get appointed to the civil service (with the exception of the church and the army), while opportunities for education and employment gradually increase.

Political developments of the 1960s accelerated the emergence of a wider women's movement (the Panhellenic Association of Women in 1964). Many women joined this organization and solutions were promoted to problems related to employment, equal pay, protection of motherhood and social security. Women's activities were restrained due to the coming into power of the military dictatorship in 1967. Social action was halted once again. The junta's approach to the role of women in family life and in the workplace was included in the 1968 manifesto: 'The Revolution honours the Greek woman for her biological mission as a mother and is aware for the importance of this role.'

From 1975 to the End of the Twentieth Century

Following the collapse of the dictatorship, a flourishing period for the women's movement begins. Many new high-aiming organizations are created,[11] fully enriched with new demands brought about by changes in Greek society, permitting activities in the direction of political targets. The Coordinating Commission of Representatives of Women's Organizations is established, an informal group of cooperation demanding the transformation and promotion of Family Law. The Federation of

Greek Women (OGE) and the Union of Greek Women (EGE) are also founded in 1976, aiming at achieving higher participation of women in the workforce, legalization of abortion and modernization of Family Law.

Greece, therefore, entered a new phase. Sociopolitical upheavals became history and democracy was stabilized, permitting the development of social struggles and offering suitable ground for women to seek an upgraded role in Greek society. The main feature of these struggles after 1974 has been that various pursuits acquired a political character, assisting women to become more conscious of current economic, social and political problems. Another characteristic of this period has been that women's struggles address the masses and have a geographical influence through the foundation of local organizations and branches all over Greece.[12] Similarly the struggle focuses specifically on four sectors; namely education, employment, politics and combating violence.

The Constitution of 1975 guaranteed the principle of equality between men and women. Since 1981 there have been significant legislative and institutional changes to ensure equality between the sexes and the elimination of all discriminations against women in the context of the harmonization of Greek legislation with international conventions and European community directives. In December 1982 the Greek Parliament ratified the new Family Law (Law 1329/83), abolishing all outdated provisions of Civil Law, and introduced progressive regulations, such as the right of women to maintain their family name after marriage. The government also considered that changing the mentality of the past was important, and therefore established an official state agency responsible for promoting the issue of equality in 1985, the 'General Secretariat for Equality' (Law 1558/85). In July 1983 Regional Equality Commissions and Offices were set up in every prefecture. Their members were representatives of national and non-governmental organizations as well as women's organizations. These Commissions and offices were institutionalized by virtue of Presidential Decree 370/89.[13] For the first time the equality of sexes is officially acknowledged by the state as a necessity, not only as a component of social justice, but also, mainly, as a prerequisite for economic and social development.

In the late 1980s the Coordinating Committee of Women's Organizations and Party Women's Sections was established with the main aim of furthering the demand for participation of a critical mass of women in the decision-making process, particularly in positions of authority, by means of a quota system (at least by 35%). During the same period (1989) women's sections of GSEE (General Confederation of Labour in Greece) and ADEDI (Confederation of Public Employees' Unions) became particularly active.

However, real equality had still not been achieved, as social prejudices and socioeconomic discriminations against women continued to play a more important role than the equality provided by the Constitution and the laws.

Unfortunately, the mobilization of women proved to be inadequate in eradicating the stereotypes and mentality of the time. The participation of women in democratic institutions still remains very low. In the 1990s the 'Cross-Party Women's Collaboration Committee' was established within the framework of the European Network 'Women in Decision-Making'. Its evolution into the 'Political Association of Women', the co-founders of which are representatives of all Greek political parties, except for the Communist Party, as well as prominent figures of the wider political spectrum, in practice meant real action to reinforce political participation of women. The first positive results became apparent in the 1994 and 1999 Euro-elections and the general elections of 9 April 2000.

WOMEN AND EDUCATION

Following the independence of Greece, only boys were admitted to the first schools, thus establishing the notion that women were only second class citizens whose only role in life being child bearing. It was only in 1836 that 'Arsakion Ladies' School' was founded and the education of girls undertaken through private initiative. It was also at that time that the first women intellectuals came to the fore. Usually members of wealthy families and capable of receiving an education in Europe, these women played a primary role in the tuition of women in Greece, founding ladies' colleges and other institutions, and editing various women's publications. It was from these ladies' colleges that the very first educated Greek women and teachers, educated in Greece, graduated. Up until the beginning of the twentieth century cultured women fought for the right of women to participate in education and it was upon their initiative that various schools and other professional institutions were founded in the traditional female fields of dress-making, cookery, textiles, etc. Education throughout the nineteenth century and the first decade of the twentieth was exclusively in private hands where girls from the wealthier sections of society could participate. Lessons by and large covered practical topics that prepared girls for their traditional role in society, that is to become good mothers and wives.

Women were admitted to universities and polytechnics for first time in 1897.[14] In the early twentieth century they began to pursue participation in education, under the guidance of wealthy educated women of the time. This was not an easy or socially acceptable task. In the course of subsequent decades women continued to demand, among other things, the combating of illiteracy, which remained at high levels, as illustrated by the earlier example of the 1934 local elections.

The 'Association for Women's Rights' set up a special committee aiming at achieving greater education of women with the specific intention of combating female illiteracy. It founded schools where poor women were able to receive tuition in the letters and arts, such as the Sunday School of Workers, the Higher Women's School and the Evening School, which was officially recognized by the state and upgraded to an Evening Commercial School in 1953. The 'Association of Greek Women Scientists' was founded in 1924 and by the time Metaxas seized power (1936) a great number of kindergartens and technical schools had been founded through the initiative of women.[15]

Equality in education was institutionalized in the 1975 Constitution. Under article 16 (paragraph 1,2,3,4) art and science, research and teaching may be freely pursued and all Greek citizens are entitled to free education without any sex discrimination. Despite this, social prejudices continued to affect the dynamics of the educational system, resulting in the perpetuation of gender discriminations.

Discrimination does not entail exclusion of women from various grades of education. Yet, there are differences in the choices of the respective sexes regarding science and art, thus demonstrating the effects of social concepts and stereotypes which restrained the educational and professional role of women.

In Greece, up until 1977, 'separatist' schools of secondary female and male education were, as a rule, centres of training of a practical and/or scientific direction for men and a classical and/or theoretical orientation for women. The different educational curricula, but mainly the different expectations of parents, teachers as well as society as a whole, dictated the educational and professional choices of the sexes and specified different approaches to work and life in general. The specific social and cultural stereotypes that exist in Greek society pass through the Greek educational system (text-books, educational programmes and practices) resulting in the perpetuation of inequality.[16] However, school text-books changed during the 1980s to reflect changes in women's role in society.

The percentages of boys' and girls' participation in the several educational levels are approximately similar; however lately the number of women (57%) following higher education has surpassed that of men and it is very often the case that their academic standard is far higher.[17] It is noteworthy that where procedures are objective and meritocratic women usually triumph. For instance, in the ASEP examination (Higher Committee for Personnel Recruitment) for appointment in the public sector women prevail over men.[18] Some differentiation appear in higher education, particularly in the division of sexes within several disciplines, a fact linked to the prevailing mentality and the concept of social roles of men and women.[19]

According to data from the country's last census of 1991, the percentage of illiterate women is higher than the corresponding percentage among men. This percentage is differentiated by geographical area, the highest being among women of rural areas and by age, the highest being among older age groups. The high rates of illiteracy, especially among older women, is mainly due to the fact that Greece has gone through long periods of internal and external upheavals. The General Secretariat for Equality has taken a number of measures in order to combat illiteracy, which is especially prevalent among women of the mountainous, island and remote areas, in order to promote equality of opportunity in education.[20]

The issue of vocational training and specialization in relation to new technologies surely signifies the cornerstone of a political widening of the choice for women. The relationship between education and employment is an area requiring further research and analysis. One needs to examine whether changes in education go step-by-step with the needs imposed by the modern world and by new technologies, and whether education helps people perform multiple roles and functions both inside and outside the workplace.

Evolutions in education should be analysed in accordance with the social environment, the mentality, motives, value-system and expectations of young people. We need to examine the relationship between the subjects young people choose to follow and the opportunities for employment in order to be able to understand the prospects and limitations of the current educational system. It is certain that as work conditions get better for women, and stereotypes are reversed, their participation in education in non-traditional fields will become higher.

WOMEN AND EMPLOYMENT

The idea of women as salaried personnel was not taken for granted until recently. It was not seen as a constant and necessary role for women as well as for society as a whole. The child-bearing role of women throughout history was tantamount to the concept of family and it became an end in itself in terms of their accomplishment as human beings. This perspective was prevalent throughout the centuries and it was responsible for shaping the absolute conviction, both by males and females, that this was the role women were called upon to play as well as the reason for their existence. While women were prevented from engaging in paid employment, in real life they never stopped working without any pay, especially within the household or even outside of it.

Mass participation of women in paid employment coincided with the Industrial Revolution. Around the middle of the nineteenth century, certain industrial and other small-industry activities emerged in Greece and women hesitantly started to be appointed as salaried employees. Despite the appalling working conditions and the absence of social approval, certain 'female' professions emerged as the only recourse, especially for women in extreme financial need who succumbed to the demand for a cheap and submissive labour force. During the first half of the twentieth century every working woman was considered more or less morally suspect. The first jobs that women were obliged to perform did not require any professional or educational skills, even the most elementary. Their usual occupations were as housemaids, farmworkers, cleaning ladies, dress-makers, even porters. Trade-unionism for women was unknown, while legislation regulating terms and conditions of female work were non-existent. Inequality in all fields of legislation was maintained throughout the 1970s. Gender discrimination was, up until then, generally acceptable and considered natural.[21]

As the twentieth century advanced, a certain elementary consciousness began to develop amongst working women, who started participating in political and trade-unionist activities. Although there had been female clubs and institutions, such as those established by factory women, who in 1913 founded a union called 'Female Life', teaching was the first occupation whereby women of middle and higher strata gained access to salaried employment.[22] Later on the participation of women was expanded into other types of salaried employment; however, the presence of the female population in the field of production was considered to be largely due to the influx of female refugees into the country, who entered the labour market on a massive scale in the mid-1920s. As has been already pointed out, many of the female refugees from Asia Minor were very well educated and able to enter the labour market, thus creating new forms of employment and acting as a driving-force to Greek women in general.

Women's participation in paid employment grew during the first half of the twentieth century: it started at 16% in 1907 and rose to 20% by 1920, thereafter it reached 23.2% in 1928 and 26.8% in 1951.[23] In the division of labour men and women held different positions and status. Men engaged in engineering, tanning, timber and the food industry, while women, especially those of the lower social class, were largely in textiles and dress-making as well as in tobacco and paper production lines. Teaching continued to be the most popular profession for the most cultured women; in 1945 women teachers represented 46.2% of the total female workforce in the public service; the rest were cashiers, telephonists, typists and the like.[24] Their presence in official positions and ministries caused considerable reaction, even from inside the House of Parliament, where Members of Parliament criticized them as superficial and irresponsible, and often recommended they be dismissed from the public sector. In the early twentieth century some women scientists founded the Union of Greek Scientists (1924) which was in close cooperation with women's organizations and played a determining role in the establishment of women in the fields of education and employment generally.

Within the framework of Venizelos' labour policy, a law was passed in 1912 which formed the foundation of the special protective legislation relating to women's and children's employment. Specifically, it prevented night and Sunday work in industrial units and in certain heavy and unhygienic posts, and defined the upper limit of daily work to ten hours. In parallel, a group of Work Inspectors was formed to supervise strict compliance with standing legislation. Many reports written at the time, however, stated that legislation was not complied with, and at the same time underlined certain facets of the industrial work of women in comparison to those of men, namely hard work, time schedules over those permitted by law, low wages, absence of technical education and lack of opportunities for promotion. The Law for collective agreements which was applied after Metaxas' dictatorship put an end to claims for the equality of women's salaries to those of men and implemented the division of labour according to gender. In 1935 recruitment of women in the public sector was forbidden – with only a few exceptions – within the framework of restructuring the public sector.

Existing limitations regarding women's careers in the civil service were eased a little later, in 1952, when Greece ratified the UN Convention for Human Rights. This provided, *inter alia*, that women were entitled to be appointed to public posts and that they may exercise public functions on an equal basis to men without any distinction whatsoever. Any remaining discrimination was withdrawn following the introduction of new legislation in 1955. However, women continued to be excluded from ecclesiastical functions, the armed forces, city and country police, the coastguard and fire brigade. In the last case, however, women were allowed to be employed in auxiliary duties. There still existed certain antiquated beliefs concerning the abilities of women, which for many years kept them confined to lower paid jobs with no potential for promotion.[25]

During the 1970s and 1980s a significant increase in the female workforce was observed in Greece which was analogous to that noted in other European Union countries one decade later. In the 1990s women gained access to almost all professional sectors of employment. Despite this, prejudices still exist. It is noteworthy that while the proportion of women with higher and postgraduate education is higher (37%) than that of men (34%), their participation in managerial and highly specialized positions is only 4.9% and 22.3% respectively. On the other hand, women comprise 41.4% of low-level employees and make up 99.8% of cleaning staff.[26]

In 1996 24% of women were employed in agriculture, 13.7% in industry and 62.4% in the service sector, which from 1970 onwards became particularly overcrowded. Moreover, the occupations falling under the category of service sector are supposed to be 'female' and seasonal, such as tourism, therefore discouraging the participation of men.[27]

The inequality between men and women can be confirmed by a number of statistics. Eurostat's data reveal that Greek women receive only 68% of the earnings of men, and as time goes on, the disparity between women's and men's earnings in most sectors is getting wider.[28] This is mainly due to the fact that very often women occupy lower-paid posts, even if they are more educated and skilled than men. Moreover, women are not very likely to engage in managerial positions or posts related to new technologies. It is noteworthy that according to UN assessments, 75% of non-paid labour is done by women. Additionally, the great majority of women are engaged in part-time or temporary employment. According to 1999 Eurostat data, Greek women lag far behind their counterparts in Europe in terms of remuneration and they have a long road ahead in order to achieve equal pay with men, as both the state and their employers undervalue their performance.[29] Despite the fact that the 1975 Constitution stipulates that all working people, irrespective of sex, are entitled to equal pay for equal work, inequalities still remain. This is in large part due to difficulties with comparing and evaluating different kinds of work

Unemployment constitutes another problem affecting women in particular. According to 1997 UN data, the long-term unemployment rate for women was as high as 62.2%, whereas the corresponding percentage for men was 45.8%. Unemployment of women aged between 15 and 64 was twice as high as that of men (15% compared to 6.4%). In the year 1996–97 women's unemployment declined for the first time since 1981 by 0.7%.[30]

The main features of female employment over the last decade are the increase in women's participation in the labour force, the increase of their participation in the service sector, the decline of their participation in industry (with only a few exceptions) and the increase of their participation in agriculture, for first time after a continuous decline over the last 15 years.[31] Despite an increase in women's participation in numerical terms, there has not been any increase in their participation in senior positions, nor has there been any improvement in the inequality of earnings between men and women.

It is obvious that occupational segregation by gender has no legal foundation, but is based on economic, social and cultural factors; therefore, it would not be an exaggeration to argue that equal opportunities are closely connected to the culture of each country and the quality of its political system. The above factors have a direct impact upon the social division of labour, the educational system and the choices that women make when entering the labour market. A woman's position at work is related, to a great extent, to her position within the family, as well as to her choices regarding her educational orientation. Different choices made when women have entered education have resulted in the creation of two different kinds of labour markets, which can be identified purely in terms of gender. In parallel, the traditional role of a woman in the family, the division of labour by gender, the preservation of double standards of sexual morality and social stereotypes are catalytic factors in her development in the professional arena.

THE NEW 'SOCIAL CONTRACT'

If one looks at the latest developments, one can see that the dividing line between the public and the private is becoming more uncertain. More women, as well as more men, are facing conflicting responsibilities both in their private and public lives. The challenge of modern society is how to ensure that these two spheres of life can achieve compatibility and complement each other. The 'social contract' which is effective to date, distributes specific roles and responsibilities to men and women in compliance with traditional spheres of influence. However, this contract seems to differ a great deal from Greek day-to-day reality and from those factors determining the life of men and women.

Despite the need for redistribution of responsibilities in private life, as a counterbalance to the redistribution of professional and financial responsibilities, 'the contract of sexes' remains to a large extent unchanged. Women are still obliged to adapt their life in such a way so as to reconcile many different and conflicting roles. Those who are in a more sound financial position may usually employ someone to take care of the domestic work; some others may delay having children or decide not to have children at all. Demographic indicators show that many women are compelled to look after elderly relatives. Care for the children, as well as dependent spouses, objectively hinder professional progress and the personal development of women.

Compromising strategies in the present case do not seem to be the solution. The real cause – the traditional division and incompatibility between the two spheres – remains unchanged, but with a much greater social and political cost (increasing stress for people, especially for women, diminishing care for people in need, low fertility rate, increase in the rates of divorce, and reduced productivity).

Brave measures are necessary in order to achieve a solution to problems and the contradictions arising from an 'old-fashioned' or

outmoded contract between the two sexes. This means that responsibilities within and outside the domestic environment should be balanced
and fairly shared on a daily basis and for life. It also means that a new
institutional and social framework should reflect the changes that have
taken place to date, and support equality of opportunity for men and
women in private and public life.

WOMEN AND POLITICS

As already mentioned, the motto 'voting rights for women' was first
heard in the 'Ladies' Newspaper' at the end of the nineteenth century.
In the period between the wars the first women's organizations became
particularly active in demanding a woman's right to vote. Despite their
immense contribution in their country's struggle for national independence, Greek women became entitled to vote 100 years later than their
male counterparts, and they only acquired full political rights in 1952.
It was in the 1953 general elections that the first woman Member of
Parliament, Eleni Skouras, was elected, in Thessaloniki.[32]

In 1956 Lina Tsaldaris became the first female Minister, taking over
the Ministry of Social Welfare, and the first female mayor was elected,
in Corfu, together with 135 women municipal councillors all over
Greece.[33] Despite important changes in the status, role and contribution
of women in society in the second half of the century, real equality has
not yet been achieved since women are still poorer and less powerful
than men. The results of the latest general elections (April 2000) have
definitely conveyed an optimistic message. There has been a 63.4%
increase in the number of female parliamentarians (31 out of 300, that
is 10.3% compared to 6.3% of the previous Parliament). Despite this,
Greece remains a patriarchal and male-dominated society. Unfortunately, both men and women are still attached to outdated stereotypes
and prejudices with regard to the role of the sexes in political life. At the
same time, the 'patriarchal' structures of political parties, the electoral
system – which requires great financial resources and qualities usually
loathed by women – fierce competition and unequal distribution of
family responsibilities between the sexes, are all factors discouraging
women from participating in public life.

Furthermore, wage differentials seem to have a negative effect upon
women's decision to participate in the public field. It is certain that as
long as women fill the low-paid occupational categories, unemployment
among women will remain high; similarly, the more women who are
engaged in part-time and temporary employment, the more their influence in political developments will diminish.

It is certain that there is a dialectical relationship between the economic activity of women and their participation in political decision-making centres. However, the fact that social, economic and cultural factors have played an important role in encouraging gender inequality does not absolve political parties and those in power from their responsibility in perpetuating inequalities between men and women.

It is about time that political parties adopt policies, structures and training programmes, as well as an appropriate electoral system, that will take into consideration the problems that women face today, and promote equal opportunities and facilitate women's access to public life. While women themselves will have to work very hard towards the participation they deserve in political life, efforts must also be made by the state through the adoption of specific policies and legislative measures, such as the quota system.

Women's participation in political decision-making centres is becoming imperative, not only in Greece, but in the world as a whole. The European Network 'Women in Decision-Making' (1992–96) has put forward a number of arguments for the necessity of the inclusion of women in the decision-making process. The following arguments have been adopted and further developed by the Political Association of Women in Greece in the last three years:

REINFORCEMENT OF DEMOCRACY

In any society, democracy is based upon the participation of all people in the process of decision-making. Women constitute half of the population and are entitled to be represented proportionately.

Application of the Principle of Gender Equality

Equality is a universal human right. The division of labour and double standards should be abolished; both men and women are entitled to participate on equal terms in both private and public spheres, so that the historical exclusion of women can be transcended.

Efficient Use of Human Resources

Women constitute half of the world's pool of potential talent and ability and their under-representation deprives society of the efficient use of human resources.

Enrichment of Political Culture with Different Interests
and Value-Systems

Women's historical exclusion from decision-making and their confinement within the private domain has led to gender differences in values
and interests. In any democratic society political decisions should reflect
the interests and values of all the people.

Rejuvenation of Political Culture

The different principles, ideas and values of women are more compatible with the social reality and political climate of our times and can
contribute to the renewal of the political agenda and political life.

Following from the above, the main aim of the Greek General
Secretariat for Equality is to promote gender equality and equal opportunity perspectives in all government policies and implement the principle of equality in all bills, laws and decisions of an administrative
nature.[34]

EUROPEAN POLICY FOR EQUAL OPPORTUNITIES

The European policy for equal opportunities deserves particular attention, as the European Union constitutes an institutional framework
within which Greece, as well as other member states, can stimulate
action and take up initiatives for their benefit. The contribution of the
European Union to the promotion of equal opportunities has been
profound over the last 40 years. Since its creation, the European
Community has recognized the principle of equal pay (Treaty of Rome,
1957) and, on this basis, has developed a consistent set of legal provisions aimed at guaranteeing equal rights to employment access, vocational training, working conditions and, to a large extent, social
protection. In the 4th World Conference on Women, the greatest
worldwide gathering of women ever which took place in Beijing in
1995, the European Union exercised a considerable influence, stating
that women's rights are human rights and therefore women are entitled
to equal treatment and rights. Furthermore, it contributed enormously
to the adoption of a commonly accepted Platform of Action.

Efforts to promote equal opportunities are being strengthened in
many aspects of the European Union's policies and programmes. The
key concept in these efforts is that of 'mainstreaming', which denotes a
more global approach to equality and calls for the integration of a
gender perspective and analysis into all policies, programmes and
actions of the Community. Finally, the Treaty of Amsterdam, which

came into effect on 1 May 1999, has strengthened the legal framework within which gender equality operates and has stated for the first time that gender equality is a key priority of the European Union and its member states. The Council Recommendation (02/12/1996) recognized that the balanced participation of men and women in decision-making is a prerequisite for democracy to function properly, thus pointing the way forward for gender equality and asking all member states to adopt strategies that would promote equal opportunities in the political decision centres. Unfortunately, Greece has not responded to this demand, as no particular legislative measures or policies have been adopted to date (European Community 1997).

WOMEN'S ROLE IN THE TWENTY-FIRST CENTURY – A NEW VALUE-SYSTEM FOR A NEW ENVIRONMENT

At the start of the twenty-first century women are faced with a number of challenges. There is a clear need to explore new ways of settling differences, create a more humane society and make an effort for the fairer distribution of power and resources – that is, to identify a new political culture. It is becoming obvious that none of the problems of our times can ever be adequately solved without the contribution, the ideas and the political participation of women.

The socioeconomic conditions that have prevailed over the centuries and the different spheres within which the sexes have found themselves – men in the public sphere and women in the private – has resulted in the development of two separate worlds with different value-systems. There are, therefore, two different cultures based upon different value-systems. Women, as a whole, are historically associated with non-violence; their value-system is associated with dialogue, compromise, reconciliation and the settling of differences by peaceful means. This value-system can hopefully provide an alternative to the current culture of violence, while at the same time it can help the development of a new political culture characterized by peace, cooperation and respect for differences. It is believed that if politics adopted women's values, there would be more social solidarity among people and nations, and no bloody wars and conflicts due to religious fanaticism and extreme nationalism. Additionally, there would be more awareness about social issues related to quality of life, such as the protection of the environment, social policy and welfare, health care, education and combating drug-use.

Examining the role of women in the twenty-first century, we have to consider the new environment created by rapid technological change and the widening application of information and communication technologies (ITC). The role of women can be profound in this context. Concerns regarding the impact of ITCs are twofold: the first has to do with employment, that is whether these technologies actually destroy more jobs than they create; the second is related to democracy and equality, that is whether the complexity of these technologies will widen the gap between developed and less developed areas, between the rich and the poor, men and women and between the young and the old. To meet these concerns we need public policies which can help us reap the benefits of technological progress and achieve a fair distribution of potential prosperity. Information Society should be *about* people and should be used *for* people and *by* people to unlock the power of information, not to create inequalities between the information rich and the information poor. Considering the sensitivity and awareness of women to social issues, in their hands, Information Society could well become a tool for the creation of an inclusive society. The participation of women in politics is becoming imperative in a world that is deprived of its humanity. As Professor Francis Fukuyama advocated in his article titled 'If women ruled the world':

> It could be certainly predicted that a greater participation of women in politics would lead to a less violent world. Athena, the Greek goddess of wisdom and war, may have been the female model in ancient times, however, in the contemporary world, female influence is definitely catalytic against militarism and for peace.

The Greek government is making efforts towards this direction. It has adopted a new perspective in its relationship to the neighbouring countries of southeastern Europe and therefore it has paved the way for the consolidation of peace, stability and security in the region. At the same time, it has taken up initiatives for assisting neighbouring countries in need. These are initiatives women have wholeheartedly welcomed.

Today, Greece plays a profound role in the consolidation of peace and stability in the region by encouraging the transition from the culture of violence to the culture of peace and by applauding the coexistence and cooperation with people of different cultures and ethnic backgrounds. Being rather optimistic, we could argue that the feminist vision of a world where peace, sustainable development, solidarity, equality, prosperity and social justice prevail is gradually becoming a reality.

NOTES

1. UN Human Development report (New York, Oxford: Oxford University Press, 1999) p. 142.
2. *To Vima* 13 April 2000; *to Pontiki* 26 April 2000.
3. For more information about the development of the feminist movement in Europe and the United States, including a comparison with the Greek situation, see Moscou-Sakorrafou, 1990, p. 54; and Daraki, 1995, p. 368).
4. PASOK's Women Section, *4th Congress Political and Ideological Positions for the Pre-Congress Dialogue* (Athens, 1994).
5. K. Pantazi-Tzifa, *The Status of Women in Greece* (Athens: Nea Sinora-A.A.Livani, 1984).
6. General Secretariat for Equality, n.d.
7. P. Daraki, *The Vision for Women's Equality* (Athens: Kastaniotis, 1995) p. 263.
8. S. Moskou-Sakorrafou, *The History of the Feminist Movement in Greece* (Athens: National Statistical Service of Greece, 1999) p. 190.
9. See P. Daraki, *The Vision for Women's Equality*, p. 271.
10. *Ibid.*, p. 279.
11. For more details about women's organisations in Greece and their goals see Daraki, *The Vision for Women's Equality*, p. 314 and General Secretariat for Equality, n.d.
12. See K. Pantazi-Tzifa, *The Status of Women in Greece* (Athens, 1984).
13. General Secretariat for Equality, *National Report of Greece. The Status of Women in Greece: Developments During the Period 1984–1994* (Athens: National Printhouse, 1995).
14. See P. Daraki, *The Vision for Women's Equality*, p. 212.
15. *Ibid.*, pp. 270–1; see S. Moskou-Sakorrafou, *The History of the Feminist Movement in Greece*, p. 156.
16. A. Karamanou, *Greek Women in Education and Employment* (Athens: OAED, 1984).
17. The participation of women in highest and higher technical education is as follows (National Statistical Service of Greece 1999; Pantazi-Tzifa 1984, 85; Karamanou 1984, 51):

	Highest education	Higher technical education
1973–74	34%	62%
1978–79	40%	52%
1994–95	55%	52%
1998–99	57%	55%

18. *Avgi*, 23 July 1998, *Ta Nea*, 23 July 1998, *Ta Nea*, 18 September 1998, *Kathimerini*, 18 September 1998.
19. An example of this discrimination can be seen in the participation of women in technical and ecclesiastical education, which in the year 1998–99 was as low as 19% (National Statistical Service of Greece 1999).
20. General Secretariat for Equality, *National Report of Greece on the Implementation of the Beijing Platform for the Action* (Athens: National Printhouse, 1999) p. 29.
21. I. Avdi-Kalkani, *Working Woman in Greece* (Athens: Kastaniotis, 1978).
22. *Kathimerini, 7 Days*, 2 September 1999, p. 3
23. *Ibid.*, p. 6.
24. *Ibid.*, p. 11.
25. See I. Avdi-Kalkani, *Working Woman in Greece*, p. 67; M. Nikolaidou, *Women in Greece: Employment and Emancipation* (Athens: Kastaniotis, 1978) pp. 38–40.
26. *Oikonomikos Taxidromos*, 17 February 2000, pp. 44–5.
27. *Ibid.*, 9 September 1999; see also *General Secretariat for Equality*, 1999.
28. See *Oikonomikos Taxidromos*, 26 August 1999, p.15.
29. *Ta Nea*, 22–23 January 2000.
30. See *General Secretariat for Equality*, 1999, p. 19.
31. *Ibid.*
32. *Ibid.*
33. *Ibid.*
34. *Ibid.*

15

The Greek-American Community: Past Achievements and Future Opportunities

CHARLES MOSKOS

Greeks began arriving in America in significant numbers starting in the 1890s. At that time, more Greeks lived outside of Greece than in Greece proper. Greece had achieved independence from the Ottoman Empire in 1821, but it was only after the First World War that the modern Greek state attained the borders that approximate it today and even these borders did not become final until after the Second World War. Many Greek immigrants thus came from the remaining parts of the Ottoman Empire, the surrounding Balkan countries, and Egypt. Greek immigrants also came from Cyprus, which did not become independent from British rule until 1960.

All told, an estimated 800,000 Greeks have crossed over to American shores.[1] About two thirds of these arrivals have made America their permanent home. Whether from Greece proper or outside, the Greek immigrants were culturally a relatively homogeneous group. Nearly all were adherents of the Greek Orthodox faith and spoke standard Greek, with a few years of grammar school in the old country being common. Thus, the Greek-American community from its inception was remarkably homogeneous in its ethnicity. Only when intermarriage became widespread in recent decades was this homogeneity altered.

IMMIGRATION PERIODS

We can divide Greek immigration into five distinct periods. Over 500,000 Greeks came to America during the Great Wave (1890–1924) which ended when Congressional legislation severely restricted immigration. The early community was in large measure a bachelor's community inasmuch as less than one in five Greek immigrants were women. The ratio of males to females among Greek-born Americans was a remarkably high 2.8 to 1 even in 1930, and a still disproportionate 1.6 to 1 as late as 1960.

The Closed Door period (1925–45) lasted through to the end of the Second World War. Only some 30,000 Greeks came to this country, many of whom were brides of immigrants already settled in America. Many such marriages were arranged across the ocean, with a goodly number being 'picture brides' who came from the same or nearby village of their prospective grooms. The usual pattern was for Greek immigrant women not to work outside of the home, though there were always exceptions to this rule. In the early immigrant families husbands were often much older than wives, which gave a distinctive cast to the family constellation.

The third period of post-war migration (1946–65), began after the doors opened somewhat under provisions for displaced persons. Some 75,000 Greeks arrived in the two decades following the Second World War. In addition to unskilled workers, the new immigrants also included a number of Greek professionals as well as Greek students attending colleges and universities in America.

The New Wave (1966–79) occurred when immigration laws were changed to allow easier entrance for the relatives of persons already here. About 160,000 Greeks came to the United States under the new legislation. Unlike previous eras, the sex ratio was fairly evenly balanced, with some of the immigrant families including young children, a first in Greek immigrant history.

The current phase, which begins in 1980, is a period of declining migration. During the 1980s approximately 2,500 Greeks annually were coming to America. In the 1990s the figure dropped to 1,500. Factoring in the probable number of returnees, there is no longer any net Greek increase in this country from immigration. Also to be noted, since the 1960s, a low birth rate means the American-born generations have not been replacing themselves. With no renewal of immigration in sight and with little likelihood of a rise in the birthrate, the Greek-American population will shrink in the years to come.

The most recent US census (1990) lists approximately one million persons who claimed to be of Greek ancestry, of whom about two thirds were entirely of Greek ancestry. This is far lower than the two to three million figure often used by Greek-American community leaders. In terms of region, Greeks were over-represented in the northeast, under-represented in the south, and proportionately represented in the rest of the country. Well over half of all Greek-Americans live in or near one of ten American cities: New York (200,000), Chicago (100,000), Boston and nearby mill towns (100,000), Los Angeles (45,000), Detroit (40,000), Philadelphia (25,000), and 20,000 each in Baltimore, Cleveland and Pittsburgh.

By using available census and immigration figures and by making some assumptions on birth and death rates, we can estimate the generational distribution of Greek-Americans in the year 2000 as follows: first generation (immigrants) 200,000; second generation 350,000; third generation 300,000; and fourth generation 150,000. The proportion of those with some non-Greek ancestry increases with succeeding generations.

HISTORY

The flood of Greek immigrants who arrived in American between 1890 and 1924 can be traced along three major routes: (1) Greeks going to the western states to work on railroad gangs and in mines; (2) Greeks going to New England mill towns to work in the textile and shoe factories; and (3) Greeks who went to the large northern cities, principally New York and Chicago, and worked in factories, or found employment as busboys, dishwashers, bootblacks and peddlers. Thus, like most other immigrants, Greeks initially made up a proletarian class.

A very few years after the start of mass migration, however, there also began within the Greek immigrant colony that process of internal social stratification that is characteristic of American society as a whole. The beginnings of a Greek-American middle class can be detected by 1910. Certainly, by the 1920s there was a considerable number of Greeks who had become owners of small businesses. The entrepreneurial ability of many of the Greek immigrants was consistently noted by every American observer of the Greek immigrants in the early decades of this century. The early Greek shopkeepers concentrated on a narrow, but familiar, range of enterprises: candy stores, bootblack and shoe repair parlours, dry cleaners, florists, produce stores, bars and taverns, and, most notably, restaurants.

The intent of the vast majority of immigrants was to come to America to make money and then return to their home villages to live lives of comfort. The migration experience was a culture shock for women and men alike – for which it took many Greek immigrants years to adjust. Some never did. To move into an urban setting, not to know the English language, to be targets of hostility by both nativistic Americans and other immigrant groups was a painful transition. Yet, the basic fact remained that almost all of the immigrants were able to make more money in America than they would in the old country. Slowly, but inevitably, the majority of the Greek immigrants came to the realization that their future was to be found in their new home.

THE GREEK ORTHODOX CHURCH

When a sufficient number of Greeks had settled in one place, the practice was to establish a local Greek Orthodox Church. Among the earliest church communities were those in New Orleans, New York, Chicago and Boston. By 1916 there were about 60 Greek churches in the United States, and about 200 in 1930. In the early years, the Greek churches in America came under the authority of the Church of Greece. But political conflict that occurred in Greece carried over into America with vying bishops belonging to the various factions. Order came in 1931 when the Greek Orthodox churches in America came under the administrative as well as spiritual authority of the Ecumenical Patriarch of Constantinople.

In the United States, the Church is officially known as the Greek Orthodox Archdiocese of America. From 1931 to 1948, Archbishop Athenagoras served as head of the Archdiocese. When Athenagoras was elevated to the Patriarchate in 1948, his successor was Archbishop Michael. Following Michael's death in 1959, Archbishop Iakovos headed the Archdiocese until his retirement in 1996. Iakovos became a major religious figure in American society and also assumed the role of ethnic spokesman for the Greek community in America. Iakovos was succeeded by Archbishop Spyridon, whose term, marred by acrimony, lasted only three years. In 1999, Archbishop Demetrios was selected by Patriarch Bartholomew to head the American Archdiocese.

The administration of the Greek Orthodox Archdiocese in America is centralized in the New York headquarters. By 2000, the Greek Orthodox Archdiocese consisted of some 130,000 dues-paying families and slightly over 500 churches in the United States. (Another dozen or so Greek Orthodox churches existed outside of the Archdocesean framework.)

As the American-born generations replaced the immigrants as the numerically dominant group, a process of Americanization in the Church became evident. English began to be introduced into the liturgy in the 1960s and by the 1990s a policy of 'flexible bilingualism', with varying mixtures of Greek and English dependent on the parish's linguistic make-up, seemed to be working fairly well.

Another development was a reassessment of women's role in the Church, although it was not nearly as pronounced as the feminism appearing in mainstream denominations. The issue of ordination for women has not seriously emerged in the Greek Orthodox Church, but there is a growing sentiment to revive the ancient ecclesiastical order of female deacons as has been done already with male deacons. Traditionally, the major outlet for women in the Church was the Philoptochos ('friends of the poor'), a female association. Since the

1970s, the overall trend is clearly toward greater representation of lay women in leadership positions.

Perhaps the strongest measure of the trend toward the Americanization of the Church can be found in the increasing incorporation of non-Greeks. Some of these are converts from other Christian denominations, but most are non-Greeks converted to Orthodoxy for reasons of marriage. According to Archdiocesan statistics, mixed couples accounted for three out of ten church marriages in the 1960s; by the 1990s the figure was seven in ten. We must keep in mind, however, that these numbers refer only to weddings conducted within the Greek Orthodox Church. We can assume that virtually all Greek-Americans who marry outside the Church marry non-Greeks. The high rate of intermarriage has changed its meaning. Intermarriage no longer carries a stigma in the community; thus it is much easier for exogamous Greek-Americans and their spouses who marry within the Church to continue an active membership in the Greek community.

The Greek-American community has had to change its position on intermarriage in the face of its frequency. The initial edict of the immigrant parents was to tell their children that all Greek potential marriage partners were better than all non-Greek. The next line of defence, typical of the second generation, was to acknowledge that there are equal measures of good and bad in all nationalities, but the sharing of a common Greek background makes for a better marriage. (Interestingly enough, the available Archdiocesan data, though not conclusive, show a somewhat lower divorce rate among couples in which one of the partners was not ethnically Greek.) The final argument, a common recourse for the third generation, is that if one does marry a non-Greek, one must be sure that the spouse is able to adapt to the family kinship system and be willing to become Greek Orthodox.

A generation ago, to be Greek-American almost always meant to know the Greek language, for the immigrant as a native tongue, for the children of the immigrants with various degrees of fluency. But learning and using Greek requires conscious effort and the effort by and large was not being made by second-generation parents for their children, much less for the children of mixed marriages.

As the Church in America enters the twenty-first century, changes of some magnitude are evident. In addition to the demographic changes caused by intermarriage and the end of immigration, there are signs of both a move toward a more pan-Orthodox identity in this country, that is, through closer interaction with co-religionists coming from Russian, Eastern European and Arabic traditions. As the immigrant past fades, the move toward pan-Orthodoxy in America will undoubtedly continue to gain ground. This also corresponds with a move toward a more pious Orthodoxy as reflected in the appearance and proliferation of Eastern

Orthodox monasteries in this country in the 1980s and 1990s. The appearance of the Orthodox Christian Laity in 1987, comprised mainly of second-generation Church activists, marked a major step toward adaptation to American realities and consideration of an autocephalous Orthodox Church in America.

MAKING IT IN AMERICA

Of course, not all Greek-Americans have done well in financial or occupational terms. But, the overall situation is one of unique success on the American scene. Greek-Americans born in the United States have one of the highest educational levels of any ethnic group. According to the US census, the children of Greek immigrants are twice more likely to have a college degree than are native-born whites.

Seven Greek-Americans – Peter Angelos, Michael Jaharis, Peter Karamanos, Theodore Leonsis, Peter Nicholas, Alex Spanos and Roy Vagelos – have appeared on Forbes list of the 400 richest Americans. This is a ratio four times greater than the proportion of Greek-Americans in the general population. Angelos and Spanos are also the owners of major sports teams, respectively, the Baltimore Orioles (baseball) and San Diego Chargers (football).

The Greek-American imprint has also been significant in science and academia. Dr George Papanicolaou invented the test for cervical cancer in 1943, universally known as the 'Pap smear'. This test has saved millions of women's lives. Papanicolaou is the only Greek-American, so far, to have had a United States postage stamp issued in his honour. Greek-Americans have also served as presidents of major institutions of higher learning. John Brademas, Peter Liacouras and Constantine Papadakis have been presidents, respectively, of New York University, Temple University and Drexel University.

Spyros Skouras, along with his brothers Charles and George, became movie magnates with Spyros reaching the apex of Hollywood when he became president of Twentieth Century-Fox in the 1940s. Two of the most distinguished directors in modern cinema are John Cassavetes and Elia Kazan. Probably the most famous Greek-American movie actor was Telly Savalas, whose role as a Greek-American policeman became a popular cliché.

Nowhere has the Greek-American presence been more notable than in politics. By 2000, twelve Greek-Americans had been elected to the House of Representatives at one time or another and three to the US Senate: Paul Sarbanes, Paul Tsongas and Olympia Snowe. Spiro T. Agnew, though never active in the Greek-American community, was the son of a Greek immigrant, had been elected vice-president of the United

States (a position from which he resigned in 1973 following a financial scandal). A threshold of great importance was certainly crossed with the nomination of Michael S. Dukakis, the son of Greek immigrants, as the 1988 Democratic Party candidate for president of the United States. (Michael's first cousin, Olympia Dukakis, is an actress of renown.) In the Bill Clinton Administration, Greek-Americans served in key positions. These included George Stephanopoulos as the President's chief of staff in Clinton's first term, and George Tenet as director of the Central Intelligence Agency. John Podesta, President Clinton's Chief of Staff as of 2000, has an Italian father and a mother whose parents came from the Peloponnese.

ACROSS THE GENERATIONS

If the immigrant Greek family in America could not exactly replicate that of the old country, it was not for lack of trying. Husbands insisted on their moral authority over their spouses, though the formal submissions of the wife could mask her practical dominance in household affairs. Mothers and fathers tried to enforce a strict disciplinary code over their children, though this could be softened by frequent parental indulgences, or subverted by clandestine activities with American friends outside the home. Spanking was common, but both parents were physically affectionate toward their offspring with much kissing of young children. Children were included in adult activities as age segregation was alien to the Greek immigrant mind. In their adolescent years, sons were given much more leeway and were much more likely to be supported in a university education than daughters. A generalized respect for elders is ingrained in both the Greek and Greek-American cultural norms. This is complemented by the notion that grandparents are expected to 'spoil' their grandchildren.

To be sure, assimilative processes are always at work. Even though most second-generation Greek-Americans were familiar with the Greek language, and many could speak it quite well, English became the language of American-born Greeks in their own homes as well as on the outside. While vestiges of patriarchy persisted, egalitarian relations between the spouses became more the mode along with much more equal treatment of sons and daughters. The major celebration accorded the nameday, the traditional day of the saint after which a person is named, has given way to the American custom of the birthday celebration. Yet some patterns continue. A taste for Greek food and a liking of Greek music and dancing often carries over into the third and fourth generations.

The intersect between ethnicity, class and family structure is a complex one. It is generally agreed, however, that those immigrant parents who displayed a more open attitude toward American influences were more successful in passing on Greek ethnicity than those parents who tried to resist totally all American encroachments. Efforts to rear children as though they were living in Greece were more common among blue-collar than middle-class immigrants. To pose the alternatives as all or nothing Greek, as many traditional parents were inclined, could lead some of their adult children to forsake their Greek background entirely. But the much more characteristic outcome has been one of continuing – though changing in form – Greek identity across the generations.

The family, which in the old country was a tightly knit unit that included uncles, aunts and cousins, has become modelled after the nuclear family. Though an aged parent is much more likely to live with one of her or his grown children in a Greek-American setting than is typical of contemporary American society, the pattern of aged parents living on their own or in nursing homes has become more prevalent. Divorce, which was rare and brought shame to Greek-American families before the Second World War, approaches middle-class American proportions in the contemporary period.

No better illustration of the coexistence of Greek and American customs is found than in the Greek-American funeral. Attendance is high including distant relatives and casual friends as well as close friends and relatives. If the deceased was an old person, there will not be excessive gravity. Before the Second World War, wakes were commonly held in the home of the deceased and, following the funeral, a meal was prepared at home by some of the female relatives for the mourners. Today, the wake is held at a funeral home, always Greek-owned if such exists in the area. The next day there is a service at church, the internment at the cemetery, and a post-funeral meal at a restaurant. The entire funerary event remains – though now refracted through commercial establishment – a major manifestation of the collective consciousness of the Greek-American community.

VOLUNTARY ASSOCIATIONS

The first Greek associations to form in this country were the *topika somateia*, groups of immigrants who came from the same village or region in the home country. The *topika somateia* gained a second wind in the late 1960s with the arrival of large numbers of new immigrants. Much of this momentum carried through into the 1990s along with the rise of second-generation leadership. Predictions of the demise of such parochial organizations have been premature.

Since its founding in 1922, the AHEPA (from American Hellenic Educational Progressive Association) has been pre-eminent among Greek-American secular associations. Influenced by Masonic ritual, the AHEPA represented the aspiration of a rising middle class and was committed to Americanizing its membership by adopting English as the official language. (The GAPA, from Greek American Progressive Association, a counter-organization that used Greek as its language, had become moribund by the 1960s.) The AHEPA's annual conventions are premier social events in Greek America, and since the 1970s the AHEPA has shifted its goals toward support of charitable activities and maintenance of Hellenic identity. In the 1980s and 1990s, it began to have an image of an ageing organization, but the current leadership seems to be committed to reversing this perception.

Another organizational development reflected the rise of a new generation of business and professional persons. Usually covering a metropolitan area, these organizations held fund-raisers and sponsored cultural programmes. The United Hellenic American Congress (UHAC), founded in 1975, was based in Chicago and became a national organization. Other organizations formed in the 1970s to promote Greek-American causes and to serve as a forum for Greek-American issues were Krikos ('link') and Axios ('worthy') in Los Angeles. On a different scale was the Hellenic American Neighborhood Action Committee (HANAC), which evolved into one of the major social service agencies in the greater New York area. Also notable was the 1990 founding of the Greek-American Women's Network (GAWN), a departure from previous women's organizations which were essentially auxiliaries of male organizations.

THE PRESS AND ACADEMIA

The first Greek newspaper in the United States appeared in 1892 in Boston. Since that time, well over a hundred Greek newspapers in America have appeared at one time or another. Two New York dailies, the conservative *Atlantis* (1894–1971) and the liberal *Ethnikos Kirix* (1915-present), dominated the national scene from their inception. Another Greek language newspaper, *Proini,* began daily publication in New York City in 1977.

Over time, older Greek-American newspapers began to shift from Greek to English and new ones emerged using English from the start. Among the more successful are the *Greek American Review* in New York, *Greek Press* and *Greek Star* in Chicago, *Hellenic Chronicle* in Boston, *Hellenic Journal* in San Francisco and *Hellenic News of America* in Pennsylvania. Both *Proini* and *Ethnikos Kirix* have inaugurated weekly

English editions, respectively, *The Greek-American* and *The National Herald*, which are widely acknowledged to have raised the standards in Greek-American journalism.

As for magazines, *Greek Accent* (1980–88) was the first magazine geared to a Greek-American audience with a professional format and art work. *Odyssey*, another high quality magazine, appeared in 1993 with insightful coverage of developments in Greece and the Greek diaspora. What also made *Odyssey* notable was that although published in Athens, the main readership was in the United States.

Some 30 American colleges and universities offer programmes in modern Greek-language instruction along with courses in literature, culture and history. Major programmes were founded at New York University (the recipient of a $15 million award from the Alexander S. Onassis Foundation), Queens College of the City University of New York (with the largest student enrolment), Princeton University, Columbia University, Ohio State University, Harvard University, University of Florida, University of Missouri in St. Louis, San Francisco State University, Temple University and Wayne State University. Many other programmes, often reflecting the energies and commitment of a single faculty member, had a tenuous existence within their institutions' budget.

The Modern Greek Studies Association (MGSA) was established in 1968 and although primarily American in membership had international representation in its officers and conferences. The MGSA publishes the *Journal of Modern Greek Studies*. Also noteworthy are the scholarly periodicals *Journal of the Hellenic Diaspora* and *Journal of Modern Hellenism*.

GREEK-AMERICANS AND GREECE

During the Balkan Wars (1912–13), some 45,000 immigrants returned to volunteer to fight in the Greek army. In the immediate post-First World War period, the political schism in Greece between the supporters of King Constantine I and the liberal prime minister Eleftherios Venizelos cleaved the Greek community in America as well. Following the Second World War, the Greek-American community strongly supported the pro-Western government in the Greek civil war, though elements of leftist support for the communist side were not absent.

The Turkish invasion of Cyprus in 1974 affected the Greek-American community profoundly. One important consequence was the formation of what came to be known as the 'Greek lobby'. The major entities were the American Hellenic Institute (AHI), headed by Eugene Rossides, which worked closely with the AHEPA, and the United Hellenic

American Congress (UHAC), chaired by Andrew A. Athens, with its close ties to the Archdiocese. In 1995 Athens was elected president of the newly formed World Council of Hellenes Abroad (SAE), an international organization of Greek communities from around the world supported by the Greek government. Complementing UHAC was the National Coordinated Effort of Hellenes (CEH), led by Andrew E. Manatos, and the International Coordinating Committee, Justice for Cyprus (PSEKA), headed by Philip Christopher. In 1994 the Western Policy Centre, directed by John Sitilides, was established as the first think-tank in Greek America.

Though the various groups sometimes differed on strategy and personality conflicts were not absent, they generally complemented rather than competed with one another. In addition to the Turkish occupation of northern Cyprus, Greek-American leadership also took active roles in supporting the civil rights of the Greek minority in Albania and in opposing Turkey's expansionist moves in the Aegean, and the irredentist claims of the Former Yugoslavia Republic of Macedonia on northern Greece.

The continuing support that Americans of Greek ancestry give to the causes of the old country, despite foreign policy differences between Athens and Washington, show that they ultimately take their bearings not from developments in Greece, or even from Greece's foreign relations with the United States, but rather from a deep and abiding belief that what is good for America is good for Greece and vice versa.

But for most Greek-Americans, the ties with Greece are personal rather than political. A cardinal feature of Greek-American ethnicity is the trip back to the old country. The advent of air travel made trips to Greece easily within reach of the Greek-American community. Among American-born Greeks, a large number, probably a majority, have visited the ancestral homeland as least once.

THE AMERICAN CASE: TYPICAL OR NOT OF THE GREEK DIASPORA?

If we can locate one dominant characteristic of the Greek-American experience it would be 'embourgeoisment'. Nearly all immigrants entered the United States as unskilled workers, but a significant portion became proprietors of their own small businesses. The children and grandchildren of the immigrants have moved, in the main, into middle-class vocations and into the professions. In basic respects, this has also been the experience of the Greek immigrants and their descendants in other English-speaking countries such as Canada and Australia as well as South Africa. One has the same impression of the Greeks in the United

Kingdom, though, surprisingly enough, this community has yet to find its historian.[2]

The Greek communities of Latin America also remain largely *terra incognita* from a scholarly standpoint. But it is probably fair to state that, on the whole, their situation approximates the overall upward mobility of Greeks in the United States, Canada, Australia and South Africa. Surely, the most well-known Greek abroad was Aristotle Onassis who had both Argentine and Greek citizenship.

Other regions have somewhat different historical patterns. In Germany, the large numbers of Greek guest workers or *gastarbeiter* peaked in the 1970s and 1980s. The Greeks in Germany, and elsewhere in northern Europe, present a purer case of a diaspora as the large majority keep very close ties with the home country and do not envision themselves or their children settling in Germany for good. The Greeks in the former Soviet Union present a special case as they are poverty stricken and many are also seeking to return to the ancestral homeland. Indeed, alleviating the plight of the Greeks in the former Soviet Union has become one of the major policy goals of the Council of Hellenes Abroad (SAE).

As Greek America enters the twenty-first century, the end of the immigrants' story is in sight. A similar future will occur within the next generation in most of the other major countries which have received large numbers of Greek immigrants. Although processes of assimilation are undeniable, there has been a persistent attachment to a 'Greek identity', however hard to define that sentiment might be, well into many of the second and third generation.

A useful distinction can be made between acculturation and assimilation. Acculturation refers to the acquisition by the immigrants and their descendants of the cultural behaviour – language, norms, customs – of the new society. Assimilation implies the entrance of the ethnics into the very fabric – the social cliques, business life, civic associations and, eventually, the families – of the host society. Usually acculturation proceeds faster than assimilation. The pattern for Greek-Americans, however, is different. Acculturation has lagged behind assimilation. This is the only way to understand continuing Greek Orthodox affiliation and attachment to the old country in the face of such assimilative measures as educational attainment, economic ascendancy, political representation and even intermarriage. But for this ethnic identity to continue in later generations requires rethinking and accompanying policies.

The Greek Orthodox Church has been the primary transmitter of Greek ethnic identity in the overseas community. But as intermarriage becomes the rule rather than the exception, as fewer parishioners have command of the Greek language, as more non-Greek converts enter the Church, a distinction can be made between sacred and secular ethnicity.

As Hellenism in the Church becomes less prominent, the maintenance of Greek identity outside Greece must follow a different path. The key to bolstering Greek ethnicity is to foster connections of the descendants of Greek immigrants with the old country. The advent of inexpensive flights makes travel to Greece more feasible than ever before. Today's youth – and here we include those of Greek stock, mixed parentage and even philhellene non-Greeks – will be the future of Hellenism abroad.

Well designed education programmes in Greece can be the major means to foster a Greek ethnic identity and a revival of the Greek language in the later generations of the diaspora. For example, more and more college students are spending a 'junior year abroad'. What better country for Greek-American (Australian, Canadian, etc.) youth to do so than Greece? Already over a half dozen American college programmes can be found in Greece. Likewise, excellent summer courses in Modern Greek and Greek culture already exist. Thinking ahead, we would easily envision an exchange programme of a high school year in Greece or a 'fifth year' of study in Greece following college graduation in one's home country. Many persons beyond student age would also find a language and culture vacation in the old country very attractive. At the same time, Hellenic language and studies programmes should be fostered in those countries with significant numbers of the progeny of Greek immigrants. Certainly, such programmes have proven to be successful in the United States.

For Hellenism to have a future in the diaspora, we must proceed along two avenues, the religious and the ethnic. Each is different, yet complementary to the other. By opening up to the spiritually hungry in new lands, the Greek Orthodox Church will bring more non-Greeks into contact with Greek ethnicity. By becoming more Greek in an ethnic, notably linguistic, sense, more people will find their way to Greek Orthodoxy in a spiritual manner.

In sum, as our Orthodox membership becomes wider, our Greek ethnic identity must become deeper. This in turn will involve reciprocal ties between the Greek nation and the progeny of those Greeks who have emigrated abroad. Such is the way for Hellenism to have a future in America and elsewhere in the diaspora.

NOTES

1. T. Saloutos, *The Greeks in the United States* (Cambridge: Harvard University Press, 1964); H. Psomiades and A. Sourby (eds) *The Greek American Community in Transition* (New York: Pella, 1982); A. Scourby, *The Greek Americans* (Boston: Twaye, 1984); C. Moskos, *Greek Americans: Struggle and Success* (New Brunswick, NJ: Transaction, 1989); D. Georgakas and C. Moskos (eds) *New Directions in Greek American Studies* (New York: Pella, 1991); G. Kourvetakis, *Studies on Greek Americans* (Boulder, CO: East European Monographs, 1997).

2. Hellenic Studies Forum, *Greeks in English Speaking Countries* (Melbourne: Ellinikon, 1993); C. P. Ioannides, *Greeks in English Speaking Countries* (New York: Caratzas, 1997); R. Glogg, *The Greek Diaspora in the Twentieth Century* (London: Macmillan, 1999); A. K. Kyrou and S. H. Frangos, 'Central Works on the Greek Diaspora' in J. O. Iatrides (ed.) *Bibliography of Modern Greek Sources* (Ohio: Kent State University Press, 2001) and in S. E. Constantinidis (ed.) *Greece in Modern Times* (Lanham, MD: Scarecrow Press, 1999) pp. 355–78.

PART V

16

Greek–Turkish Relations:
A New Era?

BYRON THEODOROPOULOS

Have we really entered a new era in Greek–Turkish relations? Do we really see a 'window of opportunity' open before us, a chance for peace and constructive neighbourly coexistence?

I suggest that this is a gate rather than a window, albeit a gate standing ajar. We find ourselves at the threshold and it is now up to us, Greeks and Turks, whether we throw this gate wide open and step beyond or whether we hesitatingly (or stubbornly) refuse to make this step. This is, therefore, a moment of decision and it would seem imperative on the one hand to look back and take stock of what we have done in the past and on the other hand to look forward and envisage what we can do in the future.

I have been following the course of Greek–Turkish relations for the last 55 years, since I first entered the diplomatic service. I still remember the time when our two countries were both apprehensive of the growing Soviet aggression along our borders. We both gratefully accepted the measure of security which was offered to us under the Truman Doctrine. We both benefited from US economic assistance. We both joined simultaneously the Council of Europe. We both took part, with the other UN members, in the Korean War. We both were admitted at the same time to NATO as full members. We both concluded in 1953 and 1954 the Tripartite Pacts with Yugoslavia. It was a time when no problems seem to trouble our coexistence and cooperation. And then … then all hell broke loose!

The reason was Cyprus. I have followed the Cyprus conflict for years, even for decades, as it continued to widen, spilling over into bilateral Greek–Turkish relations, the Greek minority in Turkey and the Aegean. It started with the 'pogrom' against the Greeks living in Turkey and their mass expulsion. It then widened into the Aegean, where new claims were raised by Turkey against Greece, first on the continental

shelf, then in air-space, then in maritime space, then even on the land
territory of the islands, until it culminated with the *casus belli* threat,
from which Turkey has not yet withdrawn. Each time I wondered:
Where were all these claims before? How can it be that Turkey has
neglected for decades to make known and to safeguard her alleged
'rights' in the sea- or air-space which she now invokes? How could she
so belatedly discover the 'correct' interpretation of the Lausanne Treaty
of 1923, more than 70 years after the Treaty was signed? Of course
there was no neglect on Turkey's part. These were all new claims. The
effort to change the *status quo* in the Aegean started as a tactical decision by Turkey. It seems that when the Cypriot question arose in the
early 1950s, Ankara considered it more expedient not only to localise
the differences between Greek and Turkish Cypriots on Cyprus, but also
to widen the area of confrontation to include the totality of Greek–
Turkish relations, in the belief that exercising direct pressure on Greece
would weaken Greece's position in the Cyprus problem.

However, what had begun as supposedly useful tactics of Turkish
diplomacy over the question of Cyprus has in the course of decades
acquired an existence and an impetus of its own. Thus Turkey now
maintains that the Cyprus question has been solved once and for all and
there is nothing left to negotiate, while the only pending problems are
the bilateral Greek–Turkish ones. Only recently a statement was issued
by the Turkish Foreign Minister to the effect that 'Cyprus has nothing to
do with Greek–Turkish bilateral problems'! This is surprising to some-
body who has followed the course of Greek–Turkish relations since the
end of the war. It is also misleading, and above all shows up the absur-
dity of the situation. It means that in the minds of Turkish policy-makers
the question at the heart of Greek–Turkish tension has been settled
according to Turkey's aims and what remains is only the bilateral
confrontation originally adopted as a tactical expedient in a dispute now
'solved'. This, however, has lead the Greeks inevitably to suspect that
the Cyprus problem was only the beginning of a larger scheme to establish a dominant Turkish position of quasi 'co-sovereignty' in the Aegean
and to gradually reduce Greece to 'junior partner' status. Needless to say
nobody in Greece believes that Turkey is acting defensively against
Greek 'aggression', since Greece has not raised any claims on Turkey.

It is, however, a sterile, even counter-productive, exercise to go into
the past and continue with mutual recriminations about the responsibility for starting the conflict. If I have gone into the history, it is only to
show how absurd the origins of today's tension are, how artificially they
were brought about and how the present Greek–Turkish relationship is
plagued by a number of problems which one might call contrived or
simply 'pseudo-problems'.

We certainly do not want to continue looking back. Our task ought to be to look ahead beyond the threshold of that half-opened gate. This is the time to think about the future while learning the lessons of the past. One might then in that spirit ask a number of questions of all the sides involved.

I would for example ask my fellow Greeks:

• Does the Greek air defence really need an air-space of 10 nautical miles?
• What are the benefits Greece expects to derive from eventually extending her territorial waters to 12 n.m. along the totality of her Aegean coastline?
• Does the Aegean continental shelf have any economic significance? Or is Greece only anxious to prevent the enclavement of her islands of the Eastern Aegean in a Turkish continental shelf in order to preclude further Turkish claims on the islands themselves?

I would also turn to my Turkish friends and ask only one question, which is, admittedly, much more difficult to answer:

• Is the confrontation with Greece really and seriously the first priority of Turkish foreign policy?

This single, seemingly simple question implies of course a series of other questions:

• Does Turkey not have other, more weighty problems?
• What about her three neighbours, Iran, Iraq and Syria, who would seem to require more vigilance?
• What about the Caucasus, where the situation continues to be rather fluid and where the Russian presence makes itself more and more felt?
• Do other internal problems, such as the Kurdish one, deserve a higher priority than sovereignty over some rocky islands of the Aegean?
• Are the chronic problems of the Turkish economy, such as high inflation and low GDP, less pressing than the conflict about the Aegean continental shelf?
• Does the confrontation with Greece improve or worsen the prospect of Turkey's eventual accession to the EU?

In other words, why does Turkish foreign policy consider the confrontation with Greece her main preoccupation? Would a climate of peace and friendship with Greece not prove beneficial for Turkey, in particular in view of her desire to accede to the EU?

Both Greece and Turkey could, no doubt, find reasonable answers to these questions and thus step beyond the threshold into the opening gate of peaceful neighbourly relations. Nevertheless one cannot ignore the fact that – whatever the Turkish side maintains about the Cyprus question having been solved – Cyprus is still a problem and that there is no solution in sight. It would, therefore, seem appropriate to ask some questions of both Cypriot sides:

• Are the Greek Cypriots determined to pay any price in order to achieve the re-unification of the island, even if that price proves to be unbearably high? The perspective of only minor territorial modifications of the present 'Green Line'; the possibility of a new constitution under which the Turkish Cypriot side would have practically the last word in all vital problems; the fact that the prosperous south will have to assist for an indefinite period the poorer north; the very remote possibility of the Greek Cypriots enjoying within a reasonable time freedom of movement, of establishment and of property in the north: does all this seem to the Greek Cypriot side a fair price for the island's re-unification?

The question to be asked of the Turkish Cypriots might be: If one day the Greek Cypriot side come to the conclusion that the price asked by the north for re-unification is too high and therefore final separation preferable, what then? The south fulfils all requirements to become a full member of the EU. What would that mean then for the north if they are excluded from such a development? Would northern Cyprus qualify for EU accession? What will be the future prospect for an independent Turkish Cypriot statelet separated from the south not by a 'Green Line' but by an international border? Another question: How to explain the fact that a great many Cyprus-born Turks have emigrated from the north in increasing numbers? Is this perhaps a sign that they have preferred to 'vote with their feet', thus indicating that the future of the north does not seem promising as long as the present separation continues?

These may all be 'rhetorical' questions. Still, rhetorical questions have their rationale. In this case it is to show that in this game, which has lasted for decades, both sides are losing. This is the reason why I would suggest a time for reflection at the threshold of the new era, in order to evaluate what we on both sides have to win or lose by continuing this game. Mutual recriminations about the responsibility for this situation may go on and on, as they have already *ad nauseam*. What should we now reflect upon? My answer would be to reflect about two things closely connected to one another. Firstly, consider the world around us as it is taking shape at the beginning of a new century. Secondly, think about the real, long-term interest of our two countries.

On the first question, the world is now a very different place than 50 years ago, when Greece and Turkey started their confrontation. The word 'globalization' may be overblown and overused nowadays. The fact, however, remains that the traditional concept of the territorial boundaries of the states is continually losing its power and that sovereign rights of the single states are either ignored by technology or willingly transferred by the states themselves to bigger entities such the EU. Who would have believed 50 years ago that news and ideas no longer know frontiers? Who would have believed that huge amounts of capital, disregarding national boundaries, would move freely around the world within seconds? Who would have anticipated that the European national states would cede sovereign decisions on monetary policy to a European Central Bank? Can we, in this new global environment, really insist on pursuing narrow 'parish' politics?

These facts alone should convince us that our peoples deserve a different perspective on their future. Of course, some voices may be raised asking why we should, in the name of globalization, neglect our national interests. This answers the second question mentioned above. It is obvious that decades of confrontation have brought no advantages, but only losses, to our peoples. The enormous burden of military expenditure on both sides of the Aegean should alone suffice to show that both Greece and Turkey have been playing a 'lose-lose game', while believing or pretending that they are defending their interests. A game, moreover, that continues at a crucial time when Turkey wants to undertake the important step of becoming a full EU member and Greece is joining the Euro.

It is understandable that an outside observer might point out that the French–German relationship after the last war is the proper example for Greece and Turkey to follow. This sounds very reasonable, but it ignores the historical-psychological background. Franco–German rivalry may go back to the partition of the Carolingian Reich, but it has always been a rivalry among equals, where each side in turn won the upper hand for a certain time. In the case of the Greek–Turkish relationship the decisive historical-psychological fact is that the major part of Hellenism was for almost five centuries held in slavery by Ottoman masters and that the Greeks had to fight hard for decades to recover their independence. From the Turkish side history may look different, namely that the former master can hardly tolerate an upstart, former subject, people at his borders. Therefore the historical-psychological context is totally different. One should refrain from drawing misleading historical parallels, such as the Franco-German one. Besides, neither France nor Germany raises claims on each other's territory any longer, as Turkey does on Greece.

Other outside observers may remark that, since this is admittedly a 'lose-lose game', both sides, Greece and Turkey, ought to try somehow to 'meet each other half-way'. This may sound reasonable, but ignores the fact that by piling up claim upon claim Turkey has over the years pushed the middle line of the road more and more towards the Greek side, leaving an extremely narrow margin for a meaningful negotiation. Practically all Aegean problems have indeed been successively raised unilaterally by Turkey in her effort to change the *status quo* in the Aegean at the expense of Greece, while on the other hand Greece is asking nothing from Turkey. (Greece has even abstained until now from extending her territorial waters to 12 n.m., although this would be in conformity to the UN Convention on the Law of the Sea.) One should further note that while the Greek minority living in Turkey has, through pressure and intimidation, been practically reduced to a handful of people, the Muslim minority in Thrace is multiplying and thriving.

It is obvious that there is an ever-smaller space for any kind of a meaningful *do ut des* deal between the two countries, and this asymmetrical situation makes a future negotiation extremely difficult. This is the reason why Greece considers that Turkey should be the first to take a number of steps to restore a climate of mutual trust. After all, it is Turkey who still threatens Greece with *casus belli*, raises claims even on Greek land territory and refuses to have the dispute concerning the continental shelf resolved by the International Court of Justice in conformity with international law. Unfortunately, while Greece has by positive action facilitated the opening of EU accession negotiations for Turkey, the only Turkish gesture in response was to reduce the number of violations of Greek air-space. Moreover, only recently the Turkish Foreign Minister raised questions about the Muslim minority in northern Greece, thus signalling the re-activation of yet another area of confrontation. (It is, to say the least, surprising to hear minority problems in another country raised by Turkey, who is well known for the treatment she reserved over the years to the Armenian and the Greek minorities while still having a huge open problem with the Kurds.)

Therefore, it is understandable that it is a difficult decision for Turkey to revert to the *status quo ante Cyprus* in the bilateral relations. Neither the present policies of the West nor the past history of the Turks makes it easy.

Some Western countries, in particular the US, do not assist Turkey enough to realize the benefits of peaceful neighbourly relations with Greece. On the contrary, Turkey is being given the impression that the West needs Turkey so badly that it would be willing to tolerate any behaviour by Turkey on the international scene. This was the case in the decades of the Cold War. Since then the West has given the Turks to understand that even now Turkey is the 'indispensable nation' and that the West is willing to close both eyes if Turkey violates the human rights of her citizens or bullies her neighbours.

On the other hand, the past weighs heavily on Turkey's public policies. A series of enlightened reformers throughout the nineteenth and twentieth centuries have fought to bring Turkey into the mainstream of Europe. The results have been patchy. In more than one aspect Turkish public policy is still far below the accepted European standards. We see this today in the Greek–Turkish context. Turkey, for example, is threatening a neighbour with war in case this neighour applies an internationally valid Convention (UN on the Law of the Sea). Turkey further refuses the authority of the ICJ. Last, but not least, Turkey challenges the validity of international treaties (1923 Lausanne; 1931 Dodecanese) and seeks their 're-interpretation'. This tendency to ignore generally accepted standards of international law is particularly worrying. On the subject of the Lausanne Treaty, I recently heard an eminent retired Turkish diplomat maintaining that the Treaty is not a legal, but rather a political and military document which is, therefore, subject to 're-interpretations'! This position was repeated in a text by the Chief of the Turkish General Staff, saying that 'no legal concept or rule can justify Turkey's limitation inside her territorial waters and her exclusion from a sea which she alone was using for centuries and with which she has unbreakable ties of geography, history, economy, society and security'!

There is indeed a profound dichotomy between the East and the West in Turkey's body politic. It was and still is an arduous and demanding task to bring Turkey closer to Europe. Kemal Atatürk said: 'We come from the East and we go to the West.' He thus expressed in a few words the deep identity problem within modern Turkey. This is a problem not easy to overcome. All the more so because the West, towards which Kemal and all the reformers before and after him aspired, is not a stationary construction but rather a moving train which Turkey has to catch. Those striving and struggling today in Turkey to overcome the natural inertia of traditional thinking, who work to propel Turkey towards an eventual full membership in the EU with all the advantages but also obligations that this entails, deserve encouragement and assistance. The commitment to EU membership as regards democratic governance and respect of human rights may indeed cause second thoughts among the Turkish political establishment. It should not be taken for granted that Turkey will want to take the European route under any circumstances if accession requires full compliance to European standards as regards respect of international law. This should be taken into account by some European governments. If they, for reasons of their own bilateral interests, signal that they are inclined to ignore Turkey's disregard of Western standards and values and offer her 'a bargain price' for EU accession, they will have given Turkey the wrong message. They will have encouraged Turkey to remain thinking of and acting out an outdated past, believing that she can accede to the EU on her own terms. Recent statements heard in Ankara against Greece should sound a warning. All the more so because they come from the Foreign Minister and the Chief of the General Staff, as quoted above. These are signs possibly marking a reversal of the recent hopeful trend, and they should alert at least the EU governments that Turkey may revert to the tactics of bullying Greece in the belief that she can count on the Europeans' desire not to estrange Turkey. This may have the opposite effect and encourage Turkey to continue her old ways rather than converge towards the standards and values of the EU. This would be bad for the EU and bad for Turkey.

I have tried to point out the dangers on the road ahead, not in order to discourage the pursuit towards the new era but in order to show the difficulties and pitfalls which lie ahead. It is my firm belief that we have both, Greece and Turkey, suffered enough from decades of confrontation. We definitely have other priorities in our national lives beyond the dispute about the 'grey areas' in the Aegean.

17

The Future of Greece in the European Union

LOUKAS TSOUKALIS

MEMBERSHIP MEANS ADJUSTMENT

Let me start with some preliminary remarks about membership of the EU and what it concretely entails for a country like Greece. The Union is now much more than the incomplete common market it had been for many years. Integration has both widened and deepened; and high politics has been added, albeit slowly and half-heartedly, to what had been wrongly described in the past as low politics. Yet, the fundamental characteristic of the European construction has not changed much until now: it is mainly about economics in the wider sense of the term.

European economic integration encompasses three processes: the opening (and regulation) of the internal market for goods, services, persons and capital; the redistribution of resources, mainly through structural policies; and now, economic and monetary union (EMU), which covers the whole macroeconomic dimension. Thus, integration is not only about economic liberalization; it should also be seen as an attempt to establish a new form of governance between the nation-state and increasingly global markets.[1]

The success or failure of a country's EU membership depends largely on the ability of its economic agents to survive in a highly competitive environment, and hence to cope with continuous change. It also depends on its collective ability to play an active part in a never-ending process of negotiations that take place at different levels and that involve representatives of both governments and private interests. The everyday functioning of the EU is still more about diplomacy than it is about democracy.[2] Each country needs to actively defend its interests, however defined, in negotiations where arguments interact with power politics and shifting alliances against the background of jointly established rules.

Membership of the EU has been a formidable challenge for Greece.

Before accession, the country had a long history of high external protection and extensive state intervention in the economy, usually arbitrary and non-transparent. Interestingly enough, external protection and state intervention had survived the Association Agreement signed with the EEC of Six back in 1961. Tariffs had come down as a result, but various forms of non-tariff protection proved to be highly endurable: they survived even some years after Greece's accession to what was still the European Community (EC) in 1981.

As a member of the EC and now the EU, Greece has had to adjust to open and highly competitive markets. It also has had to adjust to the requirements of joint rule-setting in Brussels, which now covers not only different barriers to entry into the domestic market but also inflation, budget deficits and interest rates. Economic sovereignty in the Union has indeed become a relative concept. Greece experienced considerable difficulties in adjusting to the new economic reality, much more so than the two Iberian countries that joined five years later.[3] Greece's economic maladjustment, which lasted for several years, at least partly explains the tensions that developed between it and both European institutions and partner countries.[4]

Greece often asked for exceptions in order to protect its domestic producers. Either deliberately or because of administrative inefficiency, Greece was slow in implementing European directives and regulations and was sometimes accused of wasting the money allocated to it through the Structural Funds. In the meantime, trade deficits kept on growing, financed in part through EU transfers, while the figures for inflation, budget deficits and interest rates remained way above those of any other EU country.

It was certainly not just a question of economic adjustment. The problems experienced by Greece as a member of the EU had also much to do with the functioning of the state and its institutions. The Greek state is both omni-present and fundamentally weak. Its pervasive influence is intimately linked to a clientele system, which it has been precisely intended to serve. It is extremely vulnerable to political parties and organized groups, while its institutions remain weak, inflexible and inefficient in performing the traditional Weberian functions. The Greek state has been aptly described as a colossus with feet of clay.[5]

... AND MANY TRIED TO DELAY IT

Greece's European adjustment came with considerable delay, especially when compared with the experience of the two Iberian countries which joined the EC five years later than Greece; but it did come in the end. Membership of the EC/EU has acted as a catalyst, a legitimator and an instrument of external discipline for this transformation of Greece. It helped to change the internal balance of forces between reformers/modernizers on the one hand and conservatives/populists on the other.

The process of reform/modernization (what matters, of course, is not the name but the contents) has been long and difficult, characterized by strong domestic resistance to change. It is only natural that resistance to change should come from those who expect to lose from it. Thus, any political economy analysis of reform needs to identify potential losers, which is also what politicians carrying the banner of reform need to do. Once identified, potential losers can be dealt with in different ways. Divide and rule is an old and frequently practised method. There is also the possibility of compensation, usually in a limited number of cases, or even incorporation in a wider, positive-sum game.

The experience of Greece during the 1980s and 1990s suggests that potential losers from the kind of reform associated with EU membership were numerous – and that some of them were politically powerful. Although potential winners were perhaps the majority in absolute numbers, they were generally dispersed and badly organized. A non-exhaustive list of losers from adjustment to EU membership would include a significant part of Greek business, accustomed to external protection and heavily dependent on state favouritism, especially through public procurement contracts. Who said that all businesspeople believe in free competition? The opening of the Greek economy to European and international competition has led to considerable restructuring and some de-industrialization. The list of losers would also include most organized labour, which can be found in the large state-controlled sector, characterized by over-employment, relatively high pay and low productivity.

The same list would certainly include a large part of the political class, which had developed and exploited its comparative advantage in the operation of the clientele system, a system that flourishes in protected markets and under non-transparent rules. The list of losers would also include other, less well-organized groups of society, such as many small businesses and the lesser skilled. Unable to adjust to a very competitive environment, but also unable to offer effective political resistance, they are, unavoidably, being sacrificed on the altar of economic restructuring.

Faced with such a situation, Greek governments tried for more than ten years following accession to avoid or simply postpone adjustment, which would have been politically costly. At the same time, they showed great readiness to throw money at any group in society able to make enough noise around it. In the process they have created another category of losers, one that conveniently happened to be disenfranchised because of age. By that, I mean the younger generations and those not yet born, who will have to bear the full burden of delayed adjustment, not to mention the burden of servicing the large public debt accumulated mostly during the 1980s. The welfare state in Greece has been largely built on the basis of inter-generational redistribution, and this is certainly not something the post-1974 political system should be proud of.

In the second half of the 1990s, the process of reform/modernization acquired a new momentum. The big turning point came when Constantine Simitis was elected leader of PASOK and Prime Minister in 1996. Greece then entered a phase of economic stabilization and convergence with the rest of the EU, coupled with a more determined effort at privatization and restructuring. Previous attempts in this direction had proved short-lived; but the margin of manoeuvre has become increasingly narrower with time. The prospect of economic marginalization in the context of the EU, the rapidly rising cost of the servicing of the debt, and the increasing difficulties in the financing of deficits left Greek governments with very limited options.

Macroeconomic stabilization produced quick results, and Greece was able to fulfil the Maastricht criteria for admission to EMU on the basis of the 1998 figures. It joined the other eleven members of the euro-zone in January 2001. In the process of bringing down inflation rates and public deficits, many Greeks discovered, to their surprise, that there is no necessary trade-off between macroeconomic stabilization and growth. Thus, this recent period has been characterized by a substantial improvement in terms of economic growth.

REFORMERS AND MODERNIZERS

There is a great deal, however, that remains to be done. The biggest challenge for reform lies in the state and its institutions. This promises to be a long, drawn-out and painful process in which the benefits for those who undertake the reform are mostly of a long-term nature, while the costs are more immediate; a highly unattractive combination for most politicians.

The Greek state has generally catered for specific interests and the perpetuation of the clientele system. Today, Greece needs state institutions which provide stable and transparent rules of the game, flexible regulation of markets, macroeconomic stability, the promotion and management of economic change, and, last but not least, the development of new forms of social solidarity for the losers. The above would imply a radical change in the relationship between the state and the market in Greece, which is largely what membership of the EU is all about.

The pensions time-bomb is ticking away, and Greece is facing a similar demographic problem as most of the other countries of the EU.

It is slowly experimenting with greater flexibility in labour markets, while rules need to catch up with current practice in the market. A disproportionately large part of Greek GDP is being produced in the so-called informal sector of the economy.

The education system remains rigid and thus not easily adaptable to the requirements of a rapidly changing economic and technological environment. An ever-increasing number of Greek students seek their university education abroad, thus creating a safety valve which reduces the pressure for reform. Meanwhile, a highly ambitious effort has begun to overhaul the ailing public health system.

Privatization of state-controlled enterprises and the liberalization of public utilities have so far proceeded at a slow pace. There is much at stake here, the biggest danger being that inefficient (and corrupt?) state monopolies will be replaced by private monopolies if public regulation and competition rules remain lax. The process of reform in recent years has been accompanied by a strong concentration of economic power inside Greece. Although some of it was arguably the unavoidable price for much delayed economic restructuring, the rest is simply a reflection of the weakness of regulatory authorities.

Having been traditionally an exporter of labour, Greece has become in the course of the last ten years or so a country of immigrants, and in a big way. Its land and sea frontiers are long and porous, the differences in the standards of living with all the neighbouring countries are huge, and domestic demand for cheap labour, especially in the unregulated sector of the economy, remains substantial. This has proved as difficult a problem to handle in Greece as in the rest of western Europe. As a corollary to immigration, Greece is now being faced with the challenge of multiculturalism.

The domestic political scene has undergone a major transformation. Greek politics has become less polarized and personalized – and perhaps verging on the boring for the taste of some Greeks, used to charismatic leaders and interminable fights between good and evil. What is interesting, however, is that the division between reform/modernization on the one hand and conservatism/populism on the other does not always follow party lines.

In times when ideological differences are not always easy to discern and the range of political choices becomes rather narrow, there is a big risk of vacuous talk and populist rhetoric. There is no shortage of candidates to perform those functions in any part of the world. In a country where politics has been about anything and everything, and where political parties, either directly or through state institutions, try to exercise control over everything from admission to hospitals to the running of universities and sports, civil society has remained underdeveloped. The quality of democracy in Greece largely depends on the strengthening of independent groups and associations of citizens, which can act as effective controls on the all-expansive tendencies of the state. The relatively recent mushrooming of citizens' movements, mainly on environmental and human rights issues, is therefore a most encouraging sign.

EURO-ENTHUSIASM AND OPINION POLLS

Membership of the EU brings with it numerous constraints, be they the product of open markets, of common rules for bank assets and the protection of the environment, or the need to conform with the convergence criteria as an entry ticket for the final stage of EMU. On the other hand, EU policies and rules can sometimes serve as a convenient scapegoat for unpopular policies at home. Greek governments have frequently made use of the European scapegoat, whenever domestic support was in short supply. They have tried to capitalize on the generally high levels of public support for the EU at home, thus sometimes risking a boomerang effect.

EU membership enjoys high levels of support in Greece. This support has been repeatedly confirmed in opinion polls conducted in the country, and it has also been manifested in the attitude of most political parties and in the votes taken in the Greek Parliament. But there seems to be a contradiction between the apparent love for the EU on the one hand, manifested by the large majority of Greeks, and the strong resistance offered by many of the same people to the things that membership of the Union actually implies. This apparent contradiction may suggest that the Greeks have tended to adopt a rather selective (and often inconsistent) approach to EU membership.

For the cynical observer, Greek popular support for the EU could be explained in terms of the transfers of funds which now represent approximately 4 to 5 per cent (net transfers) of GDP per annum. There is, of course, something real in this argument, which equally well applies to a country like Ireland where membership of the Union is also very popular. Nevertheless, in the case of Greece transfers through the Structural Funds and the CAP have also had a negative aspect. Coupled with Greece's improved access to external borrowing, linked to membership of this club of advanced European economies, transfers from the EU enabled Greek politicians in the past to delay adjustment, while also providing an extra breathing space for the old clientele system.

For Greece, there is much more to EU membership than access to funds. The Union is generally seen as providing a stable political environment for a country with a turbulent history; a catalyst for political, economic and social modernization, which is, of course, resisted by potential losers; and a valuable alliance, even without military means, for a country which finds itself in a very unstable neighbourhood and which perceives a serious threat to its external security.

In other words, many Greeks consider the EU as a protection mechanism against their own bad, collective self and also a kind of insurance, inadequate though admittedly it may be, against external risks. For some Greeks, membership of the EU has always been considered as a means of changing the internal balance of forces and thus strengthening the political coalition for reform/modernization. The number of reformers/modernizers has been steadily on the increase over the years. Thus, Greece combines some of the characteristics of Ireland and Portugal (the pursuit of economic development and modernization) with the feeling of external vulnerability found in a country like Finland. There is undoubtedly much more at stake in Greece with EU membership than in most other countries of the Union.

Attitudes towards EMU provide a good illustration of the above. The popularity of Greece's membership of EMU has been repeatedly confirmed by large majorities in opinion polls, although here again we come up against the old problem of consistency, namely that every Greek in favour of EMU is not necessarily prepared to pay the price associated with membership. Support for EMU is easy to explain. The search for a collective shield against the enormous instability of exchange markets is coupled with the fear of the political marginalization that would follow should Greece be left out for long of the most important part of the European construction. Experience seems to suggest that monetary stability would be more effectively guaranteed if responsibility for decisions in the area of monetary policy were to be transferred to the European Central Bank in Frankfurt. In this respect, Greece is not very different from most other members of the EU.

It is one thing to secure membership of EMU, and another to ensure that the Greek economy performs well in this new environment. Greece has entered a long and difficult phase of structural reform, including cutting the state-controlled sector of the economy down to size, overhauling the social security system, and adjusting Greek public administration to the rapidly shifting reality of European integration and globalization. There is still a long distance to travel in this direction with many obstacles on the way. It is almost certain that many of those obstacles will be created by people who otherwise profess to be Euro-enthusiasts.

There is an undercurrent of nationalism in Greek society, which is evident mostly among groups of people who perceive themselves as potential losers in times of rapid change. This helps to explain the periodic outbursts of anti-European feelings in Greece, which spring from the darker parts of the collective Greek psyche, stirred by populist politicians and the country's sensationalist mass media. On such occasions, one is painfully reminded of the vulnerability of many Greeks to conspiracy theories and the persistence of what Diamantouros calls an 'underdog culture'.[6] This may in turn suggest that public support for the EU may not be as deep as those not very careful readers of opinion polls seem to think.

GOOD NEIGHBOURLY RELATIONS

If in economic and political terms Greece is gradually becoming like any other European country, this is still not true of foreign policy. The reason is simple: the Greeks live in the rough neighbourhood of the Balkans, where nation-states have a relatively short history, national frontiers are not generally considered as sacrosanct, and ethnic minorities are frequently manipulated in order to destabilize neighbours and thus lay claims on a possible future redrawing of political maps.

The collapse of the old communist order on Greece's northern frontier may have opened the way for the establishment of democratic régimes, but its first effect was to unleash the old nationalist (and irredentist) forces that had been kept in deep freeze during the Cold War. This new environment presented Greece with many problems and risks, but also with new opportunities.[7] In the early years, it tended to exaggerate the former and ignore the latter. It gradually learned its lesson the hard way and, in the process, it became a crucial part of the solution to the Balkan problem.

Although relatively poor by EU standards, Greece is an economic giant in the region. In money terms, its GDP is now bigger than the GDP of Albania, Bulgaria, Romania, the FYR of Macedonia, and new Yugoslavia put together, with a population approximately five times that of Greece. At current exchange rates, Greek GDP per capita is also approximately four times the GDP per capita of Turkey. Trade with its northern neighbours has grown, despite the economic difficulties experienced by the countries in the region; and Greek investment has also increased rapidly – arguably the most important contribution that Greece can make to stabilization in the region. Greece's economic and political weight is further strengthened by its membership of both the EU and NATO, as long as the policies pursued by Athens do not diverge widely from those of its partners and allies. This has become increasingly true in recent times.

Greece is fundamentally a *status quo* country in a part of the world where the *status quo* is being challenged from many directions. Worried about the instability on its northern frontier, it also perceives a direct threat to its territorial integrity emanating from Turkey. The long list of unresolved bilateral issues between Greece and its NATO ally on the other side of the Aegean Sea, the continuing problem of Cyprus affecting directly both Greece and Turkey, the military build-up on both sides, and the repeated threats of war from Turkish generals and politicians are not figments of the otherwise fertile imagination of the Greeks.

Indeed, living with Turkey as a neighbour is by no means a guarantee of an easy and comfortable life for most of the countries sharing a frontier with Turkey. The relatively recent memory of an empire, the large size and strategic position of the country, the serious instability of its political system, coupled with huge internal disparities and the threat of Islamic fundamentalism, the dominant position of the army in domestic politics, and the institutionalization of state violence, all combine to make Turkey a difficult country to deal with.

Nobody could, of course, seriously argue that Greece has no share of responsibility for the poor state of relations with its eastern neighbour. Yet Greece has a vested interest in the economic development and political stability of Turkey. The last thing that Greeks should want is a poor and internally divided Turkey, one more vulnerable to the temptation offered by political Islam and military adventures abroad. In this respect, Greece has a common interest with its European and American allies.

Support for Turkey's *rapprochement* with the EU, leading eventually to full membership of the Union, should be entirely consistent with the above objectives; and this therefore needs to receive Greece's full support. It has not always been so in the past. An important step in this direction was taken at the European Council of Helsinki in December 1999, when Turkey was adopted as an official candidate for EU membership, with the full agreement of Greece.

As with all other candidates, Turkey's accession to the EU will depend on the fulfilment of the so-called Copenhagen criteria, including most notably the proper functioning of democratic institutions, the rule of law, the protection of human rights and the respect of minorities. Since Turkey's democratic record still leaves much to be desired, the road to Brussels may prove to be quite bumpy. The prospect of EU membership may, however, help to shift the internal balance of forces in Turkey in favour of those who support democratic reforms and the process of Europeanization of the country. Greece, more than any other member of the EU, should have a vested interest in such an outcome.

Cyprus is one of the six countries in the so-called fast track leading to membership of the EU, and it is likely to be able to fulfil the basic criteria for membership more easily than the other candidates. Yet, it remains a divided country, and the crucial question is whether early accession to the EU can act as a catalyst for an internal political settlement between the two communities on the island or whether the internal settlement should be considered as a pre-condition for accession.

Not surprisingly, the governments in Athens and Nicosia have opted for the former, fearing that if accession were to be made conditional on an internal settlement, which in turns means conditional on the willingness of Turkish Cypriots and Turkey to play the game, the accession of Cyprus would risk being written off *ad calendas Graecas*. The European Council of Helsinki took some reassuring steps in this direction.

MOVING IN THE RIGHT DIRECTION

Greece has travelled a long distance since the fall of the colonels' dictatorship in 1974. Democracy has been consolidated, and this has been achieved in an extremely peaceful manner. Greek democracy has had its share of demagogues, and public opinion sometimes has fallen prey to populist rhetoric. This is, of course, not totally unknown in other democracies. It could be argued that, for several years, economic stabilization and much needed structural reforms were sacrificed on the altar of democratic consolidation.

Membership of the European Union has acted as a powerful catalyst for domestic reform/modernization. Adjustment to the requirements of membership of this very unusual club, in which the most advanced democracies and mixed economies of Europe experiment in new forms of pooling of sovereignty, has been difficult and rather painful for Greece. Resistance to change from organized groups proved powerful enough to delay the process of adjustment for many years. The forces of reform/modernization have now taken the upper hand, although there is still much that needs to be done.

Greece does not have the luxury enjoyed by many western European countries for whom external threat has become a rather abstract notion since the disintegration of the Soviet empire. Developments in the Balkans, coupled with continuing tension in relations with Turkey, often tended in the past to create a siege mentality in Greek society. In the early 1990s this reached a dangerous peak, when a group of politicians across the political spectrum apparently decided to invest heavily in nationalist shares. They were strongly encouraged by a large section of the media. Again, this is, undoubtedly, no Greek monopoly. Things have improved quite dramatically in recent years, arguably the product of greater collective self-confidence.

Greek diplomacy has often experienced difficulties in finding the right combination of the language of might, right and common interests. It has often placed almost exclusive emphasis on what it perceives as right on issues of foreign policy, while not paying enough attention to the need for building coalitions and identifying common interests with other countries. It has thus failed to appreciate that moralizing in international relations is mostly the privilege of the strong, as so many US politicians never fail to remind us.

For Greece, membership of the EU certainly constitutes the most important element of its domestic and foreign policy. But the country happens to exist in an unstable neighbourhood; and no kind of foreign policy can transport it away from that location. Moreover, it will, unfortunately, remain on the frontier of the Union for many years to come, because none of its neighbours is likely to be able to fulfil the criteria for membership for some time. Guarding frontier posts requires continuous vigilance and *sang-froid*. It also requires skilful diplomacy. Greece needs to act as a stabilizing force in the region.

Greece will need to combine domestic reforms with careful diplomacy abroad. Structural reforms can only succeed if social cohesion is preserved. On the other hand, national interests can only be defended successfully through alliances, formal or *ad hoc*. Given the nature of the European Union, the recipe for a successful membership of Greece should contain more domestic reform and less high politics. It is my strong impression that Greece has been steadily moving in this direction.

NOTES

1. L. Tsoukalis, *The New European Economy Entanglement* (Athens: Hellenic Foundation for European and Foreign Policy, 1997).
2. B. Laffan, 'The Politics of Identity and Political Order in Europe', *Journal of Common Market Studies* (March 1996).
3. See also J. M. Maravall, *Regimes, Politics and Markets: Democratisation and Economic Change in Southern and Eastern Europe* (Oxford: Oxford University Press, 1997).
4. See also K. Featherstone and K. Ifantis, *Greece in a Changing Europe: Between European Integration and Balkan Disintegration?* (Manchester: Manchester University Press, 1996) and P. Kazakos and P. C. Ioakimidis, *Greece and EC Membership Evaluated* (London: Pinter Publications, 1994).
5. D. Sotiropoulos, 'A Colossus with Feet of Clay: The State in Post-Authoritarian Greece', in H. G. Psomiades and S. Thomadakis (eds) *Greece, the New European the Changing International Order* (New York: Pella Publishing, 1993).
6. N. P. Diamandouros, *Cultural Dualism and Political Change in Post-Authoritarian Greece* (Madrid: Centro Juan March de Estudios Avanzados en Ciencias Sociales, 1994).
7. T. Veremis, *Greece's Balkan Entanglement* (Athens: Hellenic Foundation for European and Foreign Policy, 1995).

Index